The AMERICAN FRONTIER

*A social
and literary record*

The AMERICAN FRONTIER

*A social
and literary
record*

C. MERTON BABCOCK

Holt, Rinehart and Winston, Inc.

NEW YORK   CHICAGO   SAN FRANCISCO

TORONTO   LONDON

Archibald MacLeish quotation on opposite page from his essay, "Sweet Land of Liberty," Collier's, July 1955

Robert Frost quotation on page x from *Complete Poems of Robert Frost.* Copyright 1942 by Robert Frost. Reprinted by permission of Holt, Rinehart and Winston, Inc.

For Jackie
wherever she is
is West

———

WEST IS A COUNTRY IN THE MIND,
AND SO ETERNAL.

Archibald MacLeish

Contents

PART 4   THE FRONTIERSMAN

PART 5   THE AMERICAN INDIAN

PART 6   MANIFEST DESTINY

PART 7   LITERARY SKETCHES

PART 8   RELIGION

Contents

PART 9   POLITICS AND GOVERNMENT

PART 10   LANGUAGE

PART 11   HUMOR

PART 12   THE FRONTIER IN RETROSPECT

THE GIFT OUTRIGHT

The land was ours before we were the land's.
She was our land more than a hundred years
Before we were her people. She was ours
In Massachusetts, in Virgina,
But we were England's, still colonials,
Possessing what we still were unpossessed by,
Possessed by what we now no more possessed.
Something we were withholding made us weak
Until we found out that it was ourselves
We were withholding from our land of living,
And forthwith found salvation in surrender.
Such as we were we gave ourselves outright
(The deed of gift was many deeds of war)
To the land vaguely realizing westward,
But still unstoried, artless, unenhanced,
Such as she was, such as she would become.

ROBERT FROST

The AMERICAN FRONTIER

*A social
and literary record*

Introduction

I

In most European countries the word *frontier* denotes a boundary between two separate countries, somewhat fixed and permanent in character; in America, it connotes a moving, shifting, and progressive line of demarcation between settled and unsettled areas. For this reason, frontier America, which refused to be fenced in by natural, social, or political barriers, is more properly thought of as a direction, or possibly a momentum, than as a geographical expanse or cultural region. Frederick Jackson Turner, who became famous for his interest in the effects of migration on American democracy, has defined the frontier as that point at which civilized people advance or move into a wilderness or uncivilized territory where land may be had for the taking.

One should not suppose, however, that this transitory sense of the frontier applies only to America. As Emerson Hough once said, "The frontier knows no country; it lies also in other lands and in other times than our own." Walter Prescott Webb, in a more specific manner, has pointed out that the Boers in South Africa and the English in Australia were faced with the same kinds of conditions that Americans and Canadians experienced in their progress westward across North America. The Webb thesis proposes that all of America was once a frontier and that the European exodus to the New World may be said to explain the

1

development of Western civilization. Thus, in a very real sense, Americans had pioneering in the marrow of their bones.

The colonists who fastened themselves to the soil in Virginia and Massachusetts had no adequate conception of the incalculable dimensions of their backyard. Cotton Mather spoke of New England as bounded by the "Atlantic Sea Eastward" and the "Connecticut River Westward," not realizing that it was nearly as far to the western ocean beyond the river as it was to terra firma across the Atlantic. "The map of America is a map of endlessness," wrote Archibald MacLeish, and a recent British visitor to the United States, staggered by the expansiveness of the country, described it as "a continental landmass where forty-eight States straddle an area which, translated into Euro-Africo-Asian terms, would stretch from Copenhagen to Tripoli and from Cherbourg to Astrakham." An American frontiersman would have said, "Why, sir, on the north we are bounded by the aurora borealis, on the east by the rising sun, on the south by the procession of the equinoxes, and on the west by the day of judgment." What the pioneers faced as they looked into the sunset was a bundle of geography that the "weightiest words in the dictionary" could not describe, a parcel of earth too vast to be comprehended in a single thought.

II

The first pioneers to front the Appalachian Highlands were from Virginia, Maryland, and Pennsylvania. As soon as the United States had declared its independence from Britain, people from the Carolinas and Virginia poured into Tennessee and Kentucky. People from the Middle Atlantic States and from New England moved toward the St. Lawrence River and the Great Lakes. Settlements in what are now Indiana, Illinois, and Missouri occurred within the first decade of the nation's history. The spirit of adventure and exploration which had filled the sails of ships that brought civilized people to the uncivilized shores of the American continent was not easily shaken off. Compelled by some uncontrollable impulse, the braver and bolder and more daring settlers moved deeper and deeper into the West, and the history of these people has ever followed the sun.

By 1783, the Mississippi River marked the western boundary of civilized America, and people moved into the open plains faster than the political limits of the nation could be defined. Jefferson's purchase of Louisiana (1803), followed by the Lewis and Clark expedition (1804–1806), invited settlers into western Minnesota, the Dakotas, Iowa, Nebraska, and Kansas. The War of 1812 opened up the gulf territories south of Tennessee as far west as the Mississippi, which had become a thoroughfare of commercial traffic by the 1830s. In less than a half century the remaining details of the continental land grab—the largest real-estate transaction in history—had been worked out: settlement of a dispute with Spain over Florida (1819), acquisition of Texas (1845), settlement of the Oregon boundary (1846), acquisition of California (1848), the Gadsden Purchase of territories on the Mexican border (1853), and the purchase of Alaska (1867).

Expansion of the nation's territories from coast to coast gave a sudden spurt to westering, and jumping-off places like Independence, Saint Joseph, and Council Bluffs boomed with excitement. The geographical area of the United States had twice doubled, and Americans were making a mad dash for the wide-open spaces across both the geography and history of the country. Furthermore, the very existence of unsettled territories was a carte blanche invitation to Europeans. During the century of the greatest frontier activity, some thirty-five million people came to America from overseas, many of whom joined the westward processions. Nearly ten million people crossed the Mississippi within two decades. Never before in history were so many people on the move. Herbert Quick called it "a nation on wheels, an empire in the commotion and pangs of birth."

For a while the Rocky Mountains halted through traffic to the Far West, but not for long. Discovery of gold on Sutter's plantation in California (1848), along the beds of Cripple Creek in Colorado (1850), in the Virginia Range of Western Nevada (1859), and in the Black Hills of South Dakota (1874) started a series of stampedes which all but choked the mountain passes and caused stopping-off places like Denver, Leadville, Deadwood, and

Virginia City (now a ghost town) to skip an entire chapter in the history of their development. Temporary camps mushroomed into existence as wealthy and luxurious urban centers, never having gone through an intermediate stage in their metamorphoses. There was no time for nature to take her usual courses. Within a few weeks after the strike near Clear Creek, Colorado (1859), the name "Gregory's Diggings" was changed to "Mountain City," because it had suddenly acquired a municipality, a newspaper, and thousands of inhabitants. In less than six months, however, its story was finished. The gold had petered out, and the people had moved to another bonanza. The Comstock Lode in Nevada, on the other hand, held up for twenty years, yielding during that time $300,000,000 worth of gold and silver.

The glittering dollar had long been a guiding star for trappers and fur traders who ferreted out the remotest haunts and retreats of the Western wilds in their quest for pelts. John Jacob Astor's amalgamation of the fur-trading companies of the West and Northwest (1808) marked the beginnings of big business in frontier territory. After the Civil War and the completion of a trans-continental railroad (1869), industrialism boomed, and all manner of opportunists, speculators, and entrepreneurs vied with one another for a concession in the West and a stake in the future of the country.

But progress depended upon the settlement of large numbers of workaday people upon the land, and the promise of a private piece of Mother Earth on which to work out one's destiny furnished the necessary enticement. Passage of the Homestead Act (1862) made it possible for anyone to acquire 160 acres of land free, if he would live on it for five years, pay a nominal filing charge, and meet certain other minimal conditions. To the more visionary Americans, such an opportunity must have seemed like Jefferson's dream of Arcadia come true. Emerging from the thickly wooded areas along the rivers, pioneers were more than a little exhilarated at first sight of the endless prairies—the seas of glistening grass—the rolling, heaving oceans of virgin land. In sober contemplation of the lavish prospects, men were charged with a new sense of power and mastery. Enthusiasm came out of hiding and waved her magic wand. Frontiersmen spoke of savannas "with grass as high as your shoulders and the air perfumed with the blossoms of exotic trees." The smell of romance was in the air. The western sky was painted with gold.

III

The idea that the American West is a land of promise, a paradise of plenty, a veritable Canaan "flowing with milk and honey" captivated the minds of the more hopeful people who inspected the picturesque landscapes, and the myth of abundance that grew out of this idea persists in the American consciousness. Abraham Lincoln saw the great interior region of the United States as "one of the most important in the world" in its potential. He referred to the open prairies as the "Egypt of the West." Walt Whitman, equally complimentary, described the same expanses as "more lovely and fertile in their unplough'd innocence than the fair and valuable fields of New York's, Pennsylvania's, Maryland's, or Virginia's richest farms."

Some observers, however, were not satisfied to view the wonders of the West at a vantage point sufficiently removed from reality as to obliterate the more disagreeable facts about much of the un-settled territory. James Fenimore Cooper realized that the "great prairies" west of the Mississippi were "incapable of sustaining a dense population." In his introduction to *The Prairie*, he said, "They resemble the steppes of Tartary more than any other known portion of the world." Mark Twain, in *Roughing It*, also spoke of the overrated lushness of Western landscapes. California, he decided, "is best contemplated at a distance, because although its grass blades are tall, they stand up vindictively straight and self-sufficient, and are unsociably wide apart, with uncomely spots of barren sand between."

Explorers who took a close look at the American West employed, in their reports, such disparaging terms as "desert," "Siberia," and "land of starvation." The testimony of such men as Zebulon Pike, Stephen H. Long, Jedediah Smith, and especially of John Wesley Powell, leader of the Rocky Mountain Scientific

Exploring Expedition, all but exploded the breadbasket myth and helped create a picture of the West as a region of savages, of wild beasts, of deserts, of whirlwinds and dust storms, of sagebrush, cactus, and prairie dogs. "Out here," said Carl Sandburg's Texas range rider, "the only windbreak is the North Star." Many a frontiersman, half jokingly, half seriously, proposed giving the whole domain back to the Indians.

Frederick Jackson Turner, whose paper on "The Significance of the Frontier in American History" (1893) called for a reassessment of the impact of the frontier on American character and American civilization, endorsed an agrarian philosophy so uncritically as to invite repeated attacks. He argued that environmental factors were largely responsible for the transformation of Old World ideas into American institutions, and, although his thesis strongly influenced the writing of American history for nearly a half century, scholars eventually discovered that some facts in the American experience cannot be accounted for on the basis of his theory. Henry Nash Smith, in *Virgin Land*, for example, argued that, while Turner had affirmed an admirable set of values, the philosophy and the myth of abundance proves highly unsatisfactory in interpreting such realities of American life as were brought about by the Industrial Revolution. Wallace Stegner, another interpreter of the frontier, emphasized the unresponsiveness of nature to man's will and tireless efforts, in his highly convincing novel *The Big Rock Candy Mountain*. Walter Prescott Webb qualified Turner's thesis by showing that the destiny of the West was primarily shaped by the unimpeachable fact of the "great American desert" and by the frontiersman's adjustment to that fact.

But in spite of the academic hullabaloo that depreciated the importance of Turner's frontier hypothesis, the famous Wisconsin historian was not without his staunch defenders. Woodrow Wilson, endorsing Turner's ideas at the time they were first expounded, called the history of the United States, not one of "origins," but of "developments." In our own time, the distinguished frontier historian Ray Allen Billington has challenged the most carping critics to disprove Turner's basic postulate, referring to the frontier hypothesis as "our historical declaration of independence."

IV

Advocates of territorial expansion and exponents of the idea of a "manifest design of Providence" in the occupation of the American continent clung to the cornucopian myth as a means of furthering their own ends. "We are the pioneers of the world," they assured themselves, "the advance guard, sent on through the wilderness of untried things, to break a new path in the New World that is ours." Based on the theories that the American continent is a "new Canaan," that Americans of Anglo-Saxon heritage are "God's chosen people," and that the nation has a divine mission to perform in spreading the light of Christianity and democracy to the world, the doctrine of Manifest Destiny is a kind of rationalization and justification of America's highhanded methods in acquiring the western territories. This flagwaving variety of nationalism may be defined as the shotgun marriage of moral idealism and land hunger. It is white savagery in the garb of civilization. Running from aggression, the frontiersman became himself an aggressor. His method of dealing with the red man, for example, was to dispossess him of his land, lock him up on a reservation at the point of a gun, and then hand him a Bible.

Thoughtful people found themselves asking such questions as: Can Americans masquerade vice as virtue and get away with it? Can "boomer" tactics in the acquisition of land be reconciled with a theory of natural rights? Can a Christian people unwrite a history that is bathed in blood?

Americans justified their usurpation of Indian lands and their infringement of the red man's prior claim to the open prairies on the basis of their alleged superior rights as agents of Almighty God. Theodore Roosevelt proposed that the Indians "never had any real ownership" in the country at all. "To most of the land on which we found them," he said, "they had no stronger claim than that of having a few years previously butchered the original occupants." It became clear, almost from the beginning, that "where a paleface comes, a red man cannot stay." The blood of the red man and the blood of the white man run in different directions. The two cultures are basically antagonistic. All attempts at reconciliation came to nothing. Frontiersmen, not having time to argue or legislate matters, pushed the Indians into undesirable regions of the country, cut off their principal source of food and clothing, and virtually starved them to death. "These people must die out," wrote Horace Greeley. "There is no help for them. God has given this earth to those who will subdue and cultivate it, and it is vain to struggle against His righteous decree."

In the more permanently settled sections of the country where the Indian had long since ceased to constitute a threat to civilization, attitudes were quite different from those on the frontier. Jefferson, in his dealings with the red man, had decided the Indian to be "in body and mind equal to the white man." Poets and writers, notably Washington Irving, Henry Wadsworth Longfellow, Walt Whitman, and Helen Hunt Jackson, glorified the Indian as a "noble savage," and missionaries, reformers, and even members of Congress did their best to refute the popular frontier notion that "the only good Indian is a dead Indian." But the influence of such humanitarians had little effect in establishing a national policy of fair treatment for the children of the wilderness or of promoting anything like universal respect for their rights. The right of might and the force of numbers prevailed as usual. The pleas of the Indians combined with the petitions of righteous whites, for example, could not sway Andrew Jackson from his decision to remove the Cherokees from North Carolina and Georgia along the "trail of tears" to the arid territories west of the Mississippi. Joaquin Miller, in California, was all but ostracized by the whites because of his fraternal attitude toward the "savages" and his willingness to live with them.

V

One of the things, beside an ax and a rifle and a few rude implements for housekeeping, that the frontiersman took with him into the West was his Bible. While Mark Twain may have been right when he said that the name of the desperado Slade was feared more in those parts than that of the Almighty, the rumor that there was "no God west of the Mississippi" was unfounded. In the earliest settlements it was, of course, some time before a sufficient number of people had clustered together to warrant building a church, but as the West became more and more settled, churches sprang into existence wherever towns and villages appeared. Few settlements in the more flourishing parts of the country, said Cooper, existed fifteen years without reaching the church-building stage of their development. Another writer described the New England exodus to California as a religious crusade: "Bibles in one hand and good New England civilization in the other."

Perhaps the religion of the West is best described as spiritual hunger. Gospel meetings offered the frontier people opportunity for much-needed companionship. The church became a haven from loneliness and isolation and supplied a means of releasing pent-up frustrations caused by the strain of hard work, the vicissitudes of life, adverse experiences with the Indians, and open warfare with the elements of nature, that, as Ole Rölvaag made so dramatically clear in *Giants in the Earth*, could actually unhinge men's minds. The church was also an important cohesive agent in unifying the people of a community. This was especially true in Utah, where the Mormon church was the center of social, civic, and judicial, as well as religious affairs.

The frontier was as hard on religious bigotry as it was on social snobbery. Religious fervor, accompanied by a high degree of emotionalism and enthusiasm, eclipsed all doctrinal differences among congregations. In one instance, a baptized Episcopalian donated money for the erection of a Presbyterian church. When asked to explain, he said, "I do as I please, and I please to help my neighbors, who will help me in some other way, if not in this; besides, they are Christians as well as myself, and I mean to have a pew, and go and hear their parson till I can hear one of my own church." When confronted with the idea that he might be converted, he replied, "Well, then I shall be a Presbyterian, and my wife and myself will be of the same mind; we are not afraid of looking the truth in the face in America, let it come out of what pulpit it may."

The so-called social graces were pretty much lost in the frontier shuffle. People had little time for ornamentation of any kind, especially during the initial stages of settlement. Gentility did not really suit the frontier, and most attempts to import or create the embellishments and baubles of refinement or to imitate the antics of a cultural aristocracy produced nothing more than lavish, uncouth, gaudy, and preposterous displays of pretension. Church organizations did establish some schools and colleges in the West and men and women were thus afforded opportunity to work out their social and cultural salvation in the face of frontier crudities, but Western schools usually promoted nationalism rather than culture, partly because of a frontier predisposition to practicality, partly because of people's desperate need for identification with something larger than themselves, and partly because of the wide adoption of *McGuffey's Reader* in which a doctrine of nationalism was implicit. Considering the intellectual wilderness in which schoolmasters carved out a pedagogical career, they were pioneers in the strictest sense of the word.

The influx of ministers, missionaries, gospel peddlers and social reformers into frontier territories brought about the enforcement of strict moral codes. At one time in the Comstock mining country, bank games were forbidden on penalty of "final banishment from the district." One woman of the second generation of pioneers explained that when her father arrived in the frontier settlement of Steamboat Springs, Colorado, "there were four saloons impartially distributed along the trail that later became Main Street." "Within a year," she said, "the townspeople had driven the saloons across the river that flowed along one side of the village, and there the pariahs set up a colony of their own, called 'Brooklyn.'" When a certain prostitute, living on the sinful side of the river, died, she had to be smuggled into the whitewashed district under cover of night and disguised as a Negress before she could be buried in the cemetery.

VI

It has become all but axiomatic that frontiersmen of the Old West would "shoot first and ask questions afterward," that all differences were settled with rifles at twenty paces. Actually, however, the frontiers of America were not the lawless places they were reputed to be. While it is true that wickedness and debauchery existed in the camps and newly formed towns, that men turned to vice as a form of amusement to bring relief from hard work and rugged living, and that lynch law and vigilance committees often took the place of constables and courts, there were but few more infractions of law and order in the West than in other parts of the country. Samuel Boyles, then editor of the Springfield, Massachusetts, *Republican*, who visited the Far West in 1865, testified that the order and decorum of the streets of San Francisco and Portland were as perfect as those of Boston. "The San Francisco police system is admirable," he said, "and a woman may walk the streets of this city in the evening with less danger of insult and annoyance than in those of Springfield."

Miners' law established the tone of Western justice. While the hangman's rope often served as a statute book and trials were quick and efficient, accused persons were given a fair chance to defend themselves and the regulations of the diggings were enforced in daylight by impartial men publicly chosen. The miners, cut off as they were from the "fountains of justice which every American citizen should enjoy," realized the necessity of organizing a body politic "for mutual protection against the lawless and for meting out justice between man and man." When city, county, and state organizations came into being, the temporary courts were glad to be relieved of the responsibility of maintaining order and decorum.

Frontier politics, like frontier religion, was impassioned, emotional, and rampageous. Westerners were essentially men of action, better riflemen than statesmen and better orators than logicians. Andrew Jackson became their symbol as well as their ideal in political matters. People admired "Old Hickory" for his courage, his daring, his unpolished approach to problems, his warring spirit, his rugged individualism, his outspokenness, his belief in equality. Davy Crockett was of the same stamp, a typical frontier politician. So was Mrs. Mary E. Lease of Kansas—"Patrick Henry in Petticoats"—who, when the price of corn dropped so low that people began to burn it for fuel, proposed they raise "less corn and more hell."

Crockett was quick to perceive that laughter and liquor will win more votes than law and logic. "A good joke and a good drink" won him a seat in Congress, and his clangorous vocal qualities rubbed off on the Buncombe school of politicians who perfected a brand of oratory that may be described as a blend of frontier tall talk, spread-eagleism, and hallelujah. To say that buckskin politicians were rambunctious is to put it mildly. A onetime Speaker of the House in Arkansas, provoked by a wisecrack from the floor, deserted the chair, reached for his bowie knife, and after a considerable scuffle, "thrust his blade to the hilt in the innocent member's breast."

Power politics also figured significantly in the settlement of the West. In the early stages of California history, for example, the state was virtually controlled by the Southern Pacific Railroad—a fact that Frank Norris made much of in his novel The Octopus. In the Dakota Territory, Alexander McKenzie, representing the Northern Pacific Railroad, employed extremely unethical practices to secure passage of legislation that would move the territorial capital from Yankton to "some undesignated spot," in the sole interests of the railroad company. The history of western expansion is full of similar instances of sharp practices and juggling chicanery. The frontier town became, as Thomas D. Clark has pointed out, "a bubble of the eternal optimism of the American promoter."

VII

Tall talk, or bombastic outspokenness, came naturally to people living on the ragged edges of civilization. Frontier lingo was spiked with impetuous indecorum, startling picturesqueness, wayward unrefinement, and swaggering magniloquence. Words like *sockdologer, absquatulate, high falutin, flabbergast, blizzard, spandangalous,* and *splurge* were bandied about with gusto and conviction. "Improper" place names like *Greasyridge, Dry Bones, Bubbleup, Pickpocket, Wounded Knee, Jackass Gulch, Tombstone, Boot Hill, Red Horse,* and verbal distortions like *Smackover* for *Sumac Covert* or *Picketwire* for *Purgatoire* reflect an uproarious and riotous freedom of speech.

Figurative language, with its wild hyperbole and fantastic metaphor, had the same tempestuous, slaphappy disturbance. "Such a fog," wrote one Westerner, "one could chew it up and spit it out. With a sharp knife it might be cut in hunks and stored for dry weather." Booster talk and chamber-of-commerce rhetoric, such as those that punctuate so profusely the pages of Sinclair Lewis's *Babbitt*, are direct descendents of frontier verbal inflation. "Georgia soil is so rich," wrote a patriotic "Buzzard," "that when we throw corn to the chickens, they have to catch it on the fly or eat if off the stalk."

A lusty and earthy folklore, closely related to tall talk, developed among backwoodsmen and pioneers. The West, loaded as it was with mystery, was just right for mythmaking. Superstition possessed the minds of men, who acquired mighty proportions in imagination as they contemplated such fabulous terrors as the venomous hoop snake that supposedly spun through swamps and brakes killing trees on contact, the lashing whip snake that drove cattle to frenzy with its infernal tail, and the hissing serpent that exhaled a subtle gas laden with mortal disease. Thus was created a mountain of make-believe. Thus was created the fabulous "ringtailed roarer," or frontier screamer—a superhuman figure, half man and half myth, half horse and half alligator, who, "sired by a hurricane," "could strike as hard as fourth-proof lightning, "chaw chain cables for 'bakey,' " "take gun powder for snuff," and "drink steam without flinching."

Among numerous varieties of the roarer, or frontier hero, that emerged, four deserve special mention: the riverboatman, the backwoodsman, the Indian fighter, and the outlaw. Mike Fink, first and last of the boatmen, attained heroic proportions because of his unbelievable accomplishments on the river and because of the mysterious circumstances shrouding his death. Davy Crockett, whose coonskin cap and Kentucky rifle became widely recognized as symbols of the taming of the wilderness, attained mythological status before the fatal Alamo escapade by virtue of his backwoods ingenuity and his uncanny mental agility. Andrew Jackson—Bonaparte of the backwoods—grew in heroic stature as historians of the oral tradition recounted his exploits against the savage Indians, adding new details with every telling. Jesse James—"the greatest bandit and freebooter that ever figured in the pages of a country's history"—attempted to adjust the unequal distribution of wealth in his own way. An American Robin Hood with a double dose of rebellion in his blood, he became a symbol of man's eternal quest for freedom from the lock-step patterns of civilization. The treacherous act that ended his reckless career made him a popular hero and a national legend.

VIII

The stalwart men who subdued the West and made it safe for settlement were great talkers but poor readers. Timothy Flint said, "The people here are not yet a reading people. They are too busy, too much occupied in making farms and speculations, to think of literature." While taking a back seat to practically no one in the art of storytelling, the frontiersman rarely outdistanced his New England cousins in the realm of ideas, in spite of the fact that some of our greatest writers—men like Emerson, Whitman, and Melville—were firmly convinced that, if we were ever to produce a literature that could be called genuinely American, it must somehow reflect the ideas that are associated with the West—that part of the country least influenced by British styles and standards. It was Melville who said, "Let us believe, then, once for all, that there is no hope for us in these smooth, pleasing writers that know their powers." "No American writer should write like an Englishman or a Frenchman," he argued. "Let him write like a man, for then he will be sure to write like an American."

Western humor was, to be sure, a masculine literature, or "subliterature," as one writer has called it. Augustus Baldwin Longstreet was the dean of a group of yarn spinners who set forth the details of backwoodsmanship in hilarious colors. He made it clear that his *Georgia Scenes* (1835) were not mere "fancy sketches," but authentic accounts of real people, places, and events that he had known personally, and that his aim was "to supply a chasm in history which has always been overlooked—the manners, customs, amusements, wit, dialect, as they appear in all grades of society to an ear and eye witness to them." Besides accomplishing this laudable objective, in a style full of zest, exhilaration, and tomfoolery, Longstreet and other Western humorists of the same stripe presented frontier folk as human beings equipped with ambitions, passions, foibles, and clownish eccentricities. And if the writing of such precursors of local-color fiction as Madison Tenas, Johnson J. Hooper, William T. Thompson, Thomas Bangs Thorpe, John S. Robb, Joseph G. Baldwin, and George Washington Harris seems crude and awkward, it is probably because frontier times were out of kilter and backwoods society in a state of general uproar. A sense of unparalleled comicality and horseplay ruled out any semblance of formality and deportment.

The West abounded with yarns and stories and linguistic oddities which made up a unique oral tradition. "The nearer sundown," declared one frontier scribe, "the more original the character and odd the expression." Mark Twain—the only member of the clan to attain real eminence as a writer—defended the tall tale as a literary genre in "How to Tell a Story" (1899). His "Celebrated Jumping Frog of Calaveras County," published in the New York *Saturday Press* (1865), had been a "classic of the mining camps" for years, "rehearsed around campfires and in convivial gatherings." In the long run, this kind of literary pay dirt earned far greater dividends for the famous frontier author than all the precious metal he unearthed in the Nevada diggings.

Newspapers and magazines served an important function in frontier territories, not so much by reporting the news, which circulated effectively by word of mouth, but by publishing the ruminations and scribblings of backwoods literati, who attracted the attention of a large number of unsophisticated readers with their waggish neologisms, verbal extravagances, tall tales, blue-ribbon lies, outlandish character sketches, preposterous parodies, and sky-splitting boasts. The writing, denounced as banal, unethical, and disgustingly amoral by the sort of critics whom Crockett called "vermin that I shan't so much as stop to brush off," was often shrewd, penetrating, and refreshingly cynical. It recorded colloquial speechways, belittled backwoods nincompoopery, criticized social and political snobbery, interpreted and lampooned provincial manners, and helped both writer and reader maintain a semblance of sanity amid the hurdy-gurdy of frontier life.

IX

While most of the literature of the nineteenth-century West can be catalogued as travel accounts, autobiographies, journals of expeditions, diaries, histories, political propaganda, topographical studies, and religious treatises, some highly imaginative works also appeared. The first novel of importance produced in frontier territory was Judge H. H. Brackenridge's *Modern Chivalry* (1792), which the editor of the *Literary World* called "a kind of aboriginal classic." Another frontier classic was William Littell's *Festoons of Fancy* (1814), a satirical take-off on fraudulent practices of pioneer politicians and land speculators in Kentucky. Early romantic tales included James Hall's *Legends of the West* (1832), F. W. Thomas's *Clinton Bradshaw* (1835), and Benjamin Drake's *Tales and Sketches of the Queen City* (1839). Besides a distinguished list of nonfiction books, Timothy Flint also wrote several novels which have been called "racy and readable."

Local-color fiction, which pictured life in isolated regional areas with varying degrees of accuracy, began to appear around the middle of the century. Caroline Kirkland, who is especially remembered for *A New Home—Who'll Follow?* (1839), wrote a number of unromantic stories of frontier life in Michigan which were collected in *Western Clearings* (1846). Bret Harte's melodramatic *The Luck of Roaring Camp and Other Sketches* (1870), Mark Twain's *Roughing It* (1872) (a duke's mixture of fact and fancy) and William Wright's *History of the Big Bonanza* (1876) present pictures of frontier life in the gold fields of California and Nevada. Superbly drawn character sketches from rural Georgia may be found in Richard Malcolm Johnston's *Dukesborough Tales* (1871); and a happy marriage of genial humor and homely realism in Edward Eggleston's widely read Hoosier pieces, which began to appear in the 1870s. In sharp contrast to Eggleston's nostalgic style are E. W. Howe's rather bitter *Story of a Country Town* (1883), Joseph Kirkland's *Zury: The Meanest Man in Spring County* (1887), and Hamlin Garland's caustically critical *Main*

Traveled Roads (1891), all of which anticipate such twentieth-century realists as Sinclair Lewis and Sherwood Anderson.

James Fenimore Cooper was possibly the first to recognize the drama of the West for what it really was: the struggle between the forces of primitive nature and of civilized society for the soul of man. As Russel Nye so aptly phrased it: "When Natty Bumppo walked into American fiction and leaned on his long rifle, the American novel came of age." Cooper equipped his hero with a psychological conflict and a neurotic compulsion which matched the realities of frontier experience. The Leatherstocking sought self-expression by perpetually retreating westward in order to escape advancing civilization, which, forever breathing down his neck, tried to thwart his efforts to be free. He was caught between what Emerson called "the Establishment and the Movement"—"the party of the Past and the party of the Future." It was precisely the fact of Leatherstocking's innate moral sense at sword's points with the moralities of regularized society that constituted his dilemma.

The same dilemma may be discerned in Melville's *Moby Dick* and in Mark Twain's *Adventures of Huckleberry Finn*, two classic studies of frontier America concerned with attempted escapes from the pressures of social discipline. Melville's Ishmael flees to the open sea by taking passage on the *Pequod* which is "not so much bound to any haven ahead as rushing from all havens astern." Huck Finn is forever lighting out for the territory in a mad flight from respectability and decency. In both novels, the search for identity in an untrammeled environment proves futile, and neither author offers a satisfactory solution to the perplexing problem of individuality versus conformity which forever faces the people of a nation for whom freedom is a sacred birthright.

The cattleman's frontier became a subject for serious fiction near the end of the nineteenth-century when Owen Wister, Alfred Henry Lewis, and Andy Adams began publishing their stories and accounts of rodeos, roundups, cattle drives, and other wrangling affairs of American cowpunchers. Of these writers, Adams was most realistic—so much so, in fact, that his stories might easily pass as history. Lewis was most fanciful. Owen Wister's *The Virginian* (1902), which combines honest realism with humor and melodrama, may be called the granddaddy of modern horse opera.

After Wister, Western fiction of the cattle range degenerated rapidly into a kind of patterned unrealism that gives readers a falsified, superficial, and overglamorous picture of what the West really was like. Out of scores of names of Western fiction writers who made frontier heroics their specialty, only one deserves honorable mention. Eugene Manlove Rhodes, for his fidelity to facts and for his vitality of expression, has been distinguished by De Voto as "the novelist of the Cattle Kingdom."

Some pertinent facts about Western experience, however, are more adequately expressed in fiction than elsewhere: the frontiersman's victimization by social and economic as well as geographical and natural forces beyond his power to control; the incalculable importance of the land to sensitive people unable to cope with the invidious manipulations of the money-changers; the futility of theoretical and traditional solutions to problems of survival in the wilderness; the death grip of loneliness on the careers of women who followed their husbands into the uncharted West; the bitter rewards of unbounded faith in the myth of abundance; the fierceness and brutality of the struggle with the raw and unbecoming facts of life in the plains country; the high price of impetuosity in matters of judicial decision. Significant writers include Frank Norris (*The Octopus*, 1901), Willa Cather (*O Pioneers!*, 1913), Ole Rölvaag (*Giants in the Earth*, 1927), H. L. Davis (*Honey in the Horn*, 1935), Mari Sandoz (*Old Jules*, 1935), Wallace Stegner (*The Big Rock Candy Mountain*, 1938), Walter Van Tilburg Clark (*The Oxbow Incident*, 1940), and A. B. Guthrie, Jr. (*The Big Sky*, 1947, and *The Way West*, 1949).

X

The frontier officially was declared closed some three-quarters of a century ago, even though the free lands had not all been taken up. By 1890, the Indians had been largely subdued and the unsettled parts of the country were "so broken into by isolated bodies of settlement" that no distinct line of separation could be defined. But the migrations did not stop, in spite of the firm conviction, as expressed by Henry Demarest Lloyd, that "our young men can no longer go West; they must go up or down." Although the forced halt at the shores of the Pacific was considered by some to be "a much more serious affair than that which brought our ancestors to a pause before the barriers of the Atlantic," the driving force that carried pioneers through the wilderness, across the plains, and over the mountains to the Pacific had not yet fizzled out. People could still "breathe independence with the air of the mountains and the woods," and the largest exodus was still to come. During the period from 1940 to 1960, the states in the Rocky Mountain West and the Pacific Coast West increased their populations by nearly fourteen million people.

America, in many ways, is still "westward-tilted." The geographical center of population is now on the verge of crossing the Mississippi. But direction is no longer important. Nowadays, in covered wagons of the air, modern pioneers encircle the globe in less time than it took the overland migrants to push their prairie schooners from Leavenworth to Junction City. Although the new West is one of make-believe, of celluloid dreams, of "one-armed bandits," and of "Cadillac cowboys," the spirit and dynamics of the old West remain integral parts of the nation's make-up. The frontier was never one of geography, really, but of the mind, which may well account for its apparent timelessness. "The New Frontier" is a reality, and John F. Kennedy's Peace Corps has inspired thousands of young people to shove off for hinterlands far beyond the borders of the continental United States, to seek, not tillable lands, but new opportunities—opportunities for adventure, for service, for self-realization, for active participation in working out the destiny of the American people.

Perhaps the frontier influence on modern America is most evident in our impulsive mobility, our unshakable faith in progress (despite repeated failures and setbacks of one kind and another), and our incomparable propensity for building. The very history of America is a story of process, of movement, of unfolding, of westering.

An Englishman, viewing New York City for the first time, is reported as saying, "It will be wonderful when it is finished." The truth of the matter is that, should America ever become finished, the frontier really will be closed.

part 1

PERSPECTIVES

⤙ HENRY DAVID THOREAU

Westward I Go Free

Henry David Thoreau (1817–1862) in his essay "Walking" (1862) has contrasted, as he says, "absolute freedom and wildness" with "a freedom and culture merely civil." In so doing, he gives expression to a movement that symbolizes the westward migrations of Americans across the continent. He speaks of a magnetic force that impels people to quit what Emerson called the "Establishment" and to join what he called the "Movement." The spiritual dimension of Thoreau's thought, in the selection reprinted here, has a recognizable kinship with Whitman's "Passage to India."

What is it that makes it so hard sometimes to determine whither we will walk? I believe that there is a subtle magnetism in Nature, which, if we unconsciously yield to it, will direct us aright. It is not indifferent to us which way we walk. There is a right way; but we are very liable from heedlessness and stupidity to take the wrong one. We could fain take that walk, never yet taken by us through this actual world, which is perfectly symbolical of the path which we love to travel in the interior and ideal world; and sometimes, no doubt, we find it difficult to choose our direction, because it does not yet exist distinctly in our idea.

When I go out of the house for a walk, uncertain as yet whither I will bend my steps, and submit myself to my instinct to decide for me, I find, strange and whimsical as it may seem, that

From "Walking," *Atlantic Monthly*, June 1862. Editor's title.

I finally and inevitably settle southwest, toward some particular wood or meadow or deserted pasture or hill in that direction. My needle is slow to settle—varies a few degrees and does not always point due southwest, it is true, and it has good authority for this variation, but it always settles between west and south-southwest. The future lies that way to me, and the earth seems more unexhausted and richer on that side. The outline which would bound my walks would be not a circle, but a parabola, or rather like one of those cometary orbits which have been thought to be non-returning curves, in this case opening westward, in which my house occupies the place of the sun. I turn round and round irresolute sometimes for a quarter of an hour, until I decide, for a thousandth time, that I will walk into the southwest or west. Eastward I go only by force, but westward I go free. Thither no business leads me. It is hard for me to believe that I shall find fair landscapes or sufficient wildness and freedom behind the eastern horizon. I am not excited by the prospect of a walk thither; but I believe that the forest which I see in the western horizon stretches uninterruptedly toward the setting sun, and there are no towns nor cities in it of enough consequence to disturb me. Let me live where I will, on this side is the city, on that the wilderness, and ever I am leaving the city more and more and withdrawing into the wilderness. I should not lay so much stress on this fact if I did not believe that something like this is the prevailing tendency of my countrymen. I must walk toward Oregon, and not toward Europe. And that way the nation is moving, and I may say that mankind progress from east to west. Within a few years we have witnessed the phenomenon of a southeastward migration, in the settlement of Australia; but this affects us as a retrograde movement, and, judging from the moral and physical character of the first generation of Australians, has not yet proved a successful experiment. The eastern Tartars think that there is nothing west beyond Tibet. "The world ends there," say they; "beyond, there is nothing but a shoreless sea." It is unmitigated East where they live.

We go eastward to realize history and study the works of art and literature, retracing the steps of the race; we go westward as into the future, with a spirit of enterprise and adventure. The Atlantic is a Lethean stream; in our passage over which we have had an opportunity to forget the Old World and its institutions. If we do not succeed this time, there is perhaps one more chance for the race left before it arrives on the banks of the Styx; and that is in the Lethe of the Pacific, which is three times as wide.

I know not how significant it is, or how far it is an evidence of singularity, that an individual should thus consent in his pettiest walk with the general movement of the race; but I know that something akin to the migratory instinct in birds and quadrupeds —which, in some instances, is known to have affected the squirrel tribe, impelling them to a general and mysterious movement in which they were seen, say some, crossing the broadest rivers, each on its particular chip, with its tail raised for a sail, and bridging narrower streams with their dead—that something like the furor which affects the domestic cattle in the spring, and which is referred to a worm in their tails, affects both nations and individuals, either perennially or from time to time. Not a flock of wild geese cackles over our town but it to some extent unsettles the value of real estate here; and, if I were a broker, I should probably take that disturbance into account.

> Than longen folk to gon on pilgrimages,
> And palmers for to seken strange strondes.

Every sunset which I witness inspires me with the desire to go to a West as distant and as fair as that into which the sun goes down. He appears to migrate westward daily, and tempt us to follow him. He is the Great Western Pioneer whom the nations follow. We dream all night of those mountain ridges in the horizon, though they may be of vapor only, which were last gilded by his rays. The island of Atlantis and the islands and gardens of the Hesperides, a sort of terrestrial paradise, appear to have been the Great West of the ancients, enveloped in mystery and poetry. Who has not seen in imagination, when looking into the sunset sky, the gardens of the Hesperides, and the foundation of all those fables?

Columbus felt the westward tendency more strongly than any before. He obeyed it, and found a New World for Castile and

Leon. The herd of men in those days scented fresh pastures from afar.

> And now the sun had stretched out all the hills,
> And now was dropped into the western bay;
> At last *he* rose, and twitched his mantle blue;
> Tomorrow to fresh woods and pastures new.

Where on the globe can there be found an area of equal extent with that occupied by the bulk of our States, so fertile and so rich and varied in its productions, and at the same time so habitable by the European, as this is? Michaux, who knew but part of them, says that "the species of large trees are much more numerous in North America than in Europe; in the United States there are more than one hundred and forty species that exceed thirty feet in height; in France there are but thirty that attain this size." Later botanists more than confirm his observations. Humboldt came to America to realize his youthful dreams of a tropical vegetation, and he beheld it in its greatest perfection in the primitive forests of the Amazon, the most gigantic wilderness on the earth, which he has so eloquently described. The geographer Guyot, himself a European, goes farther—farther than I am ready to follow him; yet not when he says, "As the plant is made for the animal, as the vegetable world is made for the animal world, America is made for the man of the Old World. . . . The man of the Old World sets out upon his way. Leaving the highlands of Asia, he descends from station to station toward Europe. Each of his steps is marked by a new civilization superior to the preceding, by a greater power of development. Arrived at the Atlantic, he pauses on the shore of this unknown ocean, the bounds of which he knows not, and turns upon his footprints for an instant." When he has exhausted the rich soil of Europe and reinvigorated himself, "then recommences his adventurous career westward as in the earliest ages." So far Guyot.

From this western impulse coming in contact with the barrier of the Atlantic sprang the commerce and enterprise of modern times. The younger Michaux, in his "Travels West of the Alleghanies in 1802," says that the common inquiry in the newly settled West was, " 'From what part of the world have you come?' As if these vast and fertile regions would naturally be the place of meeting and common country of the inhabitants of the globe."

To use an obsolete Latin word, I might say, *Ex Oriente lux; ex Occidente frux*. From the East light; from the West fruit.

Sir Francis Head, an English traveler and a Governor General of Canada, tells us that "in both the northern and southern hemispheres of the New World Nature has not only outlined her works on a larger scale, but has painted the whole picture with brighter and more costly colors than she used in delineating and in beautifying the Old World. . . . The heavens of America appear infinitely higher, the sky is bluer, the air is fresher, the cold is intenser, the moon looks larger, the stars are brighter, the thunder is louder, the lightning is vivider, the wind is stronger, the rain is heavier, the mountains are higher, the rivers longer, the forests bigger, the plains broader." This statement will do at least to set against Buffon's account of this part of the world and its productions.

Linnaeus said long ago, "*Nescio quae facies laeta, glabra plantis Americanis*": I know not what there is of joyous and smooth in the aspect of American plants; and I think that in this country there are no, or at most very few, *Africanae bestiae*, African beasts, as the Romans called them, and that in this respect also it is peculiarly fitted for the habitation of man. We are told that within three miles of the center of the East Indian city of Singapore, some of the inhabitants are annually carried off by tigers; but the traveler can lie down in the woods at night almost anywhere in North America without fear of wild beasts.

These are encouraging testimonies. If the moon looks larger here than in Europe, probably the sun looks larger also. If the heavens of America appear infinitely higher and the stars brighter, I trust that these facts are symbolical of the height to which the philosophy and poetry and religion of her inhabitants may one day soar. At length, perchance, the immaterial heaven will appear as much higher to the American mind, and the intimations that star it as much brighter. For I believe that climate does thus react on man —as there is something in the mountain air that feeds the spirit and inspires. Will not man grow to greater perfection intellectually as well as physically under these influences? Or is it unimportant how many foggy days there are in his life? I trust that we shall be more imaginative, that our thoughts will be clearer, fresher, and more ethereal, as our sky; our understanding more comprehensive and broader, like our plains; our intellect generally on a grander scale, like our thunder and lightning, our rivers and mountains and forests; and our hearts shall even correspond in breadth and depth and grandeur to our inland seas. Perchance there will appear to the traveler something, he knows not what, of *laeta* and *glabra*, of joyous and serene, in our very faces. Else to what end does the world go on, and why was America discovered?

To Americans I hardly need to say,

> Westward the star of empire takes its way

As a true patriot, I should be ashamed to think that Adam in paradise was more favorably situated on the whole than the back-woodsman in this country.

Our sympathies in Massachusetts are not confined to New England; though we may be estranged from the South, we sympathize with the West. There is the home of the younger sons, as among the Scandinavians they took to the sea for their inheritance. It is too late to be studying Hebrew; it is more important to understand even the slang of today.

Some months ago I went to see a panorama of the Rhine. It was like a dream of the Middle Ages. I floated down its historic stream in something more than imagination, under bridges built by the Romans and repaired by later heroes, past cities and castles whose very names were music to my ears, and each of which was the subject of a legend. There were Ehrenbreitstein and Rolands-eck and Coblentz, which I knew only in history. They were ruins that interested me chiefly. There seemed to come up from its waters and its vine-clad hills and valleys a hushed music as of Crusaders departing for the Holy Land. I floated along under the spell of enchantment, as if I had been transported to a heroic age and breathed an atmosphere of chivalry.

Soon after, I went to see a panorama of the Mississippi; and as I worked my way up the river in the light of today and saw the steamboats wooding up, counted the rising cities, gazed on the fresh ruins of Nauvoo, beheld the Indians moving west across the stream, and, as before I had looked up the Moselle, now looked' up the Ohio and the Missouri and heard the legends of Dubuque and of Wenona's Cliff—still thinking more of the future than of the past or present—I saw that this was a Rhine stream of a different kind, that the foundations of castles were yet to be laid, and the famous bridges were yet to be thrown over the river; and I felt that this was the heroic age itself, though we know it not, for the hero is commonly the simplest and obscurest of men.

✒ FREDERICK JACKSON TURNER

The Significance
of the Frontier
in American History

When Frederick Jackson Turner (1861–1932) read his paper on "The Significance of the Frontier in American History" at a meeting of the American Historical Association in Chicago, July 1893, he started an academic debate that is still not settled. The famous University of Wisconsin historian, supporting agrarian idealism and cultural environmentalism, introduced what has been called a "safety-valve" theory of colonization of unsettled territories. His thesis that the American character and American institutions grew out of man's experience in taming the frontier is at variance with the so-called "germ" theory that contends that civilized man took the seeds of culture with him into the West. For a pro and con discussion of Turner's ideas see George Rogers Taylor, *The Turner Thesis*, in Problems in American Civilization Series (Boston, 1956). See also Ray Allen Billington's foreword to *The Frontier in American History* by Frederick Jackson Turner (New York, 1962).

In a recent bulletin of the Superintendent of the Census for 1890 appear these significant words: "Up to and including 1880 the country had a frontier of settlement, but at present the unsettled area has been so broken into by isolated bodies of settlement that there can hardly be said to be a frontier line. In the discussion of its extent, its westward movement, etc., it can not, therefore, any longer have a place in the census reports." This brief official statement marks the closing of a great historic movement. Up to our own day American history has been in a large degree the history of the colonization of the Great West. The existence of an area of free land, its continuous recession, and the advance of American settlement westward, explain American development.

Behind institutions, behind constitutional forms and modifications, lie the vital forces that call these organs into life and shape them to meet changing conditions. The peculiarity of American institutions is the fact that they have been compelled to adapt themselves to the changes of an expanding people—to the changes involved in crossing a continent, in winning a wilderness, and in developing at each area of this progress out of the primitive economic and political conditions of the frontier into the complexity of city life. Said Calhoun in 1817, "We are great, and rapidly—I was about to say fearfully—growing!" So saying, he touched the distinguishing feature of American life. All peoples show development; the germ theory of politics has been sufficiently emphasized. In the case of most nations, however, the development has occurred in a limited area; and if the nation has expanded, it has met other growing peoples whom it has conquered. But in the case of the United States we have a different phenomenon. Limiting our attention to the Atlantic coast, we have the familiar phenomenon of the evolution of institutions in a limited area, such as the rise of representative government; the differentiation of simple colonial governments into complex organs; the progress from primitive industrial society, without division of labor, up to manufacturing civilization. But we have in addition to this a recurrence of the process of evolution in each western area reached in the process of expansion. Thus American development has exhibited not merely advance along a single line, but a return to primitive conditions on a continually advancing frontier line, and a new development for that area. American social development has been continually beginning over again on the frontier. This perennial rebirth, this fluidity of American life, this expansion westward with its new opportunities, its continuous touch with the simplicity of primitive society, furnish the forces dominating American character. The true point of view in the history of this nation is not the Atlantic coast, it is the Great West. Even the slavery struggle, which is made so exclusive an object of attention by writers like Professor von Holst, occupies its important place in American history because of its relation to westward expansion.

In this advance, the frontier is the outer edge of the wave— the meeting point between savagery and civilization. Much has been written about the frontier from the point of view of border warfare and the chase, but as a field for the serious study of the economist and the historian it has been neglected.

The American frontier is sharply distinguished from the European frontier—a fortified boundary line running through dense populations. The most significant thing about the American frontier is, that it lies at the hither edge of free land. In the census reports it is treated as the margin of that settlement which has a density of two or more to the square mile. The term is an elastic one, and for our purposes does not need sharp definition. We shall consider the whole frontier belt, including the Indian country and the outer margin of the "settled area" of the census reports. This paper will make no attempt to treat the subject exhaustively; its aim is simply to call attention to the frontier

as a fertile field for investigation, and to suggest some of the
problems which arise in connection with it.

In the settlement of America we have to observe how European life entered the continent, and how America modified and
developed that life and reacted on Europe. Our early history is
the study of European germs developing in an American environment. Too exclusive attention has been paid by institutional
students to the Germanic origins, too little to the American
factors. The frontier is the line of most rapid and effective Ameri-
canization. The wilderness masters the colonist. It finds him a
European in dress, industries, tools, modes of travel, and thought.
It takes him from the railroad car and puts him in the birch
canoe. It strips off the garments of civilization and arrays him in
the hunting shirt and the moccasin. It puts him in the log cabin
of the Cherokee and Iroquois and runs an Indian palisade around
him. Before long he has gone to planting Indian corn and plowing with a sharp stick; he shouts the war cry and takes the scalp
in orthodox Indian fashion. In short, at the frontier the environment is at first too strong for the man. He must accept the conditions which it furnishes, or perish, and so he fits himself into
the Indian clearings and follows the Indian trails. Little by little
he transforms the wilderness, but the outcome is not the old
Europe, not simply the development of Germanic germs, any
more than the first phenomenon was a case of reversion to the
Germanic mark. The fact is, that here is a new product that is
American. At first, the frontier was the Atlantic coast. It was
the frontier of Europe in a very real sense. Moving westward, the
frontier became more and more American. As successive terminal
moraines result from successive glaciations, so each frontier leaves
its traces behind it, and when it becomes a settled area the region
still partakes of the frontier characteristics. Thus the advance of
the frontier has meant a steady movement away from the influence of Europe, a steady growth of independence on American
lines. And to study this advance, the men who grew up under
these conditions, and the political, economic, and social results
of it, is to study the really American part of our history.

In the course of the seventeenth century the frontier was advanced up the Atlantic river courses, just beyond the "fall line,"

and the tidewater region became the settled area. In the first half of the eighteenth century another advance occurred. Traders followed the Delaware and Shawnese Indians to the Ohio as early as the end of the first quarter of the century. . . . In the period of the Revolution the frontier crossed the Alleghanies into Kentucky and Tennessee, and the upper waters of the Ohio were settled. When the first census was taken in 1790, the continuous settled area was bounded by a line which ran near the coast of Maine, and included New England except a portion of Vermont and New Hampshire, New York along the Hudson and up the Mohawk about Schenectady, eastern and southern Pennsylvania, Virginia well across the Shenandoah Valley, and the Carolinas and eastern Georgia. . . . The "West," as a self-conscious section, began to evolve. . . .

In the middle of this century the line indicated by the present eastern boundary of Indian Territory, Nebraska, and Kansas marked the frontier of the Indian country. Minnesota and Wisconsin still exhibited frontier conditions, but the distinctive frontier of the period is found in California, where the gold discoveries had sent a sudden tide of adventurous miners, and in Oregon, and the settlements in Utah. . . .

By 1880 the settled area had been pushed into northern Michigan, Wisconsin, and Minnesota, along Dakota rivers, and in the Black Hills region, and was ascending the rivers of Kansas and Nebraska. The development of mines in Colorado had drawn isolated frontier settlements into that region, and Montana and Idaho were receiving settlers.

In these successive frontiers we find natural boundary lines which have served to mark and to affect the characteristics of the frontiers, namely: the "fall line"; the Alleghany Mountains; the Mississippi; the Missouri where its direction approximates north and south; the line of the arid lands, approximately the ninety-ninth meridian; and the Rocky Mountains. The fall line marked the frontier of the seventeenth century; the Alleghanies that of the eighteenth; the Mississippi that of the first quarter of the nineteenth; the Missouri that of the middle of this century (omitting the California movement); and the belt of the

Rocky Mountains and the arid tract, the present frontier. Each was won by series of Indian wars. . . .

The Atlantic frontier was compounded of fisherman, fur-trader, miner, cattle-raiser, and farmer. Excepting the fisherman, each type of industry was on the march toward the West, impelled by an irresistible attraction. Each passed in successive waves across the continent. Stand at Cumberland Gap and watch the procession of civilization, marching single file—the buffalo following the trail to the salt springs, the Indian, the fur-trader and hunter, the cattle-raiser, the pioneer farmer—and the frontier has passed by. Stand at South Pass in the Rockies a century later and see the same procession with wider intervals between. The unequal rate of advance compels us to distinguish the frontier into the trader's frontier, the rancher's frontier, or the miner's frontier, and the farmer's frontier. When the mines and the cow pens were still near the fall line the traders' pack trains were tinkling across the Alleghenies, and the French on the Great Lakes were fortifying their posts, alarmed by the British trader's birch canoe. When the trappers scaled the Rockies, the farmer was still near the mouth of the Missouri.

Why was it that the Indian trader passed so rapidly across the continent? What effects followed from the trader's frontier? The trade was coeval with American discovery. The Norsemen, Vespucius, Verrazani, Hudson, John Smith, all trafficked for furs. the Plymouth pilgrims settled in Indian cornfields, and their first return cargo was of beaver and lumber. The records of the various New England colonies show how steadily exploration was carried into the wilderness by this trade. What is true for New England is, as would be expected, even plainer for the rest of the colonies. All along the coast from Maine to Georgia the Indian trade opened up the river courses. Steadily the trader passed westward, utilizing the older lines of French trade. The Ohio, the Great Lakes, the Mississippi, the Missouri, and the Platte, the lines of western advance, were ascended by traders. They found the passes in the Rocky Mountains and guided Lewis and Clark, Frémont, and Bidwell. The explanation of the rapidity of this advance is connected with the effects of the trader on the Indian. The trading post left the unarmed tribes at the mercy of those that had purchased fire-arms—a truth which the Iroquois Indians wrote in blood, and so the remote and unvisted tribes gave eager welcome to the trader. "The savages," wrote La Salle, "take better care of us French than of their own children; from us only can they get guns and goods." This accounts for the trader's power and the rapidity of his advance. Thus the disintegrating forces of civilization entered the wilderness. Every river valley and Indian trail became a fissure in Indian society, and so that society became honeycombed. Long before the pioneer farmer appeared on the scene, primitive Indian life had passed away. The farmers met Indians armed with guns. The trading frontier, while steadily undermining Indian power by making the tribes ultimately dependent on the whites, yet, through its sale of guns, gave to the Indian increased power of resistance to the farming frontier. French colonization was dominated by its trading frontier; English colonization by its farming frontier. There was an antagonism between the two frontiers as between the two nations. Said Duquesne to the Iroquois, "Are you ignorant of the difference between the king of England and the king of France? Go see the forts that our king has established and you will see that you can still hunt under their very walls. They have been placed for your advantage in places which you frequent. The English, on the contrary, are no sooner in possession of a place than the game is driven away. The forest falls before them as they advance, and the soil is laid bare so that you can scarce find the wherewithal to erect a shelter for the night."

And yet, in spite of this opposition of the interests of the trader and the farmer, the Indian trade pioneered the way for civilization. The buffalo trail became the Indian trail, and this became the trader's "trace"; the trails widened into roads, and the roads into turnpikes, and these in turn were transformed into railroads. The same origin can be shown for the railroads of the South, the Far West, and the Dominion of Canada. The trading posts reached by these trails were on the sites of Indian villages which had been placed in positions suggested by nature; and these trading posts, situated so as to command the water systems of the country, have grown into such cities as Albany, Pittsburgh, Detroit, Chicago, St. Louis, Council Bluffs, and Kansas City. Thus civilization in America has followed the arteries made by geology, pouring an ever richer tide through them, until at last the slender paths of aboriginal intercourse have been broadened and interwoven into the complex mazes of modern commercial lines; the wilderness has been interpenetrated by lines of civilization growing ever more numerous. It is like the steady growth of a complex nervous system for the originally simple, inert continent. If one would understand why we are to-day one nation, rather than a collection of isolated states, he must study this economic and social consolidation of the country. . . .

The exploitation of the beasts took hunter and trader to the west, the exploitation of the grasses took the rancher west, and the exploitation of the virgin soil of the river valleys and prairies attracted the farmer. Good soils have been the most continuous attraction to the farmer's frontier. The land hunger of the Virginians drew them down the rivers into Carolina, in early colonial days; the search for soils took the Massachusetts men to Pennsylvania and to New York. As the eastern lands were taken up migration flowed across them to the west. Daniel Boone, the great backwoodsman, who combined the occupations of hunter, trader, cattle-raiser, farmer, and surveyor—learning, probably from the traders, of the fertility of the lands of the upper Yadkin, where the traders were wont to rest as they took their way to the Indians, left his Pennsylvania home with his father, and passed down the Great Valley road to that stream. Learning from a trader of the game and rich pastures of Kentucky, he pioneered the way for the farmers to that region. Thence he passed to the frontier of Missouri, where his settlement was long a landmark on the frontier. Here again he helped to open the way for civilization, finding salt licks, and trails, and land. His son was among the earliest trappers in the passes of the Rocky Mountains, and his party are said to have been the first to camp on the present site of Denver. His grandson, Col. A. J. Boone, of Colorado, was a power among the Indians of the Rocky Mountains, and was appointed an agent by the government. Kit Carson's mother was a Boone. Thus this family epitomizes the backwoodsman's advance across the continent. . . .

Omitting those of the pioneer farmers who move from the love of adventure, the advance of the more steady farmer is easy to understand. Obviously the immigrant was attracted by the cheap lands of the frontier, and even the native farmer felt their influence strongly. Year by year the farmers who lived on soil whose returns were diminished by unrotated crops were offered the virgin soil of the frontier at nominal prices. Their growing families demanded more lands, and these were dear. The competition of the unexhausted, cheap, and easily tilled prairie lands compelled the farmer either to go west and continue the exhaustion of the soil on a new frontier, or to adopt intensive culture. Thus the census of 1890 shows, in the Northwest, many counties in which there is an absolute or a relative decrease of population. These States have been sending farmers to advance the frontier on the plains, and have themselves begun to turn to intensive farming and to manufacture. A decade before this, Ohio had shown the same transition stage. Thus the demand for land and the love of wilderness freedom drew the frontier ever onward.

Having now roughly outlined the various kinds of frontiers, and their modes of advance, chiefly from the point of view of the frontier itself, we may next inquire what were the influences on the East and on the New World. . . .

First, we note that the frontier promoted the formation of a composite nationality for the American people. The coast was preponderantly English, but the later tides of continental immigration flowed across to the free lands. This was the case from the early colonial days. The Scotch-Irish and the Palatine Germans, or "Pennsylvania Dutch," furnished the dominant element in the stock of the colonial frontier. With these peoples were also the freed indented servants, or redemptioners, who at the expiration of their time of service passed to the frontier. . . . Very generally these redemptions were of non-English stock. In the crucible of the frontier the immigrants were Americanized, liberated, and fused into a mixed race, English in neither nationality nor characteristics. The process has gone on from the early days to our own. . . .

In another way the advance of the frontier decreased our dependence on England. The coast, particularly of the South, lacked diversified industries, and was dependent on England for the bulk of its supplies. In the South there was even a dependence on the Northern colonies for articles of food. . . . Before long the frontier created a demand for merchants. As it retreated from the coast it became less and less possible for England to bring her supplies directly to the consumer's wharfs, and carry away staple crops, and staple crops began to give way to diversified agriculture for a time. The effect of this phase of the frontier action upon the northern section is perceived when we realize how the advance of the frontier aroused seaboard cities like Boston, New York, and Baltimore, to engage in rivalry for what Washington called "the extensive and valuable trade of a rising empire."

The legislation which most developed the powers of the national government, and played the largest part in its activity, was conditioned on the frontier. Writers have discussed the subjects of tariff, land, and internal improvement, as subsidiary to the slavery question. . . . This is a wrong perspective. The pioneer needed the goods of the coast, and so the grand series of internal improvement and railroad legislation began, with potent nationalizing effects. Over internal improvements occurred great debates, in which grave constitutional questions were discussed. Sectional groupings appear in the votes, profoundly significant for the historian. Loose construction increased as the nation marched westward. But the West was not content with bringing the farm to the factory. Under the lead of Clay—"Harry of the West"—protective tariffs were passed, with the cry of bringing the factory to the farm. The disposition of the public lands was a third important subject of national legislation influenced by the frontier.

The public domain has been a force of profound importance in the nationalization and development of the government. The effects of the struggle of the landed and the landless States, and of the Ordinance of 1787, need no discussion. Administratively the frontier called out some of the highest and most vitalizing activities of the general government. The purchase of Louisiana was perhaps the constitutional turning point in the history of the Republic, inasmuch as it afforded both a new area for national legislation and the occasion of the downfall of the policy of strict construction. But the purchase of Louisiana was called out by frontier needs and demands. As frontier States accrued to the Union the national power grew. In a speech on the dedication of the Calhoun monument Mr. Lamar explained: "In 1789 the States were the creators of the Federal Government; in 1861 the Federal Government was the creator of a large majority of the States.". . .

It is safe to say that the legislation with regard to land, tariff, and internal improvements—the American system of the nationalizing Whig party—was conditioned on frontier ideas and needs. But it was not merely in legislative action that the frontier worked against the sectionalism of the coast. The economic and social characteristics of the frontier worked against sectionalism. The men of the frontier had closer resemblances to the Middle region than to either of the other sections. Pennsylvania had been the seed-plot of frontier emigration, and, although she passed on her settlers along the Great Valley into the west of Virginia and the Carolinas, yet the industrial society of these Southern frontiersmen was always more like that of the Middle region than like that of the tide-water portion of the South, which later came to spread its industrial type throughout the South.

The Middle region, entered by New York harbor, was an open door to all Europe. The tide-water part of the South represented typical Englishmen, modified by a warm climate and servile labor, and living in baronial fashion on great plantations; New England stood for a special English movement—Puritanism. The middle region was less English than the other sections. It had a wide mixture of nationalities, a varied society, the mixed town and country system of local government, a varied economic life, many religious sects. In short, it was a region mediating between New England and the South, and the East and the West. It represented that composite nationality which the contemporary United States exhibits, that juxtaposition of non-English groups, occupying a valley or a little settlement, and presenting reflections of the map of Europe in their variety. It was democratic and nonsectional, if not national; "easy, tolerant, and contented"; rooted strongly in material prosperity. It was typical of the modern United States. . . .

It was this nationalizing tendency of the West that transformed the democracy of Jefferson into the national republicanism of Monroe and the democracy of Andrew Jackson. The West of the War of 1812, the West of Clay, and Benton and Harrison, and Andrew Jackson, shut off by the Middle States and the mountains from the coast sections, had a solidarity of its own with national tendencies. On the tide of the Father of Waters, North and South met and mingled into a nation. Interstate migration went steadily on—a process of cross-fertilization of ideas and institutions. The fierce struggle of the sections over slavery on the western frontier does not diminish the truth of this statement; it proves the truth of it. Slavery was a sectional trait that would not down, but in the West it could not remain sectional. It was the greatest of frontiersmen who declared: "I believe this Government can not endure permanently half slave and half free. It will become all of one thing or all of the other." Nothing works for nationalism like intercourse within the nation. Mobility of population is death to localism, and the western frontier worked irresistibly in unsettling population. The effect reached back from the frontier and affected profoundly the Atlantic coast and even the Old World.

But the most important effect of the frontier has been in the promotion of democracy here and in Europe. As has been indicated, the frontier is productive of individualism. Complex society is precipitated by the wilderness into a kind of primitive organization based on the family. The tendency is anti-social. It produces antipathy to control, and particularly to any direct control. The tax-gatherer is viewed as a representative of oppression. Prof. Osgood, in an able article, has pointed out that the frontier conditions prevalent in the colonies are important factors in the explanation of the American Revolution, where individual liberty was sometimes confused with absence of all effective government. The same conditions aid in explaining the difficulty of instituting a strong government in the period of the confederacy. The frontier individualism has from the beginning promoted democracy.

The frontier States that came into the Union in the first quarter of a century of its existence came in with democratic suffrage provisions, and had reactive effects of the highest importance upon the older States whose peoples were being attracted there. An extension of the franchise became essential. It was *western* New York that forced an extension of suffrage in the constitutional convention of that State in 1821; and it was *western* Virginia that compelled the tide-water region to put a more liberal suffrage provision in the constitution framed in 1830, and to give to the frontier region a more nearly proportionate representation with the tide-water aristocracy. The rise of democracy as an effective force in the nation came in with western preponderance under Jackson and William Henry Harrison, and it meant the triumph of the frontier—with all of its good and with all of its evil elements. . . .

So long as free land exists, the opportunity for a competency exists, and economic power secures political power. But the democracy born of free land, strong in selfishness and individualism, intolerant of administrative experience and education, and pressing individual liberty beyond its proper bounds, has its dangers as well as its benefits. Individualism in America has allowed a laxity in regard to governmental affairs which has rendered possible the spoils system and all the manifest evils that follow from the lack of a highly developed civic spirit. . . .

From the conditions of frontier life came intellectual traits of profound importance. The works of travelers along each frontier from colonial days onward describe certain common traits, and these traits have, while softening down, still persisted as survivals in the place of their origin, even when a higher social organization succeeded. The result is that to the frontier the American intellect owes its striking characteristics. That coarseness and strength combined with acuteness and inquisitiveness; that practical, inventive turn of mind, quick to find expedients; that masterful grasp of material things, lacking in the artistic but powerful to effect great ends; that restless, nervous energy; that dominant individualism, working for good and for evil, and withal that buoyancy and exuberance which comes with freedom—these are traits of the frontier, or traits called out elsewhere because of the existence of the frontier. Since the days when the fleet of Columbus sailed into the waters of the New World, America has been another name for opportunity, and the people of the United States have taken their tone from the incessant expansion which has not only been open but has even been forced upon them. He would be a rash prophet who should assert that the expansive character of American life has now entirely ceased. Movement has been its dominant fact, and unless this training has no effect upon a people, the American energy will continually demand a wider field for its exercise. But never again will such gifts of free land offer themselves. For a moment, at the frontier, the bonds of custom are broken and unrestraint is triumphant. There is not *tabula rasa*. The stubborn American environment is there with its imperious summons to accept its conditions; the inherited ways of doing things are also there; and yet, in spite of environment, and in spite of custom, each frontier did indeed furnish a new field of opportunity, a gate of escape from the bondage of the past; and freshness, and confidence, and scorn of older society, impatience of its restraints and its ideas, and indifference to its lessons, have accompanied the frontier. What the Mediterranean sea was to the Greeks, breaking the bond of custom, offering new experiences, calling out new institutions and activities, that, and more, the ever retreating frontier has been to the United States directly, and to the nations of Europe more remotely. And now, four centuries from the discovery of America, at the end of a hundred years of life under the Constitution, the frontier has gone, and with its going has closed the first period of American history.

↙ *WALTER PRESCOTT WEBB*

The Western World Frontier

Walter Prescott Webb (1888–1963), distinguished professor of history at the University of Texas, grew up in western Texas. "It was there," he said, "that I touched the hem of the garment of the frontier, received my earliest impressions of the struggle of a people with a new and arid country." In this essay, Webb takes us on a grand tour of the world's fron-

"The Western World Frontier" by Walter Prescott Webb, reprinted with permission of the copyright owners, the Regents of the University of Wisconsin, from *The Frontier in Perspective*, by Walter D. Wyman and Clifton B. Kroeber, editors, 1957, the University of Wisconsin Press.

tiers since 1500. Rather than opposing Turner's position with regard to the influence of frontier life on
people, Webb has enlarged the frame of reference to
include Africa, Australia, New Zealand, and both
North and South America in what he calls *The
Great Frontier*, the title of a book he published in
1952. According to his theory, which may be called
the "Webb thesis," in the interaction between the
world frontier and Europe lies one of the important keys to modern civilization.

When Frederick Jackson Turner launched his frontier
thesis, he must at times have wondered what the effect would be
on his future reputation. Would it be more sensible to follow the
tradition of his elders and glean the fields they had harvested, either
substantiating their views or modifying them so little as not to disturb their sacred principles? His other choice was to strike out for
himself and have a look at the country from a vantage point which
others had not used. Though I am not an authority on Turner's
life, I dare say he made his important decision not from considerations of policy, but because of an inner compulsion which drove
him to make it regardless of the effect it might have on his career.
A statesman has been described as a man who perceives a single
truth of tomorrow. Occasionally there comes a historian who perceives an important truth of yesterday, discovers a set of relationships which throws a light on the past, and, if he sets it forth, and
it is eventually accepted by a reasonable number of people, finds a
place as an interpreter. No interpretation of history based on a
general idea is ever universally accepted, and no interpreter escapes
the tonic of criticism.

It would be bad taste for me to elaborate the basic idea that the
frontier exerted a profound influence on American life, culture,
and institutions. That idea is accepted and has by now pervaded
all the fields of thought about this country. That idea is permeat-
ing other lands similar to this, such as Canada, Australia, South
Africa, and New Zealand. It is also being considered in the Latin-
American countries to the south, and it will in the future be examined elsewhere.

I am submitting here what seems to me to be a truth of yesterday, an extension of the idea that the frontier exerted a far-reaching influence, not only on American life and institutions, but on all of Western civilization, and therefore on world history. The idea I am advancing is as simple as the one Turner announced and that others have elaborated. The American argument runs that there was for a long period a settled East and an unsettled West, a civilized region and a frontier region, that people were moving from the settled region into the unsettled one, that the process of moving and occupying raw land had its effects on those who moved, and that the whole long process had a reflex effect on the older region whence the people came. We may differ as to the extent of the influence, but it would require a strangely perverse mind to deny that there was some effect.

Here we have a principle of history demonstrated to be applicable in this country. It is gradually dawning on thinkers about other frontier countries that it is applicable in other countries too. If this principle of frontier influence is applicable in all the separate parts of the frontier, in Canada, Australia, South Africa, and New Zealand, in the twenty republics of Latin America, then this influence was exerted wherever the people of Western Europe took over frontier lands. In each of these countries there was in the beginning a little "East" and a greater "West." In each of them the little "East" ate into the greater "West," gradually reducing the West until in each country we can say there is no longer raw frontier. Also in each country, as in the United States, the process of eating up the frontier exerted influence on those who did the eating and had some reflex effect on those who did not participate. Thus, in each of the frontier countries, the scholars who have considered the frontier principle have followed the American lead and examined their own frontier as if it were an isolated example confined to their own country.

This limited procedure has been necessary and is invaluable. It was the method of Bacon, who believed that we should examine many details before inducing a general conclusion. This minute examination of the many little frontiers, little "Easts" and little "Wests," has resulted in the accumulation of a wealth of data about the processes that went on and has revealed a small central core of uniformity. The invasion of the little "West," the area of free land, has always had some effect on the little "East," on the civilization of that particular fragment.

The next step is to assemble all the little "Wests," all the fragments of the frontier, into the whole frontier, the greater "West," and when we have done this, we have a greater frontier than we have previously been examining; we have the whole instead of a parcel of parts of which the United States is only one. This whole Great Frontier originally would have comprised the three and one half continents and the thousands of islands opened up by Columbus and his associates. This is a synthesis that was inevitable and is logical, once the idea of frontier has been accepted as a force in history.

But once we perform this act of synthesis and visualize all the scattered parts of the frontier brought together into a Great Frontier, we ask ourselves what of the little "Easts" and the little "Wests" with which we have been so concerned in such fragments as the United States and other dominions. We are for the moment looking at the whole frontier as analogous to the American West, thus merging the little "Easts" and the little "Wests" into one big "East." We have only lost—and that temporarily— the fragmentary "Easts," replicas of a greater "East," the existence of which has almost escaped notice. What we need look for now is the Mother East that gave birth to the little "Easts" tucked away on the fringes of the distant new lands. Our chief difficulty is psychological in that we have been concerned hitherto with the struggles and activities of the children and have lost sight of the home where the mother of all the little "Easts" resides. By an act of resolution, and at the expense perhaps of some preconceptions, we need to focus attention on the Mother East, which we can see by now is none other than Western Europe. Western Europe is the "East" in the American sense, bearing the same relation to the Great Frontier that the Atlantic Coast settlements long bore to the traditional American West. The name I have applied to Western Europe to set it off from the Great Frontier is the Metropolis. Since all of the frontier did not lie to the west of Europe, we must get away from our figurative use of East and West and substitute respectively the Metropolis and the Great Frontier. When we do this, we are in position to view the interaction and relation be-

tween the whole things rather than the relation between two parts
—the civilized part and the frontier part—of a fragment of one of
them only.

It is necessary for us to back away from the detail, the fragment,
and have a fresh look at the *whole* Frontier and the *whole* Metropolis as they interacted on each other after 1500. There are advantages and disadvantages in shifting to this longer perspective
and to this larger geographical canvas.

The disadvantages are: Since the whole frontier is greater than
any of its parts, so the task of thinking about it is of greater scope
and magnitude. The whole frontier is a complex thing, varying
with the varied geography and dissimilar people, whereas a single
frontier has both geographic unity and a measure of cultural unity.
It is difficult for one person to know all the lands and the languages and literatures, but he who shrinks from difficulties should
not elect to be a historian.

It would seem that the advantages of taking the long perspective
and looking at the whole frontier instead of a part of it overbalance
the difficulties. The fundamental gain derived from the long perspective and the world view is this: It enables us to see the whole,
the Great Frontier on the one hand and the whole of Metropolis
on the other. We see the extent of the forest, its relation to what is
around it, and we see over the centuries the people of the Metropolis moving out on it, nibbling tentatively at its edges along the
Atlantic seaboard, upward from the Cape, inward from Sydney and
Melbourne, and inward from the South American shore. From all
these points, the migrating hordes from the Metropolis move in
rough unison on the forest and the plain, and eventually they
claim a simultaneous victory on a broad intercontinental field
because they have destroyed that which so challenged and lured
them.

When we view this interaction from this high vantage point,
things seem to fall into place. What in closer perspective appeared
as separate and disconnected historical phenomena now appear as
scattered manifestations of a single action. For example, I mentioned the little "Easts" and the little "Wests" with which we
have been so busy. We now see that they are cut of the same two
cloths. The little "Easts" are but extended fingers of the Metrop-

olis; the little "Wests" are what is left in various places of the original Great Frontier.

When from this same vantage point we observe the interaction between the Metropolis and the Great Frontier over a period of four and one-half centuries, we feel that we have perhaps found one of the important keys to modern Western civilization. In this interaction, we see a prime example of Toynbee's challenge and response; we see a backdrop of Spengler's philosophy of rise and decay, which he probably did not see. This interaction between these two gigantic forces developed so much power that, like a diesel engine, it picked up all the other historical movements, such as the price revolution, the commercial revolution, the industrial revolution, and the democratic revolutions, and moved them like a long train down the track. Whatever got in the way of this inter-action was altered or destroyed; whatever harmonized with it or served it, prospered. In the long perspective, both capitalism and democracy appear as by-products of the interaction, the use of the precious metals as a medium of exchange appears as an episode now ended, and the rise of modern Negro slavery appears as a device adopted by the Metropolitans in order that they might have cheap and permanent labor with which to hew their fortunes out of the raw materials of the Great Frontier. Before this interaction, the old ideas about economics, based on scarcity, were wrecked because they were not applicable to the new age of plenty. Mer-cantilism gave way to laissez faire, which lasted only as long as the frontier lasted. These are some of the vistas that open up when we view the whole Frontier and its relation to the whole Metropolis, vistas which cannot ordinarily be reached by the most minute ex-amination of a single frontier fragment.

What has been said above applies to the period of the open frontier, say from 1500 to about 1900. By 1900 or thereabout, the first phase was over because the Metropolis had in effect eaten up the Frontier. The challenge to the Metropolis prior to that date was the challenge of the open frontier: the challenge since that date is that of a closed frontier. The Metropolis has destroyed the Frontier and now for the first time in several centuries must stew in its own juice. There is no longer the dramatic interaction to which I have attributed such power and influence. There is no longer the dynamism to which we were accustomed, no longer the free migration of people or the return cargoes of windfall wealth. Many practices, ideas, and institutions which arose and served well when the interaction was going on have been discarded, and all—even democracy and capitalism—are being modified. The precious metals no longer serve as a medium of exchange; laissez faire has been discarded and slavery abolished; the freewheeling individual, the pampered pet of the frontier era, is being brought under control and required to reassume some responsibility to the society in which he lives. To put the same fact in another form, the state is reasserting its sovereignty. The vaunted freedoms of which we boast, both economic and political, appear as incidental to a temporary situation which enabled the sovereign to release the individual from accustomed obligations and duties to the state. The sovereign could release the individual because he was reaping such harvests from the new lands that he could dispense with services he had formerly needed and required.

With the windfall prizes of the Great Frontier all appropriated, the nations realigned—the "haves" on one side and the "have-nots" on the other. An important difference between them was that members of the first group had frontier possessions, or were of the frontier, while those of the second group had none. The two groups have fought two wars which may in retrospect appear as an attempted adjustment to the closed world frontier. These wars resulted in the two groups' approaching nearer to each other, not because the "have-nots" have more but because the "haves" now have less. Another such war could very well bring them to stand on common ground where neither has anything. With the Frontier swallowed up, there is no escape to a new frontier by the enlarged Metropolis, which must now face a condition comparable to that which obtained when the society was released by the opening of the Great Frontier in 1500.

These are some vistas—not too pleasant—that appear when we take the long perspective and view the *end* of the interaction between the Metropolis and the Great Frontier. What we view now is a condition created by the cessation of the interaction. There is no interaction because one of the leading characters is dead. The Metropolis has destroyed the Frontier and stands triumphant in the midst of the magnificent ruins. We may recall Byron's description of Rome:

> The Niobe of nations! There she stands
> Childless and crownless, in her voiceless woe;
> An empty urn within her withered hand,
> Whose holy dust was scattered long ago.

part 2

TRAIL BLAZERS

The Discovery, Purchase, and Settlement of Kentucke

John Filson (c. 1747–1788), the first historian of
Kentucky and the original biographer of Daniel
Boone, moved into the backwoods in 1783 in order
to collect information about the frontier and some
of the pioneers. From the information he was able
to collect, he wrote his manuscript, which contained
*The Discovery, Settlement, and Present State of
Kentucke: The Adventures of Col. Daniel Boone,*
and a new and accurate map of Kentucky and adjoining country drawn from actual surveys. Filson
returned East in 1784 and had his book published.
It went through several editions, including some in
London and Paris. Boone was delighted with his
"ghost-written" autobiography. Colonel R. T. Dur-
rett gathered together the scanty memorials of the
romantic pioneer, and published *John Filson, the
First Historian of Kentucky* (Louisville and Cincinnati, 1884).

The first white man we have certain accounts of, who
discovered this province, was one James M'Bride, who, in company
with some others, in the year 1754, passing down the Ohio in
Canoes, landed at the mouth of Kentucke river, and there marked
a tree, with the first letter of his name, and the date, which remain
to this day. These men reconnoitred the country, and returned
home with the pleasing news of their discovery of the best tract

---

From *The Discovery, Purchase and Settlement of Kentucke* (Wilmington,
Del.: James Adams, 1784), pp. 7–38 *passim.*

of land in North-America, and probably in the world. From this period it remained concealed till about the year 1767, when one John Finley, and some others, trading with the Indians, fortunately travelled over the fertile region, now called Kentucke, then but known to the Indians, by the name of the Dark and Bloody Ground, and sometimes the Middle Ground. This country greatly engaged Mr. Finley's attention. Some time after, disputes arising between the Indians and traders, he was obliged to decamp; and returned to his place of residence in North-Carolina, where he communicated his discovery to Col. Daniel Boon, and a few more, who conceiving it to be an interesting object, agreed in the year 1769 to undertake a journey in order to explore it. After a long fatiguing march, over a mountainous wilderness, in a westward direction, they at length arrived upon its borders; and from the top of an eminence, with joy and wonder, descried the beautiful landscape of Kentucke. Here they encamped, and some went to hunt provisions, which were readily procured, there being plenty of game, while Col. Boon and John Finley made a tour through the country, which they found far exceeding their expectations, and returning to camp, informed their companions of their discoveries: But in spite of this promising beginning, this company, meeting with nothing but hardships and adversity, grew exceedingly disheartened, and was plundered, dispersed, and killed by the Indians, except Col. Boon, who continued an inhabitant of the wilderness until the year 1771, when he returned home.

About this time Kentucke had drawn the attention of several gentlemen. Doctor Walker of Virginia, with a number more, made a tour westward for discoveries, endeavouring to find the Ohio river; and afterwards he and General Lewis, at Fort Stanwix, purchased from the Five Nations of Indians the lands lying on the north side of Kentucke. Col. Donaldson, of Virginia, being employed by the State to run a line from six miles above the Long Island, on Holstein, to the mouth of the great Kenhawa, and finding thereby that an extensive tract of excellent country would be cut off to the Indians, was solicited, by the inhabitants of Clench and Holstein, to purchase the lands lying on the north side of Kentucke river from the Five Nations. This purchase he compleated for five hundred pounds, specie. It was then agreed, to fix a boundary line, running from the long Island on Holstein to the head of Kentucke river; thence down the same to the mouth, thence up the Ohio, to the mouth of Great Kenhawa; but this valuable purchase the State refused to confirm.

Col. Henderson, of North-Carolina, being informed of this country by Col. Boon, he, and some other gentlemen, held a treaty with the Cherokee Indians at Wataga, in March 1775, and then purchased from them the lands lying on the south side of Kentucke river for goods, at valuable rates, to the amount of six thousand pounds, specie.

Soon after this purchase, the State of Virginia took the alarm, agreed to pay the money Col. Donaldson had contracted for, and then disputed Col. Henderson's right of purchase, as a private gentlemen of another state, in behalf of himself: However, for his eminent services to this country, and for having been instrumental in making so valuable an acquisition to Virginia that state was pleased to reward him with a tract of land, at the mouth of Green River, to the amount of two hundred thousand acres; and the state of North-Carolina gave him the like quantity in Powel's Valley. This region was formerly claimed by various tribes of Indians; whose title, if they had any, originated in such a manner, as to render it doubtful which ought to possess it: Hence this fertile spot became an object of contention, a theatre of war, from which it was properly denominated the Bloody-Grounds. Their contentions not being likely to decide the Right to any particular tribe, as soon as Mr. Henderson and his friends proposed to purchase, the Indians agreed to sell; and notwithstanding the valuable Consideration they received, have continued ever since troublesome neighbours to the new settlers. . . .

Soil and Produce

The soil of Kentucke is of a loose, deep black mould, without sand, in the first rate lands about two or three feet deep, and exceeding luxurious in all its productions. In some the wood, as the natural consequence of too rich a soil, is of little value, appearing like dead timber and large stumps in a field lately cleared. These parts are not considerable. The country in general may be considered as well timbered, producing large trees of many kinds, and to be exceeded by no country in variety. Those which are peculiar to Kentucke are the sugar-tree, which grows in all parts in great plenty, and furnishes every family with plenty of excellent sugar. The honey-locust is curiously surrounded with large thorny spikes, bearing broad and long pods in form of peas, has a sweet taste, and makes excellent beer.

The coffee-tree greatly resembles the black oak, grows large, and also bears a pod, in which is enclosed good coffee. The pappa-tree does not grow to a great size, is a soft wood, bears a fine fruit much like a cucumber in shape and size, and tastes sweet. The cucumber-tree is small and soft, with remarkable leaves, bears a fruit much resembling that from which it is named. Black mulberry-trees are in abundance. The wild cherry-tree is here frequent, of a large size, and supplies the inhabitants with boards for all their buildings. Here also is the buck-eye, an exceeding soft wood, bearing a remarkable black fruit, and some other kinds of trees not common elsewhere. Here is great plenty of fine cane, on which the cattle feed, and grow fat. This plant in general grows from three to twelve feet high, of a hard substance, with joints at eight or ten inches distance along the stalk, from which proceed leaves resembling those of the willow. There are many cane brakes so thick and tall that it is difficult to pass through them. Where no cane grows there is abundance of wild-rye, clover, and buffalo-grass, covering vast tracts of country, and affording excellent food for cattle. The fields are covered with abundance of wild herbage not common to other countries. The Shawanese sallad, wild lettuce, and pepper-grass, and many more, as yet unknown to the inhabitants, but which, no doubt, have excellent virtues. . . .

Quadrupeds

Among the native animals are the urus, or zorax, described by Cesar, which we call a buffalo, much resembling a large bull, of a great size, with a large head, thick short crooked horns, and broader in his forepart than behind. Upon his shoulder is a large lump of flesh, covered with a thick boss of long wool and curly hair, of a dark brown colour. They do not rise from the ground as our cattle, but spring up at once upon their feet; are of a broad make and clumsy appearance, with short legs, but run fast, and turn not aside for any thing when chased, except a standing tree. They weigh from five to ten hundred weight, are excellent meat, supplying the inhabitants in many parts with beef, and their hides make good leather. I have heard a hunter assert, he saw above one thousand buffaloes at the Blue Licks at once; so numerous were they before the first settlers had wantonly sported away their lives. There still remains a great number in the exterior parts of the settlement. They feed upon cane and grass, as other cattle, and are innocent harmless creatures.

There are still to be found many deer, elks, and bears, within the settlement, and many more on the borders of it. There are also panthers, wildcats, and wolves. . . .

Inhabitants

An accurate account is kept of all the male inhabitants above the age of sixteen, who are rated towards the expences of the government by the name of Tithables; from which, by allowing that those so enrolled amount to a fourth part of the whole inhabitants, we may conclude that Kentucke contains, at present, upwards of thirty thousand souls: So amazingly rapid has been the settlement in a few years. Numbers are daily arriving, and multitudes expected this Fall; which gives a well grounded expectation that the country will be exceedingly populous in a short time. The inhabitants, at present, have not extraordinary good houses, as usual in a newly settled country.

They are, in general, polite, humane, hospitable, and very complaisant. Being collected from different parts of the continent, they have a diversity of manners, customs and religions, which may in time perhaps be modified to one uniform. As yet united to the State of Virginia, they are governed by her wholesome laws, which are virtuously executed, and with excellent decorum. Schools for education are formed, and a college is appointed by act of Assembly of Virginia, to be founded under the conduct of trustees in Kentucke, and endowed with lands for its use. An excellent library is likewise bestowed upon this seminary, by the Rev. John Todd, of Virginia.

The Anabaptists were the first that promoted public worship in Kentucke; and the Presbyterians have formed three large congregations near Harrod's station, and have engaged the Rev. David Rice, of Virginia, to be their pastor. At Lexington, 35 miles from these, they have formed another large congregation, and invited the Rev. Mr. Rankin, of Virginia, to undertake that charge among them. At present there are no other religious societies formed, although several other sects have numerous adherents. But from these early movements it is hoped that Kentucke will eminently shine in learning and piety, which will fulfil the wish of every virtuous citizen. . . .

Rights of Land

The proprietors of the Kentucke lands obtain their patents from Virginia, and their rights are of three kinds, viz. Those which arise from military service, from settlement and pre-emption, or from warrants from the treasury. The military rights are held by officers, or their representatives, as a reward for services done in one of the two last wars. The Settlement and pre-emption rights arise from occupation. Every man who, before March, 1780, had remained in the country one year, or raised a crop of corn, was allowed to have a settlement of four hundred acres, and a pre-emption adjoining it of one thousand acres. Every man who had only built a cabbin, or made any improvement by himself or others, was entitled to a pre-emption of one thousand acres where such improvement was made.

In March, 1780, the settlement and pre-emption rights ceased, and treasury warrants were afterwards issued, authorizing their possessor to locate the quantity of land mentioned in them, wherever it could be found vacant in Virginia. . . .

The validity of the right of Virginia to this extensive western territory has been disputed by some, but without reason. The western boundary of that state, by charter, restricted by the treaty of Paris, in 1763, is fixed upon the Ohio River. She has purchased the soil from the Indians, has first settled it, and established wholesome laws for the regulation and government of the inhabitants; and therefore we conclude, that the right of Virginia to Kentucke is as permanent as the independence of America.

Trade of Kentucke

A convenient situation for commerce is the grand hinge upon which the population, riches and happiness of every country greatly depends. I believe many conceive the situation of Kentucke to be unfavourable in this respect. I confess when I first visited this country I was of the opinion of other misinformed men, that the best channel was from Philadelphia or Baltimore, by the way of Pittsburg, and from thence down the Ohio; and upon account of the difficulties and expences attending this route, for which there is no remedy, that goods would ever be dear. This opinion I have since reprobated, as the effect of ignorance of the trade up the Mississippi from New Orleans, or Mantchac, at the river or gut Iberville.

Those who are acquainted with America know the Mississippi and Ohio rivers to be the key to the northern parts of the western continent. These are the principal channels through which that extensive region, bathed by their waters, and enriched by the many streams they receive, communicate with the sea, and may truly be considered as the great passage made by the Hand of Nature for a variety of valuable purposes, and principally to promote the happiness and benefit of mankind; amongst which, the conveyance of the produce of that immense and fertile country lying westward of the United States is not the least. . . .

Explorations
in the American Desert

Jedediah Strong Smith (1799–1831) was the first white man to cross the Sierra Nevada mountains and the treacherous Great Salt Lake Desert. Arriving in Saint Louis in 1822, he joined the William H. Ashley expedition to the fur-trading regions of the far West. He, more than any other, was the "breaker of trails" to California and the Pacific Northwest. During his extraordinary wide travels, he discovered rich fur-trading and trapping country and stimulated the westward movement of thousands of American pioneers. Charting an overland route from Salt Lake to Lower California, he explored the entire length of that Mexican province. Refused residence in California, he forced his way against tremendous odds to Fort Vancouver on the Columbia, barely escaping death at the hands of the Mohave Indians. He was killed by a band of Comanches in 1831.

See H. C. Dale, *The Ashley-Smith Explorations* (Cleveland, 1917); and a biography by Maurice Sullivan (1936).

Little Lake of Bear River, July 17th 1827. Genl. Wm. Clark, Supt. of Indian Affairs

Sir, My situation in this country has enabled me to collect information respecting a section of the country which has hitherto been measurably veiled in obscurity to the citizens of the United States. I allude to the country S.W. of the *Great Salt Lake* west of the Rocky mountains.

I started about the 22d of August 1826, from the Great Salt

From *Missouri Republican* (St. Louis, Mo.), October 11, 1827. Editor's title.

Lake, with a party of fifteen men, for the purpose of exploring the country S.W. which was entirely unknown to me, and of which I could collect no satisfactory information from the Indians who inhabit this country on its N.E. borders.

My general course on leaving the Salt Lake was S.W. and W. Passing the Little Uta Lake and ascending Ashley's river, which empties into the Little Uta Lake. From this lake I found no more signs of buffalo; there are a few antelope and mountain sheep, and an abundance of *black tailed hares*. On Ashley's river, I found a nation of Indians who call themselves *Sampatch*; they were friendly disposed towards us. I passed over a range of mountains running S.E. and N.W. and struck a river running S.W. which I called *Adams River*, in compliment to our President. The water is of a muddy cast, and is a little brackish. The country is mountainous to East; towards the West there are sandy plains and detached rocky hills.

Passing down this river some distance, I fell in with a nation of Indians who call themselves *Pa-Ulches* (those Indians as well as those last mentioned, wear rabbit skin robes) who raise some little corn and pumpkins. The country is nearly destitute of game of any description, except a few hares. Here (about ten days march down it) the river turns to the South East. On the S.W. side of the river there is a cave, the entrance of which is about 10 or 15 feet high, and 5 or 6 feet in width; after descending about 15 feet, a room opens out from 25 to 30 in length and 15 to 20 feet in width; the roof, sides and floor are solid rock salt, a sample of which I send you, with some other articles which will be hereafter described. I here found a kind of plant of the prickly pear kind, which I called the cabbage pear, the largest of which grows about two feet and a half high and 1½ feet in diameter; upon examination I found it to be nearly of the substance of a turnip, altho' by no means palatable; its form was similar to that of an egg, being smaller at the ground and top than in the middle; it is covered with pricks similar to the prickly pear with which you are acquainted.

There are here also a number of shrubs and small trees with which I was not acquainted previous to my route there, and which

I cannot at present describe satisfactorily, as it would take more space than I can here allot.

The *Pa Ulches* have a number of marble pipes, one of which I obtained and send you, altho it has been broken since I have had it in my possession; they told me there was a quantity of the same material in their country. I also obtained of them a knife of *flint*, which I send you, but it has likewise been broken by accident.

I followed Adams river two days further to where it empties into the Seedekeeden a South East course. I crossed the Seed-skeeder, and went down it four days a south east course; I here found the country remarkably barren, rocky, and mountainous; there are a good many rapids in the river, but at this place a valley opens out about 5 to 15 miles in width, which on the river banks is timbered and fertile. I here found a nation of Indians who call themselves *Ammuchabas*; they cultivate the soil, and raise corn, beans, pumpkins, watermelons and muskmelons in abundance, and also a little wheat and cotton. I was now nearly destitute of horses, and had learned what it was to do without food; I therefore remained fifteen days and recruited my men, and I was enabled also to exchange my horses and purchase a few more of a few runaway Indians who stole some horses of the Spaniards. I here got information of the Spanish country (the Californias) and obtained two guides, recrossed the Seedskadeer, which I afterwards found emptied into the Gulf of California about 80 miles from this place by the name of the Collarado; many render the river *Gild* from the East.

I travelled a west course fifteen days over a country of complete barrens, generally travelling from morning until night without water. I crossed a Salt plain about 20 miles long and 8 wide; on the surface was a crust of beautiful white salt, quite thin. Under this surface there is a layer of salt from a half to one and a half inches in depth; between this and the upper layer there is about four inches of yellowish sand.

On my arrival in the province of Upper California, I was looked upon with suspicion, and was compelled to appear in presence of the Governor of the Californias residing at San Diego, where, by the assistance of some American gentlemen (especially Capt. W. H. Cunningham of the ship Courier from Boston) I was enabled to obtain permission to return with my men the route I came, and purchased such supplies as I stood in want of. The Governor would not allow me to trade up the Sea coast towards Bodaga. I returned to my party and purchased such articles as were necessary, and went Eastward of the Spanish settlements on the route I had come in. I then steered my course N.W. keeping from 150 miles to 200 miles from the sea coast. A very high range of mountains lay on the East. After travelling three hundred miles in that direction through a country somewhat fertile, in which there was a great many Indians, mostly naked and destitute of arms, with the exception of a few Bows and Arrows and what is very singular amongst Indians, they cut their hair to the length of three inches; they proved to be friendly; their manner of living is on fish, roots, acorns and grass.

On my arrival at the river which I named the *Wim-mul-che* (named after a tribe of Indians which resides on it, of that name) I found a few beaver, and elk, deer, and antelope in abundance. I here made a small hunt, and attempted to take my party across the [mountain] which I before mentioned, and which I called *Mount Joseph*, to come on and join my partners at the Great Salt Lake. I found the snow so deep on Mount Joseph that I could not cross my horses, five of which starved to death; I was compelled therefore to return to the valley which I had left, and there, leaving my party, I started with two men, seven horses and two mules, which I loaded with hay for the horses and provisions for ourselves, and started on the 20th of May, and succeeded in crossing it in eight days, having lost only two horses and one mule. I found the snow on the top of this mountain from 4 to 8 feet deep, but it was so consolidated by the heat of the sun that my horses only sunk from half a foot to one foot deep.

After travelling twenty days from the east side of Mount Joseph, I struck the S.W. corner of the Great Salt Lake, travelling over a country completely barren and destitute of game. We frequently travelled without water sometimes for two days over sandy deserts, where there was no sign of vegetation and when we found water in some of the rocky hills, we most generally found some Indians who appeared the most miserable of the human race having nothing to subsist on (nor any clothing) except grass seed, grasshoppers, etc. When we arrived at the Salt Lake, we had but one horses and one mule remaining, which were so feeble and poor that they could scarce carry the little camp equipage which I had along; the balance of my horses I was compelled to eat as they gave out.

The company are now starting, and therefore must close my communication. Yours respectfully,

(signed)   Jedediah S. Smith, of the firm of
Smith, Jackson and Sublette.

⚓ *WASHINGTON IRVING*

The Fur Trade in the Pacific

Astoria—the first white settlement in the Oregon country—was named for John Jacob Astor who established a fur-trading post (1811) on the site where Lewis and Clark had camped in 1805. From materials furnished by Astor himself, Washington Irving (1783–1859), with the help of his nephew and biographer Pierre M. Irving, wrote his two-volume *Astoria: Or Anecdotes of an Enterprise beyond the Rocky Mountains* (1836). It contains, in addition to stories of fur-trading expeditions by land and by sea, some biographical detail from the life of the West's first business magnate.

The selection reprinted here explains Astor's plan to promote and protect American enterprise in the fur-trading industry. See also Alexander Ross, *The*

From *Astoria*, vol. 1 (New York: G. P. Putnam's Sons, 1895), chap. 2, pp. 31–40.

Fur Hunters of the Far West: A Narrative of Adventures in the Oregon and Rocky Mountains (London, 1855); Hiram M. Chittenden, The American Fur Trade of the Far West (3 vols., New York, 1902); and Bernard De Voto, Across the Wide Missouri (Boston, 1947).

While the various companies we have noticed were pushing their enterprises far and wide in the wilds of Canada, and along the course of the great western waters, other adventurers, intent on the same objects, were traversing the watery wastes of the Pacific and skirting the northwest coast of America. The last voyage of that renowned but unfortunate discoverer, Captain Cook, had made known the vast quantities of the sea-otter to be found along that coast, and the immense prices to be obtained for its fur in China. It was as if a new gold coast had been discovered. Individuals from various countries dashed into this lucrative traffic, so that in the year 1792, there were twenty-one vessesl under different flags, plying along the coast and trading with the natives. The greater part of them were American, and owned by Boston merchants. They generally remained on the coast and about the adjacent seas, for two years, carrying on as wandering and adventurous a commerce on the water as did the traders and trappers on land. Their trade extended along the whole coast from California to the high northern latitudes. They would run in near shore, anchor, and wait for the natives to come off in their canoes with peltries. The trade exhausted at one place, they would up anchor and off to another. In this way they would consume the summer, and when autumn came on, would run down to the Sandwich Islands and winter in some friendly and plentiful harbor. In the following year they would resume their summer trade, commencing at California and proceeding north: and, having in the course of the two seasons collected a sufficient cargo of peltries, would make the best of their way to China. Here they would sell their furs, take in teas, nankeens, and other merchandise, and return to Boston, after an absence of two or three years.

The people, however, who entered most extensively and effectively in the fur trade of the Pacific, were the Russians. Instead of making casual voyages, in transient ships, they established regular trading houses in the high latitudes, along the northwest coast of America, and upon the chain of the Aleutian Islands between Kamtschatka and the promontory of Alaska.

To promote and protect these enterprises, a company was incorporated by the Russian government with exclusive privileges, and a capital of two hundred and sixty thousand pounds sterling; and the sovereignty of that part of the American continent, along the coast of which the posts had been established, was claimed by the Russian crown on the plea that the land had been discovered and occupied by its subjects.

As China was the grand mart for the furs collected in these quarters, the Russians had the advantage over their competitors in the trade. The latter had to take their peltries to Canton, which, however, was a mere receiving mart, from when they had to be distributed over the interior of the empire and sent to the northern parts, where there was the chief consumption. The Russians, on the contrary, carried their furs, by a shorter voyage, directly to the northern parts of the Chinese empire; thus being able to afford them in the market without the additional cost of internal transportation.

We come now to the immediate field of operation of the great enterprise we have undertaken to illustrate.

Among the American ships which traded along the northwest coast in 1792, was the *Columbia*, Captain Gray, of Boston. In the course of her voyage she discovered the mouth of a large river in lat. 46° 19′ north. Entering it with some difficulty, on account of sand-bars and breakers, she came to anchor in a spacious bay. A boat was well manned, and sent on shore to a village on the beach, but all the inhabitants fled excepting the aged and infirm. The kind manner in which these were treated, and the presents given to them, gradually lured back the others, and a friendly intercourse took place. They had never seen a ship or a white man. When they had first described the *Columbia*, they had supposed it a floating island; then some monster of the deep; but when they saw the boat putting for shore with human beings on board, they considered them cannibals sent by the Great Spirit to ravage the country and devour the inhabitants. Captain Gray did not ascend the river farther than the bay in question, which continues to bear his name. After putting to sea, he fell in with the celebrated discoverer, Vancouver, and informed him of his discovery, furnishing him with a chart which he had made of the river. Vancouver visited the river, and his lieutenant, Broughton, explored it by the aid of Captain Gray's chart; ascending it upwards of one hundred miles, until within view of a snowy mountain, to which he gave the name of Mount Hood, which it still retains.

The existence of this river, however, was known long before the visits of Gray and Vancouver, but the information concerning it was vague and indefinite, being gathered from the reports of Indians. It was spoken of by travellers as the Oregon, and as the Great River of the West. A Spanish ship is said to have been wrecked at the mouth, several of the crew of which lived for some time among the natives. The *Columbia*, however, is believed to be the first ship that made a regular discovery and anchored within its waters, and it has since generally borne the name of that vessel.

As early as 1763, shortly after the acquisition of the Canadas by Great Britain, Captain Jonathan Carver, who had been in the British provincial army, projected a journey across the continent between the forty-third and forty-sixth degrees of northern latitude to the shores of the Pacific Ocean. His objects were to ascertain the breadth of the continent at its broadest part, and to determine on some place on the shores of the Pacific, where government might establish a post to facilitate the discovery of a northwest passage, or a communication between Hudson's Bay and the Pacific Ocean. This place he presumed would be somewhere about the Straits of Annian, at which point he supposed the Oregon disembogued itself. It was his opinion, also, that a settlement on this extremity of America would disclose new sources of trade, promote many useful discoveries, and open a more direct communication with China and the English settlements in the East Indies, than that by the Cape of Good Hope or the Straits of Magellan.* This enterprising and intrepid traveller was twice baffled in individual efforts to accomplish this great journey. In 1774 he was joined in the scheme by Richard Whitworth, a member of Parliament, and

---

* Carver's *Travels*, Introd., b. iii. Philad., 1796.

a man of wealth. Their enterprise was projected on a broad and bold plan. They were to take with them fifty or sixty men, artificers and mariners. With these they were to make their way up one of the branches of the Missouri, explore the mountains for the source of the Oregon, or the River of the West, and sail down that river to its supposed exit, near the Straits of Annian. Here they were to erect a fort, and build the vessels necessary to carry their discoveries by sea into effect. Their plan had the sanction of the British government, and grants and other requisites were nearly completed, when the breaking out of the American Revolution once more defeated the undertaking.*

The expedition of Sir Alexander Mackenzie in 1793, across the continent to the Pacific Ocean, which he reached in lat. 52° 20′ 48″, again suggested the possibility of linking together the trade of both sides of the continent. In lat. 52° 30′ he had descended a river for some distance which flowed towards the south, and was called by the natives Tacoutche Tesse, and which he erroneously supposed to be the Columbia. It was afterwards ascertained that it emptied itself in lat. 49°, whereas the mouth of the Columbia is about three degrees farther south.

When Mackenzie some years subsequently published an account of his expeditions, he suggested the policy of opening an intercourse between the Atlantic and Pacific oceans, and forming regular establishments through the interior and at both extremes, as well as along the coasts and islands. By this means, he observed the entire command of the fur trade of North America might be obtained from lat. 48° north, to the pole, excepting that portion held by the Russians, for as to the American adventurers who had hitherto enjoyed the traffic along the northwest coast, they would instantly disappear, he added, before a well regulated trade.

A scheme of this kind, however, was too vast and hazardous for individual enterprise; it could only be undertaken by a company under the sanction and protection of a government; and as there might be a clashing of claims between the Hudson's Bay and Northwest Company, the one holding by right of charter, the other by right of possession, he proposed that the two companies should

---

* Carver's *Travels*, p. 360. Philad., 1796.

coalesce in this great undertaking. The long cherished jealousies of these two companies, however, were too deep and strong to allow them to listen to such counsel.

In the meantime the attention of the American government was attracted to the subject, and the memorable expedition under Messrs. Lewis and Clarke, fitted out. These gentlemen, in 1804, accomplished the enterprise which had been projected by Carver and Whitworth, in 1774. They ascended the Missouri, passed through the stupendous gates of the Rocky Mountains, hitherto unknown to white men; discovered and explored the upper waters of the Columbia, and followed that river down to its mouth, where their countryman, Gray, had anchored about twelve years previously. Here they passed the winter, and returned across the mountains in the following spring. The reports published by them of their expedition, demonstrated the practicability of establishing a line of communication across the continent, from the Atlantic to the Pacific Ocean.

It was then that the idea presented itself to the mind of Mr. Astor, of grasping with his individual hand this great enterprise, which for years had been dubiously yet desirously contemplated by powerful associations and maternal governments. For some time he revolved the idea in his mind, gradually extending and maturing his plans as his means of executing them augmented. The main feature of his scheme was to establish a line of trading posts along the Missouri and the Columbia, to the mouth of the latter, where was to be founded the chief trading house or mart. Inferior posts would be established in the interior, and on all the tributary streams of the Columbia, to trade with the Indians; these posts would draw their supplies from the main establishment, and bring to it the peltries they collected. Coasting craft would be built and fitted out, also, at the mouth of the Columbia, to trade, at favorable seasons, all along the northwest coast, and return with the proceeds of their voyages, to this place of deposit. Thus all the Indian trade, both of the interior and the coast, would converge to this point, and thence derive its sustenance.

A ship was to be sent annually from New York to this main establishment with reinforcements and supplies, and with merchandise suited to the trade. It would take on board the furs collected during the preceding year, carry them to Canton, invest the proceeds in the rich merchandise of China, and return thus freighted to New York.

As, in extending the American trade along the coast to the northward, it might be brought into the vicinity of the Russian Fur Company, and produce a hostile rivalry, it was part of the plan of Mr. Astor to conciliate the good-will of that company by the most amicable and beneficial arrangements. The Russian establishment was chiefly dependent for its supplies upon transient trading vessels from the United States. These vessels, however, were often of more harm than advantage. Being owned by private adventurers, or casual voyagers, who cared only for present profit, and had no interest in the permanent prosperity of the trade, they were reckless in their dealings with the natives, and made no scruple of supplying them with fire-arms. In this way several fierce tribes in the vicinity of the Russian posts, or within the range of their trading excursions, were furnished with deadly means of warfare, and rendered troublesome and dangerous neighbors.

The Russian government had made representations to that of the United States of these malpractices on the part of its citizens, and urged to have this traffic in arms prohibited; but, as it did not infringe any municipal law, our government could not interfere. Yet, still it regarded with solicitude a traffic which, if persisted in, might give offence to Russia, at that time almost the only friendly power to us. In this dilemma the government had applied to Mr. Astor, as one conversant in this branch of trade, for information that might point out a way to remedy the evil. This circumstance had suggested to him the idea of supplying the Russian establishment regularly by means of the annual ship that should visit the settlement at the mouth of the Columbia (or Oregon); by this means the casual trading vessels would be excluded from those parts of the coast where their malpractices were so injurious to the Russians.

Such is a brief outline of the enterprise projected by Mr. Astor, but which continually expanded in his mind. Indeed, it is due to him to say that he was not actuated by mere motives of individual profit. He was already wealthy beyond the ordinary desires of man, but he now aspired to that honorable fame which is awarded to

men of similar scope of mind, who by their great commercial
enterprises have enriched nations, peopled wilderness, and extended the bounds of empire. He considered his projected establishment at the mouth of the Columbia as the emporium to an
immense commerce; as a colony that would form the germ of a
wide civilization; that would, in fact, carry the American population across the Rocky Mountains and spread it along the shores
of the Pacific, as it already animated the shores of the Atlantic.

↗ JESSE APPLEGATE

A Day with the
Cow Column

Jesse Applegate (1811–1888), "prince of pioneers,"
was captain of the cow column in the great emigration of 1843 to Oregon. His capacity for organization, his physical stamina, and his knowledge of
surveying, mathematics, political science, and law
were superior qualifications for leadership in a frontier territory. As an engineer, he opened up a much
needed wagon route over the western section of the
Oregon trail. As a member of the legislative com-
mission of the provisional government that ruled
Oregon until 1849, he was responsible for the adoption of the new constitution, for the passage of many
workable laws, and for the institution of wholesome
relationships between American settlers and the British Hudson's Bay Company. That he could wield a
pen effectively is demonstrated by "A Day with the
Cow Column in 1843," written as an address to be

From *Oregon Historical Society Quarterly*, vol. 1 no. 4 (December 1900),
pp. 371–383. By permission of the Oregon Historical Society.

delivered at the fourth annual reunion of the Oregon
Pioneer Association in 1876.

For further information about the author or his
work see Maude A. Rucker, *The Oregon Trail and
Some of Its Blazers* (New York, 1930); and Jesse
A. Applegate, *A Day with the Cow Column in 1843
and Recollections of My Boyhood*, edited by Joseph
Schafer (Chicago, 1934).

The migration of a large body of men, women and children across the continent to Oregon was, in the year 1843, strictly
an experiment; not only in respect to numbers, but to the outfit of
the migrating party.

Before that date, two or three missionaries had performed the
journey on horseback, driving a few cows with them. Three or four
wagons drawn by oxen had reached Fort Hall, on Snake River, but
it was the honest opinion of the most of those who had traveled
the route down Snake River that no large number of cattle could
be subsisted on its scanty pasturage, or wagons taken over a route
so rugged and mountainous.

The emigrants were also assured that the Sioux would be much
opposed to the passage of so large a body through their country,
and would probably resist it on account of the emigrants destroying
and frightening away the buffaloes, which had been diminishing in
number.

The migrating body numbered over one thousand souls, with
about one hundred and twenty wagons, drawn by six-ox teams,
averaging about six yokes to the team, and several thousand loose
horses and cattle.

The emigrants first organized and attempted to travel in one
body, but it was soon found that no progress could be made with
a body so cumbrous, and as yet as averse to all discipline. And at
the crossing of the "Big Blue" it divided into two columns, which
traveled in supporting distance of each other as far as Independence Rock, on the Sweet Water.

From this point, all danger from Indians being over, the emigrants separated into small parties better suited to the narrow
mountain paths and small pastures in their front. Before the

division on the Blue River there was some just cause for discontent in respect to loose cattle. Some of the emigrants had only their teams, while others had large herds in addition which must share the pastures and be guarded and driven by the whole body.

This discontent had its effect in the division on the Blue, those not encumbered with or having but few loose cattle attached themselves to the light column; those having more than four or five cows had of necessity to join the heavy or cow column. Hence the cow column, being much larger than the other and encumbered with its large herds had to use greater exertion and observe a more rigid discipline to keep pace with the more agile consort. It is with the cow or more clumsy column that I propose to journey with the reader for a single day.

It is four o'clock A.M.; the sentinels on duty have discharged their rifles—the signal that the hours of sleep are over; and every wagon and tent is pouring forth its night tenants, and slow-kindling smokes begin largely to rise and float away on the morning air. Sixty men start from the corral, spreading as they make through the vast herd of cattle and horses that form a semicircle around the encampment, the most distant perhaps two miles away.

The herders pass to the extreme verge and carefully examine for trails beyond, to see that none of the animals have strayed or been stolen during the night. This morning no trails lead beyond the outside animals in sight, and by five o'clock the herders begin to contract the great moving circle and the well-trained animals move slowly toward camp, clipping here and there a thistle or tempting bunch of grass on the way. In about an hour five thousand animals are close up to the encampment, and the teamsters are busy selecting their teams and driving them inside the "corral" to be yoked. The corral is a circle one hundred yards deep, formed with wagons connected strongly with each other, the wagon in the rear being connected with the wagon in front by its tongue and ox chains. It is a strong barrier that the most vicious ox cannot break, and in case of an attack of the Sioux would be no contemptible entrenchment.

From six to seven o'clock is a busy time; breakfast is to be eaten, the tents struck, the wagons loaded, and the teams yoked and brought up in readiness to be attached to their respective wagons.

All know when, at seven o'clock, the signal to march sounds, that those not ready to take their proper places in the line of march must fall into the dusty rear for the day.

There are sixty wagons. They have been divided into fifteen divisions or platoons of four wagons each, and each platoon is entitled to lead in its turn. The leading platoon of today will be the rear one tomorrow, and will bring up the rear unless some teamster, through indolence or negligence, has lost his place in the line, and is condemned to that uncomfortable post. It is within ten minutes of seven; the corral but now a strong barricade is everywhere broken, the teams being attached to the wagons. The women and children have taken their places in them. The pilot (a borderer who has passed his life on the verge of civilization, and has been chosen to the post of leader from his knowledge of the savage and his experience in travel through roadless wastes) stands ready in the midst of his pioneers, and aids, to mount and lead the way. Ten or fifteen young men, not today on duty, form another cluster. They are ready to start on a buffalo hunt, are well mounted, and well armed as they need be, for the unfriendly Sioux have driven the buffalo out of the Platte, and the hunters must ride fifteen or twenty miles to reach them. The cow drivers are hastening, as they get ready, to the rear of their charge, to collect and prepare them for the day's march.

It is on the stroke of seven; the rushing to and fro, the cracking of the whips, the loud command to oxen, and what seems to be the inextricable confusion of the last ten minutes has ceased. Fortunately every one has been found and every teamster is at his post. The clear notes of the trumpet sound in the front; the pilot and his guards mount their horses, the leading division of wagons moves out of the encampment, and takes up the line of march, the rest fall into their places with the precision of clock work, until the spot so lately full of life sinks back into that solitude that seems to reign over the broad plain and rushing river as the caravan draws its lazy length toward the distant El Dorado. It is with the hunters we will briskly canter towards the bold but smooth and grassy bluffs that bound the broad valley, for we are not yet in sight of the grander but less beautiful scenery (of the Chimney Rock, Court House, and other bluffs, so nearly resem-

bling giant castles and palaces) made by the passage of the Platte
through the Highlands near Laramie. We have been traveling
briskly for more than an hour. We have reached the top of the
bluff, and now have turned to view the wonderful panorama
spread before us. To those who have not been on the Platte my
powers of description are wholly inadequate to convey an idea of
the vast extent and grandeur of the picture, and the rare beauty
and distinctness of its detail. No haze or fog obscures objects in
the pure transparent atmosphere of this lofty region. To those accustomed only to the murky air of the sea-board, no correct judgment of distance can be formed by sight, and objects which they
think they can reach in a two hours' walk may be a day's travel
away; and though the evening air is a better conductor of sound,
on the high plain during the day the report of the loudest rifle
sounds little louder than the bursting of a cap; and while the report can be heard but a few hundred yards, the smoke of the
discharge may be seen for miles. So extended is the view from the
bluff on which the hunters stand that the broad river glowing
under the morning sun like a sheet of silver, and the broader
emerald valley that borders it stretch away in the distance until
they narrow at almost two points in the horizon, and when first
seen, the vast pile of the Wind River mountain, though hundreds
of miles away, looks clear and distinct as a white cottage on the
plain.

We are full six miles away from the line of march; though
everything is dwarfed by distance, it is seen distinctly. The caravan
has been about two hours in motion and is now extended as widely
as a prudent regard for safety will permit. First, near the bank of
the shining river, is a company of horsemen; they seem to have
found an obstruction, for the main body has halted while three
or four ride rapidly along the bank of the creek or slough. They
are hunting a favorable crossing for the wagons; while we look
they have succeeded; it has apparently required no work to make
is passable, for all but one of the party have passed on and he has
raised a flag, no doubt a signal to the wagons to steer their course
to where he stands. The leading teamster sees him though he is
yet two miles off, and steers his course directly towards him, all
the wagons following in his track. They (the wagons) form a line

three quarters of a mile in length; some of the teamsters ride upon the front of their wagons, some walk beside their teams; scattered along the line companies of women and children are taking exercise on foot; they gather bouquets of rare and beautiful flowers that line the way; near them stalks a stately greyhound or an Irish wolf dog, apparently proud of keeping watch and ward over his master's wife and children.

Next comes a band of horses; two or three men or boys follow them, the docile and sagacious animals scarce needing this attention, for they have learned to follow in the rear of the wagons, and know that at noon they will be allowed to graze and rest. Their knowledge of time seems as accurate as of the place they are to occupy in the line, and even a full-blown thistle will scarcely tempt them to straggle or halt until the dinner hour has arrived. Not so with the large herd of horned beasts that bring up the rear; lazy, selfish and unsocial, it has been a task to get them in motion, the strong always ready to domineer over the weak, halt in the front and forbid the weaker to pass them. They seem to move only in fear of the driver's whip; though in the morning full to repletion, they have not been driven an hour before their hunger and thirst seem to indicate a fast of days' duration. Through all the long day their greed is never sated nor their thirst quenched, nor is there a moment of relaxation of the tedious and vexatious labors of their drivers, although to all others the march furnishes some season of relaxation or enjoyment. For the cow-drivers there is none.

But from the standpoint of the hunters the vexations are not apparent; the crack of the whips and loud objurgations are lost in the distance. Nothing of the moving panorama, smooth and orderly as it appears, has more attractions for the eye than that vast square column in which all colors are mingled, moving here slowly and there briskly, as impelled by horsemen riding furiously in front and rear.

But the picture, in its grandeur, its wonderful mingling of colors and distinctness of detail, is forgotten in contemplation of the singular people who give it life and animation. No other race of men with the means at their command would undertake so great a journey; none save these could successfully perform it with no previous preparation, relying only on the fertility of their invention to devise the means to overcome each danger and difficulty as it arose. They have undertaken to perform, with slow moving oxen, a journey of two thousand miles. The way lies over trackless wastes, wide and deep rivers, rugged and lofty mountains, and is beset with hostile savages. Yet, whether it were a deep river with no tree upon its banks, a rugged defile where even a loose horse could not pass, a hill too steep for him to climb, or a threatened attack of an enemy, they are always found ready and equal to the occasion, and always conquerors. May we not call them men of destiny? They are people changed in no essential particulars from their ancestors, who have followed closely on the footsteps of the receding savage, from the Atlantic sea-board to the valley of the Mississippi.

But while we have been gazing at the picture in the valley, the hunters have been examining the high plain in the other direction. Some dark moving objects have been discovered in the distance, and all are closely watching them to discover what they are, for in the atmosphere of the plains a flock of crows marching miles away, or a band of buffaloes or Indians at ten times the distance, look alike, and many ludicrous mistakes occur. But these are buffaloes, for two have stuck their heads together and are alternately pushing each other back. The hunters mount and away in pursuit, and I, a poor cow-driver, must hurry back to my daily toil, and take a scolding from my fellow herders for so long playing truant.

The pilot, by measuring the ground and timing the speed of the wagons and the walk of his horses, has determined the rate of each, so as to enable him to select the nooning place, as nearly as the requisite grass and water can be had at the end of five hours' travel of the wagons. Today, the ground being favorable, little time has been lost in preparing the road, so that he and his pioneers are at the nooning place an hour in advance of the wagons, which time is spent in preparing convenient watering places for the animals and digging little wells near the bank of the Platte. As the teams are not unyoked, but simply turned loose from the wagons, a corral is not formed at noon, but the wagons are drawn up in columns, four abreast, the leading wagon of each platoon on the left—the platoons being formed with that view. This brings friends together at noon as well as at night.

Today an extra session of the Council is being held, to settle a dispute that does not admit of delay, between a proprietor and a young man who has undertaken to do a man's service on the journey for bed and board. Many such engagements exist and much interest is taken in the manner this high court, from which there is no appeal, will define the rights of each party in such engagements. The Council was a high court in the most exalted sense. It was a Senate composed of the ablest and most respected fathers of the emigration. It exercised both legislative and judicial powers, and its laws and decisions proved it equal [to] and worthy of the high trust reposed in it. Its sessions were usually held on days when the caravan was not moving. It first took the state of the little commonwealth into consideration; revised or repealed rules defective or obsolete, and exacted such others as the exigencies seemed to require. The commonwealth being cared for, it next resolved itself into a court, to hear and settle private disputes and grievances. The offender and aggrieved appeared before it, witnesses were examined, and the parties wre heard by themselves and sometimes by counsel. The judges thus being made fully acquainted with the case, and being in no way influenced or cramped by technicalities, decided all cases according to their merits. There was but little use for lawyers before this court, for no plea was entertained which was calculated to defeat the ends of justice. Many of these judges have since won honors in higher spheres. They have aided to establish on the broad basis of right and universal liberty two of the pillars of our great Republic in the Occident. Some of the young men who appeared before them as advocates have themselves sat upon the highest judicial tribunals, commanded armies, been Governors of States, and taken high positions in the Senate of the nation.

It is now one o'clock; the bugle has sounded, and the caravan has resumed its westward journey. It is in the same order, but the evening is far less animated than the morning march; a drowsiness has fallen apparently on man and beast; teamsters drop asleep on their perches and even when walking by their teams, and the words of command are now addressed to the slowly creeping oxen in the softened tenor of women or the piping treble of children, while the snores of teamsters make a droning accompaniment.

But a little incident breaks the the monotony of the march. An emigrant's wife whose state of health has caused Dr. Whitman to travel near the wagon for the day, is now taken with violent illness. The doctor has had the wagon driven out of the line, a tent pitched and a fire kindled. Many conjectures are hazarded in regard to this mysterious proceeding, and as to why this lone wagon is to be left behind.

And we too must leave it, hasten to the front and note the proceedings, for the sun is now getting low in the west, and at length the painstaking pilot is standing ready to conduct the train in the circle which he has previously measured and marked out, which is to form the invariable fortification for the night. The leading wagons follow him so nearly round the circle, that but a wagon length separates them. Each wagon follows in its track, the rear closing on the front, until its tongue and ox chains will perfectly reach from one to the other, and so accurate the measurement and perfect the practice, that the hindmost wagon of the train always precisely closes the gateway. As each wagon is brought into position it is dropped from its team (the teams being inside the circle), the team unyoked, and the yokes and chains are used to connect the wagon strongly with that in its front. Within ten minutes from the time the leading wagon halted, the barricade is formed, the teams unyoked and driven out to pasture.

Everyone is busy preparing fires of buffalo chips to cook the evening meal, pitching tents and otherwise preparing for the night. There are anxious watchers for the absent wagon, for there are many matrons who may be afflicted like its inmate before the journey is over; and they fear the strange and startling practice of this Oregon doctor will be dangerous. But as sun goes down, the absent wagon rolls into camp, the bright, speaking face and cheery look of the doctor, who rides in advance, declares without words that all is well, and both mother and child are comfortable. I would fain now and here pay a passing tribute to that noble, devoted man, Dr. Whitman. I will obtrude no other name upon the reader, nor would I his, were he of our party or even living, but his stay with us was transient, though the good he did us permanent, and he has long since died at his post.

From the time he joined us on the Platte until he left us at Fort Hall, his great experience and indomitable energy were of priceless value to the migrating column. His constant advice, which we knew was based upon a knowledge of the road before us, was— "travel, TRAVEL, TRAVEL—nothing else will take you to the end of your journey; nothing is wise that does not help you along, nothing is good for you that causes a moment's delay." His great authority as a physician and complete success in the case above referred to saved us many prolonged and perhaps ruinous delays from similar causes, and it is no disparagement to others to say, that to no other individual are the emigrants of 1843 so much indebted for the successful conclusion of their journey as to Dr. Marcus Whitman.

All able to bear arms in the party have been formed into three companies, and each of these into four watches. Every third night it is the duty of one of these companies to keep watch and ward over the camp, and it is so arranged that each watch takes its turn of guard duty through the different watches of the night. Those forming the first watch tonight will be second on duty, then third and fourth, which brings them through all the watches of the night. They begin at eight o'clock P.M. and end at four o'clock A.M.

It is not yet eight o'clock when the first watch is to be set; the evening meal is just over, and the corral now free from the intrusion of the cattle or horses, groups of children are scattered over it. The larger are taking a game of romps, "the wee toddling things" are being taught that great achievement that distinguishes man from the lower animals. Before a tent near the river a violin makes lively music, and some youths and maidens have improvised a dance upon the green; in another quarter a flute gives its mellow and melancholy notes to the still air, which as they float away over the quiet river seem a lament for the past rather than a hope for the future. It has been a prosperous day; more than twenty miles have been accomplished of the great journey. The encampment is a good one; one of the causes that threatened much future delay has just been removed by the skill and energy of "that good angel," Dr. Whitman, and it has lifted a load from the hearts of the elders. Many of these are assembled around the good Doctor at the tent of the pilot (which is his home for the time being), and are giving grave attention to his wise and energetic counsel.

The careworn pilot sits aloof, quietly smoking his pipe, for he knows the brave Doctor is "strengthening his hands."

But time passes; the watch is set for the night, the council of old men has broken up and each has returned to his own quarter. The flute has whispered its last lament to the deepening night, the violin is silent and the dancers have dispersed. Enamored youth have whispered a tender "good night" in the ears of blushing maidens, or stolen a kiss from the lips of some future bride—for Cupid here as elsewhere has been busy bringing together congenial hearts, and among those simple people he alone is consulted in forming the marriage tie. Even the Doctor and the pilot have finished their confidential interview and have separated for the night. All is hushed and repose from the fatigue of the day, save the vigilant guard, and the wakeful leader who still has cares upon his mind that forbid sleep.

He hears the ten o'clock relief taking post and the "all well" report of the returned guard; the night deepens, yet he seeks not the needed repose. At length a sentinel hurries to him with the welcome report that a party is approaching—as yet too far away for its character to be determined, and he instantly hurries out in the direction seen. This he does both from inclination and duty, for in times past the camp had been unnecessarily alarmed by timid or inexperienced sentinels, causing much confusion and fright amongst women and children, and it had been made a rule that all extraordinary incidents of the night should be reported directly to the pilot, who alone had the authority to call out the military strength of the column or so much of it as was in his judgment necessary to prevent a stampede or repel an enemy.

Tonight he is at no loss to determine that the approaching party are our missing hunters, and that they have met with success, and he only waits until by some further signal he can know that no ill has happened to them. This is not long wanting. He does not even await their arrival, but the last care of the day being removed, and the last duty performed, he too seeks the rest that will enable him to go through the same routine tomorrow. But here I leave him, for my task is also done, and unlike his, it is to be repeated no more.

part 3

PIONEER
SETTLEMENTS

⌁ EMERSON HOUGH

Society in the
Cow Country

Emerson Hough (1857–1923) was firmly convinced
that "the story of the West is a story of the time of
heroes" and that, "of those who appear large upon
the fading page of that day, none may claim greater
stature than the chief figure of the cattle range." A
devoted lover of the out-of-doors, Hough was practically a nomad, but found time to manage the
periodical *Field and Stream* for a number of years
and to edit a column "Out-of-Doors" in the *Saturday
Evening Post*. Evidence of his glorified and somewhat
stereotypical version of frontier life may be discovered
in *Story of the Cowboy* (1897), *The Passing of the
Frontier* (1918), and *The Covered Wagon* (1922),
which has been extremely popular as a motion
picture.

Among the little cow towns of the frontier the searcher
for vivid things might have found abundance of material. Society
was certainly a mixed matter enough. It was a womanless society
for the most part, hence with some added virtues and lost vices,
as well as with certain inversions of that phase. The inhabitants
might be cowboys, half-breeds, gamblers, teamsters, hunters,
freighters, small storekeepers, petty officials, dissipated professional
men. The town was simply an eddy in the troubled stream of
Western immigration, and it caught the odd bits of drift wood
and wreck—the flotsam and jetsam of a chaotic flood.

From *The Cowboy*, vol. 2 (New York: The Brampton Society, 1897),
chap. 13, pp. 237–259 *passim*.

In the life of a modern business comunity a man must beware
of too much wisdom. The specialist is the man who succeeds, and
having once set his hand to an occupation, one dare never leave
it, under penalty of failure in what he has chosen as his life work.
In the city he who shifts and changes his employment loses the
confidence of his fellow-mortals, who agree that he should know
how to do one thing and nothing else, and should continue to
do it diligently all his life. In the West all this was different.
Versatility was a necessity. The successful man must know how
to do many things. The gleanings of any one field of activity were
too small to afford a living of themselves. This fact was accepted
by the citizens of the country, sometimes with the grim humour
which marked the West. A young lawyer in a Western town had
out a sign which read, "John Jones, Attorney-at-Law. Real Estate
and Insurance. Collections promptly attended to at all hours of
the day and night. Good Ohio cider for sale at 5 cents a glass." A
storekeeper had on his window the legend, "Wall Paper and
Marriage Licenses," thus announcing two commodities for which
there was but very small demand. One of the prominent citizens
of such a town was a gambler, a farmer, a fighter, and a school
teacher all in one. One of the leaders of the rustlers and cattle
thieves who made a little cow town their headquarters was a
Methodist minister. It was not unusual for a justice of the peace
to be a barber. The leading minister of a certain thriving cow
town, which experienced a "boom" in the early railroad days, eked
out his scanty salary by working as a sign painter during the week.
There seemed to the minds of the inhabitants of the country
nothing incongruous in this mixing up of occupations, it being
taken for granted that a man would endeavour to make a living
in the ways for which he seemed best fitted.

In any early cow town or mining camp of the West there was
sure to be a man from Leavenworth. No apparent reason for this
curious fact seems ever to have been given, yet it is certainly true
that no such town ever was settled without a man from Leavenworth to take part in the inauguration. He was apt afterward to
be one of the town officers. He was nearly always a lawyer, or
claimed to have once been one. He was sure to be the first justice

of the peace, and in that capacity of high dignity presented an interesting spectacle. The early Western justice of the peace was a curious being at best. Apt to be fully alive to his own importance, he presided at his sessions with a wisdom and solemnity not to be equalled in the most august courts of the land. It was rarely that the justice knew much law, but he nearly always was acquainted with the parties to any suit and with the prisoner who happened to be at bar, and usually he had a pretty accurate idea of what he was going to do with the case before it came up for trial. It may have been such a justice as this of whom the story is told that he made the defendant's lawyer sit down when he arose to reply to the arguments of the prosecution, saying that the counsel's talk served to "confuse the mind of the court." Yet the frontier justice of the peace usually came well within the bounds of common sense in his decisions, as witness the ruling of that Texas justice who gravely declared "unconstitutional" a certain State law which restricted the sale of liquor in his town in many unwelcome ways, he holding that such a law must necessarily be contrary to public policy and against good morals. This man was later elected to the State senate.

The first female inhabitants of the town were also sure to come from Kansas. There seems to be no special reason for this curious feature of the fauna of the cow town in the early days, and it seems difficult to tell why all the men seemed to have left Leavenworth and all the women to have abandoned the State of Kansas, though the fact remained none the less apparent. The family from Kansas nearly always came in a wagon, and among the family there were usually two or three girls, sure to become objects of admiration for a large cowboy contingent in a short period of time. There never was a cow town which did not have a family including "them girls from Kansas," and their fame was sure to be known abroad all over the local range. One by one the girls from Kansas disappeared down the tortuous road of matrimony, yet still the supply seemed unexhausted, more girls coming from Kansas in some mysterious way.

There was always a Jew merchant in any cow town, who handled the bulk of the business in general supplies. The infallible instinct of his kind led him to a place so free with its money and so loose in its business ideas. The Jew did not come from Kansas, but dropped down from above, came up from below, or blew in upon the wind, no one knew how, but he was always there. He advertised in the local paper, complaining about the rates, of course. "Keep your eye on Whitman" read his advertisement, and "Geep you eye on Viteman" was the burden of his talk to his customers. It was indeed a very wise thing to keep your eye on Whiteman, though perhaps the latter did not mean it in that way in his boastful advice.

There was always a sheriff in a cow town, and he was always the same sort of man—quiet, courageous, just, and much respected by his fellow-men. The public of the cow town had little real respect for the courts, and the judicial side of the law was sometimes farcical; but, by some queer inversion of the matter, all had respect for the executive side of the law, and indeed, recognised that side alone as the law itself. The sheriff was the law. He was worthy of this feeling, for nearly always he was a strong and noble nature, worthy of an unqualified admiration.

There was always a barber in a cow town, and when a town was so run down that it could not support a barber it was spoken of with contempt. There might not be any minister of the Gospel or any church, but there were two or three saloons, which served as town hall and general clubrooms, being the meeting places of the inhabitants. There was no dentist or doctor, though there might be a druggist, who kept half a dozen or so jars and bottles. If a cowpuncher wanted a little alum to cure a hide, the druggist charged him at about the rate of ten or fifteen dollars a pound for it, according to the extent of the need he had just then for the money. If the druggist was playing in fair luck at the time in the nightly poker game, alum was cheaper.

There was always a little newspaper, a whimsical, curious little affair, which lived in some strange fashion, and whose columns showed a medley of registered and published brands and marks for the members of the cattle association living in that district, this business being almost the only source of revenue for the newspaper. Of news there was none, except such as all men knew. The editor of the paper had a certain prestige in political matters, but led withal an existence properly to be termed extra hazardous. The editor always drank whisky when he could get it, just as everybody else did, it being quite too much to ask that he should depart from popular custom; but the paper was ground out from the hand press every week, or almost every week, with a regularity which under the circumstances was very commendable. Sooner or later, if one paper began to make more than a living, another paper came in, and then life assumed an added interest with the inhabitants. Both papers were then read, so that everybody might see what one editor was saying of the other. The second editor was nearly always a more vindictive man than the first one, and he drank more whisky, and wrote worse English and had a redder nose; but he added life to the town, and he was sure of a fair showing until at some unfortunate time he said the wrong thing. This wrong thing was never far away in the journalism of the range. It behooved the editor to be careful in his criticism of any one, and always to be sure to "boom the town," no matter what else might be omitted.

One of the owners of the saloons was sure to be a gambler as well as a dispenser of fluids. He had more money than anybody else, and also a surer chance of sudden death. He always killed one or two men before his own time came, but his time came some day. He was then properly mourned and buried, and the affair was discreetly mentioned in the papers. If it seemed that the gambler's partner was getting too "bad" to be needed in the economy of the town, he was asked to "move on," and this he was wise enough to do. Another gambler came in then.

The lawyer of the town was something of a personage. His library did not amount to so much, consisting probably of not more than two or three books, not very many, for one can not carry many books when on foot, and the lawyer nearly always walked into town; but the lawyer had all the authorities in his head, and so did not need a library. The lawyer was naturally a candidate for the territorial council, for county assessor, or anything else that had any pay attached to it. Of strictly legal work there was not much to do, but the lawyer always remembered his dignity, and you could always tell him in a crowd, for he was the only man in the town who did not wear "chaps" or overalls. The lawyer and the county surveyor sometimes had work to do in settling the lines of a homestead or some such thing when water rights were in dispute. He had no occasion to prosecute or defend any client for theft, for everybody in that country was afraid to steal; and burglary was a crime unknown. It was rarely that a man was prosecuted for horse stealing; never, unless the sheriff got to him first. A "killing" sometimes gave the lawyer a chance, but this was not a thing to make much stir about, and very often the killer was set free, because it was usually certain that the other man would have killed him if he could, and that is defence at law. Much more interesting was it when a man was shot and not killed, alike for the rarity of the occasion and for its probable consequences. Everybody wondered then which would be the one to get killed when he was well and around shooting again.

The cow town was very proud of any public improvements, very resentful of any attempt to cast slight upon such improvements, and very jealous of the pretensions of any other town of its neighbourhood. It being rumoured that a certain foothills city over toward the edge of the range was to have a railroad tunnel which would add to its attractions, it was gravely suggested by the citizens of a rival town located well out on the plains that the latter should also have a tunnel, and not allow itself to be surpassed in the "race of progress" by any "one-armed sheep-herding village." The county surveyor lost popularity because he tried to point out how expensive it would be to construct a tunnel out on the prairie.

The first coal-burning stove, the first piano, the first full-length mirror to come to town made each an occasion of popular rejoicing. At a time when all was progressing as usual in the leading saloon of such a town one evening, two of the players at a card table, without word of warning, arose and began shooting at each other in the celeritous yet painstaking fashion of the country. They were both caught by friends before any damage was done to either man, but the aim of one being disconcerted by the grasp upon his wrist, his bullet missed its mark and shattered the stove door, on the big new stove which was the boast of the community. For this careless shooting he received a general censure. . . .

In the communities of the frontier men were sometimes apt to be a trifle touchy and suspicious of their fellow-men, perhaps a bit ultra in their notions of personal honour and personal rights.

A cowpuncher from the Two Hat outfit was once heard explaining a little instance of this. "It was this a' way," said he, speaking of the recent killing over on Crooked Creek of Bill Peterson, who had been shot by his neighbour, a man by name of Sanders. "Peterson an' Sanders had both of 'em started hen ranches, allowin' to make plenty o' money next year, when the hens had sort o' got used to the range an' begun to do well on the feed. Sanders, he come in there first, an' he 'lowed he wouldn't have no one to buck aginst in the aig business, but Peterson he moves in on the creek too, and lays out his ranch right up agin Sanders, an' that makes Sanders plenty mad. Them two fellers, they got so blame jealous of each other they used to be afraid to go to sleep, for fear the other feller would think up some scheme or other. The wild cats and coyotes got in among the corrals like, an' before long they mighty nigh cleaned up the whold cavvieyard o' hens fer both of 'em, but they couldn't see it that way, an' each accused the other of stealin' his hens, which of course we knowed meant trouble some day.

"Fin'ly, these fellers got so jealous of each other that one feller he'd stay out in his hen pasture all day, a-herdin' back the grasshoppers to keep 'em from goin' on to the other feller's range— which them grasshoppers is shore good feed fer hens. Peterson, he consults a lawyer about this, and he comes back and tells Sanders that grasshoppers is critters *ferry natoory*,[1] or somethin' o' that sort, and so they belongs to everybody alike. Sanders he says he don't care a d—n about that, he aint goin, to have Peterson's hens a-eatin' his 'hoppers, because he saw the place first. So they at last got to sort o' havin' it in fer each other. One day Sanders he came down to me an' ast me to lend him my gun, because his was out o' order, an' he had to kill Peterson purty soon. So I let him take my gun, which is a shore daisy, an' next mornin' he laid fer Peterson when he come out the house. Peterson he saw him, an' he come out a-shootin', but Sanders he was a leetle too quick fer him. Sanders he quit the ranch then, an' now you kaint get a aig in this whole country fer a dollar a aig, not noways."

In the rude conditions of the society of the frontier the man of

---

[1] *ferae naturae* (L): Of a wild nature; not domesticated. [Ed. Note]

"sand" was the man most respected. If one allowed himself to be "run over" by the first person, he might as well be prepared to meet the contempt of all the others. Sooner or later a man was put to the test and "sized up" for what sort of timber he contained. If he proved himself able to take care of himself, he was much less apt to meet trouble thereafter. The man who was willing to mind his own business was not apt to meet with the professional bully or bad man of the town. The latter was a person who understood the theory of killing and escaping the law. He was confident in his own ability to pull quick, and it was his plan to so irritate his antagonist that the latter would "go for his gun." After that it was a case of self-defence. In the great cities the man who draws a deadly weapon is severely handled by the law, but in the old days on the frontier the bearing of arms was a necessity, and their general use made all men familiar with them and deprived them of half their terror. The stranger in the cow town was at first much troubled when he heard of a "killing" next door to him, but soon he became accustomed to such things and came to think little of them. The fashions of a country are its own and are not easily changed by a few; the change is apt to operate in quite the opposite direction. It is not the case that all the dwellers on the frontier were brave men, but courage is much a matter of association, and comes partly from habit after long acquaintance with scenes of danger and violence. The citizens of the cow town all wore guns, and did not feel fully dressed without such appurtenances. There was but one respectable way of settling a quarrel. It was not referred to the community, but to the individual, for in that land the individual was the supreme arbiter. None the less, many a coward's heart has beaten above a pistol belt, and nowhere in the world was such a fact more swiftly and unerringly determined than in a primitive community such as that in question. Upon the other hand, the rudest of the inhabitants of that community would recognise the quality of actual courage very quickly, and the man who stood highest in the esteem of his fellow-men was he who had the reputation of being a "square man," not "looking for trouble," but always ready to meet it if it came.

A wealthy and respected cattleman of a certain part of the cow range had a niece who ran away and married a renegade ranch foreman against whom she had been warned. This man soon began to abuse her, and she returned to her former home. The quarrel was patched up, but the girl's uncle sent word to the husband that if she ever was obliged to come back home again, she should never again go away to live with him. The husband sent back word that he would kill the uncle on sight. To this the cowman made no reply, but he always rode abroad with a rifle across his lap. One day he had word that his enemy was about to waylay him, and accordingly he was upon the lookout for him. As he entered the edge of a bit of wood, he saw the dutiful relative waiting for him, but luckily looking in the wrong direction. The wind being in his favour, the cowman drove up within a short distance of the man who was seeking to kill him, and then calling to him, killed him in his tracks when he turned. In this act he was upheld by all the society of the range, and was never in the least called to account for it, as it was thought he had done quite what was right and needful. He was never molested by any more relatives after that. This incident was long ago forgotten in his history, and a quieter, more respected, or more useful citizen does not live than he is to-day, nor one more marked for his mildness and even-tempered disposition. He did only what in his time and under his surroundings was the fit and needful thing to do. . . .

Sometimes in the winter season society in the cow town would be enlivened by a ball. Such a ball was a singular and somewhat austere event, and one which it would be difficult to match to-day in all the land. The news of the coming ball spread after the mysterious fashion of the plains, so that in some way it became known in a short time far and wide across the range. The cowboys fifty miles away were sure to hear of it and to be on hand, coming horseback from their ranches, each man clad in what he thought was his best. The entire populace of the cow town was there, the ballroom being the largest room to be found in the town, wherever that might chance to be. Refreshments were on hand, sometimes actually cake, made by the fair hands of the girls from Kansas. A fiddler was obtained from some place, for where a few men are gathered together there is always sure to be a fiddler; and this well meaning, if not always melodious, individual was certain to have a hard night's work ahead of him.

Of course there was a great scarcity of lady partners, for the men outnumbered the women a dozen to one. No woman, whatever her personal description, needed to fear being slighted at such a ball. There were no wall flowers on the range. The Mexican wash-woman was sure of a partner for every dance, and the big girl from Kansas, the little girl from Kansas, the wife of the man from Missouri, and all the other ladies of the country there assembled, were fairly in danger of having their heads turned at the praise of their own loveliness. In the Southwest such a dance was called a *baille*, and among the women attending it were sure to be some dark-eyed *señoritas* with *mantilla* and *reboso*, whose costume made contrast with the calico and gingham of the "American" ladies. The dancing costume of the men was various, but it was held matter of course if a cowboy chose to dance in his regulation garb, "chaps," spurs and all. In the more advanced stages of society it became etiquette for a gentleman to lay aside his gun when engaging in the dance, but he nearly always retained a pistol or knife somewhere about him, for he knew there might be occasion to use it. Sometimes the cowpuncher danced with his hat on, but this later became improper. There are few more startling spectacles, when one pauses to think of it from a distance, than a cowboy quadrille in which there was a Mexican woman with only one leg, a girl from Kansas who had red hair, and two cowboys who wore full range costume.

Between dances the cowpuncher entertained his fair one with the polite small talk of the place; surmises that the weekly mail had been delayed by some mule getting "alkalied over on the flats"; talk of the last hold-up of the mail; statistics of the number of cattle shipped last year, and the probable number to be shipped this; details of the last "killing" in the part of the country from which the cowpuncher came, etc. Meantime the lady was complimented openly upon her good points and those of her costume, not to her personal displeasure, for human nature is much the same no matter where the ball is held. It sometimes happened that the lady was not averse to sharing with her escort of a bit of the liquid refreshments that were provided. The effects of this, the stir of the dancing, the music, the whirl and go of it all, so unusual in the experiences of most of the attendants, kept things moving in a fashion that became more and more lively as the hours passed by. The belated range man, riding full gallop to town, could see from a distance the red lights of the windows at the hall, and could hear afar the sound of revelry by night. Excited by this, he spurred on his horse the faster, answering to the dancers with the shrill yell of the plains, so that all might know another man was coming to join in the frolic. He cast his bridle rein over the nearest corral post, and forthwith rushed in to mingle with the others in a merriment that was sure to last to daybreak. Out of this ball, as out of other balls, were sure to arise happiness, heartburnings, jealousies, and some marriages. An engagement on the plains was usually soon followed by a marriage, and such an engagement was not made to be broken to the advantage of another man, there was apt to be trouble over it between the men. Sometimes the night of the ball did not pass without such trouble. Any such affair was apt to be handled most delicately in the next issue of the paper; although funeral notices were not customary there, the papers being printed only each week or so.

The cow town was sure to have among its dwellers some of the odd characters which drifted about the West in the old times, men who had somehow gotten a warp into their natures, and had ceased to fit in with the specifications of civilization. Such men might be teamsters, cowboys, or those mysterious beings who in some way manage always to live without doing any work—these not to be called tramps, for the tramp was something unknown in the cow town. Such a man might have a little cabin of his own, with a fireplace and a bed of blankets. Nearly all the male population of the town was made up of single men, and of these nearly all did their own cooking, living in a desultory, happy-go-lucky sort of fashion, with no regularity in any habits. Some of these men were educated, and had known other conditions of life. Bitterer cynics never lived than some of these wrecks of the range. There was Tom O—, a cowpuncher, apparently as ignorant and illiterate as any man that ever walked, but who had his Shakes-

peare at his tongue's end, and could quote Byron by the yard.
Tom's only song was—

"I never loved a fond gazel-l-e!"

The song rarely got further along than that. A cheerful fatalist,
Tom accepted the fact that luck was against him, and looked upon
life as the grimmest of jokes, prepared for his edification. No
matter how ill his fortune, Tom never complained, even as he
never hoped. He had, too, a certain amount of enterprise in his
character. At last accounts he was headed for the Indian Nations,
it being his expressed intention to marry an Indian woman and so
become a member of the tribe, this being the easiest way open
to fortune which offered to his mind. He had several wives scattered over the range at different points, and at times he was wont
to discuss the good and bad points of these with the utmost
candour and impartiality, thus showing himself a liberal and philo-
sophical man. . . .

In short, the cow town of the good old times was a gathering of
men of most heterogeneous sorts, a mass of particles which could
not mix or blend. Of types there was abundance, for each man was
a study of himself. He had lived alone, forced to defend himself
and to support himself under the most varying and trying circumstances, very often cut off from all manner of human aid or
companionship for months at a time. Needing his self-reliance, his
self-reliance grew. Forced to be independent, his independence
grew. Many of these men had been crowded out of the herd in
the States, and had so wandered far away from the original pastures
of their fellows. They met in the great and kindly country of the
old West, a number of these rogues of the herd, and it was a
rough sort of herd they made up among themselves. They could
not blend; not until again the sweep of the original herd had
caught up with them, and perforce taken them in again among
its numbers. Then, as they saw the inevitable, as they saw the old
West gone forever, leaving no place whither they might wander
farther, they turned their hands to the ways of civilization, and
did as best they could. In many cases they became quiet and

useful and diligent citizens, who to-day resent the raking up of the grotesque features of their past, and have a contempt for the men who try to write about that past with feigned wisdom and unfeigned sensationalism. Among those citizens of the old cow town were many strange characters, but also many noble ones, many lovable ones. A friend in that society was really a friend. Alike the basest and the grandest traits of human nature were shown in the daily life of the place. Honour was something more than a name, and truth something less than a jest. The cynicisms were large, they were never petty. The surroundings were large, the men were large, their character was large. Good manhood was something respected, and true womanhood something revered. We do very ill if we find only grotesque and ludicrous things in such a society as this. . . .

⚡ J. ROSS BROWNE

Washoe Revisited

John Ross Browne (1821–1875), immortalized in *Moby Dick* as one of Melville's whaling authors, traveled widely in Zanzibar, in the Far East, in Germany, in Scandinavia, and in western America. Among a number of pieces which he wrote for *Harper's Magazine* are three articles about California and Washoe (Nevada) published in 1865. The selection reprinted here is the second of these three: an eye-witness account of the goings on in Virginia City during gold-rush days. A short sketch of Browne's career was published in *Harper's* on February 22, 1868.

From *Harper's Monthly Magazine*, June 1865, pp. 1–12.

I was prepared to find great changes on the route from Carson to Virginia City. At Empire City—which was nothing but a sage-desert inhabited by Dutch Nick on the occasion of my early exploration—I was quite bewildered with the busy scenes of life and industry. Quartz-mills and saw-mills had completely usurped the valley along the head of the Carson River; and now the hammering of stamps, the hissing of steam, the whirling clouds of smoke from tall chimneys, and the confused clamor of voices from a busy multitude, reminded one of a manufacturing city. Here, indeed, was progress of a substantial kind.

Further beyond, at Silver City, there were similar evidences of prosperity. From the descent into the cañon through the Devil's Gate, and up the grade to Gold Hill, it is almost a continuous line of quartz-mills, tunnels, dumps, sluices, water-wheels, frame shanties, and grog-shops.

Gold Hill itself has swelled into the proportions of a city. It is now practically a continuation of Virginia. Here the evidences of busy enterprise are peculiarly striking. The whole hill is riddled and honey-combed with shafts and tunnels. Engine-houses for hoisting are perched on points apparently inaccessible; quartz-mills of various capacities line the sides of the cañon; the main street is well flanked by brick stores, hotels, express-offices, saloons, restaurants, groggeries, and all those attractive places of resort which go to make up a flourishing mining town. Even a newspaper is printed here, which I know to be a spirited and popular institution, having been viciously assailed by the same. A runaway team of horses, charging full tilt down the street, greeted our arrival in a lively and characteristic manner, and came very near capsizing our stage. One man was run over some distance below, and partially crushed; but as somebody was killed nearly every day, such a meagre result afforded no general satisfaction.

Descending the slope of the ridge that divides Gold Hill from Virginia City a strange scene attracts the eye. He who gazes upon it for the first time is apt to doubt if it be real. Perhaps there is not another spot upon the face of the globe that presents a scene so weird and desolate in its natural aspect, yet so replete with busy life, so animate with human interest. It is as if a wondrous battle raged, in which the combatants were man and earth. Myriads of swarthy, bearded, dust-covered men are piercing into the grim old mountains, ripping them open, thrusting murderous holes through their naked bodies; piling up engines to cut out their vital arteries; stamping and crushing up with infernal machines their disemboweled fragments, and holding fiendish revels amidst the chaos of destruction; while the mighty earth, blasted, barren, and scarred by the tempests of ages, fiercely affronts the foe—smiting him with disease and death; scoffing at his puny assaults with a grim scorn; ever grand in his desolation, ever dominant in the infinity of his endurance. "Come!" he seems to mutter, "dig, delve, pierce, and bore, with your picks, your shovels, and your infernal machines; wring out of my veins a few globules of the precious blood; hoard it, spend it, gamble for it, bring perdition to your souls with it—do what you will, puny insects! Sooner or later the death-blow smites you, and Earth swallows you! From earth you came—to earth you go again!"

The city lies on a rugged slope, and is singularly diversified in its uprisings and downfallings. It is difficult to determine, by any system of observation or measurement, upon what principle it was laid out. My impression is that it was never laid out at all, but followed the dips, spurs, and angles of the immortal Comstock. Some of the streets run straight enough; others seem to dodge about at acute angles in search of an open space, as miners explore the subterranean regions in search of a lead. The cross streets must have been forgotten in the original plan—if ever there was a plan about this eccentric city. Sometimes they happen accidentally at the most unexpected points; and sometimes they don't happen at all where you are sure to require them. A man in a hurry to get from the upper slope of the town to any opposite point below must try it under-ground or over the roofs of the houses, or take the customary circuit of half a mile. Every body seems to have built wherever he could secure a lot. The two main streets, it must be admitted, are so far regular as to follow pretty nearly the direction of the Comstock lead. On the lower slope, or plateau, the town, as viewed from any neighboring eminence, presents much the appearance of a vast number of shingle-roofs shaken down at random, like a jumbled pack of cards. All the streets are narrow, except where there are but few houses, and there they are wide enough at present. The business part of the town has been built up with astonishing rapidity. In the spring of 1860 there was nothing of it save a few frame shanties and canvas tents, and one or two rough stone cabins. It now presents some of the distinguishing features of a metropolitan city. Large and substantial brick houses, three or four stories high, with ornamental fronts, have filled up most of the gaps, and many more are still in progress of erection. The oddity of the plan, and variety of its architecture —combining most of the styles known to the ancients, and some but little known to the moderns—give this famous city a grotesque, if not picturesque, appearance, which is rather increased upon a close inspection. . . .

Entering the main street you pass on the upper side huge piles of earth and ore, hoisted out of the shafts or run out of the tunnels, and cast over the "dumps." The hill-sides, for a distance of more than a mile, are perfectly honeycombed. Steam-engines are puffing off their steam; smoke-stacks are blackening the air with their thick volumes of smoke; quartz-batteries are battering; hammers are hammering; subterranean blasts are bursting up the earth; picks and crow-bars are picking and crashing into the precious rocks; shanties are springing up, and carpenters are sawing and ripping and nailing; store-keepers are rolling their merchandise in and out along the way-side; fruit vendors are peddling their fruits; wagoners are tumbling out and piling in their freights of dry goods and ore; saloons are glittering with their gaudy bars and fancy glasses, and many-colored liquors, and thirsty men are swilling the burning poison; auctioneers, surrounded by eager and gaping crowds of speculators, are shouting off the stocks of delinquent stockholders; organ-grinders are grinding their organs and torturing consumptive monkeys; hurdy-gurdy girls are singing bacchanalian songs in bacchanalian dens; Jew clothiers are selling off prodigious assortments of worthless garments at ruinous prices; billstickers are sticking up bills of auctions, theatres, and new saloons; newsboys are crying the city papers with the latest telegraphic news; stages are dashing off with passengers for "Reese;" and stages are dashing in with passengers from "Frisco;" and the inevitable Wells, Fargo, and Co. are distributing letters, packages, and papers to the hungry multitude, amidst tempting piles of silver bricks and wonderful complications of scales, letter-boxes, clerks, account-books, and twenty-dollar pieces. All is life, excitement, avarice, lust, deviltry, and enterprise. A strange city truly, abounding in strange exhibitions and startling combinations of the human passions. Where upon earth is there such another place? . . .

Making due allowance for the atmosphere of exaggeration through which a visitor sees every thing in this wonderful mining metropolis, its progress has been sufficiently remarkable to palliate in some measure the extraordinary flights of fancy in which its inhabitants are prone to indulge. I was not prepared to see so great a change within the brief period of three years; for when people assure me "the world never saw any thing like it," "California is left in the shade," "San Francisco is eclipsed" "Montgomery Street is nowhere now," my incredulity is excited, and it takes some little time to judge of the true state of the case without prejudice. Speaking then strictly within bounds, the growth of this city is remarkable. When it is considered that the surrounding country affords but few facilities for the construction of houses; that lumber has to be hauled a considerable distance at great expense; that lime, bricks, iron-works, sashes, doors, etc., cost three or four times what similar articles do in San Francisco; that much indispensable material can only be had by transporting it over the mountains a distance of more than a hundred and fifty miles; and that the average of mechanical labor, living, and other expenses is correspondingly higher than in California, it is really wonderful how much has been done in so short a space of time.

Yet, allowing all this, what would be the impressions of a Fejee Islander sent upon a mission of inquiry to this strange place? His earliest glimpse of the main street would reveal the curious fact that it is paved with a conglomerate of dust, mud, splintered planks, old boots, clippings of tinware, and playing-cards. It is especially prolific in the matter of cards. Mules are said to fatten on them during seasons of scarcity when the straw gives out. The next marvelous fact that would strike the observation of this wild native is that so many people live in so many saloons, and do nothing from morning till night, and from night till morning again, but drink fiery liquids and indulge in profane language. How can all these ablebodied men afford to be idle? Who pays their expenses?

And why do they carry pistols, knives, and other deadly weapons, when no harm could possibly befall them if they went unarmed and devoted themselves to some useful occupation? Has the God of the white men done them such an injury in furnishing all this silver for their use that they should treat His name with contempt and disrespect? Why do they send missionaries to the Fejee Islands and leave their own country in such a dreadful state of neglect? The Fejeeans devour their enemies occasionally as a war measure; the white man swallows his enemy all the time without regard to measure. Truly the white man is a very uncertain native! Fejeeans can't rely upon him.

When I was about to start on my trip to Washoe, friends from Virginia assured me I would find hotels there almost, if not quite, equal to the best in San Francisco. There was but little difference, they said, except in the matter of extent. The Virginia hotels were quite as good, though not quite so large. Of course I believed all they told me. Now I really don't consider myself fastidious on the subject of hotels. Having traveled in many different countries I have enjoyed an extensive experience in the way of accommodations, from my mother-earth to the foretop of a whale-ship, from an Indian wigwam to a Parisian hotel, from an African palm-tree to an Arctic snowbank. I have slept in the same bed with two donkeys, a camel, half a dozen Arabs, several goats, and a horse. I have slept on beds alive with snakes, lizards, scorpions, centipeds, bugs, and fleas—beds in which men stricken with the plague had died horrible deaths—beds that might reasonably be suspected of small-pox, measles, and Asiatic cholera. I have slept in beds of rivers and beds of sand, and on the bare bed rock. Standing, sitting, lying down, doubled up, and hanging over; twisted, punched, jammed and elbowed by drunken men; snored at in the ears; sat upon and smothered by the nightmare; burnt by fires, rained upon, snowed upon, and bitten by frost—in all these positions, and subject to all these discomforts, I have slept with comparative satisfaction. There are pleasanter ways of sleeping, to be sure, but there are times when any way is a blessing. In respect to the matter of eating I am even less particular. Frogs, horse-leeches, snails, and grasshoppers are luxuries to what I have eaten. It has pleased Providence to favor me with appetites and tastes appropriate to a great variety of circumstances and many conditions of life. These facts serve to show that I am not fastidious on the subject of personal accommodations.

Perhaps my experience in Virginia was exceptional; perhaps misfortune was determined to try me to the utmost extremity. I endeavored to find accommodations at a hotel recommended as the best in the place. and was shown a room over the kitchen stove, in which the thermometer ranged at about 130 to 150 degrees of Fahrenheit. To be lodged and baked at the rate of $2 per night, cash in advance, was more than I could stand, so I asked for another room. There was but one more, and that was preempted by a lodger who might or might not come back and claim possession in the middle of the night. It had no windows except one that opened into the passage, and the bed was so arranged that every other lodger in the house could take a passing observation of the sleeper and enjoy his style of sleeping. Nay, it was not beyond the resources of the photographic art to secure his negative and print his likeness for general distribution. It was bad enough to be smothered for want of light and air; but I had no idea of paying $2 a night for the poor privilege of showing people how I looked with my eyes shut, and possibly my mouth open. A man may have an attack of nightmare, his countenance may be distorted by horrible dreams; he may laugh immoderately at a very bad pun made in his sleep—in all which conditions of body and mind he doubtless presents an interesting spectacle to the critical eyes of a stranger, but he doesn't like to wake up suddenly and be caught in the act.

The next hotel to which I was recommended was eligibly located on a street composed principally of grog-shops and gambling-houses. I was favored with a frontroom about eight feet square. The walls were constructed of boards fancifully decorated with paper, and afforded this facility to a lodger—that he could hear all that was going on in the adjacent rooms. The partitions might deceive the eye, but the ear received the full benefit of the various oaths, ejaculations, conversations, and perambulations in which his neighbors indulged. As for the bed, I don't know how long it had been in use, or what race of people had hitherto slept in it, but the sheets and blankets seemed to be sadly discolored by age—or lack of soap and water. It would be safe to say washing was not considered a paying investment by the managers of this establishment. Having been over twenty-four hours without sleep or rest I made an attempt to procure a small supply, but miserably failed in consequence of an interesting conversation carried on in the passage between the chamber-maids, waiters, and other ladies and gentlemen respecting the last free fight. From what I could gather this was considered the best neighborhood in the city for free fights. Within the past two weeks three or four men had been shot, stabbed, or maimed close by the door. "Oh, it's a lively place, you bet!" said one of the ladies (the chamber-maid, I think), "an oncommon lively place—reely hexcitin'. I look out of the winder every mornin' jist to see how many dead men are layin' around. I declare to gracious the bullets flies around here sometimes like hailstones!" "An' shur," said a voice in that rich brogue which can never be mistaken, "it's no wondher the boys shud be killin' an' murtherin' themselves forninst the door, whin they're all just like me, dyin' in love wid yer beauteeful self!" A smart slap and a general laugh followed this suggestion. "Git away wid ye, Dinnis; yer always up to yer mischief! As I was sayin', no later than this mornin', I see two men a poppin' away at each other wid six-shooters—a big man an' a little man. The big man he staggered an' fell right under the winder, wid his head on the curb-stone, an' his legs a stickin' right up in the air. He was all over blood, and when the boys picked him up he was dead as a brickbat. 'Tother chap he run into a saloon. You better b'leeve this is a lively neighborhood. I tell you hailstones is nothink to the way the bullets flies around." "That's so," chimes in another female voice; "I see myself, with my own eyes, Jack's corpse an' two more carried away in the last month. If I'd a had a six-shooter then you bet they'd a carried away the fellow that nipped Jack!"

Now taking into view the picturesque spectacle that a few dead men dabbled in blood must present to the eye on a fine morning, and the chances of a miscellaneous ball carrying away the top of one's cranium, or penetrating the thin board wall and ranging upward through his body as he lies in bed, I considered it best to seek a more secluded neighborhood, where the scenery was of a less stimulating character and the hail-storms not quite so heavy.

By the kind aid of a friend I secured comparatively agreeable quarters in a private lodging-house kept by a widow lady. The rooms were good and the beds clean, and the price not extravagant for this locality—$12 a week without board.

So much for the famous hotels of Virginia. If there are any better, neither myself, nor some fellow-travelers who told me their experiences, succeeded in finding them. The concurrent testimony was that they are dirty, ill-kept, badly attended by rough, ill-mannered waiters—noisy to such a degree that a sober man can get but little rest, day or night, and extravagantly high in proportion to the small comfort they afford. One of the newspapers published a statement which the author probably intended for a joke, but which is doubtless founded upon fact—namely, that a certain hotel advertised for 300 chickens to serve the same number of guests. Only one chicken could be had for love or money—a very ancient rooster, which was made into soup and afterward served up in the form of a fricassee for the 300 guests. The flavor was considered extremely delicate—what there was of it; and there was plenty of it such as it was.

Still if we are to credit what the Virginia newspapers say—and it would be dangerous to intimate that they ever deal in any thing save the truth—there are other cities on the eastern slope of the Sierras which afford equally attractive accommodations. On the occasion of the recent Senatorial contest at Carson City, the prevailing rates charged for lodgings, according to the Virginia *Enterprise*, were as follows: "For a bed in a house, barn, blacksmithshop, or hay-yard (none to be had—all having been engaged shortly before election); horse-blanket in an old sugar hogshead per night, $10; crockery-crate, with straw, $7.50; without straw, $5.75; for cellar-door, $4; for roosting on a smooth pole, $3.50; pole, common, rough, $3; plaza fence, $2.50; walking up and down the Warm Springs road—if cloudy, $1.50; if clear, $1.25. (In case the clouds are very thick and low $1.75 is generally asked.) Very good roosting in a pine-tree, back of Camp Nye, may still be had free, but we understand that a company is being formed to monopolize all the more accessible trees. We believe they propose to improve by putting two pins in the bottom of each tree, or keep a man to boost regular customers. They talk of charging six bits."

I could scarcely credit this, if it were not that a friend of mine, who visited Reese River last summer, related some experiences of a corroborative character. Unable to secure lodgings elsewhere, he undertook to find accommodations in a vacant sheep corral. The proprietor happening to come home about midnight found him spread out under the lee of the fence. "Look-a-here, stranger!" said he, gruffly, "that's all well enough, but I gen'rally collect in advance. Just fork over four bits or mizzle!" My friend indignantly mizzled. Cursing the progressive spirit of the age, he walked some distance out of town, and was about to finish the night under the lee of a big quartz boulder, when a fierce-looking speculator, with a six-shooter in his hand, suddenly appeared from a cavity in the rock, saying, "No yer don't! Take a fool's advice now, and git! When you go a prospectin' around ov nights agin, jest steer ov this boulder ef you please!" In vain my friend attempted to explain. The rising wrath of the squatter was not to be appeased by soft words, and the click of the trigger, as he raised his pistol and drew a bead, warned the trespasser that it was time to be off. He found lodgings that night on the public highway to Virginia City and San Francisco.

↙ *HAMLIN GARLAND*

The Land of the Dakotas

Hamlin Garland (1860–1940) was born in a pioneer log cabin in Wisconsin. In 1869, his people moved to Iowa onto what he called a "Middle Border" farm.

Reprinted with permission of the publisher from *A Son of the Middle Border* by Hamlin Garland. Copyright 1917 by Hamlin Garland. Renewed 1945 by Mary I. Lord and Constance G. Williams. © 1962 by The Macmillan Company.

In 1881, he helped his father establish a home in
Ordway, South Dakota, a few miles northeast of
Aberdeen on the James River. The following chapter
from *A Son of the Middle Border* (1917) concerns
Garland's Dakota experience. The author professed
cultural regionalism as a sort of literary creed, and is
especially remembered for *Main Traveled Roads*
(1890), one of the early expressions of naturalism in
American literature.

The movement of settlers toward Dakota had now become
an exodus, a stampede. Hardly anything else was talked about as
neighbors met one another on the road or at the Burr Oak school-
house on Sundays. Every man who could sell out had gone west
or was going. In vain did the county papers and Farmer's Institute
lecturers advise cattle raising and plead for diversified tillage, pre-
dicting wealth for those who held on; farmer after farmer joined
the march to Kansas, Nebraska, and Dakota. "We are wheat
raisers," they said, "and we intend to keep in the wheat belt."

Our own family group was breaking up. My uncle David of
pioneer spirit had already gone to the far Missouri Valley. Rachel
had moved to Georgia, and Grandad McClintock was with his
daughters, Samantha and Deborah, in western Minnesota. My
mother, thus widely separated from her kin, resigned herself once
more to the thought of founding a new home. Once more she
sang, "O'er the hills in legions, boys," with such spirit as she
could command, her clear voice a little touched with the huskiness
of regret.

I confess I sympathized in some degree with my father's new
design. There was something large and fine in the business of
wheat-growing, and to have a plague of insects arise just as our
harvesting machinery was reaching such perfection that we could
handle our entire crop without hired help was a tragic, abominable
injustice. I could not blame him for his resentment and dismay.

My personal plans were now confused and wavering. I had no
intention of joining this westward march; on the contrary, I was
looking toward employment as a teacher, therefore my last weeks
at the Seminary were shadowed by a cloud of uncertainty and

vague alarm. It seemed a time of change, and immense, far-reaching, portentous readjustment. Our homestead was sold, my world was broken up. "What am I to do?" was my question.

Father had settled upon Ordway, Brown County, South Dakota, as his future home, and immediately after my graduation, he and my brother set forth into the new country to prepare the way for the family's removal, leaving me to go ahead with the harvest alone. It fell out, therefore, that immediately after my flowery oration on *Going West* I found myself more of a slave to the cattle than ever before in my life.

Help was scarce; I could not secure even so much as a boy to aid in milking the cows; I was obliged to work double time in order to set up the sheaves of barley which were in danger of mouldering on the wet ground. I worked with a kind of bitter, desperate pleasure, saying, "This is the last time I shall ever lift a bundle of this accursed stuff."

And then, to make the situation worse, in raising some heavy machinery connected with the self-binder. I strained my side so seriously that I was unable to walk. This brought the harvesting to a stand, and made my father's return necessary. For several weeks I hobbled about, bent like a gnome, and so helped to reap what the chinch bugs had left, while my mother prepared to "follow the sunset" with her "Boss."

September first was the day set for saying goodbye to Dry Run, and it so happened that her wedding anniversary fell close upon the same date and our neighbors, having quietly passed the word around, came together one Sunday afternoon to combine a farewell dinner with a Silver Wedding "surprise party."

Mother saw nothing strange in the coming of the first two carriages, the Buttons often came driving in that way—but when the Babcocks, the Coles, and the Gilchrists clattered in with smiling faces, we all stood in the yard transfixed with amazement. "What's the meaning of all this?" asked my father.

No one explained. The women calmly clambered down from their vehicles, bearing baskets and bottles and knobby parcels, and began instant and concerted bustle of preparation. The men tied their horses to the fence and hunted up saw-horses and planks, and soon a long table was spread beneath the trees on the lawn.

One by one other teams came whirling into the yard. The assembly resembled a "vandoo" as Asa Walker said. "It's worse than that," laughed Mrs. Turner. "It's a silver wedding and a 'send off' combined."

They would not let either the "bride" or the "groom" do a thing, and with smiling resignation my mother folded her hands and sank into a chair. "All right," she said. "I am perfectly willing to sit by and see you do the work. I won't have another chance right away." And there was something sad in her voice. She could not forget that this was the beginning of a new pioneering adventure.

The shadows were long on the grass when at the close of the supper old John Gammons rose to make a speech and present the silver tea set. His voice was tremulous with emotion as he spoke of the loss which the neighborhood was about to suffer, and tears were in many eyes when father made reply. The old soldier's voice failed him several times during his utterance of the few short sentences he was able to frame, and at last he was obliged to take his seat, and blow his nose very hard on his big bandanna handkerchief to conceal his emotion.

It was a very touching and beautiful moment to me, for as I looked around upon that little group of men and women, rough-handed, bent and worn with toil, silent and shadowed with the sorrow of parting, I realized as never before the high place my parents had won in the estimation of their neighbors. It affected me still more deeply to see my father stammer and flush with uncontrollable emotion. I had thought the event deeply important before, but I now perceived that our going was all of a piece with the West's elemental restlessness. I could not express what I felt then, and I can recover but little of it now, but the pain which filled my throat comes back to me mixed with a singular longing to relive it.

There, on a low mound in the midst of the prairie, in the shadow of the house we had built, beneath the slender trees we had planted, we were bidding farewell to one cycle of emigration and entering upon another. The border line had moved on, and my indomitable Dad was moving with it. I shivered with dread of the irrevocable decision thus forced upon me. I heard a clanging as of great gates behind me and the field of the future was wide and wan.

From this spot we had seen the wild prairies disappear. On every hand wheat and corn and clover had taken the place of the wild oat, the hazelbush and the rose. Our house, a commonplace frame cabin, took on grace. Here Hattie had died. Our yard was ugly, but there Jessie's small feet had worn a slender path. Each of our lives was knit into these hedges and rooted in these fields and yet, notwithstanding all this, in response to some powerful yearning call, my father was about to set out for the fifth time into the still more remote and untrodden west. Small wonder that my mother sat with bowed head and tear-blinded eyes, while these good and faithful friends crowded around her to say goodbye.

She had no enemies and no hatreds. Her rich singing voice, her smiling face, her ready sympathy with those who suffered, had endeared her to every home into which she had gone, even as a momentary visitor. No woman in childbirth, no afflicted family within a radius of five miles had ever called for her in vain. Death knew her well, for she had closed the eyes of youth and age, and yet she remained the same laughing, bounteous, wholesouled mother of men that she had been in the valley of the Neshonoc. Nothing could permanently cloud her face or embitter the sunny sweetness of her creed.

One by one the women put their worn, ungraceful arms about her, kissed her with trembling lips, and went away in silent grief. The scene became too painful for me at last, and I fled away from it—out into the fields, bitterly asking, "Why should this suffering be? Why should mother be wrenched from all her dearest friends and forced to move away to a strange land?"

I did not see the actual packing up and moving of the household goods, for I had determined to set forth in advance and independently, eager to be my own master, and at the moment I did not feel in the least like pioneering.

Some two years before, when the failure of our crop had made the matter of my continuing at school an issue between my father and myself, I had said, "If you will send me to school until I graduate, I will ask nothing further of you," and these words I now took a stern pleasure in upholding. Without a dollar of my own,

I announced my intention to fare forth into the world on the strength of my two hands, but my father, who was in reality a most affectionate parent, offered me thirty dollars to pay my carfare.

This I accepted, feeling that I had abundantly earned this money, and after a sad parting with my mother and my little sister, set out one September morning for Osage. At the moment I was oppressed with the thought that this was the fork in the trail, that my family and I had started on differing roads. I had become a man. With all the ways of the world before me I suffered from a feeling of doubt. The open gate allured me, but the homely scenes I was leaving suddenly put forth a latent magic.

I knew every foot of this farm. I had traversed it scores of times in every direction, following the plow, the harrow, or the seeder. With a great lumber wagon at my side I had husked corn from every acre of it, and now I was leaving it with no intention of returning. My action, like that of my father, was final. As I looked back up the lane at the tall Lombardy poplar trees bent like sabres in the warm western wind, the landscape I was leaving seemed suddenly very beautiful, and the old home very peaceful and very desirable. Nevertheless I went on.

Try as I may, I cannot bring back out of the darkness of that night any memory of how I spent the time. I must have called upon some of my classmates, but I cannot lay hold upon a single word or look or phrase from any of them. Deeply as I felt my distinction in thus riding forth into the world, all the tender incidents of farewell are lost to me. Perhaps my boyish self-absorption prevented me from recording outside impressions, for the idea of travelling, of crossing the State line, profoundly engaged me. Up to this time, notwithstanding all my dreams of conquest in far countries, I had never ridden in a railway coach! Can you wonder therefore that I trembled with joyous excitement as I paced the platform next morning waiting for the chariot of my romance? The fact that it was a decayed little coach at the end of a "mixed accommodation train" on a stub road did not matter. I was ecstatic.

However, I was well dressed, and my inexperience appeared only in a certain tense watchfulness. I closely observed what went on around me and was careful to do nothing which could be misconstrued as ignorance. Thrilling with excitement, feeling the mighty significance of my departure, I entered quietly and took my seat, while the train roared on through Mitchell and St. Ansgar, the little towns in which I had played my part as an actor,—on into distant climes and marvellous cities. My emotion was all very boyish, but very natural as I look back upon it.

The town in which I spent my first night abroad should have been called Thebes or Athens or Palmyra; but it was not. On the contrary, it was named Ramsey, after an old pioneer, and no one but a youth of fervid imagination at the close of his first day of adventure in the world would have found it worth a second glance. To me it was both beautiful and inspiring, for the reason that it was new territory and because it was the home of Alice, my most brilliant school mate, and while I had in mind some notion of a conference with the county superintendent of schools, my real reason for stopping off was a desire to see this girl whom I greatly admired.

I smile as I recall the feeling of pride with which I stepped into the 'bus and started for the Grand Central Hotel. And yet, after all, values are relative. That boy had something which I have lost. I would give much of my present knowledge of the world for the keen savor of life which filled my nostrils at that time.

The sound of a violin is mingled with my memories of Ramsey, and the talk of a group of rough men around the bar-room stove is full of savage charm. A tall, pale man, with long hair and big black eyes, one who impressed me as being a man of refinement and culture, reduced by drink to poverty and to rebellious bitterness of soul, stands out in powerful relief—a tragic and moving figure.

Here, too, I heard my first splendid singer. A patent medicine cart was in the street and one of its troupe, a basso, sang *Rocked in the Cradle of the Deep* with such art that I listened with delight. His lion-like pose, his mighty voice, his studied phrasing, revealed to me higher qualities of musical art than I had hitherto known.

From this singer, I went directly to Alice's home. I must have appeared singularly exalted as I faced her. The entire family was in the sitting room as I entered—but after a few kindly inquiries concerning my people and some general remarks they each and all slipped away, leaving me alone with the girl—in the good old-fashioned American way.

It would seem that in this farewell call I was permitting myself an exaggeration of what had been to Alice only a pleasant association, for she greeted me composedly and waited for me to justify my presence.

After a few moments of explanation, I suggested that we go out and hear the singing of the "troupe." To this she consented, and rose quietly—she never did anything hurriedly or with girlish alertness—and put on her hat. Although so young, she had the dignity of a woman, and her face, pale as a silver moon, was calm and sweet, only her big gray eyes expressed the maiden mystery. She read my adoration and was a little afraid of it.

As we walked, I spoke of the good days at "the Sem," of our classmates, and their future, and this led me to the announcement of my own plans. "I shall teach," I said. "I hope to be able to work into a professorship in literature some day.—What do you intend to do?"

"I shall go on with my studies for a while," she replied. "I may go to some eastern college for a few years."

"You must not become too learned," I urged. "You'll forget me."

She did not protest this as a coquette might have done. On the contrary, she remained silent, and I was aware that while she liked and respected me, she was not profoundly moved by this farewell call. Nevertheless I hoped, and in that hope I repeated, "You will write to me, won't you?"

"Of course!" she replied, and again I experienced a chilling perception that her words arose from friendliness rather than from tenderness, but I was glad of even this restrained promise, and I added, "I shall write often, for I shall be lonely—for a while."

As I walked on, the girl's soft warm arm in mine, a feeling of uncertainty, of disquiet, took possession of me. "Success," seemed a long way off and the road to it long and hard. However, I said nothing further concerning my doubts.

The street that night had all the enchantment of Granada to me. The girl's voice rippled with a music like that of the fountain Lindarazza, and when I caught glimpses of her sweet, serious face beneath her hat-rim, I dreaded our parting. The nearer to her gate we drew the more tremulous my voice became, and the more uncertain my step.

At last on the door-step she turned and said, "Won't you come in again?"

In her tone was friendly dismissal, but I would not have it so. "You will write to me, won't you?" I pleaded with choking utterance.

She was moved (by pity perhaps).

"Why, yes, with pleasure," she answered. "Goodbye, I hope you'll succeed. I'm sure you will."

She extended her hand and I, recalling the instructions of my most romantic fiction, raised it to my lips. "Goodbye!" I huskily said, and turned away.

My next night was spent in Faribault. Here I touched storied ground, for near this town Edward Eggleston had laid the scene of his novel, *The Mystery of Metropolisville* and my imagination responded to the magic which lay in the influence of the man of letters. I wrote to Alice a long and impassioned account of my sensations as I stood beside the Cannonball River.

My search for a school proving futile, I pushed on to the town of Farmington, where the Dakota branch of the Milwaukee railroad crossed my line of march. Here I felt to its full the compelling power of the swift stream of immigration surging to the west. The little village had doubled in size almost in a day. It was a junction point, a place of transfer, and its thin-walled unpainted pine hotels were packed with men, women and children laden with bags and bundles (all bound for the west) and the joyous excitement of these adventurers compelled me to change my plan. I decided to try some of the newer counties in western Minnesota. Romance was still in the West for me.

I slept that night on the floor in company with four or five young Iowa farmers, and the smell of clean white shavings, the wailing of tired children, the excited muttering of fathers, the plaintive voices of mothers, came through the partitions at intervals, producing in my mind an effect which will never pass away. It seemed to me at the moment as if all America were in process of change, all hurrying to overtake the vanishing line of the middle border, and the women at least were secretly or openly doubtful of the outcome. Woman is not by nature an explorer. She is the home-lover.

Early the next morning I bought a ticket for Aberdeen, and entered the train crammed with movers who had found the "prairie schooner" all too slow. The epoch of the canvas-covered wagon had passed. The era of the locomotive, the day of the chartered car, had arrived. Free land was receding at railroad speed, the borderline could be overtaken only by steam, and every man was in haste to arrive.

All that day we rumbled and rattled into a strange country, feeding our little engine with logs of wood, which we stopped occasionally to secure from long ricks which lined the banks of the river. At Chaska, at Granite Falls, I stepped off, but did not succeed in finding employment. It is probable that being filled with the desire of exploration I only half-heartedly sought for work; at any rate, on the third day, I found myself far out upon the unbroken plain where only the hair-like buffalo grass grew—beyond trees, beyond the plow, but not beyond settlement, for here at the end of my third day's ride at Millbank, I found a hamlet six months old, and the flock of shining yellow pine shanties strewn upon the sod, gave me an illogical delight, but then I was twenty-one—and it was sunset in the Land of the Dakotas!

All around me that night the talk was all of land, land! Nearly every man I met was bound for the "Jim River valley," and each voice was aquiver with hope, each eye alight with anticipation of certain success. Even the women had begun to catch something of this enthusiasm, for the night was very beautiful and the next day promised fair.

Again I slept on a cot in a room of rough pine, slept dreamlessly, and was out early enough to witness the coming of dawn—a wonderful moment that sunrise was to me. Again, as eleven years before, I felt myself a part of the new world, a world fresh from the hand of God. To the east nothing could be seen but a vague expanse of yellow plain, misty purple in its hollows, but to the west rose a long low wall of hills, the Eastern Coteaux, up which a red line of prairie fire was slowly creeping.

It was middle September. The air, magnificently crisp and clear, filled me with desire of exploration, with vague resolution to do and dare. The sound of horses and mules calling for their feed, the clatter of hammers and the rasping of saws gave evidence of eager builders, of alert adventurers, and I was hotly impatient to get forward.

At eight o'clock the engine drew out, pulling after it a dozen box-cars laden with stock and household goods, and on the roof of a freight caboose, together with several other young Jasons, I rode, bound for the valley of the James.

It was a marvellous adventure. All the morning we rattled and rumbled along, our engine snorting with effort, struggling with a load almost too great for its strength. By noon we were up amid the rounded grassy hills of the Sisseton Reservation where only the coyote ranged and the Sioux made residence.

Here we caught our first glimpse of the James River valley, which seemed to us at the moment as illimitable as the ocean and as level as a floor and then pitching and tossing over the rough track, with our cars leaping and twisting like a herd of frightened buffaloes, we charged down the western slope, down into a level land of ripened grass, where blackbirds chattered in the willows, and prairie chickens called from the tall rushes which grew beside the sluggish streams.

Aberdeen was the end of the line, and when we came into it that night it seemed a near neighbor to Sitting Bull and the bison. And so, indeed, it was, for a buffalo bull had been hunted across its site less than a year before.

It was twelve miles from here to where my father had set his stakes for his new home, hence I must have stayed all night in some small hotel, but that experience has also faded from my mind. I remember only my walk across the dead-level plain next day. For the first time I set foot upon a landscape without a tree to break its sere expanse—and I was at once intensely interested in a long flock of gulls, apparently rolling along the sod, busily gathering their morning meal of frosted locusts. The ones left behind kept flying over the ones in front so that a ceaseless change of leadership took place.

There was beauty in this plain, delicate beauty and a weird

charm, despite its lack of undulation. Its lonely unplowed sweep gave me the satisfying sensation of being at last among the men who held the outposts,—sentinels for the marching millions who were approaching from the east. For two hours I walked, seeing Aberdeen fade to a series of wavering, grotesque notches on the southern horizon line, while to the north an equally irregular and insubstantial line of shadows gradually took on weight and color until it became the village in which my father was at this very moment busy in founding his new home.

My experienced eyes saw the deep, rich soil, and my youthful imagination looking into the future, supplied the trees and vines and flowers which were to make this land a garden.

I was converted. I had no doubts. It seemed at the moment that my father had acted wisely in leaving his Iowa farm in order to claim his share of Uncle Sam's rapidly-lessening unclaimed land.

～ *MARTHA L. SMITH*

Going to God's Country

Martha L. Smith (1862–1949) and her husband Hans Hamilton Smith, having spent twenty-eight years in what they called "the rocky country of Missouri," decided to go west. In September 1890, with washtubs, buckets, chairs, and dozens of things tied to the outside of their rigs, they and their five little children bade their friends and relatives good-by and led a band of seven wagons through the high sagebrush of the Indian Territory in search of "God's country." The following excerpts from Mrs. Smith's

From *Going to God's Country*. (Boston: The Christopher Company, copyright 1941).

personal recollections, *Going to God's Country*
(1941), not only tell the story of a search for a way
of life, but also point up a profound truth that the
Smiths discovered while they wandered about the
country looking for a suitable place to settle down.

Old Missouri was after all a prety toughf place. I hated to
leave it though for it was all I knew. But we were going to God's
Country. We were going to a new land and get rich. Then we
could have a real home of our own. But we didn't know what was
ahead of us. . . .

We hadn't gotten ten miles from home when it began to rain
and did we have fun for it rained for one whole week. We did not
see the sunlight for four days. It was almost imposabele to build
a camp fire so we found some grocery stores where we could get
a few crackers. It hapend that we allready had buter which we
had taken with us. A ten pound crock of buter which I had made
myself. We did manage sometimes to make a pot of coffe. And
while in Missouri we could get milk from the farmers, so that
helped out with the litel folks.

And the rocky roads were awful. It rained so much, day and
night, that we got oil cloth and made covers for the horses and
mules. We had one span each.

We finly came to Sock River and was it booming. Full from
bank to bank. And with just an old reck of a boat to fery across.
We were delaid several hours. Just one wagon and team could
cross at once but we got across and we felt much beter for the
sun was shining. It was about noon so we all got out of the
wagons and had a good walk. Then we fed our teams and drug
up some dead lims and cooked one squar meal. The children
could get out of the wagons and play on the ground and was they
hapy. And so were we for it was our first squar meal in four days.

When we reached Kansas it looked so beautifull that I ask my
husband why we should not stop there. But he said that we were
going to God's Country. Everyone seemed to be so hapy now that
it had quit raining. On we went. But no so very fast, about 20
miles a day. . . .

We traveled severl days but we did not see Indians. Nor no

living human. Only our gang. But finly we began to see Indians. Hunderds of them. Horseback. Feathers on their heads and wearing britch clouchs and blankets. And all painted. Was we scerd. They would not tell us any thing about the roads. The men would take turns of watch at night but I dont think any of the grown folks slept very much for we felt like we were in danger.

It was very slow going but in a few days we were at Gray Horse Agency. That is where the Government isued rashings to the Osage Indians. We felt very hapy for the government had some white people there. The Indians had gone there to get their rashings. And a mess it was. They were having a tribal dance of some kind. So many Indians. Some half dressed, some with brich clouch, but all with feathers on their heads. And was they ugly. The white folks said we had beter camp there because it was late. Then we could get quite a distance next day. The Osages would only grunt and look so mean we were most frighent to death. We were so afraid that they would try to take our litel girls for they would sneak up and peep in our wagons. We just sat by with our shot guns and they would say "hu" and walk off. . . .

We were severl days more on the road then our next stop was Oklahoma City. . . .

We had been in the habit of lying over on Sundays so as to let the teams rest and the women folks would wash and do some baking. We would make a big fire, put our skillet on the coals, rake the coals over it and bake some buisquit and some corn pone so when we would stop for noon we would have bread. Then it would not take so long to get our meal. Just fry a litel meat was all, because there wasnt any place to buy any thing.

While we were in camp Sunday a colord man came to our camp and beged us to buy a quarter section rite in Oklahoma City for 400 dolars. But we thought it was a poor looking place. We were going to God's Country and did not want to setel among the bamboo brires. . . .

We travled miles and God only knows where all we were travling. Just one certain direction—a southwest course. There was no roads or land marks, just a path with the sage grass as high as our wagon tops. We travled on untell we got to Purcell. We had fun again. The South Canadian River was up so we had to go many miles out of our way to get to Rock Botom crossing. We was delayed another day and our food suply was geting short but we could get some things from the setlers. . . .

Since this country had just come in the year before it was very hard to get much to eat. Some of the setelers had plowed up litel patches of ground along the litel creecks and low places and had planted cabage and other garden stuff. But sometimes there wasnt any one living very close so we couldnt buy the vegetables.

When we would stop for camp I would go out and hunt and find a vegetable patch. I tried to get some of them to go with me but they said that was stealing. One time one of the women did go and we found a nice cabage patch. We got severl heads and took them in camp. I gave the rest of the folks some and you bet they ate them. We were so hungry for something green. They would eat them but they would not get them. . . .

We were all tired from the long wearysome trip. And it seemed that every river we crossed was up. Our first was Sock, the next bad river was the Arkansaw and the next was the Cimarron. And then the North Canadian and the South Canadian and hundreds of others it seemed. We went through part of Missouri, Kansas, Osage Nation, Pawnee Nation, Old Oklahoma proper, Chicsaw Nation and then we landed on the Fleet Wood Farms. It was on the Red River just across from Texas. So there we were at our cousens. And was we ever so hapy. We all drove in his lot with the seven coverd wagons. And so tired from thirty three days drive. But at last we were in God's Country. . . .

Next morning we were all out bright and early looking for some place to live. Some of the folks found some shacks and moved in. But we was a litel hard to please I guess. We staid with our cousens for two days. Still looking but nothing to be found. . . .

We were in camp there for two weeks and tryed picking a litel coton but we did not do very much for we didn't have any sacks. We worked for one week and we picked about two hunderd pounds and got 2 dolars. All this time we were looking for a place to live.

While we were in the field one day some drunk Indians came past our camp and shot our tea kitle full of holes. So we got buisy right away and bought out a man. . . .

It was stratening the house and geting ready for farm work now. We had big ideas of what we were going to make on so much land. We thought we would be able to go somehere in the States where we could buy us a home and live like white people and not like gypsies. But this was supposed to be God's Country.

We were out on the big prarie. But you could not go walking on the prarie. The catle would get you. And you could not sleep at night for cyotes and the scream of the panthers. Their noises would make the hair raise on your head. And pole cats by the hunderds. But we stayed. This was God's Country. And we were going to get rich. . . .

In the spring of 92 people began to come in and plow around big tracks of land. So we felt like we were going to have neighbors. The catlemen didn't like it very much. But the people just went rite ahead puting up fences and dugouts or just any thing to live in.

All the goverment wanted you to do was to fence and you could have all you made off the land. They did not care whether you built a house or dugout. All they wanted, or all they would requir you to do, was to put up a four wire fence. . . .

In 1892 the prarie grass was most as high as our coverd wagons. One day by some means a fire got started. We never knew how but any way it was exsiting. You could see the blaze leap. It looked like it was fifty feet in the air. We had burned a very small patch around our house. Perhaps one half an acer. We had just built us a shed for our teams and a chicken house for a cow corell. Our horses were all tied in the shed and the fire was coming so fast that we could not tell whether we would have time to get them out or what to do. It looked like our horses and our milk cows and our famly too would go up in the flames. We did manage to get the teams and harness out of the shed and close to the house. But the fire was geting very close. Just about half mile away I should judge. . . .

While we were standing in front of the hut watching the fire I just hapend to turn my head to get some of the burned grass out of my eyes and I thought that I could see some moving objects coming from the north. I wiped my eyes again and looked. Then I said to my husband, "Look, there is something coming from the north." He wiped his eyes and looked. It looked like a herd of stampeded catle. And if it was that, we were goners for they were coming toward us. We watched for a moment but it was so smokey and so much burned grass flying in the air, for the fire was coming from the south west and was blowing very hard, we couldnt see. All that we could do was to stand there and wait.

There we were, we thought, between two fires. We could plainly see the fire coming from the south west and my husband said if it was a stampeded herd of catle that we were in for something. I ask him if we hadnt beter go in the house with the childern and he said that I might but that he would watch. But I never did go in, for just about that time I wiped my eyes again and I could see that it wasnt catle. But we couldn't make out just what it was. It looked like men the best we could see through all that smoke. We just stood and looked and I told my husband perhaps it was Indians on the war path. He said it might be but he did not think so. But I do believe he thought it was Indians for he turned white. So white that I could see he was scerd. And so was I. The fire coming one way and the Indians or stampeded catle the other.

We just stood there most petrified for a few seconds and then I could see that it was men. But what kind of men. Cow boys or Indians? But all at once one man whiped ahead of the rest and then I felt like it was cow boys. And shure enoughf he just came chargen up. I felt some relief but I was shakin so I could hardly stand on my feet and so was my husband. The six litel childern in the house got over being scerd and were just playing. When we opend the door they looked so surprised to see so many cow boys. They never said a word but just looked so amased.

Then the boys said that Roof Benton had sent them for he could see the fire and thought we might be in danger and some of his catle might too. All the water I had drawd out of the well was used for when the cow boys got there they got off their horses, droped their briedl reins, went to the shed, gathered up all the old feed sacks and two of them picked up the water and walked out to the edge of the high grass. Then they all wet the feed sacks and began to set the grass a fire but they did not tell us what they were going to do. We soon found out. They were back firing. . . .

We finly got every thing in shape again. But I never looked over the prarie that way but what I could imagin that I could see smoke. It took me a long time to forget it. In fact I never did and it makes my flesh creep today when I think about that terable fire and smoke. I said to myself, "Is this God's Country or not?" . . .

It was July 1895. I comenced to wonder if God had forsaken this country. Crops was bad. And most all our money gone. And all those teams to feed. The corn all burned. Five hunderd acers of wheat and not one grain cut. It was all too short. Just a very few oats cut. The coton was about a foot high, then the jack rabits cleaned it up. We had about fifty acers of coton but it did not last long when the jack rabits took to it. And it looked like the grass was going to dry up too. No gardens. No feed for our hogs. No feed for the children. But our credit was good so we still bought goods. . . .

This new God's Country was much farther north and we would camp out while we were building. One thing was that we had a lumber yard in Geary, the place where we were going, and it wouldn't be so far to hall lumber. Our new place was just four miles from Geary. We had been going so much farther four miles would seem just like play.

We sold our building to Charley Willis, the man that had worked for us four years. He bought all of our improvements and was going to run the farm.

When it came time for us to move I felt like I wanted to stay for we had had lots of exsitement and lots of fun, lots of hardships too and lots of hard work. But it was all over now. We did like pioneering very much for you would get something out of it.

We had not found God's Country but we were sure we would find it in our new home in the Cheyenne Country. So again we were on our way. We were going to God's Country. . . .

It was not long untell a man from Kentucky came to our place and wanted to know how much we wanted for our home place. I said that I wanted to quit moving but he kept hanging around so H.H. told him that he would take ten thousand dolars. He said, "Sold." I had to have a big cry for we had bought a lot of new

furnature and we allso had the other farm. But I didn't say any
thing. I wondered where we were going to go this time. . . .

So now we were all set for another search for God's Country.
For another wild goose chase. And this time it was Oregon. My
father was there and I had a sister there too and they had been
writing what a wonderful country it was. They wrote that "Oregon
is really God's Country." We had been in search of God's Country ever since we left Missouri so we decided we would taken
another chance. We decided that it was—on to Oregon. . . .

It was a husel around to get off but this time we were going on
the train and not in the coverd wagons. I thought it would be
much beter. And of course it was. We were only five days on the
train. But believe me it was some job even then with all those litel
folks. It was a big trek across the country. Easy though. For it was
made by train.

We landed in Salem Oregon about the middle of June. It was
so difernt but it was a lovly country. Somehow I did not like
it. But we thought that we would try it. . . .

I was geting discouraged hunting for God's Country. I knew
there must be such a place. But where? We decided that maybe
Oklahoma wasnt so bad. Anyway we decided to go back. . . .

It was five days and nights of travling. But it was some difernt
for we knew where we were going. Going back to what we had
caled God's Country. We landed in Enid, Oklahoma. This was
nineteen and nine. . . .

After a while we moved from Enid back to Geary. We built
a big twelve room house. We were still looking. Looking for the
location of God's Country. Then later, we moved back to Enid
to put our daughters in the University. All the time we were
watching and watching. . . .

We found just about every kind of person in every part of the
country we lived. We worked, made friends, helped out where
we could and usually found that others were willing to help us
when we had our troubles. We were comencing to wonder if
there was a certain place that was God's Country. Or if God's
Country was everywhere? Or if God wasnt in the country—then
in what?

H.H. and I did a lot of thinking and a litel talking. We had been living out on the farm in Woodward County for three years when H.H. had a stroke of paralysis. We moved back to Enid so we could be near good doctors. He lived for two years. Then my beloved died. We had spent 48 years together hunting for God's Country. Before he died we learned something. Something teribly important.

We learned that God's Country isnt in the country. It is in the mind. As we looked back we knew that all the time we was hunting for God's Country, we had it. We worked hard. We was loyal. Honest. We was happy. For 48 years we lived together in God's Country.

part 4

THE FRONTIERSMAN

↜ J. HECTOR ST. JOHN CRÈVECOEUR

Back-settlers in America

Michel Guillaume Jean de Crèvecoeur (1735–1813), who employed the pseudonym J. Hector St. John Crèvecoeur, penetrated the American backwoods to the limits of the colonies and found delight in living close to the soil. As an American farmer, he captured the aroma of life that he transmitted to his *Letters from an American Farmer* (1782), from which the following passage is taken. His picture of the frontiersman is somewhat overembellished and romanticized because of his uncritical endorsement of the agrarian ideal. The doctrines of Rousseau appealed to Crèvecoeur's "restless and impetuous spirit," and the *Letters* reflect both revolutionary ideas and romantic tendencies. The book had disastrous effects upon some of its readers. Five-hundred Norman families are said to have perished in the Ohio wilderness as a result of its influence.

Now we arrive near the great woods, near the last inhabited districts; there men seem to be placed still farther beyond the reach of government, which in some measure leaves them to themselves. How can it pervade every corner; as they were driven there by misfortunes, necessity of beginnings, desire of acquiring large tracks of land, idleness, frequent want of economy, ancient debts; the re-union of such people does not afford a very pleasing spectacle. When discord, want of unity and friendship; when either drunkenness or idleness prevail in such remote districts;

From *Letters from an American Farmer* (New York: Fox, Duffield and Co., 1904), pp. 58–72 *passim.* Editor's title.

contention, inactivity, and wretchedness must ensue. There are not the same remedies to these evils as in a long established community. The few magistrates they have, are in general little better than the rest; they are often in a perfect state of war; that of man against man, sometimes decided by blows, sometimes by means of the law; that of man against every wild inhabitant of these venerable woods, of which they are come to dispossess them. There men appear to be no better than carnivorous animals of a superior rank, living on the flesh of wild animals when they can catch them, and when they are not able, they subsist on grain. He who would wish to see America in its proper light, and have a true idea of its feeble beginnings and barbarous rudiments, must visit our extended line of frontiers where the last settlers dwell, and where he may see the first labours of settlement, the mode of clearing the earth, in all their different appearances; where men are wholly left dependent on their native tempers, and on the spur of uncertain industry, which often fails when not sanctified by the efficacy of a few moral rules. There, remote from the power of example, and check of shame, many families exhibit the most hideous parts of our society. They are a kind of forlorn hope, preceding by ten or twelve years the most respectable army of veterans which come after them. In that space, prosperity will polish some, vice and the law will drive off the rest, who uniting again with others like themselves will recede still farther; making room for more industrious people, who will finish their improvements, convert the loghouse into a convenient habitation, and rejoicing that the first heavy labours are finished, will change in a few years that hitherto barbarous country into a fine fertile, well regulated district. Such is our progress, such is the march of the Europeans toward the interior parts of this continent. In all societies there are off-casts; this impure part serves as our precursors or pioneers; my father himself was one of that class, but he came upon honest principles, and was therefore one of the few who held fast; by good conduct and temperance, he transmitted to me his fair inheritance, when not above one in fourteen of his contemporaries had the same good fortune.

Forty years ago this smiling country was thus inhabited; it is now purged, a general decency of manners prevails throughout, and such has been the fate of our best countries. . . .

But to return to our back settlers. I must tell you, that there is something in the proximity of the woods, which is very singular. It is with men as it is with the plants and animals that grow and live in the forests; they are entirely different from those that live in the plains. I will candidly tell you all my thoughts but you are not to expect that I shall advance any reasons. By living in or near the woods, their actions are regulated by the wildness of the neighbourhood. The deer often come to eat their grain, the wolves to destroy their sheep, the bears to kill their hogs, the foxes to catch their poultry. This surrounding hostility, immediately puts the gun into their hands; they watch these animals, they kill some; and thus by defending their property, they soon become professed hunters; this is the progress; once hunters, farewell to the plough. The chase renders them ferocious, gloomy, and unsociable; a hunter wants no neighbour, he rather hates them, because he dreads the competition. In a little time their success in the woods makes them neglect their tillage. They trust to the natural fecundity of the earth, and therefore do little; carelessness in fencing, often exposes what little they sow to destruction; they are not at home to watch; in order therefore to make up the deficiency, they go oftener to the woods. That new mode of life brings along with it a new set of manners, which I cannot easily describe. These new manners being grafted on the old stock, produce a strange sort of lawless profligacy, the impressions of which are indelible. The manners of the Indian natives are respectable, compared with this European medley. Their wives and children live in sloth and inactivity; and having no proper pursuits, you may judge what education the latter receive. Their tender minds have nothing else to contemplate but the example of their parents; like them they grow up a mongrel breed, half civilized, half savage, except nature stamps on them some constitutional propensities. That rich, that voluptuous sentiment is gone that struck them so forcibly; the possession of their freeholds no longer conveys to their minds the same pleasure and pride. To all these reasons you must add, their lonely situation, and you cannot imagine what an effect on manners the great distances they live from each other has! Consider one of the last settlements in its first view: of what is it composed? Europeans who have not that sufficient share of knowledge they ought to have, in order to prosper; people who have suddenly passed from oppression, dread of government, and fear of laws, into the un-limited freedom of the woods. This sudden change must have a very great effect on most men, and on that class particularly. Eating of wild meat, whatever you may think, tends to alter their temper: though all the proof I can adduce, is, that I have seen it: and having no place of worship to resort to, what little society this might afford, is denied them. The Sunday meetings, exclusive of religious benefits, were the only social bonds that might have inspired them with some degree of emulation in neatness. Is it then surprising to see men thus situated, immersed in great and heavy labours, degenerate a little? It is rather a wonder the effect is not more diffusive. The Moravians and the Quakers are the only instances in exception to what I have advanced. The first never settle singly, it is a colony of the society which emigrates; they carry with them their forms, worship, rules, and decency: the others never begin so hard, they are always able to buy im-provements, in which there is a great advantage, for by that time the country is recovered from its first barbarity. Thus our bad people are those who are half cultivators and half hunters; and the worst of them are those who have degenerated altogether into the hunting state. As old ploughmen and new men of the woods, as Europeans and new made Indians, they contract the vices of both; they adopt the moroseness and ferocity of a native, without his mildness, or even his industry at home. If manners are not refined, at least they are rendered simple and inoffensive by tilling the earth; all our wants are supplied by it, our time is divided between labour and rest, and leaves none for the com-mission of great misdeeds. As hunters it is divided between the toil of the chase, the idleness of repose, or the indulgence of inebriation. Hunting is but a licentious idle life, and if it does not always prevert good dispositions; yet, when it is united with bad luck, it leads to want: want stimulates that propensity to rapacity and injustice, too natural to needy men, which is the fatal gradation. After this explanation of the effects which follow by living in the woods, shall we yet vainly flatter ourselves with the hope of converting the Indians? We should rather begin with converting our back-settlers; and now if I dare mention the name of religion, its sweet accents would be lost in the immensity of these woods. Men thus placed, are not fit either to receive or remember its mild instructions; they want temples and ministers, but as soon as men cease to remain at home, and begin to lead an erratic life, let them be either tawny or white, they cease to be its disciples.

Thus have I faintly and imperfectly endeavoured to trace our society from the sea to our woods! yet you must not imagine that every person who moves back, acts upon the same principles, or falls into the same degeneracy. Many families carry with them all their decency of conduct, purity of morals, and respect of religion; but these are scarce, the power of example is sometimes irresistible. Even among these back-settlers, their depravity is greater or less, according to what nation or province they belong. Were I to adduce proofs of this, I might be accused of partiality. If there happens to be some rich intervals, some fertile bottoms, in those remote districts, the people will there prefer tilling the land to hunting, and will attach themselves to it; but even on these fertile spots you may plainly perceive the inhabitants to acquire a great degree of rusticity and selfishness.

It is in consequence of this straggling situation, and the astonishing power it has on manners, that the back-settlers of both the Carolinas, Virginia, and many other parts, have been long a set of lawless people; it has been even dangerous to travel among them. Government can do nothing in so extensive a country, better it should wink at these irregularities, than that it should use means inconsistent with its usual mildness. Time will efface those stains: in proportion as the great body of population approaches them they will reform, and become polished and subordinate. Whatever has been said of the four New-England provinces, no such degeneracy of manners has ever tarnished their annals; their back-settlers have been kept within the bounds of decency, and government, by means of wise laws, and by the influence of religion. What a detestable idea such people must have given to the natives of the Europeans! They trade with them, the worst of people are permitted to do that which none but persons of the best characters should be employed in. They get drunk with them, and often defraud the Indians. Their avarice, removed from the eyes of their superiors, knows no bounds; and aided by a little superiority of knowledge, these traders deceive them, and even sometimes shed blood. Hence those shocking violations, those sudden devastations which have so often stained our frontiers, when hundreds of innocent people have been sacrificed for the crimes of a few. It was in consequence of such behaviour, that the Indians took the hatchet against the Virginians in 1774. Thus are our first steps trod, thus are our first trees felled, in general, by the most vicious of our people; and thus the path is opened for the arrival of a second and better class, the true American freeholders; the most respectable set of people in this part of the world: respectable for their industry, their happy independence, the great share of freedom they possess, the good regulation of their families, and for extending the trade and the dominion of our mother country.

Europe contains hardly any other distinctions but lords and tenants; this fair country alone is settled by freeholders, the possessors of the soil they cultivate, members of the government they obey, and the framers of their own laws, by means of their representatives. This is a thought which you have taught me to cherish; our difference from Europe, far from diminishing, rather adds to our usefulness and consequence as men and subjects. Had our forefathers remained there, they would only have crouded it, and perhaps prolonged those convulsions which had shook it so long. Every industrious European who transports himself here, may be compared to a sprout growing at the foot of a great tree; it enjoys and draws but a little portion of sap; wrench it from the parent roots, transplant it, and it will become a tree bearing fruit also. Colonists are therefore entitled to the consideration due to the most useful subjects; a hundred families barely existing in some parts of Scotland, will here in six years, cause an annual exportation of 10,000 bushels of wheat: 100 bushels being but a common quantity for an industrious family to sell, if they cultivate good land. It is here then that the idle may be employed, the useless become useful, and the poor become rich; but by riches I do not mean gold and silver, we have but little of those metals; I mean a better sort of wealth, cleared lands, cattle, good houses, good cloaths, and an increase of people to enjoy them.

There is no wonder that this country has so many charms, and presents to Europeans so many temptations to remain in it. A traveller in Europe becomes a stranger as soon as he quits his own kingdom; but it is otherwise here. We know, properly speaking, no strangers; this is every person's country; the variety of our soils, situations, climates, governments, and produce, hath something which must please every body. No sooner does an European arrive, no matter of what condition, than his eyes are opened upon the fair prospect; he hears his language spoke, he retraces many of his own country manners, he perpetually hears the names of families and towns with which he is acquainted; he sees happiness and prosperity in all places disseminated; he meets with hospitality, kindness, and plenty every where; he beholds hardly any poor, he seldom hears of punishments and executions; and he wonders at the elegance of our towns, those miracles of industry and freedom. He cannot admire enough our rural districts, our convenient roads, good taverns, and our many accommodations; he involuntarily loves a country where every thing is so lovely. When in England, he was a mere Englishman; here he stands on a larger portion of the globe, not less than its fourth part, and may see the productions of the north, in iron and naval stores; the provisions of Ireland, the grain of Egypt, the indigo, the rice of China. He does not find, as in Europe, a crouded society, where every place is over-stocked; he does not feel that perpetual collision of parties, that difficulty of beginning, that contention which oversets so many. There is room for every body in America; has he any particular talent, or industry? he exerts it in order to procure a livelihood, and it succeeds. Is he a merchant? the avenues of trade are infinite; is he eminent in any respect? he will be employed and respected. Does he love a country life? pleasant farms present themselves; he may purchase what he wants, and thereby become an American farmer. Is he a labourer, sober and industrious? he need not go many miles, nor receive many informations before he will be hired, well fed at the table of his employer, and paid four or five times more than he can get in Europe. Does he want uncultivated lands? thousands of acres present themselves, which he may purchase cheap. Whatever be his talents or inclinations, if they are moderate, he may satisfy them. I do not mean that every one who comes will grow rich in a little time; no, but he may procure an easy, decent maintenance, by his industry. Instead of starving he will be fed, instead of being idle he will have employment; and these are riches enough for such men as come over here. The rich stay in Europe, it is only the middling and the poor that emigrate. Would you wish to travel in independent idleness, from north to south, you will find easy access, and the most chearful reception at every house; society without ostentation, good cheer without pride, and every decent diversion which the country affords, with little expence. It is no wonder that the European who has lived here a few years, is desirous to remain; Europe with all its pomp, is not to be compared to this continent, for men of middle stations, or labourers.

An European, when he first arrives, seems limited in his intentions, as well as in his views; but he very suddenly alters his scale; two hundred miles formerly appeared a very great distance, it is now but a trifle; he no sooner breathes our air than he forms schemes, and embarks in designs he never would have thought of in his own country. There the plenitude of society confines many useful ideas, and often extinguishes the most laudable schemes which here ripen into maturity. Thus Europeans become Americans.

TIMOTHY DWIGHT

Two Kinds of Frontiersmen

Timothy Dwight (1752–1817), Yale University president, theologian, poet, and writer, expressed an antagonistic attitude toward the frontier and all frontiersmen. As a Calvinist, Dwight was a severe critic of deism and a firm believer in the sanctity of prop-

From *Travels in New-England and New-York* (New Haven, Conn.: the author, 1821–1822). Editor's title.

erty. He had little patience for primitivism or any philosophy that allowed relaxation of rigid social controls in community development. In the following selection from *Travels in New-England and New-York* (1882), he has contrasted two varieties of backwoodsmen, and has set forth what he believed to constitute the secret of a successful life on the land.

In the formation of Colonies, those who are first inclined to emigrate are usually such as have met with difficulties at home. These are commonly joined by persons, who, having large families and small farms, are induced for the sake of settling their children comfortably to seek for new and cheaper lands. To both are always added the discontented, the enterprizing, the ambitious, and the covetous. Many of the first and some of all these classes are found in every new American country, within ten years after its settlement has commenced. From this period kindred, friendship, and former neighborhood prompt others to follow them. Others still are allured by the prospect of gain, presented in every new country to the sagacious from the purchase and sale of lands: while not a small number are influenced by the brilliant stories, which everywhere are told concerning most tracts during the early progress of their settlement.

A considerable part of all those who *begin* the cultivation of the wilderness may be denominated *foresters*, or *Pioneers*. The business of these persons is no other than to cut down trees, build log-houses, lay open forested grounds to cultivation, and prepare the way for those who come after them. These men cannot live in regular society. They are too idle, too talkative, too passionate, too prodigal, and too shiftless to acquire either property or character. They are impatient of the restraints of law, religion, and morality; grumble about the taxes by which Rulers, Ministers, and Schoolmasters are supported; and complain incessantly, as well as bitterly, of the extortions of mechanics, farmers, merchants, and physicians to whom they are always indebted. At the same time they are usually possessed, in their own view, of uncommon wisdom; understand medical science, politics, and religion better than those who have studied them through life; and, although they manage their own concerns worse than any other men, feel perfectly satisfied that they could manage those of the nation far better than the agents to whom they are committed by the public. After displaying their own talents and worth, after censuring the weakness and wickedness of their superiours, after exposing the injustice of the community in neglecting to invest persons of such merit with public offices in many an eloquent harangue, uttered by many a kitchen fire, in every blacksmith's shop, and in every corner of the streets, and finding all their efforts vain, they become at length discouraged and under pressure of poverty, the fear of a gaol, and the consciousness of public contempt, leave their native places and betake themselves to the wilderness.

Here they are obliged either to work or to starve. They accordingly cut down some trees and girdle others; they furnish themselves with an ill-built log-house and a worse barn; and reduce a part of the forest into fields, half-enclosed and half-cultivated. The forests furnish browse; and their fields yield a stinted herbage. On this scanty provision they feed a few cattle: and with these and the penurious products of their labour, eked out by hunting and fishing, they keep their families alive.

A farm, thus far cleared, promises immediate subsistence to a better husbandman. A loghouse, thus built, presents, when repaired with moderate exertions, a shelter for his family. Such a husbandman is therefore induced by these little advantages, where the soil and situation please him, to purchase such a farm, when he would not plant himself in an absolute wilderness. The proprietor is always ready to sell: for he loves this irregular, adventurous, half-working, and half-lounging life; and hates the sober industry and prudent economy by which his bush pasture might be changed into a farm, and himself raised to thrift and independence. The bargain is soon made. The forester, receiving more money for his improvements than he ever before possessed and a price for the soil somewhat enhanced by surrounding settlements, willingly quits his house to build another like it, and his farm to girdle trees, hunt, and saunter in another place. His wife accompanies him only from a sense of duty or necessity, and secretly pines for the quiet, orderly, friendly society to which she originally bade a reluctant farewell. Her husband, in the meantime, becomes less and less a civilized man: and almost every thing in the family which is amiable and meritorious is usually the result of her principles, care, and influence.

The second proprietor is commonly a *farmer*, and with an industry and spirit, deserving no small commendation, changes the desert into a fruitful field.

This change is accomplished much more rapidly in some places than in others, as various causes, often accidental, operate. In some instances a settlement is begun by farmers and assumes the aspect of regular society from its commencement. This, to some extent, is always the fact: and the greater number of the first planters are, probably, of this description: but some of them also are foresters, and sometimes a majority.

You must have remarked a very sensible difference in the character of different towns through which I have passed. This diversity is in no small degree derived from the original character of the planters in the different cases.

The class of men who have been the principal subject of these remarks have already straggled onward from New-England, as well as from other parts of the Union, to Louisiana. In a political view their emigration is of very serious utility to the ancient settlements. All countries contain restless inhabitants, men impatient of labour; men who will contract debts without intending to pay them, who had rather talk than work, whose vanity persuades them that they are wise and prevents them from knowing that they are fools, who are delighted with innovations, who think places of power and profit due to their peculiar merits, who feel that every change from good order and established society will be beneficial to themselves, who have nothing to lose and therefore expect to be gainers by every scramble, and who, of course, spend life in disturbing others with the hope of gaining something for themselves. Under despotic governments they are awed into quiet; but in every free community they create, to a greater or less extent, continual turmoil, and have often overturned the peace, liberty, and happiness of their fellowcitizens. In the Roman Commonwealth, as before in the Republics of Greece, they were emptied out as soldiers upon the surrounding countries, and left the sober inhabitants in comparative quiet at home. It is true, they often threw these States into confusion and sometimes overturned the government. But if they had not been thus thrown off from the body politic, its life would have been of a momentary duration. As things actually were, they finally ruined all these States. For some of them had, as some of them always will have, sufficient talents to do mischief, at times, very extensive. The Gracchi, Clodius, Marius, and Mark Antony were men of this character. Of this character is every demagogue, whatever may be his circumstances. Power and profit are the only ultimate objects which every such man, with a direction as steady as that of the needle to the pole, pursues with a greediness unlimited and inextinguishable.

Formerly the energetic government established in New-England, together with the prevailing high sense of religion and morals and the continually pressing danger from the French and the savages, compelled the inhabitants into habits of regularity and good order, not surpassed perhaps in the world. But since the American Revolution, our situation has become less favourable to the existence, as well as to the efficacy, of these great means of internal peace. The former exact and decisive energy of the government has been obviously weakened. From our ancient dangers we have been delivered, and the deliverance was a distinguished blessing: but the sense of danger regularly brings with it a strong conviction that safety cannot be preserved without exact order and a ready submission to lawful authority.

The institutions and the habits of New-England, more I suspect than those of any other country, have prevented or kept down this noxious disposition, but they cannot entirely prevent either its existence or its effects. In mercy, therefore, to the sober, industrious, and well-disposed inhabitants, Providence has opened in the vast Western wilderness a retreat sufficiently alluring to draw them away from the land of their nativity. We have many troubles even now: but we should have many more if this body of foresters had remained at home.

It is however to be observed that a considerable number even of these people become sober, industrious citizens merely by the acquisition of property. The love of property to a certain degree seems indispensable to the existence of sound morals. I have never had a servant in whom I could confide except such as were desirous to earn and preserve money. The conveniences and the character, attendant on the preservation of property, fix even these restless men at times, when they find themselves really able to accumulate it, and persuade them to a course of regular industry. I have mentioned that they sell the soil of their first farms at an enhanced price, and that they gain for their improvements on them what, to themselves at least, is a considerably sum. The possession of this money removes, perhaps for the first time, the despair of acquiring property, and awakens the hope and the wish to acquire more. The secure possession of property demands, every moment, the hedge of law, and reconciles a man, originally lawless, to the restraints of government. Thus situated, he sees that reputation also is within his reach. Ambition forces him to aim at it, and compels him to a life of sobriety and decency. That his children may obtain this benefit, he is obliged to send them to school, and to unite with those around him in supporting a school-master. His neighbours are disposed to build a church and settle a Minister. A regard to his own character, to the character and feelings of his family, and very often to the solicitations of his wife, prompts him to contribute to both these objects; to attend, when they are compassed, upon the public worship of God; and perhaps to become in the end a religious man.

⤳   *TIMOTHY FLINT*

In Defense
of the Backwoodsman

Timothy Flint (1780–1840) traveled in a wagon
with a party of colonists from Salem, Massachusetts,

From *Recollections of the Last Ten Years* (Boston: Cumings, Hilliard and Co., 1826). Editor's title.

to Marietta, Ohio, when he was eight years old. His imagination was kindled by his experiences in the backwoods of frontier Ohio, of Indiana, of Kentucky, and up and down the Mississippi, Ohio, Missouri, and Arkansas rivers, which he toured for the express purposes of seeing the country and of preaching to the people. Flint's *Recollections of the Last Ten Years in the Valley of the Mississippi* (1826) was an immediate success and was reprinted in London and translated into French in Paris. On the strength of such popularity, the author decided to make literature his career. For a full account of his writings and his contributions to frontier publications see W. H. Venable, *Beginnings of Literary Culture in the Ohio Valley* (Cincinnati, 1891); and J. E. Kirkpatrick, *Timothy Flint, Pioneer, Missionary, Author, Editor, 1780–1840* (Cleveland, 1911).

The people in the Atlantic states have not yet recovered from the horror, inspired by the term "backwoodsman." This prejudice is particularly strong in New England, and is more or less felt from Maine to Georgia. When I first visited this country, I had my full share, and my family by far too much for their comfort. In approaching the country, I heard a thousand stories of gougings, and robberies, and shooting down with the rifle. I have travelled in these regions thousands of miles under all circumstances of exposure and danger. I have travelled alone, or in company only with such as needed protection, instead of being able to impart it; and this too, in many instances, where I was not known as a minister, or where such knowledge would have had no influence in protecting me. I never have carried the slightest weapon of defense. I scarcely remember to have experienced any thing that resembled insult, or to have felt myself in danger from the people. I have often seen men that had lost an eye. Instances of murder, numerous and horrible in their circumstances, have occurred in my vicinity. But they were such lawless rencounters, as terminate in murder every where, and in which the drunkenness, brutality, and violence were mutual. They were catastrophes, in which quiet and sober men would be in no danger of being involved. When we look round these immense regions, and consider that I have been in settlements three hundred miles from any court of justice, when we look at the position of the men, and the state of things, the wonder is, that so few outrages and murders occur. The gentlemen of the towns, even here, speak often with a certain contempt and horror of the backwoodsmen. I have read, and not without feelings of pain, the bitter representations of the learned and virtuous Dr. Dwight, in speaking of them. He represents these vast regions, as a grand reservoir for the scum of the Atlantic states. He characterizes in the mass the emigrants from New England, as discontented coblers, too proud, too much in debt, too unprincipled, too much puffed up with self-conceit, too strongly impressed that their fancied talents could not find scope in their own country, to stay there. It is true there are worthless people here, and the most so, it must be confessed, are from New England. It is true there are gamblers, and gougers, and outlaws; but there are fewer of them, than from the nature of things, and the character of the age and the world, we ought to expect. But it is unworthy of the excellent man in question so to designate this people in the mass. The backwoodsman of the west, as I have seen him, is generally an amiable and virtuous man. His general motive for coming here is to be a freeholder, to have plenty of rich land, and to be able to settle his children about him. It is a most virtuous motive. And notwithstanding all that Dr. Dwight and Talleyrand have said to the contrary, I fully believe, that nine in ten of the emigrants have come here with no other motive. You find, in truth, that he has vices and barbarisms, peculiar to his situation. His manners are rough. He wears, it may be, a long beard. He has a great quantity of bear or deer skins wrought into his household establishment, his furniture, and dress. He carries a knife, or a dirk in his bosom, and when in the woods has a rifle on his back, and a pack of dogs at his heels. An Atlantic stranger, transferred directly from one of our cities to his door, would recoil from a rencounter with him. But remember, that his rifle and his dogs are among his chief means of support and profit. Remember, that all his first days here were passed in dread of the savages. Remember, that he still encounters them, still meets bears and panthers. Enter his door, and tell him you are benighted, and wish the shelter of his cabin for the night. The welcome is indeed seemingly ungracious: "I reckon you can stay," or "I suppose we must let you stay." But this apparent ungraciousness is the harbinger of every kindness that he can bestow, and every comfort that his cabin can afford. Good coffee, corn bread and butter, venison, pork, wild and tame fowls are set before you. His wife, timid, silent, reserved, but constantly attentive to your comfort, does not sit at the table with you, but like the wives of the patriarchs, stands and attends on you. You are shown to the best bed which the house can offer. When this kind hospitality has been afforded you as long as you choose to stay, and when you depart, and speak about your bill, you are most commonly told with some slight mark of resentment, that they do not keep tavern. Even the flaxen-headed urchins will turn away from your money.

In all my extensive intercourse with these people, I do not recollect but one instance of positive rudeness and inhospitality. . . .

With this single exception, I have found the backwoodsmen to be such as I have described; a hardy, adventurous, hospitable, rough, but sincere and upright race of people. I have received so many kindnesses from them, that it becomes me always to preserve a grateful and affectionate remembrance of them. If we were to try them by the standard of New England customs and opinions, that is to say the customs of a people under entirely different circumstances, there would be many things in the picture, that would strike us offensively. They care little about ministers, and think less about paying them. They are averse to all, even the most necessary restraints. They are destitute of the forms and observances of society and religion; but they are sincere and kind without professions, and have a coarse, but substantial morality, which is often rendered more striking by the immediate contrast of the graceful bows, civility, and professions of their French Catholic neighbours, who have the observances of society and the forms of worship, with often but a scanty modicum of the blunt truth and uprightness of their unpolished neighbours.

In the towns of the upper country on the Mississippi, and especially in St. Louis, there is one species of barbarism, that is but too common; I mean the horrid practice of duelling. But be it remembered, this is the barbarism only of that small class that denominate themselves "the gentlemen." It cannot be matter of astonishment that these are common here, when we recollect, that the fierce and adventurous spirits are naturally attracted to these regions, and that it is a common proverb of the people, that when we cross the Mississippi, "we travel beyond the Sabbath." . . .

In truth, while travelling on the prairies of the Illinois and Missouri, and observing such immense tracts of rich soil, of the blackness of ink, and of exhaustless fertility,—remarking the beautiful simplicity of the limits of farms, introduced by our government, in causing the land to be all surveyed in exact squares, and thus destroying here the barbarous prescription, which has in the settled countries laid out the lands in ugly farms; and bounded them by zigzag lines,—contemplating the hedge of verdure that will bound the squares on these smooth and fertile plains,—remarking the beauty of the orchards and improvements, that must ensue,— being convinced that the climate will grow salubrious with its population and improvement,—seeing the guardian genius, Liberty, hovering over the country,—measuring the progress of the future, only by the analogy of the past,—it will be difficult for the imagination to assign limits to the future growth and prosperity of the country. Perhaps on one of these boundless plains, and contiguous to some one of these noble rivers, in view of these hoary bluffs, and where all these means of the subsistence and multiplication of the species are concentered in such ample abundance, will arise the actual "Ne plus ultra." On looking at the astonishing change, which the last ten years have introduced over the whole face of the United States, and anticipating the change of a century, I have sometimes found the famous wish of Franklin stealing into my mind, with respect to the interesting country which I am describing.

Johnny Appleseed:
A Pioneer Hero

Jonathan Chapman (1775–1847), who became the mythical Johnny Appleseed was a regularly ordained Swedenborgian missionary. He descended the Ohio River in 1806 with two canoes filled with bags of appleseeds, and for forty years wandered up and down in Ohio, Indiana, and Illinois planting apple-seeds and religious ideas. Many legends sprang up about the ragged and eccentric itinerant who, as a folk hero, became the subject of subsequent poems, paintings, and songs.

W. D. Haley's account of the personal experiences of Johnny Appleseed may well be the first published biographical sketch. For further information consult J. L. Himrod, *Johnny Appleseed* (Chicago, 1926); and *Johnny Appleseed* by Harian Hatcher and others (Patterson, N.J., 1945).

Two generations of frontier lives have accumulated stores of narratives which, like the small but beautiful tributaries of great rivers, are forgotten in the broad sweep of the larger current of history. The march of Titans sometimes tramples out the memory of smaller but more useful lives, and sensational glare often eclipses more modest but purer lights. This has been the case in the popular demand for the dime novel dilutions of Fenimore Cooper's romances of border life, which have preserved the records of Indian rapine and atrocity as the only memorials of pioneer history. But the early days of Western settlement witnessed sublimer heroisms than those of human torture, and nobler victories than those of the tomahawk and scalping-knife.

From *Harper's Monthly Magazine*, November 1871, pp. 830–836.

Among the heroes of endurance that was voluntary, and of action that was creative and not sanguinary, there was one man whose name, seldom mentioned now save by some of the few surviving pioneers, deserves to be perpetuated.

The first reliable trace of our modest hero finds him in the Territory of Ohio, in 1801, with a horse-load of apple seeds, which he planted in various places on and about the borders of Licking Creek, the first orchard thus originated by him being on the farm of Isaac Stadden, in what is now known as Licking County, in the State of Ohio. During the five succeeding years, although he was undoubtedly following the same strange occupation, we have no authentic account of his movements until we reach a pleasant spring day in 1806, when a pioneer settler in Jefferson County, Ohio, noticed a peculiar craft, with a remarkable occupant and a curious cargo, slowly dropping down with the current of the Ohio River. It was "Johnny Appleseed," by which name Jonathan Chapman was afterward known in every log-cabin from the Ohio River to the Northern lakes, and westward to the prairies of what is now the State of Indiana. With two canoes lashed together he was transporting a load of apple seeds to the Western frontier, for the purpose of creating orchards on the farthest verge of white settlements. With his canoes he passed down the Ohio to Marietta, where he entered the Muskingum, ascending the stream of that river until he reached the mouth of the Walhonding, or White Woman Creek, and still onward, up the Mohican, into the Black Fork, to the head of navigation, in the region now known as Ashland and Richland counties, on the line of the Pittsburgh and Fort Wayne Railroad, in Ohio. A long and toilsome voyage it was, as a glance at the map will show, and must have occupied a great deal of time, as the lonely traveler stopped at every inviting spot to plant the seeds and make his infant nurseries. These are the first well-authenticated facts in the history of Jonathan Chapman, whose birth, there is good reason for believing, occurred in Boston, Massachusetts, in 1775. According to this, which was his own statement in one of his less reticent moods, he was, at the time of his appearance on Licking Creek, twenty-six years of age, and whether impelled in his eccentricities by some absolute misery of the heart which could only find relief in incessant motion, or governed by a benevolent monomania, his whole after-life was devoted to the work of planting apple seeds in remote places. The seeds he gathered from the cider-presses of Western Pennsylvania; but his canoe voyage in 1806 appears to have been the only occasion upon which he adopted that method of transporting them, as all his subsequent journeys were made on foot. Having planted his stock of seeds, he would return to Pennsylvania for a fresh supply, and, as sacks made of any less substantial fabric would not endure the hard usage of the long trip through forests dense with underbrush and briers, he provided himself with leathern bags. Securely packed, the seeds were conveyed, sometimes on the back of a horse, and not unfrequently on his own shoulders, either over a part of the old Indian trail that led from Fort Duquesne to Detroit, by way of Fort Sandusky, or over what is styled in the appendix to "Hutchins's History of Boguet's Expedition in 1764" the "second route through the wilderness of Ohio," which would require him to traverse a distance of one hundred and sixty-six miles in a west-northwest direction from Fort Duquesne in order to reach the Black Fork of the Mohican.

This region, although it is now densely populated, still possesses a romantic beauty that railroads and bustling towns can not obliterate—a country of forest-clad hills and green valleys, through which numerous bright streams flow on their way to the Ohio; but when Johnny Appleseed reached some lonely log-cabin he would find himself in a veritable wilderness. The old settlers say that the margins of the streams, near which the first settlements were generally made, were thickly covered with low, matted growth of small timber, while nearer to the water was a rank mass of long grass, interlaced with morning-glory and wild pea vines, among which funereal willows and clustering alders stood like sentinels on the outpost of civilization. The hills, that rise almost to the dignity of mountains, were crowned with forest trees, and in the coverts were innumerable bears, wolves, deer, and droves of wild hogs, that were as ferocious as any beast of prey. In the grass the massasauga and other venomous reptiles lurked in such numbers that a settler named Chandler has left the fact on record that during the first season of his residence, while mowing a little prairie which formed part of his land, he killed over two hundred black rattlesnakes in an area that would involve an average destruction of one of these reptiles for each rod of land. The frontiersman, who felt himself sufficiently protected by his rifle against wild beasts and hostile Indians, found it necessary to guard against the attacks of the insidious enemies in the grass by wrapping bandages of dried grass around his buckskin leggings and moccasins; but Johnny would shoulder. his bag of apple seeds, and with bare feet penetrate to some remote spot that combined picturesqueness and fertility of soil, and there he would plant his seeds, place a slight inclosure around the place, and leave them to grow until the trees were large enough to be transplanted by the settlers, who, in the mean time, would have made their clearings in the vicinity. The sites chosen by him are, many of them, well known, and are such as an artist or a poet would select—open places on the loamy lands that border the creeks—rich, secluded spots, hemmed in by giant trees, picturesque now, but fifty years ago, with their wild surroundings and the primal silence, they must have been tenfold more so.

In personal appearance Chapman was a small, wiry man, full of restless activity; he had long dark hair, a scanty beard that was never shaved, and keen black eyes that sparkled with a peculiar brightness. His dress was of the oddest description. Generally, even in the coldest weather, he went barefooted, but sometimes, for his long journeys, he would make himself a rude pair of sandals; at other times he would wear any cast-off foot-covering he chanced to find—a boot on one foot and an old brogan or a moccasin on the other. It appears to have been a matter of conscience with him never to purchase shoes, although he was rarely without money enough to do so. On one occasion, in an unusually cold November, while he was traveling barefooted through mud and snow, a settler who happened to possess a pair of shoes that were too small for his own use forced their acceptance upon Johnny, declaring that it was sinful for a human being to travel with naked feet in such weather. A few days afterward the donor was in the village that has since become the thriving city of Mansfield, and met his beneficiary contentedly plodding along with his feet bare and half frozen. With some degree of anger he inquired for the cause of such foolish conduct, and received for reply that Johnny had overtaken a poor, barefooted family moving Westward, and as they appeared to be in much greater need of clothing than he was, he had given them the shoes. His dress was generally composed of cast-off clothing, that he had taken in payment for apple-trees; and as the pioneers were far less extravagant than their descendants in such matters, the homespun and buckskin garments that they discarded would not be very elegant or serviceable. In his later years, however, he seems to have thought that even this kind of second-hand raiment was too luxurious, as his principal garment was made of a coffee sack, in which he cut holes for his head and arms to pass through, and pronounced it "a very serviceable cloak, and as good clothing as any man need wear." In the matter of head-gear his taste was equally unique; his first experiment was with a tin vessel that served to cook his mush, but this was open to the objection that it did not protect his eyes from the beams of the sun; so he constructed a hat of pasteboard with an immense peak in front, and having thus secured an article that combined usefulness with economy, it became his permanent fashion.

Thus strangely clad, he was perpetually wandering through forests and morasses, and suddenly appearing in white settlements and Indian villages; but there must have been some rare force of gentle goodness dwelling in his looks and breathing in his words, for it is the testimony of all who knew him that, notwithstanding his ridiculous attire, he was always treated with the greatest respect by the rudest frontiersman, and what is a better test, the boys of the settlements forbore to jeer at him. With grown-up people and boys he was usually reticent, but manifested great affection for little girls, always having pieces of ribbon and gay calico to give to his little favorites. Many a grandmother in Ohio and Indiana can remember the presents she received when a child from poor homeless Johnny Appleseed. When he consented to eat with any family he would never sit down to the table until he was assured that there was an ample supply for the children; and his sympathy for their youthful troubles and his kindness toward them made him friends among all the juveniles of the borders.

The Indians also treated Johnny with the greatest kindness. By these wild and sanguinary savages he was regarded as a "great medicine man," on account of his strange appearance, eccentric actions, and, especially, the fortitude with which he could endure pain, in proof of which he would often thrust pins and needles into his flesh. His nervous sensibilities really seem to have been less acute than those of ordinary people, for his method of treating the cuts and sores that were the consequences of his barefooted wanderings through briers and thorns was to sear the wound with a redhot iron, and then cure the burn. During the war of 1812, when the frontier settlers were tortured and slaughtered by the savage allies of Great Britain, Johnny Appleseed continued his wanderings, and was never harmed by the roving bands of hostile Indians. On many occasions the impunity with which he ranged the country enabled him to give the settlers warning of approaching danger in time to allow them to take refuge in their blockhouses before the savages could attack them. Our informant refers to one of these instances, when the news of Hull's surrender came like a thunder-bolt upon the frontier. Large bands of Indians and British were destroying everything before them and murdering defenseless women and children, and even the block-houses were not always a sufficient protection. At this time Johnny travelled day and night, warning the people of the approaching danger. He visited every cabin and delivered this message: "The Spirit of the Lord is upon me, and he hath anointed me to blow the trumpet in the wilderness, and sound an alarm in the forest; for, behold, the tribes of the heathen are round about your doors, and a devouring flame followeth after them." The aged man who narrated this incident said that he could feel even now the thrill that was caused by this prophetic announcement of the wild-looking herald of danger, who aroused the family on a bright moonlight midnight with his piercing voice. Refusing all offers of food and denying himself a moment's rest, he traversed the border day and night until he had warned every settler of the approaching peril.

His diet was as meagre as his clothing. He believed it to be a sin to kill any creature for food, and thought that all that was necessary for human sustenance was produced by the soil. He was also a strenuous opponent of the waste of food, and on one occasion, on approaching a log-cabin, he observed some fragments of bread floating upon the surface of a bucket of slops that was intended for the pigs. He immediately fished them out, and when the house-wife expressed her astonishment, he told her that it was an abuse of the gifts of a merciful God to allow the smallest quantity of any thing that was designed to supply the wants of mankind to be diverted from its purpose. . . .

It was his custom, when he had been welcomed to some hospitable loghouse after a weary day of journeying, to lie down on the puncheon floor, and, after inquiring if his auditors would hear "some news right fresh from heaven," produce his few tattered books, among which would be a New Testament, and read and expound until his uncultivated hearers would catch the spirit and glow of his enthusiasm, while they scarcely comprehended his language. A lady who knew him in his later years writes in the following terms of one of these domiciliary readings of poor, self-sacrificing Johnny Appleseed: "We can hear him read now, just as he did that summer day, when we were busy quilting up stairs, and he lay near the door, his voice rising denunciatory and thrilling —strong and loud as the roar of wind and waves, then soft and soothing as the balmy airs that quivered the morning-glory leaves about his gray beard. His was a strange eloquence at times, and he was undoubtedly a man of genius." What a scene is presented to our imagination! The interior of a primitive cabin, the wide, open fire-place, where a few sticks are burning beneath the iron pot in which the evening meal is cooking; around the fire-place the attentive group, composed of the sturdy pioneer and his wife and children, listening with a reverential awe to the "news right fresh from heaven"; and reclining on the floor, clad in rags, but with his gray hairs glorified by the beams of the setting sun that flood through the open door and the unchinked logs of the humble building, this poor wanderer, with the gift of genius and eloquence, who believes with the faith of apostles and martyrs that God has appointed him a mission in the wilderness to preach the Gospel of love, and plant apple seeds that shall produce orchards for the benefit of men and women and little children whom he has never seen. If there is a sublimer faith or a more genuine eloquence in richly decorated cathedrals and under brocade vestments, it would be worth a long journey to find it.

Next to his advocacy of his peculiar religious ideas, his enthusiasm for the cultivation of apple-trees in what he termed "the only proper way"—that is, from the seed—was the absorbing object of his life. Upon this, as upon religion, he was eloquent in his appeals. He would describe the growing and ripening fruit as such a rare and beautiful gift of the Almighty with words that became pictures, until his hearers could almost see its manifold forms of beauty present before them. To his eloquence on this subject, as well as to his actual labors in planting nurseries, the country over which he traveled for so many years is largely indebted for its numerous orchards. But he denounced as absolute wickedness all devices of pruning and grafting, and would speak of the act of cutting a tree as if it were a cruelty inflicted upon a sentient being.

Not only is he entitled to the fame of being the earliest colporteur on the frontiers, but in the work of protecting animals from abuse and suffering he preceded, while, in his smaller sphere, he equaled the zeal of the good Mr. Bergh. Whenever Johnny saw an animal abused, or heard of it, he would purchase it and give it to some more humane settler, on condition that it should be kindly treated and properly cared for. It frequently happened that the long journey into the wilderness would cause the new settlers to be encumbered with lame and broken-down horses, that were turned loose to die. In the autumn Johnny would make a diligent search for all such animals, and, gathering them up, he would bargain for their food and shelter until the next spring, when he would lead them away to some good pasture for the summer. If they recovered so as to be capable of working, he would never sell them, but would lend or give them away, stipulating for their good usage. His conception of the absolute sin of inflicting pain or death upon any creature was not limited to the higher forms of animal life, but every thing that had being was to him, in the fact of its life, endowed with so much of the Divine Essence that to wound or destroy it was to inflict an injury upon some atom of Divinity. No Brahmin could be more concerned for the preservation of insect life, and the only occasion on which he destroyed a venomous reptile was a source of long regret, to which he could never refer without manifesting sadness. He had elected a suitable place for planting apple seeds on a small prairie, and in order to prepare the ground he was mowing the long grass, when he was bitten by a rattlesnake. In describing the event he sighed heavily, and said, "Poor fellow, he only just touched me, when I, in the heat of my ungodly passion, put the heel of my scythe in him, and went away. Some time afterward I went back, and there lay the poor fellow dead." Numerous anecdotes bearing upon his respect for every form of life are preserved, and form the staple of pioneer recollections. On one occasion, a cool autumnal night, when Johnny, who always camped out in preference to sleeping in a house, had built a fire near which he intended to pass the night, he noticed that the blaze attracted large numbers of mosquitoes, many of whom flew too near his fire and were burned. He immediately brought water and quenched the fire, accounting for his conduct afterward by saying, "God forbid that I should build a fire for my comfort which should be the means of destroying any of His creatures!" At another time he removed the fire he had built near a hollow log, and slept on the snow, because he found that the log contained a bear and her cubs, whom, he said, he did not wish to disturb. And this unwillingness to inflict pain or death was equally strong when he was a sufferer by it, as the following will show. Johnny had been assisting some settlers to make a road through the woods, and in the course of their work they accidentally destroyed a hornets' nest. One of the angry insects soon found a lodgment under Johnny's coffee-sack cloak, but although it stung him repeatedly he removed it with the greatest gentleness. The men who were present laughingly asked him why he did not kill it. To which he gravely replied that "It would not be right to kill the poor thing, for it did not intend to hurt me."

Theoretically he was as methodical in matters of business as any merchant. In addition to their picturesqueness, the locations of his nurseries were all fixed with a view to a probable demand for the trees by the time they had attained sufficient growth for transplanting. He would give them away to those who could not pay for them. Generally, however, he sold them for old clothing or a supply of corn meal; but he preferred to receive a note payable at some indefinite period. When this was accomplished he seemed to think that the transaction was completed in a business-like way; but if the giver of the note did not attend to its payment, the holder of it never troubled himself about its collection. His expenses for food and clothing were so very limited that, notwithstanding his freedom from the *auri sacra fames*, he was frequently in possession of more money than he cared to keep, and it was quickly disposed of for wintering infirm horses, or given to some poor family whom the ague had prostrated or the accidents of border life impoverished. In a single instance only he is known to have invested his surplus means in the purchase of land, having received a deed from Alexander Finley, of Mohican Township, Ashland County, Ohio, for a part of the southwest quarter of section twenty-six; but with his customary indifference to matters of value, Johnny failed to record the deed, and lost it. Only a few years ago the property was in litigation.

We must not leave the reader under the impression that this man's life, so full of hardship and perils, was a gloomy or unhappy one. There is an element of human pride in all martyrdom, which, if it does not soften the pains, stimulates the power of endurance. Johnny's life was made serenely happy by the conviction that he was living like the primitive Christians. Nor was he devoid of a keen humor, to which he occasionally gave vent, as the following will show. Toward the latter part of Johnny's career in Ohio an itinerant missionary found his way to the village of Mansfield, and preached to an open-air congregation. The discourse was tediously lengthy, and unnecessarily severe upon the sin of extravagance, which was beginning to manifest itself among the pioneers by an occasional indulgence in the carnal vanities of calico and "store tea." There was a good deal of the Pharisaic leaven in the preacher, who very frequently emphasized his discourse by the inquiry, "Where now is there a man who, like the primitive Christians, is traveling to heaven barefooted and clad in coarse raiment?" When this interrogation had been repeated beyond all reasonable endurance, Johnny rose from the log on which he was reclining, and advancing to the speaker, he placed one of his bare feet upon the stump which served for a pulpit, and pointing to his coffee-sack garment, he quietly said, "Here's your primitive Christian!" The well-clothed missionary hesitated and stammered and dismissed the congregation. His pet antithesis was destroyed by Johnny's personal appearance, which was far more primitive than the preacher cared to copy.

Some of the pioneers were disposed to think that Johnny's humor was the cause of an extensive practical joke; but it is

generally conceded now that a widespread annoyance was really
the result of his belief that the offensively odored weed known in
the West as the dog-fennel, but more generally styled the May-
weed, possessed valuable antimalarial virtues. He procured some
seeds of the plant in Pennsylvania, and sowed them in the vicinity
of every house in the region of his travels. The consequence was
that successive flourishing crops of the weed spread over the whole
country, and caused almost as much trouble as the disease it was
intended to ward off; and to this day the dog-fennel, introduced
by Johnny Appleseed, is one of the worst grievances of the Ohio
farmers.

In 1838—thirty-seven years after his appearance on Licking
Creek—Johnny noticed that civilization, wealth, and population
were pressing into the wilderness of Ohio. Hitherto he had easily
kept just in advance of the wave of settlement; but now towns and
churches were making their appearance, and even, at long intervals,
the stage-driver's horn broke the silence of the grand old forests,
and he felt that his work was done in the region in which he had
labored so long. He visited every house, and took a solemn farewell
of all the families. The little girls who had been delighted with his
gifts of fragments of calico and ribbons had become sober matrons,
and the boys who had wondered at his ability to bear the pain
caused by running needles into his flesh were heads of families.
With parting words of admonition he left them, and turned his
steps steadily toward the setting sun.

During the succeeding nine years he pursued his eccentric
avocation on the western border of Ohio and in Indiana. In the
summer of 1847, when his labors had literally borne fruit over a
hundred thousand square miles of territory, at the close of a warm
day, after traveling twenty miles, he entered the house of a settler
in Allen County, Indiana, and was, as usual, warmly welcomed.
He declined to eat with the family, but accepted some bread and
milk, which he partook of sitting on the door-step and gazing on
the setting sun. Later in the evening he delivered his "news right
fresh from heaven" by reading the Beatitudes. Declining other accommodation, he slept, as usual, on the floor, and in the early
morning he was found with his features all aglow with a supernal
light, and his body so near death that his tongue refused its office.

The physician, who was hastily summoned, pronounced him dying, but added that he had never seen a man in so placid a state at the approach of death. At seventy-two years of age, forty-six of which had been devoted to his self-imposed mission, he ripened into death as naturally and beautifully as the seeds of his own planting had grown into fibre and bud and blossom and the matured fruit.

Thus died one of the memorable men of pioneer times, who never inflicted pain or knew an enemy—a man of strange habits, in whom there dwelt a comprehensive love that reached with one hand downward to the lowest forms of life, and with the other upward to the very throne of God. A laboring, self-denying bene-factor of his race, homeless, solitary, and ragged, he trod the thorny earth with bare and bleeding feet, intent only upon making the wilderness fruitful. Now "no man knoweth of his sepulchre"; but his deeds will live in the fragrance of the apple blossoms he loved so well, and the story of his life, however crudely narrated, will be a perpetual proof that true heroism, pure benevolence, noble virtues, and deeds that deserve immortality may be found under meanest apparel, and far from gilded halls and towering spires.

part 5

THE AMERICAN
INDIAN

Civilizing the Red Man

James Fenimore Cooper (1789–1851) is usually considered an ardent defender of Rousseau's concept of
the "noble savage." Some of Cooper's fictional Indians are good examples of "Nature's noblemen," yet
the author of the Leatherstocking tales was not blind
to some limitations of the American aborigines, as is
quite evident in the following letter from "An American Bachelor" to a British friend.

As a rule, the red man disappears before the superior moral
and physical influence of the white, just as I believe the black man
will eventually do the same thing, unless he shall seek shelter in
some other region. In nine cases in ten, the tribes have gradually
removed west; and there is now a confused assemblage of nations
and languages collected on the immense hunting grounds of the
Prairies. . . .

The ordinary manner of the disappearance of the Indian, is by
a removal deeper into the forest. Still, many linger near the graves
of their fathers, to which their superstitions, no less than a fine
natural feeling, lend a deeper interest. The fate of the latter is
inevitable; they become victims to the abuses of civilization, without ever attaining to any of its moral elevation.

As might be supposed, numberless divisions of these people,
when the country was discovered, were found in possession of districts along the coast, and deriving a principal means of support
from the ocean. They were fishermen rather than hunters, though

---

From *Notions of the Americans Picked Up by a Traveling Bachelor* (Philadelphia: Carey, Lea, and Carey, 1828), pp. 277–289 *passim*.

the savage state ordinarily infers a resort to both pursuits. Most of these people, too, retired reluctantly from a view of "the great salt lake," but some were environed by the whites before they were properly aware of the blighting influence of the communion; and, getting gradually accustomed to their presence, they preferred remaining near the places where they had first drawn breath. Trifling districts of territory have been, in every instance in which they were sufficiently numerous to make such a provision desirable, secured to them, and on these little tracts of land many of them still remain. I have visited one or two of their establishments.

In point of civilization, comforts, and character, the Indians, who remain near the coasts, are about on a level with the lowest classes of European peasantry. Perhaps they are somewhat below the English, but I think not below the Irish peasants. They are much below the condition of the mass of the slaves. It is but another proof of the wayward vanity of man, that the latter always hold the Indians in contempt, though it is some proof that they feel their own condition to be physically better: morally, in one sense, it certainly is not.

Many of these Atlantic Indians go to sea. They are quite often found in the whalers, and, in some instances, in the vessels of war. An officer in the navy has told me that he once knew a Montauk Indian who was a captain of the main-top in a sloop of war; and in another instance, a flag officer had his gig manned by Indians. They make active and very obedient seamen, but are never remarkable for strength. The whole number of them who now go to sea, does not, however, probably exceed a hundred or two.*

---

* The writer, while in America, heard an anecdote which may give some idea of the notions of retributive justice which linger so long in the philosophy of an Indian, and which is, probably, the basis of his desire for revenge, since he is well known to be as eminently grateful as he is vindictive. The whalers always take their reward in a portion of the profits of the voyage. An Indian made several voyages in succession, in the same ship; he found, at his return, that bad luck, advances, and the supplies of an extravagant family at home, left him always in debt. "What shall I do?" was the question put to his owner, as each unfortunate balance was exhibited. "You must go to sea." To sea he went, and, as stated, for four or five years, always with the same result. At length, good fortune, with a proper amount of preventive castigation on his improvident wife, before he sailed,

I accompanied Cadwallader on a visit to a connexion, who lives within forty miles of New-York, on the adjacent island of Nassau (Long Island). The uncle of my friend was a man of extensive hereditary estate, on which there might have been a reservation of a few thousand acres of woods. While shooting over this forest, one day, the proprietor asked me if I felt any desire to see an Indian king. Surprised at such a question, in such a place, an explanation was requested. He told me that an Indian, who claimed to be a descendant of the ancient Sachems, then held his court in his woods, and that a walk of fifteen minutes would bring us into the presence of King Peter. We went.

I found this Indian, dwelling with his family, in a wigwam of a most primitive construction. It was in the form of a bee-hive, or rather of a very high dome. The covering was made of a long, tough grass, that grows near the sea, and the texture was fine and even beautiful. A post in the centre supported the fabric, which was shaped by delicate curving poles. A hole in the top admitted the light, and allowed the smoke to pass out; and the fire was near enough to the upright post to permit a kettle to be suspended from one of its knots (or cut branches) near enough to feel the influence of the heat. The door was a covering of mats, and the furniture consisted of a few rude chairs, baskets, and a bed, that was neither savage, nor yet such as marks the civilized man. The attire of the family was partly that of the one condition, and partly that of the other. The man himself was a full-blooded Indian, but his manner had that species of sullen deportment that betrays the disposition without the boldness of the savage. He complained that "basket stuff" was getting scarce, and spoke of an intention of removing his wigwam shortly to some other estate.

The manufacture of baskets and brooms is a common employment of all the Indians who reside near the settlements. They feed on game, and, sometimes, like the gypsies, they make free with poultry, though in common they are rigidly honest; nearly

---

brought the balance on his side. The money was of course tendered; but for a long time he refused to receive it, insisting that justice required that his owners should now go to sea, where it would seem he had not enjoyed himself quite as much as he believed the other party to the contract had done on shore.

always so, unless corrupted by much intercourse with the whites. With the proceeds of their labour they purchase blankets, powder, and such other indulgences as exceed their art to manufacture. King Peter, I was told, claimed a right, in virtue of his royal descent, to cut saplings to supply his materials, on any estate in the island. He was permitted to enjoy this species of feudal privilege in quiet, it being well understood that he was not to exceed a certain discretion in its exercise.

In the more interior parts of the country, I frequently met families of the Indians, either travelling, or proceeding to some village, with their wares. They were all alike, a stunted, dirty, and degraded race. Sometimes they encamped in the forests, lighted their fires, and remained for weeks in a place; and at others, they kept roaming daily, until the time arrived when they should return to their reservations.

The reservations in the old States, and with tribes that cannot aspire to the dignity of nations, are managed on a sufficiently humane principle. The laws of the State, or of the United States, have jurisdiction there, in all matters between white men, or between a white man and an Indian; but the Indians themselves are commonly permitted to control the whole of their own internal policy. Bargains, exceeding certain amounts, are not valid between them and the whites, who cannot, for instance, purchase their lands. Schools are usually provided, in the more important tribes, by the general government, and in the less, by charity. Religious instruction is also furnished by the latter means.

I saw reservations in which no mean advances had been made in civilization. Farms were imperfectly tilled, and cattle were seen grazing in the fields. Still, civilization advances slowly among a people who consider labour a degradation, in addition to the bodily dislike that all men have to its occupations.

There are many of these tribes, however, who fill a far more important, and altogether a remarkable position. There is certainly no portion of country within the admitted boundaries of the United States, in which their laws are not paramount, if they choose to exert them. Still, savage communities do exist within these limits, with whom they make treaties, against whom they wage open war, and with whom they make solemn peace. As a treaty is, by the constitution, the paramount law of the land, the several States are obliged to respect their legal provisions.

That neither the United States, nor any individual State, has ever taken possession of any land that, by usage or construction, might be decreed the property of the Indians, without a treaty and a purchase, is, I believe, certain. How far an equivalent is given, is another question: though I fancy that these bargains are quite as just as any that are ever driven between the weak and the strong, the intelligent and the ignorant. It is not pretended that the value of the territory gained is paid for; but the purchase is rather a deference to general principles of justice and humanity, than a concession to a right in the Indians, which itself might admit of a thousand legal quibbles. The treaties are sufficiently humane, and, although certain borderers, who possess the power of the white man with the disposition of the savage, do sometimes violate their conditions, there is no just reason to distrust the intentions or the conduct of the government. . . .

There is a bureau of the war department that is called the "office of the Indian affairs." A humane and discreet individual is at its head, and a good deal is endeavoured to be done in mitigating the sufferings and in meliorating the condition of the Indians, though, owing to the peculiar habits and opinions of these people, but little, I fear, is effected. I see by the report of the current year, (1827) that, in nine months, requisitions towards the support of the objects of this bureau, were made to the amount of 759,116 dollars, or at the rate of a little more than a million of dollars a year. This, you will remember, is one-tenth of the current expenditure of the whole government, and nearly as much as is paid for the support of the whole civil list, strictly speaking. . . .

The government, it would appear by the reports, puts the utmost latitude on the construction of their constitutional powers, by even paying money for the support of missionaries among the Indians. I believe, however, that the alleged and legal object of this charge, is for general instruction, though in point of fact, the teachers are missionaries. They are of all sects, Protestant and Catholic, the question of creed being never discussed at all. I see by the reports, that (in 1827) there were 1291 scholars in the different schools that come under the superintendence of the government. It is not probable that all the Indians belonging to the tribes that receive this instruction much exceed, if indeed they reach, the total number of 30,000. I think it is therefore apparent, that quite as good provision for elementary instruction is made in behalf of the Indians, as is commonly made for the people of any country, except those of the United States themselves. There is no reason to suppose that all the children who present themselves, are not taught; and there is much reason for believing that efforts are constantly making to induce all to come. The number of teachers is 293, which is quite enough to instruct ten times the number. You are not to suppose, however, that all these teachers are men hired expressly for that purpose. They are the missionaries, their wives and families, and some of them are for the purpose of instructing in the arts of life, as well as in reading and writing. Much of the expense is defrayed by charitable associations. The sum actually paid by the government for the express object of instruction, is 7,150 dollars, or enough to maintain rather more than forty teachers of stipends of 150 dollars each. It is probable that some receive more, and some less. It is said that the schools are generally in a flourishing condition.

Where there is much intercourse between the very strong and very weak, there is always a tendency in the human mind to suspect abuses of power. I shall not descend into the secret impulses that give rise to these suspicions; but in this stage of the world, there is no necessity for suspecting a nation like this of any unprovoked wrongs against a people like the savages. The inroad of the whites of the United States has never been marked by the gross injustice and brutality that have distinguished similar inroads elsewhere. The Indians have never been slain except in battle, unless by lawless individuals; never hunted by blood-hounds, or in any manner aggrieved, except in the general, and, perhaps, in some degree, justifiable invasion of a territory that they did not want, nor could not use. If the government of the United States was poor and necessitous, one might suspect it of an unjust propensity; but not only the facts, but the premises, would teach us to believe the reverse.

A great, humane, and, I think, rational project, is now in operation to bring the Indians within the pale of civilization. I shall furnish you with its outline as it is detailed in a recent report of the head of the Indian office.

Most, if not all of the Indians who reside east of the Mississippi, live within the jurisdiction of some State or of some territory. In most cases they are left to the quiet enjoyment of the scanty rights which they retain, but the people of their vicinity commonly wish to get rid of neighbours that retard civilization, and who are so often troublesome. The policy of States is sometimes adverse to their continuance. Though there is no power, except that of the United States, which can effect their removal without their own consent, the State authorities can greatly embarrass the control of the general government. A question of policy, and, perhaps, of jurisdiction, lately arose on this subject between Georgia and the general government. In the course of its disposal, the United States, in order to secure the rights of the Indians more effectually, and to prevent any future question of this sort, appear to have hit on the following plan.

West of the Mississippi they still hold large regions that belong to no State or territory. They propose to several tribes (Choctaws, Chickasaws, Cherokees, &c.) to sell their present possessions, improvements, houses, fences, stock, &c., and to receive, in return, acre for acre, with the same amount of stock, fences, and every other auxiliary of civilization they now possess. The inducements to make this exchange are as follow:—Perpetuity to their establishments, since a pledge is given that no title shall ever be granted that may raise a pretext for another removal; an organization of a republican, or, as it is termed, a territorial government for them, such as now exist in Florida, Arkansas, and Michigan; protection, by the presence of troops; and a right to send delegates to Congress, similar to that now enjoyed by the other territories.

If the plan can be effected, there is reason to think that the constant diminution in the numbers of the Indians will be checked, and that a race, about whom there is so much that is poetic and fine in recollection, will be preserved. Indeed, some of the southern tribes have already endured the collision with the white man, and are still slowly on the increase. As one of these tribes, at least, (the Chickasaws,) is included in this plan, there is just ground to hope that the dangerous point of communication has been passed, and that they may continue to advance in civilization to maturity. The chief of the bureau on Indian affairs gives it as his opinion that they (the Chickasaws) have increased about ten per cent within six years. Their whole number is computed at four thousand souls.

Should such a territory be formed, a nucleus will be created, around which all the savages of the west, who have any yearnings for a more meliorated state of existence, can rally. As there is little reluctance to mingle the white and red blood, (for the physical difference is far less than in the case of the blacks, and the Indians have never been menial slaves,) I think an amalgamation of the two races would in time occur. Those families of America who are thought to have any of the Indian blood, are rather proud of their descent, and it is a matter of boast among many of the most considerable persons of Virginia, that they are descended from the renowned Pocahontas.

The character of the American Indian has been too often faithfully described to need any repetition here. The majority of them, in or near the settlements, are an humbled and much degraded race. As you recede from the Mississippi, the finer traits of savage life become visible; and, although most of the natives of the Prairies, even there, are far from being the interesting and romantic heroes that poets love to paint, there are specimens of loftiness of spirit, of bearing, and of savage heroism, to be found among the chiefs, that might embarrass the fertility of the richest invention to equal. I met one of those heroes of the desert, and a finer physical and moral man, allowing for peculiarity of condition, it has rarely been my good fortune to encounter.

The Camp of the Wild Horse

After an absence of seventeen years in Europe, Washington Irving (1783–1859) returned to America in 1832 where he was hailed as his country's "first man of letters." His friendship with Walter Scott and his expressed love of England had, however, stamped him as an expatriate, and in order to demonstrate his nationalism, Irving turned his attention to the American West. He joined an Indian commission headed for Fort Gibson on the Arkansas River, and his experiences in this expedition make up his *A Tour of the Prairies* (1835).

Irving wrote "elegant" narratives and painted his experiences in rather lavish colors, and his account of "The Camp of the Wild Horse" has allegorical implications and some "fillagre work" that are absent from the more realistic account of the same experience by Henry Leavitt Ellsworth (1837). Irving's romantic view of the American Indians is clearly reflected in his version of the story.

See also Henry Leavitt Ellsworth, *Washington Irving on the Prairie*, edited by Stanley T. Williams and Barbara D. Simison (New York, 1937).

We had encamped in a good neighborhood for game, as the reports of rifles in various directions speedily gave notice. One of our hunters soon returned with the meat of a doe, tied up in the skin, and slung across his shoulders. Another brought a fat buck across his horse. Two other deer were brought in, and a number of turkeys. All the game was thrown down in front of the

---

From *A Tour of the Prairies* (Philadelphia: Carey, Lea and Blanchard, 1835), chap. 20.

Captain's fire, to be portioned out among the various messes. The spits and camp-kettles were soon in full employ, and throughout the evening there was a scene of hunters' feasting and profusion.

We had been disappointed this day in our hopes of meeting with buffalo, but the sight of the wild horse had been a great novelty, and gave a turn to the conversation of the camp for the evening. There were several anecdotes told of a famous gray horse, which has ranged the prairies of this neighborhood for six or seven years, setting at naught every attempt of the hunters to capture him. They say he can pace and rack (or amble) faster than the fleetest horses can run. Equally marvellous accounts were given of a black horse on the Brazos, who grazed the prairies on that river's banks in Texas. For years he outstripped all pursuit. His fame spread far and wide; offers were made for him to the amount of a thousand dollars; the boldest and most hard-riding hunters tried incessantly to make prize of him, but in vain. At length he fell a victim to his gallantry, being decoyed under a tree by a tame mare, and a noose dropped over his head by a boy perched among the branches.

The capture of the wild horse is one of the most favorite achievements of the prairie tribes, and, indeed, it is from this source that the Indian hunters chiefly supply themselves. The wild horses which range those vast grassy plains, extending from the Arkansas to the Spanish settlements, are of various forms and colors, betraying their various descents. Some resemble the common English stock, and are probably descended from horses which have escaped from our border settlements. Others are of a low but strong make, and are supposed to be of the Andalusian breed, brought out by the Spanish discoverers.

Some fanciful speculatists have seen in them descendants of the Arab stock, brought into Spain from Africa, and thence transferred to this country; and have pleased themselves with the idea, that their sires may have been of the pure coursers of the desert, that once bore Mahomet and his warlike disciples across the sandy plains of Arabia.

The habits of the Arab seem to have come with the steed. The introduction of the horse on the boundless prairies of the Far West changed the whole mode of living of their inhabitants. It gave them that facility of rapid motion, and of sudden and distant change of place, so dear to the roving propensities of man. Instead of lurking in the depths of gloomy forests, and patiently threading the mazes of a tangled wilderness on foot, like his brethren of the north, the Indian of the West is a rover of the plain; he leads a brighter and more sunshiny life; almost always on horseback, on vast flowery prairies and under cloudless skies.

I was lying by the Captain's fire, late in the evening, listening to stories about those coursers of the prairies, and weaving speculations of my own, when there was a clamor of voices and a loud cheering at the other end of the camp; and word was passed that Beatte, the half-breed, had brought in a wild horse.

In an instant every fire was deserted; the whole camp crowded to see the Indian and his prize. It was a colt about two years old, well grown, finely limbed, with bright prominent eyes, and a spirited yet gentle demeanor. He gazed about him with an air of mingled stupefaction and surprise, at the men, the horses, and the camp-fires; while the Indian stood before him with folded arms, having hold of the other end of the cord which noosed his captive, and gazing on him with a most imperturbable aspect. Beatte, as I have before observed, has a greenish olive complexion, with a strongly marked countenance, not unlike the bronze casts of Napoleon; and as he stood before his captive horse, with folded arms and fixed aspect, he looked more like a statue than a man.

If the horse, however, manifested the least restiveness, Beatte would immediately worry him with the lariat, jerking him first on one side, then on the other, so as almost to throw him on the ground; when he had thus rendered him passive, he would resume his statue-like attitude and gaze at him in silence.

The whole scene was singularly wild; the tall grove, partially illumined by the flashing fires of the camp, the horses tethered here and there among the trees, the carcasses of deer hanging around, and in the midst of all, the wild huntsman and his wild horse, with an admiring throng of rangers, almost as wild.

In the eagerness of their excitement, several of the young rangers sought to get the horse by purchase or barter, and even offered extravagant terms; but Beatte declined all their offers. "You give great price now"; said he, "tomorrow you will be sorry, and take back, and say d—d Indian!"

The young men importuned him with questions about the mode in which he took the horse, but his answers were dry and laconic; he evidently retained some pique at having been undervalued and sneered at by them; and at the same time looked down upon them with contempt as greenhorns, little versed in the noble science of woodcraft.

Afterward, however, when he was seated by our fire, I readily drew from him an account of his exploit; for, though taciturn among strangers, and little prone to boast of his actions, yet his taciturnity, like that of all Indians, had its times of relaxation.

He informed me, that on leaving the camp, he had returned to the place where we had lost sight of the wild horse. Soon getting upon its track, he followed it to the banks of the river. Here, the prints being more distinct in the sand, he perceived that one of the hoofs was broken and defective, so he gave up the pursuit.

As he was returning to the camp, he came upon a gang of six horses, which immediately made for the river. He pursued them across the stream, left his rifle on the river bank, and putting his horse to full speed, soon came up with the fugitives. He attempted to noose one of them, but the lariat hitched on one of his ears, and he shook it off. The horses dashed up a hill, he followed hard at their heels, when, of a sudden, he saw their tails whisking in the air, and they plunging down a precipice. It was too late to stop. He shut his eyes, held in his breath, and went over with them— neck or nothing. The descent was between twenty and thirty feet, but they all came down safe upon a sandy bottom.

He now succeeded in throwing his noose round a fine young horse. As he galloped alongside of him, the two horses passed each side of a sapling, and the end of the lariat was jerked out of his hand. He regained it, but an intervening tree obliged him again to let it go. Having once more caught it, and coming to a more open country, he was enabled to play the young horse with the line until he gradually checked and subdued him, so as to lead him to the place where he had left his rifle.

He had another formidable difficulty in getting him across the river, where both horses stuck for a time in the mire, and Beatte was nearly unseated from his saddle by the force of the current and the struggle of his captive. After much toil and trouble, however, he got across the stream, and brought his prize safe into camp.

For the remainder of the evening, the camp remained in a high state of excitement; nothing was talked of but the capture of wild horses; every youngster of the troop was for this harum-scarum kind of chase; every one promised himself to return from the campaign in triumph, bestriding one of these wild coursers of the prairies. Beatte had suddenly risen to great importance; he was the prime hunter, the hero of the day. Offers were made him by the best mounted rangers, to let him ride their horses in the chase, provided he would give them a share of the spoil. Beatte bore his honors in silence, and closed with none of the offers. Our stammering, chattering, gasconading little Frenchman, however, made up for his taciturnity, by vaunting as much upon the subject as if it were he that had caught the horse. Indeed he held forth so learnedly in the matter, and boasted so much of the many horses he had taken, that he began to be considered an oracle; and some of the youngsters were inclined to doubt whether he were not superior even to the taciturn Beatte.

The excitement kept the camp awake later than usual. The hum of voices, interrupted by occasional peals of laughter, was heard from the groups around the various fires, and the night was considerably advanced before all had sunk to sleep.

With the morning dawn the excitement revived, and Beatte and his wild horse were again the gaze and talk of the camp. The captive had been tied all night to a tree among the other horses. He was again led forth by Beatte, by a long halter or lariat, and, on his manifesting the least restiveness, was, as before, jerked and worried into passive submission. He appeared to be gentle and docile by nature, and had a beautifully mild expression of the eye. In his strange and forlorn situation, the poor animal seemed to seek protection and companionship in the very horse which had aided to capture him.

Seeing him thus gentle and tractable, Beatte, just as we were about to march, strapped a light pack upon his back, by way of giving him the first lesson in servitude. The native pride and independence of the animal took fire at this indignity. He reared, and plunged, and kicked, and tried in every way to get rid of the degrading burden. The Indian was too potent for him. At every paroxysm he renewed the discipline of the halter, until the poor animal, driven to despair, threw himself prostrate on the ground, and lay motionless, as if acknowledging himself vanquished. A stage hero, representing the despair of a captive prince, could not have played his part more dramatically. There was absolutely a moral grandeur in it.

The imperturbable Beatte folded his arms, and stood for a time, looking down in silence upon his captive; until seeing him perfectly subdued, he nodded his head slowly, screwed his mouth into a sardonic smile of triumph, and, with a jerk of the halter, ordered him to rise. He obeyed, and from that time forward offered no resistance. During that day he bore his pack patiently, and was led by the halter; but in two days he followed voluntarily at large among the supernumerary horses of the troop.

I could not but look with compassion upon this fine young animal, whose whole course of existence had been so suddenly reversed. From being a denizen of these vast pastures, ranging at will from plain to plain and mead to mead, cropping of every herb and flower, and drinking of every stream, he was suddenly reduced to perpetual and painful servitude, to pass his life under the harness and the curb, amid, perhaps, the din and dust and drudgery of cities. The transition in his lot was such as sometimes takes place in human affairs, and in the fortunes of towering individuals:—one day, a prince of the prairies—the next day, a pack-horse!

The Indian Hater

James Hall (1793–1868) became a writer in 1820
when, smitten with a desire to go west, he took
passage on a keelboat at Pittsburgh for Shawneetown,
Illinois. His senses were alive to every impression of
the backwoods, and his *Letters from the West*
(1828) contain sketches of scenery, manners, customs, and anecdotes connected with the first settlements in Illinois. A prolific writer, Hall published
numerous magazines and several books, principally
Legends of the West (1832), *Romance of Western
History* (1857), and *The Wilderness and the Warpath* (1845).

The story reprinted here is thought to be the
source of Herman Melville's chapters on "The Meta-
physics of Indian Hating," in *The Confidence-Man*
(1857). John T. Flanagan wrote a biography of Hall
in 1941.

Some years ago, I had occasion to travel over the beautiful
prairies of Illinois, then a frontier state, containing but few inhabitants, and those chiefly of the class called backwoodsmen. In
the course of my journey, I stopped one day at a village to rest;
and while my horse was eating his corn, and mine hostess was
picking the chicken that was to be broiled for my dinner, I stepped
into a neighbouring store to purchase some small article of which
I stood in need. I found a number of persons there, engaged,
some in buying merchandise, some in talking politics, and others
in reading the manuscript advertisements of stray horses and
constable's sales, that were pasted on the walls. There were a

From *The Wilderness and the Warpath* (New York: Wiley and Putnam,
1846), pp. 138–151.

bottle of whiskey and a pitcher of water on the counter, free for all comers, as was the hospitable fashion of those days, before temperance had got to be a tip-top virtue, or Father Mathew the greatest of modern reformers. Being not unwilling to observe a scene which might afford amusement, and to while away a few minutes in conversation, I leaned my back against the counter, and addressed myself to a person having the appearance of a substantial farmer, who answered my inquiries respecting the country with intelligence and civility.

While thus engaged, my attention was drawn to a person who stood near. He was a man who might have been about fifty years of age. His height did not exceed the ordinary stature, and his person was rather slender than otherwise; but there was something in his air and features which distinguished him from common men. The expression of his countenance was keen and daring. His forehead was elevated, his cheek bones high, his lips thin and compressed. Long exposure to the climate had tanned his complexion to a deep brown, and had hardened his skin and muscles, so as to give him the appearance of a living petrifaction. He seemed to have lived in the open air, exposed to the elements, and to every extreme of temperature.

There was nothing in the dress of this individual to attract attention; he was accosted occasionally by others, and seemed familiar with all who were present. Yet there was an air of abstraction, and standing aloof about him, so different from the noisy mirth and thoughtless deportment of those around him, that I could not help observing him. In his eye there was something peculiar, yet I could not tell in what that peculiarity consisted. It was a small grey orb, whose calm, bold, direct glances, seemed to vouch that it had not cowered with shame, or quailed in danger. There was blended in that eye a searching keenness, with a quiet vigilance—a watchful, sagacious self-possession—so often observable in the physiognomy of those who are in the habit of expecting, meeting, and overcoming peril. His heavy eyebrows had been black, but time had touched them with his pencil. He was dressed in a coarse grey hunting shirt, of home-spun cotton, girded round the waist with a broad leathern belt, tightly drawn, in which rested the long knife, with which the western hunter despatches his game, cuts his food, picks his flint and his teeth, and whittles sticks for amusement.

Upon the whole, there was about this man an expression of quiet determination, of grim and gloomy sternness, of intense but smothered passion, which stamped him as something out of the ordinary view of character; yet there were indications of openness and honesty, that forbade distrust. He was rough, but not a ruffian. His was not the unblushing front of hardy guilt, nor the lurking glance of underhanded villainy. A stranger would not have hesitated to confide in his faith or courage, but would have been extremely reluctant to provoke his hostility.

I had barely time to make these observations, when several Indians, who had strolled into the village, entered the store. The effect of their presence upon the backwoodsman, whom I have described, was instantaneous and remarkable. His eyes rolled wildly, as if he had been suddenly stung to madness, gleaming with a strange fierceness—an intense lustre, like that which flashes from the eyeballs of the panther, when crouched in a dark covert, ready to dart upon his prey. His sallow cheek was flushed; the muscles, that but a moment before seemed so rigid, became flexible, and twitched convulsively. His hand sliding quietly to the hilt of his large knife, as if by an involuntary impulse, grasped it firmly; and it was easy to perceive that a smothered fire had been disturbed, and that a single breath would be sufficient to light up a blaze. But, except these indications, he remained motionless as a statue, gazing with a look of intense ferocity at the intruders. The Indians halted when their eyes met his, and exchanged glances of intelligence with each other. Whether it was from instinct, or that they knew the man, or whether the natural sagacity of their race enabled them to read the signs of danger in his scowling visage, they seemed willing to avoid him, and returned. The backwoodsman made a motion, as if to follow; but several of the company, who had watched this silent, though momentary scene, with interest, gently withheld him, and after conversing with him a few moments in an earnest, but undertone, led him off in one direction, while the Indians rode away in another.

Having understood from the farmer, with whom I had been talking, that he was about to return home, and that my route

led through his neighbourhood, I accepted the offer of his company and guidance, and we set out together. It was a pleasant
afternoon in the fall, and as our horses trotted quietly over the
smooth prairie road, the discourse naturally fell upon the scene
we had just witnessed, and I expressed a curiosity to learn something of the history and character of the man, whose image had
impressed itself so forcibly on my mind. I was young and romantic
then, and singular as this being certainly was, his peculiarities
were probably magnified to my excited fancy.

"He is a strange, mysterious-looking being," said I, "and I should
think he must be better, or worse, than other men."

"Samuel Monson is a very good neighbour," replied the farmer,
cautiously.

"You say that in a tone," rejoined I, "which seems to imply,
that in some other respects he may not be so good."

"Well—as to that, I cannot say, of my own knowledge, that
I know any harm of the man."

"And what do other people say of him?"

The farmer hesitated, and then, with a caution very common
among people of this description, replied:

"People often say more than they can prove. It's not good, no
how, to be talking of one's neighbours; and Monson, as I said
before, is a good neighbour."

"But a bad man, as I understand."

"No—far from it—the man's well enough—"

My companion hesitated here, as gossips of both sexes are apt
to do, when conscious of a strong inclination to tell all they know
on a delicate subject; but my laudable thirst for useful knowledge
had, I suppose, awakened a benevolent desire to gratify it, and the
worthy man added, in a low tone, and looking cautiously around:

"—Except—The folks do say he are rather too keen with his
rifle."

"How so? does he shoot his neighbour's cattle?"

"No, sir—Samuel Monson is as much above a mean action as
any other man."

"What then, is he quarrelsome?"

"Oh, bless you, no! There's not a peaceabler man in the settlement; but he used to be a great Indian fighter in the last war, and

he got sort o' haunted to the woods; and folks do say that he's still rather too keen on the track of a moccasin."

"I do not exactly understand you, my dear sir.—The Indians are now quiet, I believe, and at peace with us?"

"Why yes, they are very peaceable. They never come near us, except now and then a little party comes in to trade. There's not many of them in these parts, and they live a good piece off."

"They are civil and harmless, are they not?"

"Yes, sir, quite agreeable—bating the killing of a hog once in a while—but that we don't tally—it is but just nateral to the poor savage to shoot anything that runs in the woods. They have a honing in that way, and you can't stop them, no way you can fix it."

"In what way, then, does this Monson interfere with them?"

"I did not say, stranger, that Monson done it. No, no; I wouldn't hurt no man's character; but the fact and the truth are about this: now and then an Indian are missing; and now and then one are found dead in the range;—and folks will have their notions, and their talk, and their suspicions about it—and some talk hard of Monson."

"But why charge it upon him?"

"Well, if you must have it out, stranger,—in this country we all know the bore of every man's rifle. Monson's gun carries just fifty to the pound. Now the bullet holes in all these Indians that have been shot are the same, and we know whose rifle they suit. Besides this, horse tracks have been seen on the trail of the moccasin. They were very particular tracks, and just suited the hoof of a certain horse. Then a certain man was known to be lying out in the range, about that same time; and when all these things are put together, it don't take a Philadelphia lawyer to tell who done the deed. No mistake in Sam Monson. He likes a skrimmage with them. He goes off sometimes, and is gone for weeks, and people reckon that he goes to their own hunting grounds to lie in wait for them. They do say, he can scent a red-skin like a hound, and never lets a chance slip—no how."

"But is it possible, that in a civilized country, within the reach of our laws, a wretch is permitted to hunt down his fellow-creatures like wild beasts; to murder a defenceless Indian, who comes into our territory in good faith, believing us to be what we profess, as a Christian people!"

"Well, stranger,—as to the matter of that—it is not exactly permitted; we don't know for certain who does it, and it's not any particular man's business to inquire into it, more than another. There's no love for the Indians among us, no how. Many of the people have had their kin murdered by the savages in early times; and all who have been raised in the back woods, have been learned to dislike them, and fear them. Then Monson is an honest fellow, works hard, pays his debts, and is always willing to do a good turn, and it would seem hard to break neighbourhood with him for the matter of a few Indians. People don't think the Indians of much account, no how!"

"But the wickedness of such unprovoked murder—the shame— the breach of law, the violation of hospitality!"

"Well, so it is. It are a sin; and sorry would I be to have it on my conscience. But, then, some think an Indian or so will never be missed; others, again, hate to create an interruption in the settlement; others, who pretend to know the law, say that the general government has the care of the business of the Indians, and that our state laws won't kiver the case—so they allow it's none of our business. Some folks, you know, go in heavy for state rights, and don't believe in meddling with anything that belongs to Uncle Sam; and withal Monson keeps his own counsel, and so among hands he goes his own road, and no questions asked."

All this seemed very strange to me. Border wars, we all know, are productive of feuds, which are implacable and lasting. Predatory incursions, which hardly attract the notice of the government, bring carnage and devastation, ruin and sorrow, to the fireside. Private property is wasted, and the war is against individuals, rather than the public. The actors in each scene are identified; men and families feel the sense of personal injury, and hatred and revenge are the consequence. But I was not aware that such a state of feeling existed on our own frontier. While these thoughts passed through my mind, we rode forward in silence, which was broken by my inquiring what injury this individual had suffered from the Indians, which could justify him in thus destroying them with impunity.

"Injury enough!" replied my companion: "to tell the plain sentimental truth, he has cause enough to hate them; and many a man that would not dip his own hand in the blood of an Indian, would as soon die as betray him; for few of us could lay our hands upon our hearts and say we would not do the same in his situation."

At this point of the conversation we were joined by several horsemen, who were pursuing the same road with ourselves, and joined us, in accordance with the gregarious habits of the country, which induce men to prefer a larger company to a smaller, on all occasions; and my companion being unwilling to pursue the subject in their hearing, I was unable to learn from him what injury the Indian hater had received, to provoke his sanguinary career of vengeance. Nor did another opportunity occur; for we soon came to a point where the roads diverging, obliged us to separate, and although my friendly fellow-traveller, with the usual hospitality of the country, invited me to take up my lodgings at his house for the night, I was obliged to decline the invitation, and we parted.

I continued my journey into the northwestern part of Illinois, which was then just beginning to attract the attention of settlers, and contained but few inhabitants. Delighted with this beautiful wilderness, unspoiled by art, and retaining all its native loveliness, and wishing to explore the lands lying between this tract and the Wabash, I determined, on my return, to strike directly across, through a district of country in which there were as yet no settlements, of about one hundred and fifty miles in extent. I hired an Indian guide, who was highly recommended to me, and set out under his protection.

It is not easy to describe the sensations of a traveller, unaccustomed to such scenery, on first beholding the vast prairies, which I was about to explore. Those I had heretofore seen were comparatively small; both are unique, and highly attractive, but as they differ in their features and scenic effect, I shall endeavour to describe them separately.

The smaller prairies, or those in which the plain and woodland alternate frequently, are the most beautiful. The points of woodland which make into them like so many capes or promontories, and the groves which are interspersed like islands, are in these lesser prairies always sufficiently near to be clearly defined to the eye, and to give the scene an interesting variety. We see plains, varying from a few hundred acres to several miles in extent, not perfectly level, but gently rolling or undulating, like the swelling of the ocean when nearly calm. The graceful curve of the surface is seldom broken, except when, here and there, the eye rests upon one of those huge mounds, which are so pleasing to the poet, and so perplexing to the antiquarian. The whole is overspread with grass and flowers, constituting a rich and varied carpet, in which a ground of lively green is ornamented with a profusion of the gaudiest hues, and fringed with a rich border of forest and thicket. Deep recesses in the edge of the timber resemble the bays and inlets of a lake; while occasionally a long vista, opening far back into the forest, invites the eye to roam off and refresh itself, with the calm beauty of a distant perspective.

The traveller, as he rides along over these smaller prairies, finds his eye continually attracted to the edges of the forest, and his imagination employed in tracing the beautiful outline, and in finding out resemblances between these wild scenes and the most tastefully embellished productions of art. The fairest pleasure-grounds, the noblest parks of European noblemen and princes, where millions have been expended to captivate the senses with Elysian scenes, are but mimic representations, on a reduced scale, of the beauties which are here spread by nature; for here are clumps and lawns, groves and avenues, the tangled thicket, and the solitary tree, the lengthened vista, and the secluded nook, and all the varieties of scenic attraction, but on a plan so extensive, as to offer a wide scope, and an endless succession of changes, to the eye.

There is an air of refinement here, that wins the heart,—even here, where no human residence is seen, where no foot of man intrudes, and where not an axe has ever trespassed on the beautiful domain. It is a wilderness shorn of every savage association, a desert that "blossoms as the rose." So different is the feeling awakened from anything inspired by mountain or woodland scenery, that the instant the traveller emerges from the forest into the prairie, he feels no longer solitary. The consciousness that he is travelling alone, and in a wilderness, escapes him; and he indulges in the same pleasing sensations which are enjoyed by one who, having lost his way, and wandered bewildered among the labyrinths of a savage mountain, suddenly descends into rich and highly cultivated plains, and sees around him the delightful indications of taste and comfort. The gay landscape charms him. He is encompassed by the refreshing sweetness and graceful beauty of the rural scene; and recognises at every step some well-remembered spot, or some ideal paradise in which the fancy had loved to wander, enlarged and beautified, and, as it were, retouched by nature's hand. The clusters of trees so fancifully arranged, the forest outline so gracefully curved, seem to have been disposed by the hand of taste, for the enjoyment of intelligent beings; and so complete is the illusion, that it is difficult to dispel the belief that each avenue leads to a village, and each grove conceals a splendid mansion.

Widely different was the prospect exhibited by the more northern and central districts of the State. Vast in extent, the distant forest was either beyond the reach of the eye, or was barely discernible in the shapeless outline of blue, faintly impressed on the horizon. As the smaller prairies resembled a series of larger and lesser lakes, so these boundless plains remind one of the ocean waste. Here and there a solitary tree, torn by the wind, stood alone like a dismantled mast in the ocean. As I followed my guide through this lonely region, my sensations were similar to those of the voyager, when his bark is launched upon the sea. Alone, in a wide waste, with my faithful pilot only, I was dependent on him for support, guidance, and protection. With little to diversify the path, and nothing to please the eye but the carpet of verdure, which began to pall upon the sense, a feeling of dreariness crept over me—a desolation of the spirit, such as one feels when crossed in love, or when very drowsy on a hot afternoon, after a full dinner. But these are feelings which, like the sea-sickness of the young mariner, are soon dispelled. I began to find a pleasure in gazing over this immense, unbroken waste, in watching the horizon under the vague hope of meeting a traveller, and in following the deer with my eyes as they galloped off—their agile forms growing smaller and smaller as they receded, until they shrunk into nothing.

Sometimes I descried a dark spot at an immense distance, and pointed it out to my companion with a joy like that of the seaman who discovers a sail in the distant speck which floats on the ocean. When such an object happened to be in the direction of our path, I watched it with interest as it rose and enlarged upon the vision—supposing it at one moment to be a solitary horseman, and wondering what manner of man he would turn out to be—at another supposing it might be a wild animal, or a wagon, or a pedestrian; until, after it had seemed to approach for hours, I found it to be a tree.

Nor was I entirely destitute of company; for my Pottowottomie guide proved to be both intelligent and good-humoured; and although his stock of English was but slender, and his habit of taciturnity somewhat confirmed, his conversational powers, when exerted, were quite respectable. His knowledge of the country was extensive and accurate, so that he was able, not only to choose the best route, but to point out all the localities. When we halted he kindled a fire, spread my pallet, and formed a shelter to protect me from the weather. When we came to a stream which was too deep to ford, he framed a raft to cross me over, with my baggage, while he mounted my horse and plunged into the water. Throughout the journey, his assiduities were as kind and unremitting as all his arrangements were sagacious and considerate. A higher motive than the mere pecuniary reward which he expected for his services governed his actions. He considered himself my companion; not only responsible for my safety, as a matter of contract, but kindly interested for my comfort. A genuine integrity of purpose, a native politeness and manliness of deportment, raised him above the ordinary savage, and rendered him not only a respectable, but an interesting man.

After travelling nearly five days without beholding a human habitation, we arrived at the verge of a settlement on the Wabash. We passed along a rich bottom, covered with huge trees, whose limbs were hung with immense grape vines, and whose thick shade afforded a strong contrast to the scenes we had left behind us, and then ascending a gentle rise, stood on a high bluff bank of the Wabash. A more secluded and beautiful spot has seldom been seen. A small river, with a clear stream, rippling over a rocky bed, meandered round the point on which we stood, and then turning abruptly to the left, was lost among the trees. The opposite shore was low, thickly wooded, and beautifully rich in the variety of mellow hues painted by the autumn sun.

The spot we occupied was a slip of table land, a little higher than the surrounding country. It had once been cleared for cultivation, but was now overgrown with hazel bushes, vines, and briars, while a few tall, leafless trunks, once the proudest oaks of the forest, weather-beaten and blackened by fire, still adhered tenaciously to the soil. A heap of rubbish, intermingled with logs half burnt and nearly rotten, showed the remains of what had once been a chimney, and indicated the spot where a cabin had stood, the residence of human beings—but all else had been destroyed by time or fire. We gazed on the ruins of a desolated homestead, but many years seemed to have rolled away since it had been inhabited. The clearing had been of small extent; it was now covered with a rank vegetation, which was fast restoring it to the dominion of the wilderness. One spot only, which had probably been the yard in front of the little dwelling, and had been beaten hard, was covered with a smooth green sward, unmixed with weeds or brugh; and here we stood gazing at this desolate spot, and that beautiful river. It was but a moment, and neither of us had broken silence, when the crack of a rifle was heard, and my guide, uttering a dismal yell, fell at my feet.

Recovering his senses for an instant, he grasped his gun, partly raised his body, and cast upon me a look of reproach, which I shall never forget; and then, as if satisfied by the concern and alarm of my countenance, and my prompt movement to assist him, he gave me one hand, and pointing with the other towards the woods, exclaimed—"Bad—bad, white man!—take care"—and expired. The aim had been unerring—the bullet had penetrated deep in a vital spot, and life was extinguished in a moment.

I was so much surprised and shocked at this fatal catastrophe, that I stood immoveable, thoughtless of my own safety, mourning over the stout Indian, my kind and worthy guide, who lay weltering in his gore, when I was startled by a slight rustling in the bushes close behind me, and as I turned with an involuntary shudder, a backwoodsman, rifle in hand, issued from the covert.

Advancing hastily, without the least appearance of shame or fear, until he came to the corpse, and paying not the slightest attention to me, he stood and gazed sternly at the fallen warrior. It was Monson! The fierce and gloomy picture, which had been impressed so indelibly upon my memory, stood before me in living presentation, his hand imbrued in blood, and his soul freshly steeped in murder.

"There's another of the cursed crew gone to his last account!" he exclaimed. "He is not the first, and he shall not be the last.— It's an old debt, but it shall be paid to the last drop!"

As he spoke, he gnashed his teeth, and his eyes gleamed with the malignity of gratified revenge. Then turning to me, and observing the deep abhorrence with which I shrunk back, he said gruffly,

"May be, stranger, you don't like this sort of business."

"Wretch—miscreant—murderer! begone! Approach me not," I exclaimed, shrinking back in disgust and terror, and drawing a large pistol from my belt; but, before I was aware, the backwoodsman, with a sudden spring, caught my arm, and wrested the weapon from me; and then remaining perfectly calm, while I was ready to burst with rage, he proceeded:

"This is a poor shooting-iron for a man to have about him—it might do for young men to tote in a settlement, but it's of no use in the woods—no more than a shot-gun."

"Scoundrel!" said I, "you shall repent your violence—"

"Young man!" interrupted he, very coolly, "I am no scoundrel, no more than yourself; you mistake, you do not know me."

"Murderer!" repeated I, "for such I know you to be. My life is in your power, but I dread not your vengeance! If I live, this bloody deed shall not go unpunished!"

While I was thus exhausting myself, in the expression of my rage and horror, the more politic Monson, having possessed himself of the Indian's gun, dropped it, together with my unlucky pistol, on the ground, and placing one foot on them, proceeded deliberately to load his rifle.

"Don't be alarmed, young man," said he, in reply to my last remark, "I shall not hurt a hair of your head. You cannot provoke me to it. I never harmed a Christian man, to my knowledge!"

But although his habitual command of his temper enabled him to treat the matter thus coolly, he was evidently under high excitement, and as he finished loading his piece, he exclaimed, "See here!" Then pointing to the ruins of the cabin, he proceeded in a hurried tone.

"This was my home. Here I built a house with my own labour. With the sweat of my brow I opened this clearing. Here I lived with my wife, my children, and my mother. We worked hard—lived well—and were happy."

His voice became choked; he paused, as if overcome by the recollections of the past; but after a moment's hesitation, he proceeded with the simple and vehement eloquence of passion:

"I am a rough man, stranger, but I have feelings like other men. My blood is up now, and I will tell you a tale that will explain this deed. One night—it was in the fall—just at this season—I had gathered my corn, ready for shucking, the labour of the year was done, and I was sitting by the fire with my family, with the prospect of plenty and comfort around me—when I heard the Indian yell! I never was a coward, but I knew that sound too well; and when I looked round upon the women and helpless babes, that depended on me for protection, a cold chill ran over me, and my heart seemed to die. I ran to the door, and beheld my stacks in a blaze. I caught up my gun—but in a moment a gang of yelling savages came pouring in at my door, like so many howling wolves. I fired, and one of them fell—I caught up an axe and rushed at them with such fury that I cleared the cabin. The vile varments then set fire to the roof, and we saw the flames spreading around us. What could I do?

"Stranger, you never were in such a fix, and you don't know how a man feels. Here was my poor old mother, and my wife, and my little children, unable to fight, or to escape. I burst open the door, and rushed madly out; but they pushed me back. The yelling wretches were determined to burn us in our house. The blazing timbers came falling among us—my wife hung on my neck, and called on me to save our children—our pious old mother prayed—the savage butchers roared, and laughed, and mocked us. They caught my dog, that we loved as one of the family, hung him, and then threw his carcass among us.

"I grasped my axe, and rushed out again—hoping to beat them back, until the neighbours could be alarmed, and come to our assistance. I killed several of them; but they overpowered me, bound me, and led me up to witness the ruin of all that was dear to me. Wife—children—mother—all, all perished here in the flames before my eyes. They perished in lingering torments —screaming with terror—racked with pain. I saw their agonies— heard their cries—they called on my name. Tied hand and foot, what could I do? Oh Heaven, can I ever forget it!"

The man of sorrows paused in his tragical narrative, overcome by the tender and terrible recollections that it called forth. He looked wildly around. Tears came to his relief—that hard, ferocious misanthrope, the fountains of whose tenderness seemed to have been long since broken and dried up, melted at the recital of his own griefs. Nature had resumed her sway over him. The pause was but brief; when, brushing the tears from his rough visage, he continued:

"They carried me off a prisoner. I was badly wounded, and so heart-broken, that for three days I was helpless as a child. Then a desire of revenge grew up in my heart, and I got strong. I gnawed the strings they had bound me with, and escaped from them in the night. I thought that God had spared me to be a scourge to the savage. The war with the Indians broke out soon afterwards, and I joined every expedition—I was foremost in every fight; but I could not quench my thirst for the blood of the miscreants. I swore never to forgive them, and when peace came, I continued to make war. I have made it a rule to kill every red-skin that came in my way; my revenge is not yet satisfied, and so long as I have strength to whet my knife on a stone, or ram a ball into my rifle, I shall continue to slay the savage!

"As for this fellow," he continued, "I would not have troubled him, any where else, if I had seen him in your company. I would not harm nor trouble any christian man, especially a stranger. But when he came here, setting his cursed feet on *this soil*— stepping over the ruins of my homestead, and the ashes of my family—when he intruded upon me as I sat here alone, thinking over the fate of my poor wife and children, it was not my nature to spare him—I couldn't do it.

"Let us part friends, young man, I have done you no harm; if I have hurt your feelings, I ask your pardon. Pursue your own way, and leave me to mine. If you have a grey-headed mother that prays for you, a wife and children that love you—they will welcome you, and you will be happy. I am alone;—there is none to mourn with me, no one to rejoice at my coming. When all that you cherish is torn from you in one moment, by hellish ruffians, condemn me if you can: but not till then.—That path will lead you to a house."

↗ *JOAQUIN MILLER*

Blood on the Snow

Joaquin Miller, pseudonym of Cincinnatus Heine Miller (1839?–1913), spent much of his life in the American West—in frontier Oregon, in the gold-mining camps of California, and with the Indians in the Sierras. "No one seemed to understand," he wrote, "why a man should seek to live in the heart of the Sierras for any other purpose than that of plunder." He was intensely interested in what he called the "sublime scenery" and in the "poetry and pathos of a voiceless race." His *Songs of the Sierras* (1871) brought him fame as a frontier poet. The prose selection reprinted here is from *My Own Story* (1890)—the story of his life among the Indians.

There was a tribe of Indians camped down on the rapid, rocky Klamat River—a sullen, ugly set were they, too: at least

From *My Own Story* (Chicago: Belford-Clark Co., 1890), chap. 9, pp. 85–101.

so said The Forks. Never social, hardly seeming to notice the whites, who were now thick about them, below them, above them, on the river all around them. Sometimes we would meet one on the narrow trail; he would gather his skins about him, hide his bow and arrows under their folds, and, without seeming to see any one, would move past us still as a shadow. I do not remember that I ever saw one of these Indians laugh, not even to smile. A hard-featured, half-starved set of savages, of whom the wise men of the camp prophesied no good.

The snow, unusually deep this winter, had driven them all down from the mountains, and they were compelled to camp on the river.

The game, too, had been driven down along with the Indians, but it was of but little use to them. Their bows and arrows did poor competition with the rifles of the whites in the killing of the game. The whites had fairly filled the cabins with deer and elk in their season, got the lion's share, and left the Indians almost destitute.

Another thing that made it rather more hard on the Indians than anything else, was the utter failure of the annual run of salmon the summer before, on account of the muddy water. The Klamat, which had poured from the mountain lakes to the sea as clear as glass, was now made muddy and turbid from the miners washing for gold on its banks and tributaries. The trout turned on their sides and died; the salmon from the sea came in but rarely on account of this; and what few did come were pretty safe from the spears of the Indians, because of the colored water; so that the supply, which was more than all others their bread and their meat, was entirely cut off. . . .

What made matters worse, there was a set of men, low men, of the lowest type, who would hang around those lodges at night, give the Indians whisky of the vilest sort, debauch their women, and cheat the men out of their skins and bows and arrows.

Perhaps there was a grim sort of philosophy in the red man so disposing of his bows and arrows now that the game was gone and they were of no further use. Sold them for bread for his starving babes, maybe. How many tragedies are hidden here?

How many tales of devotion, self-denial, and sacrifice, as true as the white man ever lived, as pure, and brave, and beautiful as ever gave tongue to eloquence or pen to song, sleep here with the dust of these sad and silent people on the bank of the stormy river!

In this condition of things, about mid-winter, when the snow was deep and crusted stiff, and all nature seemed dead and buried in a ruffled shroud, there was a murder. The Indians had broken out! The prophesied massacre had begun!

Killed by the Indians! It swept like a telegram through the camp. Confused and incoherent, it is true, but it gathered force and form as the tale flew on from tongue to tongue, until it assumed a frightful shape.

A man had been killed by the Indians down at the rancheria. Not much of a man, it is true.

Killed, too, down in the Indian camp when he should have been in bed, or at home, or at least in company with his kind.

All this made the miners hesitate a bit as they hurriedly gathered in at The Forks, with their long Kentucky rifles, their pistols capped and primed, and bowie-knives in their belts.

But as the gathering storm that was to sweep the Indians from the earth took shape and form, these honest men stood out in little knots, leaning on their rifles in the streets, and gravely questioned whether, all things considered, the death of the "Chicken," for that was the dead man's name, was sufficient cause for interference.

To their eternal credit these men mainly decided that it was not, and two by two they turned away, went back to their cabins, hung their rifles up on the rack, and turned their thoughts to their own affairs.

But the hangers-on about the town were terribly enraged. "A man has been killed!" they proclaimed aloud. "A man has been murdered by the savages!! We shall all be massacred! butchered! burnt!!"

In one of the saloons where men were wont to meet at night, have stag-dances, and drink lightening,[1] a short, important man,

---

[1] Whisky of inferior quality. [Ed. Note]

with the print of a glass-tumbler cut above his eye, arose and made a speech.

"Fellow-miners [he had never touched a pick in his life], I am ready to die for me country! [He was an Irishman sent out to Sydney at the Crown's expense.] What have I to live for? [Nothing whatever, as far as any one could tell.] Fellow-miners, a man has been kilt by the treacherous savages—kilt in cold blood! Fellow-miners, let us advance upon the inemy. Let us— let us—fellow-miners, let us take a drink and advance upon the inemy."

"Range around me. Rally to the bar and take a drink, every man of you, at me own ixpense."

The barkeeper, who was also proprietor of the place, a man not much above the type of the speaker, ventured a mild remonstrance at this wholesale generosity; but the pistol, flourished in a very suggestive way, settled the matter, and, with something of a groan, he set his decanters to the crowd, and became a bankrupt.

This was the beginning; they passed from saloon to saloon, or, rather, from door to door; the short, stout Irishman making speeches, and the mob gathering force and arms as it went, and then, wild with drink and excitement, moved down upon the Indians, some miles away on the bank of the river.

"Come," said the Prince[2] to me, as they passed out of town, "let us see this through. Here will be blood. We will see from the hill overlooking the camp. I hope the Indians are armed— hope to God they are 'heeled,'[3] and that they will receive the wretches warmly as they deserve."

Maybe his own wretchedness had something to do with his wrath; but I think not. I should rather say that, had he been in strength and spirits, and had his pistols, which had long since been disposed of for bread, he had met this mob face to face, and sent it back to town.

We followed not far behind the crowd of fifty or sixty men armed with pistols, rifles, knives, and hatchets.

---

[2] The author's companion, a "prince of a fellow." [Ed. Note]
[3] Armed. [Ed. Note]

The trail led to a little point overlooking the bar on which the Indian huts were huddled.

The river made a bend about there. It ground and boiled in a crescent blocked with running ice and snow. The Indians were out in the extreme curve of a horse-shoe made by the river, and we advanced from without. They were in a net. They had only a choice of deaths; death by drowning, or death at the hands of their hereditary foe.

It was nearly night; cold and sharp the wind blew up the river, and the snow flew around like feathers. Not an Indian to be seen. The thin, blue smoke came slowly up, as if afraid to leave the wigwams, and the traditional, everwatchful and wakeful Indian dog was not to be seen or heard. The men hurried down upon the camp, spreading out upon the horse-shoe as they advanced in a run.

"Stop here," said the Prince; and we stood from the wind behind a boulder that stood, tall as a cabin, upon the bar. The crowd advanced to within half a pistol shot, and gave a shout as they drew and leveled their arms. Old squaws came out— bang! bang! bang! shot after shot, and they were pierced and fell, or turned to run.

The whites, yelling, howling, screaming, were now among the lodges, shooting down at arm's length man, woman, or child. Some attempted the river, I should say, for I afterward saw streams of blood upon the ice, but not one escaped; nor was a hand raised in defense. It was all done in a little time. Instantly, as the shots and shouts began, we two advanced, we rushed into the camp, and, when we reached the spot, only now and then a shot was heard within a lodge, dispatching a wounded man or woman.

The few surviving children—for nearly all had been starved to death—had taken refuge under skins and under lodges overthrown, hidden away as little kittens will hide just old enough to spit and hiss, and hide when they first see the face of man. These were now dragged forth and shot. Not all these men who made this mob, bad as they were, did this—only a few; but enough to leave, as far as they could, no living thing.

The babies did not scream. Not a wail, not a sound. The

murdered men and women, in the few minutes that the breath took leave, did not even groan.

As we came up a man named "Shon"—at least, that was all the name I knew for him—held up a baby by the leg, a naked, bony little thing, which he had dragged from under a lodge—held it up with one hand, and with the other blew its head to pieces with his pistol.

I must stop here to say that this man Shon soon left camp, and was afterward hung by the Vigilance Committee near Lewiston, Idaho Territory; that he whined for his life like a puppy, and he died like a coward as he was. I chronicle this fact with a feeling of delight. . . .

This man threw down the body of the child among the dead, and rushed across to where a pair of ruffians had dragged up another, a little girl, naked, bony, thin as a shadow, starved into a ghost. He caught her by the hair with a howl of delight, placed the pistol to her head, and turned around to point the muzzle out of range of his companions who stood around on the other side.

The child did not cry—she did not even flinch. Perhaps she did not know what it meant; but I should rather believe she had seen so much of death there, so much misery, the steady, silent work of the monster famine through the village day after day that she did not care. I saw her face; it did not even wince. Her lips were thin and fixed, and firm as iron.

The villain, having turned her around, now lifted his arm, cocked the pistol, and—

"Stop that! Stop that, or die! You damned assassin, let go that child, or I will pitch you neck and crop into the Klamat."

The Prince had him by the throat with one hand, and with the other he wrested the pistol from his grasp and threw it into the river. The Prince had not even so much as a knife. The man did not know this, nor did the Prince care, or he had not thrown away the weapon he wrung from his hand. The Prince pushed the child behind him, and advanced toward the short, fat Sydney convict, who had turned, pistol in hand, in his direction.

"Keep your distance, or I will send you to hell across lots in a second."

The man turned away cowed and baffled. He had looked in the Prince's face, and seen his master.

As for myself, I was not only helpless, but, as was always the case on similar occasions, stupid, awkward, speechless. I went up to the little girl, however, got a robe out of one of the lodges —for they had not yet set fire to the village—and put it around her naked little body. After that, as I moved about among the dead, or stepped aside to the river to see the streams of blood on the snow and ice, she followed close as a shadow behind me, but said nothing.

Suddenly there was a sharp yell, a volley of oaths, exclamations, a scuffle, and blows.

"Scalp him! Scalp him! the little savage! Scalp him and throw him in the river!"

From out of the piles of dead somewhere, no one could tell exactly where or when, an apparition had sprung up—a naked little Indian boy, that might have been all the way from twelve to twenty, armed with a knotted war-club, and had fallen upon his foes like a fury.

The poor little hero, starved into a shadow, stood little show there, though he had been a very Hercules in courage. He was felled almost instantly by kicks and blows; and the very number of his enemies saved his life, for they could neither shoot nor stab him with safety, as they crowded and crushed around him.

How or why he was finally spared, was always a marvel. Quite likely the example of the Prince had moved some of the men to more humanity.

When the crowd that had formed a knot about him had broken up, and I first got sight of him, he was sitting on a stone with his hands between his naked legs, and blood dripping from his long hair, which fell down in strings over his forehead. He had been stunned by a grazing shot, no doubt, and had fallen among the first. He came up to his work, though, like a man, when his senses returned, and, without counting the chances, lifted his two hands to do with all his might the thing he had been taught.

Valor, such valor as that, is not a cheap or common thing. It is rare enough to be respected even by the worst of men. It is only the coward who affects to despise such courage.

The boy sat there on the stone as the village burned, the smoke from burning skins, the wild-rye straw, willow-baskets and Indian robes, ascended, and a smell of burning bodies went up to the Indians' God and the God of us all, and no one said nay, and no one approached him; the men looked at him from under their slouched hats as they moved around, but said nothing.

I pitied him. God knows I pitied him. I was a boy myself, alone, helpless, in an army of strong and unsympathetic men. I would have gone up and put my arms about the wild and splendid little savage, bloody and desperate as he was, so lonely now, so intimate with death, so pitiful! if I had dared, dared the reproach of men-brutes.

There was a sort of nobility about him; his recklessness, his desire to die, lifting his little arms against an army of strong and reckless men, his proud and defiant courage, that made me feel at once that he was above me, stronger, somehow better, than I. Still, he was a boy, and I was a boy—the only boys in the camp, and my heart went out, strong and true, toward him.

The work of destruction was now too complete. There was not found another living thing—nothing but two or three Indians that had been shot and shot, and yet seemed determined never to die, that lay in the bloody snow down toward the rim of the river.

Naked nearly, they were, and only skeletons, with the longest and blackest hair tangled and tossed, and blown in strips and strings, or in clouds out on the white and the blood-red snow, or down their tawny backs, or over their bony breasts, about their dusky forms, fierce and unconquered, with the bloodless lips set close, and blue, and cold, and firm, like steel.

The dead lay around us, piled up in places, limbs twisted with limbs in the wrestle with death; a mother embracing her boy here; an arm thrown around a neck there; as if these wild people could love as well as die.

In the village, some of the white men claimed to have found something that had been stolen. I have no idea there is any truth in it. I wish there was; then there might be some shadow of excuse for all the murders that made up this cruel tragedy, all of which is, I believe, literally true; truer than nine-tenths of the history and official reports written, wherein these people are mentioned; and I stand ready to give names, dates, and detail to all whom it may concern.

Let me not here be misunderstood. An Indian is no better than a white man. If he sins let him suffer. But I do protest against this custom of making up a case—this custom of deciding the case against him in favor of the white man, forever, on the evidence of the white man only; even though that custom be, in the language of the law, so old "that the memory of man runneth not to the contrary."

The white man and red man are much alike, with one great difference, which you must and will set down to the advantage of the latter.

The Indian has no desire for fortune; he has no wish in his wild state to accumulate wealth; and it is in his wild state that he must be judged, for it is in this condition that he is said to sin. If "money is the root of all evil," as Solomon hath it, then the Indian has not that evil, or that root of evil, or any desire for it.

It is the white man's monopoly. If an Indian love you, trusts you, or believes in you at all, he will serve you, guide you through the country, follow you to battle, fight for you, he and all his sons and kindred, and never think of the pay or profit. He would despise it if offered, beyond some presents, some tokens of remembrance, decorations, or simplest articles of use.

Again, I do vehemently protest against taking the testimony of border Indians or any Indians with whom the white man comes in constant contact, and to whom he has taught the use of money and the art of lying.

And most particularly I do protest against taking these Indians —renegades—who affiliate, mix and strike hands with the whites, as representative Indians. Better take our own "camp followers" as respectable and representative soldiers.

When you reflect that for centuries the Indians in almost every lodge on the continent, at almost every council, have talked of the whites and their aggressions, and of these things chiefly, and always with that bitterness which characterizes people who look at and see only one side of the case, then you may come to understand, a little, their eternal hatred of their hereditary enemy—how deeply seated this is, how it has become a part of their nature, and, above all, how low, fallen, and how unlike a true Indian one must be who leaves his retreating tribe and lingers in a drunken and debauched fellowship with the whites, losing all his virtues, and taking on all the vices of his enemy.

The true Indian retires before the white man's face to the forest and to the mountain tops. It is very true he leaves a surf, a sort of kelp and driftwood, and trash, the scum, the idlers, and the cowards and prostitutes of his tribe, as the sea leaves weeds and drift and kelp. But the true Indian is to be found only in his fastnesses or on the heights, gun in hand.

✎ CHIEF STANDING BEAR

What the Indian Means
to America

Chief Standing Bear (1829?–1908) of the Ogalala tribe of the Sioux Nation, following the forced removal of his people, the Lakotas, from Nebraska to Indian Territory in Kansas (1877), protested the wrongs dealt his people by the government agency, and he toured the country soliciting sympathy from the whites.

His son Luther Standing Bear (1863–1939) be-

From Land of the Spotted Eagle (Boston: Houghton Mifflin Company, 1933), chap. 9.

came hereditary chief of the tribe in 1905. At the
request of his white friends, the younger Standing
Bear wrote a number of books which detail the history of the Lakotas and which contrast the character
of the Indians with that of the whites. The following chapter from *Land of the Spotted Eagle* (Boston,
1933) argues that the Indian problem was created by
the white man. For an extensive bibliography of
readings on American Indians see Katharine C.
Turner, *Red Men Calling on the Great White
Father* (Norman, Oklahoma, 1951).

The feathered and blanketed figure of the American
Indian has come to symbolize the American continent. He is the
man who through centuries has been moulded and sculped by
the same hand that shaped its mountains, forests, and plains, and
marked the course of its rivers.

The American Indian is of the soil, whether it be the region of
forests, plains, pueblos, or mesas. He fits into the landscape, for
the hand that fashioned the continent also fashioned the man
for his surroundings. He once grew as naturally as the wild sun-
flowers; he belongs just as the buffalo belonged.

With a physique that fitted, the man developed fitting skills—
crafts which today are called American. And the body had a soul,
also formed and moulded by the same master hand of harmony.
Out of the Indian approach to existence there came a great
freedom—an intense and absorbing love for nature; a respect for
life; enriching faith in a Supreme Power; and principles of truth,
honesty, generosity, equity, and brotherhood as a guide to mun-
dane relations.

Becoming possessed of a fitting philosophy and art, it was by
them that native man perpetuated his identity; stamped it into
the history and soul of this country—made land and man one.

By living—struggling, losing, meditating, imbibing, aspiring,
achieving—he wrote himself into inerasable evidence—an evidence that can be and often has been ignored, but never totally
destroyed. Living—and all the intangible forces that constitute
that phenomenon—are brought into being by Spirit, that which
no man can alter. Only the hand of the Supreme Power can trans-

form man; only Wakan Tanka can transform the Indian. But of such deep and infinite graces finite man has little comprehension. He has, therefore, no weapons with which to slay the unassailable. He can only foolishly trample.

The white man does not understand the Indian for the reason that he does not understand America. He is too far removed from its formative processes. The roots of the tree of his life have not yet grasped the rock and soil. The white man is still troubled with primitive fears; he still has in his consciousness the perils of this frontier continent, some of its fastnesses not yet having yielded to his questing footsteps and inquiring eyes. He shudders still with the memory of the loss of his forefathers upon its scorching deserts and forbidding mountain-tops. The man from Europe is still a foreigner and an alien. And he still hates the man who questioned his path across the continent.

But in the Indian the spirit of the land is still vested; it will be until other men are able to divine and meet its rhythm. Men must be born and reborn to belong. Their bodies must be formed of the dust of their forefathers' bones.

The attempted transformation of the Indian by the white man and the chaos that has resulted are but the fruits of the white man's disobedience of a fundamental and spiritual law. The pressure that has been brought to bear upon the native people, since the cessation of armed conflict, in the attempt to force conformity of custom and habit has caused a reaction more destructive than war, and the injury has not only affected the Indian, but has extended to the white population as well. Tyranny, stupidity, and lack of vision have brought about the situation now alluded to as the 'Indian Problem.'

There is, I insist, no Indian problem as created by the Indian himself. Every problem that exists today in regard to the native population is due to the white man's cast of mind, which is unable, at least reluctant, to seek understanding and achieve adjustment in a new and a significant environment into which it has so recently come.

The white man excused his presence here by saying that he had been guided by the will of his God; and in so saying absolved himself of all responsibility for his appearance in a land occupied by other men.

Then, too, his law was a written law; his divine decalogue reposed in a book. And what better proof that his advent into this country and his subsequent acts were the result of divine will! He brought the Word! There ensued a blind worship of written history, of books, of the written word, that has denuded the spoken word of its power and sacredness. The written word became established as a criterion of the superior man—a symbol of emotional fineness. The man who could write his name on a piece of paper, whether or not he possessed the spiritual fineness to honor those words in speech, was by some miraculous formula a more highly developed and sensitized person than the one who had never had a pen in hand, but whose spoken word was inviolable and whose sense of honor and truth was paramount. With false reasoning was the quality of human character measured by man's ability to make with an implement a mark upon paper. But granting this mode of reasoning be correct and just, then where are to be placed the thousands of illiterate whites who are unable to read and write? Are they, too, 'savages'? Is not humanness a matter of heart and mind, and is it not evident in the form of relationship with men? Is not kindness more powerful than arrogance; and truth more powerful than the sword?

True, the white man brought great change. But the varied fruits of his civilization, though highly colored and inviting, are sickening and deadening. And if it be the part of civilization to maim, rob, and thwart, then what is progress?

I am going to venture that the man who sat on the ground in his tipi meditating on life and its meaning, accepting the kinship of all creatures, and acknowledging unity with the universe of things was infusing into his being the true essence of civilization. And when native man left off this form of development, his humanization was retarded in growth.

Another most powerful agent that gave native man promise of developing into a true human was the responsibility accepted by parenthood. Mating among Lakotas was motivated, of course, by the same laws of attraction that motivate all beings; however, considerable thought was given by parents of both boy and girl to the choosing of mates. And a still greater advantage accrued to the race by the law of self-mastery which the young couple voluntarily placed upon themselves as soon as they discovered they were to become parents. Immediately, and for some time after, the sole thought of the parents was in preparing the child for life. And true civilization lies in the dominance of self and not in the dominance of other men.

How far this idea would have gone in carrying my people upward and toward a better plane of existence, or how much of an influence it was in the development of their spiritual being, it is not possible to say. But it had its promises. And it cannot be gainsaid that the man who is rising to a higher estate is the man who is putting into his being the essence of humanism. It is self-effort that develops, and by this token the greatest factor today in dehumanizing races is the manner in which the machine is used—the product of one man's brain doing the work for another. The hand is the tool that has built man's mind; it, too, can refine it.

The Savage

After subjugation, after dispossession, there was cast the last abuse upon the people who so entirely resented their wrongs and punishments, and that was the stamping and the labeling of them as savages. To make this label stick has been the task of the white race and the greatest salve that it has been able to apply to its sore and troubled conscience now hardened through the habitual practice of injustice.

But all the years of calling the Indian a savage has never made him one; all the denial of his virtues has never taken them from him; and the very resistance he has made to save the things inalienably his has been his saving strength—that which will stand him in need when justice does make its belated appearance and he undertakes rehabilitation.

All sorts of feeble excuses are heard for the continued subjection of the Indian. One of the most common is that he is not yet ready to accept the society of the white man—that he is not yet ready to mingle as a social entity.

This, I maintain, is beside the question. The matter is not one of making-over the external Indian into the likeness of the white race—a process detrimental to both races. Who can say that the white man's way is better for the Indian? Where resides the human judgment with the competence to weigh and value Indian ideals and spiritual concepts; or substitute for them other values?

Then, has the white man's social order been so harmonious and ideal as to merit the respect of the Indian, and for that matter the thinking class of the white race? Is it wise to urge upon the Indian a foreign social form? Let none but the Indian answer!

Rather, let the white brother face about and cast his mental eye upon a new angle of vision. Let him look upon the Indian world as a human world; then let him see to it that human rights be accorded to the Indians. And this for the purpose of retaining for his own order of society a measure of humanity. . . .

The Living Spirit of the Indian—His Art

The spiritual health and existence of the Indian was maintained by song, magic, ritual, dance, symbolism, oratory (or council), design, handicraft, and folk-story.

Manifestly, to check or thwart this expression is to bring about spiritual decline. And it is in this condition of decline that the Indian people are today. There is but a feeble effort among the Sioux to keep alive their traditional songs and dances, while among other tribes there is but a half-hearted attempt to offset the influence of the Government school and at the same time recover from the crushing and stifling régime of the Indian Bureau.

One has but to speak of Indian verse to receive uncomprehending and unbelieving glances. Yet the Indian loved verse and into this mode of expression went his deepest feelings. Only a few ardent and advanced students seem interested; nevertheless, they have given in book form enough Indian translations to set forth the character and quality of Indian verse.

Oratory receives a little better understanding on the part of the white public, owing to the fact that oratorical compilations include those of Indian orators.

Hard as it seemingly is for the white man's ear to sense the differences, Indian songs are as varied as the many emotions which inspire them, for no two of them are alike. For instance, the Song of Victory is spirited and the notes high and remindful of an unrestrained hunter or warrior riding exultantly over the prairies. On the other hand, the song of the *Cano unye* is solemn and full of urge, for it is meant to inspire the young men to deeds of valor. Then there are the songs of death and the spiritual songs which are connected with the ceremony of initiation. These are full of the spirit of praise and worship, and so strong are some of these invocations that the very air seems as if surcharged with the presence of the Big Holy.

The Indian loved to worship. From birth to death he revered his surroundings. He considered himself born in the luxurious lap of Mother Earth and no place was to him humble. There was nothing between him and the Big Holy. The contact was immediate and personal, and the blessings of Wakan Tanka flowed over the Indian like rain showered from the sky. Wakan Tanka was not aloof, apart, and ever seeking to quell evil forces. He did not punish the animals and the birds, and likewise He did not punish man. He was not a punishing God. For there was never a question as to the supremacy of an evil power over and above the power of Good. There was but one ruling power, and that was Good.

Of course, none but an adoring one could dance for days with his face to the sacred sun, and that time is all but done. We cannot have back the days of the buffalo and beaver; we cannot win back our clean blood-stream and superb health, and we can never again expect that beautiful *rapport* we once had with Nature. The springs and lakes have dried and the mountains are bare of forests. The plow has changed the face of the world. Wi-wila is dead! No more may we heal our sick and comfort our dying with a strength founded on faith, for even the animals now fear us, and fear supplants faith.

And the Indian wants to dance! It is his way of expressing devotion, of communing with unseen power, and in keeping his tribal identity. When the Lakota heart was filled with high emotion, he danced. When he felt the benediction of the warming rays of the sun, he danced. When his blood ran hot with success of the hunt or chase, he danced. When his heart was filled with pity for the orphan, the lonely father, or bereaved mother, he danced. All the joys and exaltations of life, all his gratefulness and thankfulness, all his acknowledgments of the mysterious power that guided life, and all his aspirations for a better life, culminated in one great dance—the Sun Dance.

Today we see our young people dancing together the silly jazz —dances that add nothing to the beauty and fineness of our lives and certainly nothing to our history, while the dances that record the life annals of a people die. It is the American Indian who contributes to this country its true folk-dancing, growing, as we did, out of the soil. The dance is far older than his legends, songs, or philosophy.

Did dancing mean much to the white people they would better understand ours. Yet at the same time there is no attraction that brings people from such distances as a certain tribal dance, for the reason that the white mind senses its mystery, for even the white man's inmost feelings are unconsciously stirred by the beat of the tomtom. They are heart-beats, and once all men danced to its rhythm.

When the Indian has forgotten the music of his forefathers, when the sound of the tomtom is no more, when noisy jazz has drowned the melody of the flute, he will be a dead Indian. When the memory of his heroes are no longer told in story, and he forsakes the beautiful white buckskin for factory shoddy, he will be dead. When from him has been taken all that is his, all that he has visioned in nature, all that has come to him from infinite sources, he then, truly, will be a dead Indian. His spirit will be gone, and though he walk crowded streets, he will, in truth, be—dead!

But all this must not perish; it must live, to the end that America shall be educated no longer to regard native production of whatever tribe—folk-story, basketry, pottery, dance, song, poetry—as curios, and native artists as curiosities. For who but the man indigenous to the soil could produce its song, story, and folk-tale; who but the man who loved the dust beneath his feet could shape it and put it into undying, ceramic form; who but he who loved the reeds that grew beside still waters, and the damp roots of shrub and tree, could save it from seasonal death, and with almost superhuman patience weave it into enduring objects of beauty— into timeless art!

Regarding the 'civilization' that has been thrust upon me since the days of reservation, it has not added one whit to my sense of justice; to my reverence for the rights of life; to my love for truth, honesty, and generosity; nor to my faith in Wakan Tanka—God of the Lakotas. For after all the great religions have been preached and expounded, or have been revealed by brilliant scholars, or have been written in books and embellished in fine language with finer covers, man—all man—is still confronted with the Great Mystery.

So if today I had a young mind to direct, to start on the journey of life, and I was faced with the duty of choosing between the natural way of my forefathers and that of the white man's present way of civilization, I would, for its welfare, unhesitatingly set that child's feet in the path of my forefathers. I would raise him to be an Indian!

part 6

MANIFEST DESTINY

The Great Valley

William Davis Gallagher (1808–1894) was editor of
several Western magazines and did much to encourage literary effort in the Ohio valley. For ten
years he wrote for the Cincinnati *Gazette* and became noted for his defense of Henry Clay and for his
espousal of Whig politics. Most important of Gallagher's literary ventures was his magazine *The Hes-
perian* which was "jealously Western" in its devotion
to "freedom, education, manhood, and fair play."

The following text is from a speech Gallagher
made in Cincinnati on April 8, 1850. It details some
pertinent facts regarding the westward movement of
civilization.

On the North-American Continent, scooped out by the
hand of Omnipotence with wonderful adaptation to the wants of
man, and the purposes of his existence, lies the most stupendous
and favored Inland Valley upon which the sun shines. Having for
its eastern edge the Allegheny and the Cumberland Mountains,
and for its western the Rocky Mountains and the Black Hills, for
its northern rim the summitlands between Lake Winnipeg and the
headwaters of the Mississippi River, and for its southern the
Guadalupe Mountains and the Gulf of Mexico, it extends in one
direction over twenty-four parallels of longitude, and in the other
embraces eighteen degrees of latitude. Within it are all the varieties
of temperate climate, and all the geological and topographical
features that are essential to fit it for the residence of man. It

From a speech delivered in Cincinnati, Ohio, April 8, 1850. Editor's title.

produces in perfection all the fruits and vegetables that are most valued by civilized communities for wholesome and nutritive properties, and all the grains that are so associated with the history of mankind, as to have received the name of 'the staff of life.' Its rivers are the most wonderful known to Christendom, and its lakes are so large, and commercially so important, as to have been designated 'inland seas.' Its mineral wealth is beyond computation; the richness of its soil is inexhaustible; and its general adaptation to the purposes of agriculture, commerce, and manufactures, is unsurpassed, perhaps unequaled, by that of any other part of the earth.

Geographically, it is difficult to conceive of anything better than the position of this great valley, whose plains stretch west from the base of the Allegheny Mountains to the Mississippi River, with an almost uniform pitch in that direction, and east from the base of the Rocky Mountains to the same water, with an almost uniform pitch in this direction, the two natural divisions meeting in that great trough, and finding on its edges their lowest common level. Into the immense channel on this level, pour, generally in an east and southeast direction, the waters from the hither slopes of the Rocky Mountains, and the drainage from the western half of the great valley: into it also pour, generally in a west and southwest direction, the waters from the hither slopes of the Alleghenies, and the drainage of the eastern half of the valley: showing that not only have the two natural divisions of this Great Basin Plain an eastern and a western declivity, but that both divisions have also a common pitch to the south, which at the same time carries their surplus waters into the Gulf of Mexico, exposes their fertile bosoms to the warm and generating beams of the sun, and secures to them an unfailing prevalence of gentle and salubrious winds.

The western of these two natural divisions of the great valley under view, is for the most part a desert land, and much of it must for a long course of years remain so. Some of it, also, is totally unfitted for the abode of man, and will forever continue an uninhabited waste. But the uniformly cultivable character of the eastern division, is one of the most remarkable features of this region. This division is watered as is no other known country, and divided into uplands and lowlands, hillranges and intervening valleys, heavily-timbered tracts and naked prairies, which alternate over much of its surface in a manner the most favorable to the productive interests of life. Upland and lowland, prairie and forest, alike have a soil of great fertility, the capacity of which to produce, under good tillage, is inexhaustible.

In this division of the great valley, natural and artificial causes have induced a subdivision, the more important part of which is called the NORTH-WEST. The region thus known has an almost uniform southwestern exposure, and embraces nearly the whole of the valley north of thirty-six degrees thirty minutes, stretching from the western slopes of the Alleghenies to the Mississippi River, and beyond that great natural line ascending the western division first to the eighteenth parallel of longitude west from Washington, then to the nineteenth parallel, and finally (in Minnesota) to the twentieth. This region, as now organized and civilly divided, embraces the States of Kentucky, Ohio, Indiana, Illinois, Missouri, Michigan, Iowa, and Wisconsin, with Minnesota Territory, the aggregate superficial area of which is 478,349 square miles—to which I add a small strip of Western Virginia and Western Pennsylvania lying immediately upon the Ohio River, and on its two forming tributaries chiefly near their point of confluence, and obtain, in round numbers, the grand territor[i]al extent of 500,000 square miles, or three hundred and twenty millions of acres: a territorial superficies greater than the entire extent of the Original Thirteen States of the Union.

This is the great field of observation, that is now spread before me. And ere surveying it, with a view to my ultimate purpose, it is necessary to go back to some specific period, as a starting point from which to trace its progress. We are now just at the middle of a hundred years. The meridian line of the nineteenth century is over our heads. Fifty years is but a short time in the history of great nations: and fifty years ago the oldest State of this region, was admitted into the Union. To the beginning of this century, then, let us turn, for a moment, and see what there was in the region under view, at that time, to invite the presence of civilized man. At Pittsburgh, at Marietta, at Cincinnati, at the Falls of the Ohio, on the Muskingum, the Kentucky, the Wabash, the Upper Mississippi, and the Illinois Rivers, and scattered about at a few other points, were small villages, composed in part of hardy adventurers, soldiers, and traders, in a small degree of men of education and ambition, who had sought the region that they might grow up with it to wealth and distinction, and to some extent of religious missionaries and their converts from among the aboriginal tribes. There were none of the refinements of life here, and but few of its comforts. The whole population of the State of Kentucky was then 220,955 persons, that of what is now the State of Ohio was 45,365, and that of Indiana 4,875. And this was about all: 271,195 persons, scattered over an area of 500,000 square miles—making an average of one person to a fraction less than two square miles. On the Ohio River were a few barges and keelboats, and now and then one or two of this description of craft would ascend the Upper Mississippi to St. Louis; but the waters of the Illinois, the Wabash, and other streams, and those also of the Lakes, were still swept by the birchen bark of the Indian. Ten years later, Kentucky had a population of 406,511 persons, Ohio of 230,760, Indiana of 24,520, Missouri of 20,845, Illinois of 12,282, and Michigan of 4,762: making an ag[g]regate of 699,680, or one person on the average to about every three quarters of a mile square.

The tide of emigration had now fairly set in this direction. Little communities were pitching their tents and building their cabins on most of the better streams. The settler's ax resounded through the depths of the wilderness in all directions, and the blue smoke curled above the tops of the tall trees, at once advising newcomers of the presence of a habitation, and giving the watchful savage note of a place where he might strike at those who were encroaching on his old heritage. The Indians were now receding fast before the whites—going reluctantly, but every year further and further, their dark forms disappearing in the recesses of the wilderness, as the dusky shadows of a dark and unblest age, recede and disappear before the light of a high, christian civilization. And all this continued—and in another period of ten years, the population of the region had swelled to 1,423,622.

A new agent of civilization and settlement was now introduced. The keel of the steamboat had been plowing the waters of the West for three or four years. This description of navigation was no longer a mere experiment. Speaking relatively to what was then attempted, it had succeeded; and every time the escape of steam or the splash of the paddles woke the echoes of the still solitary shores, a requiem sounded for the departing Indian, and a song of gladness went up for the arrival of his adventurous successor. The genius of Fulton was, in the hands of these adventurers, the Lamp of Alad[d]in: it opened to them freely the doors of the Great West, frightened away their enemies, and displayed to their enraptured gaze, the many and glittering charms of this beautiful land. And still the paddles dashed the waters—and still the piercing shriek of the escapepipe woke the deep echoes—and still the child of the forest receded further and further—and still rolled on the stream of emigration, through the gaps of the Cumberland, over the hights [sic] of the Alleghenies, down into the rich valley through which coursed the calm waters of the Ohio. And another period of ten years passed—the third decade in the half century—and the population was become 2,298,390.

By this time, over nearly the whole broad bosom of the region which I have mapped out, were scattered the habitations of men, and introduced the institutions of christian, civilized life. In the interiors of its different sections, the wigwams of the savage had given place to the cabins of the newcomers, and the farmhouses of the first settlers. On the small streams, which everywhere sent up their glad voices, giving to the deep solitude a tongue that was eloquent, the hand of enterprise had taken the willing waters, and borne them to the clattering wheels of the manufactory, where they labored and yet sported, and, like virtue, were overruled and yet free. On the broad lakes, on the mighty rivers, the arm of Steam—

> That fleshless arm, whose pulses leap
> With floods of living fire,—

was propelling the gigantic hull, freighted with hundreds of human beings, coming from afar to cultivate the land, to fabricate its crude products, to engage in trade and commerce, to 'multiply and replenish the earth.' On the great natural highways, populous cities had taken the place of the primeval groves, and the schoolhouse, the church, the depots of commerce, and the elegant mansion, invited the on-coming multitudes to seek in and around them new and better homes. And the years of the fourth decade were told, and the population had swelled to 4,131,370 souls.

Still went on the work. The seat of a commerce of hundreds of millions per year, was this now populous region. The marts of its trade were filled with the surplus products of its soil, which were borne away in thousands of vessels, to feed the hungry in less-favored lands. Its flocks were feeding on unnumbered hills, and in countless fields its crops sprang up, and ripened, and bowed before the sickle. That subtle Power, which by water had brought its myriads of people to its generous bosom, and borne its rich products away in exchange for what its own soil did not yield, scorned longer to be confined to the rivers and the lakes, and their comparatively slow-moving keels. Springing upon the dry land, and seeking the iron tracks which science and labor had laid on the leveled earth, he clutched the loaded car with his invisible fingers, and bore it from point to point, for hundreds of miles, with an ease and velocity before unknown—

The beatings of his mighty heart

still sounding through the storm or the calm, and giving the only note of his approach, as he rushed through forest and field, over streams and marshes, and around the bases of many hills, with his gigantic burden. Nor was this enough. For commerce it might have been, and for bodily transit from place to place, but not for thought. And next flashed upon human genius the still more subtle essence of the electric spark; and hither came its whispering wires, stretching from hill to hill and from state to state, crossing mountains, leaping ravines, spanning rivers, and bearing to the depths of this far Interior, in the twinkling of an eye, the message spoken a thousand miles away, on the outer rim of the vast Continent. And the human tide has still rolled on and on—and the remoter forests of this region have been pierced and subdued, till the solitudes that, at the period from which this retrospect started, heard only the eternal chime of the Falls of St. Anthony, and the wild voices of the dark Chippeways, are filling with the homes of civilized man, and becoming vocal with prayers and hymns of thanksgiving to God. And the fifth decade has gone by, and seven millions now number the population of this region, which a half century ago, as was shown, contained less than 300,000 souls!

↶ THOMAS HART BENTON

The North American Road
to India

Thomas Hart Benton (1782–1858), ardent advocate
of the doctrine of "Manifest Destiny" and of government support of Western exploration, delivered his
speech on the Oregon question at a time when the
imperialistic urge was strong among Americans, and
when the possibilities for economic exploitation of
the undeveloped areas of the Northwest intrigued the
minds of visionaries. While Benton argued the
superiority of the white race above all others and
urged the building of a transcontinental road in the
interests of commerce, he was not in favor of the
annexation of Texas, of the Mexican War, or of the
settlement of the Oregon dispute at 54° 40′ on the
map. He was strongly in favor, however, of United
States occupation of the Columbia River valley and
of the material progress of the American people. The
first biography of Benton, written by Theodore
Roosevelt, was published in 1887. Since then four
others have appeared, among which is Elbert B.
Smith, *Magnificent Missourian: The Life of Thomas
Hart Benton* (Philadelphia, 1958).

The value of the country—I mean the Columbia River
and its valley—(I must repeat the limitation every time, lest I be
carried up to 54° 40′)—has been questioned on this floor and elsewhere. It has been supposed to be of little value—hardly worth the
possession, much less the acquisition; and treated rather as a
burden to be got rid of, than as a benefit to be preserved. This is a
great error, and one that only prevails on this side of the water: the

From *Speech on the Oregon Question: Delivered in the Senate of the United
States May 22, 25, and 28, 1846* (Washington, D. C.: 1846). Editor's title.

British know better; and if they held the tithe of our title, they would fight the world for what we depreciate. It is not a worthless country, but one of immense value, and that under many respects, and will be occupied by others, to our injury and annoyance, if not by ourselves for our own benefit and protection. Forty years ago it was written by Humboldt, that the banks of the Columbia presented the only situation on the northwest coast of America fit for the residence of a civilized people. Experience has confirmed the truth of this wise remark. All the rest of the coast, from the Straits of Fuca out to New Archangel, (and nothing but a fur trading post there,) remains a vacant waste, abandoned since the quarrel of Nootka Sound, and become the derelict of nations. The Columbia only invites a possessor; and for that possession, sagacious British diplomacy has been weaving its web. It is not a worthless possession; but valuable under many and large aspects; to the consideration of some of which I now proceed.

It is valuable, both as a country to be inhabited, and as a position to be held and defended. I speak of it, first, as a position, commanding the North Pacific ocean, and overlooking the eastern coast of India. The North Pacific is a rich sea, and is already the seat of a great commerce: British, French, American, Russian, and ships of other nations, frequent it. Our whaling ships cover it: our ships of war go there to protect our interests; and, great as that interest now is, it is only the beginning. Futurity will develop an immense, and various, commerce on that sea, of which the far greater part will be American. That commerce, neither in the merchant ships which carry it on, nor in the military marine which protects it, can find a port, to call its own, within twenty thousand miles of the field of its operations. The double length of the two Americas has to be run—a stormy and tempestuous cape to be doubled—to find itself in a port of its own country: while here lies one in the very edge of its field, ours by right, ready for use, and ample for every purpose of refuge and repair, protection and domination. Can we turn our back upon it? and, in turning the back, deliver it up to the British? Insane, and suicidal would be the fatal act!

To say nothing of the daily want of such a port in time of peace, its want, in time of war, becomes ruinous. Commodore Porter has often told me that, with protection from batteries in the mouth of the Columbia, he never would have put himself in a condition to be attacked under the weak, or collusive guns of a neutral port. He has told me that, with such a port for the reception of his prizes, he would not have sunk in the ocean, or hid in islands where it was often found, the three millions of British property captured in his three years' daring and dauntless cruise. Often has he told me, that, with such a port at his hand, he would never have been driven to spill upon the waters, that oil, for want of which, as a member of the British Parliament said, London had burnt darkly—had been in the dark—for a whole year. What happened to Commodore Porter and his prizes—what happened to all our merchant ships, driven from the North Pacific during the war—all this to happen again, and upon a far larger scale, is but half the evil of turning our backs now upon this commanding position; for, to do so, is to deliver it into the hands of a Power that knows the value of positions—the four quarters of the globe, and our own coasts attest that—and has her eye on this one. The very year after the renewal of the delusive convention of 1818—in the year 1819— a master ship-carpenter was despatched from London to Fort Vancouver, to begin there the repair of vessels, and even the construction of small ones; and this work has been going on ever since. She resists our possession now! If we abandon, she will retain! And her wooden walls, bristling with cannon, and issuing from the mouth of the Columbia, will give the law to the North Pacific, permitting our ships to sneak about in time of peace—sinking, seizing, or chasing them away, in time of war. As a position, then, and if nothing but a rock, or desert point, the possession of the Columbia is invaluable to us; and it becomes our duty to maintain it at all hazards.

Agriculturally the value of the country is great; and, to understand it in all its extent, this large country should be contemplated under its different divisions—the threefold natural geographical divisions under which it presents itself: the maritime, the middle, and the mountain districts.

The maritime region—the fertile part of it—is the long valley between the Cascade and the coast ranges of mountains, extending from the head of the Wah-lah-math, near the latitude of 42 degrees, to the Straits of Fuca, near latitude 49. In this valley lies the rich tidewater region of the Columbia, with the Wah-lah-math river on the south, and the Coweliske, and the Olympic district, on the north. It is a valley of near five hundred miles long, north and south, and above one hundred wide;—rich in soil, grass and timber—sufficient of itself to constitute a respectable State, and now the seat of the British commercial and military post of Vancouver, and of their great farming establishment of Nisqually.

The middle district, from the Cascade range to near the base of the Rocky Mountains, is the region called, desert, and which, in the imaginations of many, has given character to the whole country. In some respects it is a desert—barren of wood—sprinkled with sandy plains—melancholy under the sombre aspect of the gloomy artemisia—and desolate from volcanic rocks, through the chasms of which plunge the headlong streams. But this desert has its redeeming points—much water—grass—many oases—mountains capped with snow, to refresh the air, the land, and the eye—blooming valleys—a clear sky, pure air, and a supreme salubrity. It is the home of the horse! found there wild in all the perfection of his first nature—beautiful and fleet—fiery and docile—patient, enduring, and affectionate. General Clark has told me that, of the one hundred and seventy horses which he and Lewis obtained in this district, he had never seen the match in any equal number; and he had seen the finest which the sporting course, or the warlike parade, had exhibited in Virginia.

It is the home of that horse—the horse of Persia—which gallops his eighty miles a day—swimming the rivers as he comes to them—finds his own food at night, the hoof scraping away the snow when it hides the grass—gallops his eighty miles again the next day; and so on through a long and healthy life; carrying his master in the chase, or the fight, circumventing the game, and pursuing the foe, with the intelligence of reason and the fidelity of friendship. General Clark has informed me that it was necessary to keep a scout ahead, to drive away the elk and buffalo, at the sight of which all their horses immediately formed for the chase, the loose ones dashing off to surround and circumvent the game. The old hunters also have told me their marvellous stories about these horses, and that in war and hunting they had more sense than people, and as much courage, and loved it as well. The country that produces such horses, must also produce men, and cattle, and all the inferior animals; and must have many beneficent attributes to redeem it from the stigma of desolation.

The mountain division has its own peculiar features, and many of them as useful as picturesque. At the base of the mountains, a long, broad, and high bench is seen—three hundred miles long, fifty miles wide—the deposit of abraded mountains of snow and verdure through thousands of years. Lewis and Clark thus describe this great bench of land, which they twice crossed in their expedition to and from the Pacific ocean:

"The country along the Rocky Mountains, for several hundred miles in length and about fifty wide, is a high level plain; in all its parts extremely fertile, and in many places covered with a growth of tall, long-leafed pine. This plain is chiefly interrupted near the streams of water, where the hills are steep and lofty; but the soil is good, being unencumbered by much stone, and possesses more timber than the level country. Under shelter of these hills, the bottom lands skirt the margin of the rivers, and though narrow and confined, are still fertile and rarely inundated. Nearly the whole of this widespread tract is covered with a profusion of grass and plants, which are at this time (May) as high as the knee. Among these are a variety of esculent plants and roots, acquired without much difficulty, and yielding not only a nutritious, but a very agreeable food. The air is pure and dry, the climate quite as mild, if not milder, than the same parallels of latitude in the Atlantic States, and must be equally healthy, for all the disorders which we have witnessed may fairly be imputed more to the nature of the diet than to any intemperance of climate. This general observation is of course to be qualified, since in the same tract of country the degrees of the combination of heat and cold obey the influence of situation. Thus the rains of the low grounds, near our camp, are snows in the high plains; and while the sun shines with intense heat in the confined bottoms, the plains enjoy a much colder air, and the vegetation is retarded at least fifteen days, while at the foot of the mountains the snows are still many feet in depth; so that within twenty miles of our camp we observe the rigors of winter cold, the cool air of spring, and the oppressive heat of mid-summer. Even on the plains, however, where the snow has fallen, it seems to do but little injury to the grass and other plants, which, though apparently tender and susceptible, are still blooming, at the height of nearly eighteen inches through the snow. In short, this district affords many advantages to settlers, and if properly cultivated, would yield every object necessary for the subsistence and comfort of civilized man."

Other, and smaller benches of the same character, are frequently seen, inviting the farmer to make his healthy habitation and fertile field upon it.

Entering the gorges of the mountains, and a succession of everything is found which is seen in the alpine regions of Switzerland, glaciers only excepted. Magnificent mountain scenery—lakes —grassy valleys—snow-capped mountains—clear streams and fountains—coves and parks—hot and warm springs—mineral waters of many varieties—salt in the solid and fluid state—salt lakes, and even hot salt springs—wood, coal, and iron. Such are the Rocky Mountains in the long and broad section from the head of the Rio Grande del Norte, of the sunny South, to the head of the Athabasca, of the Frozen ocean. This ample, rich, and elevated mountain region is deemed, by those unacquainted with the Farthest West, to be, and to be forever, the desolate and frozen dominion of the wild beast and the savage. On the contrary, I view it as the future seat of population and power, where man is to appear in all the moral, intellectual, and physical endowments which ennoble the mountain race, and where liberty, independence, and love of virtue, are to make their last stand on earth. . . .

Commercially, the advantages of Oregon will be great—far greater than any equal portion of the Atlantic States. The eastern Asiatics, who will be their chief customer, are more numerous than our customers in western Europe—more profitable to trade with, and less dangerous to quarrel with. Their articles of commerce are richer than those of Europe; they want what the Oregons will have to spare—bread and provisions—and have no systems of policy to prevent them from purchasing these necessaries of life from those who can supply them. The sea which washes their shores is every way a better sea than the Atlantic—richer in its whale and other fisheries—in the fur regions which enclose it to the north—more fortunate in the tranquillity of its character, in its freedom from storms, gulf-streams, and icebergs—in its perfect adaptation to steam navigation—in its intermediate or half-way islands, and its myriad of rich islands on its further side;—in its freedom from maritime Powers on its coasts, except the American, which is to grow up at the mouth of the Columbia. As a people to trade with —as a sea to navigate—the Mongolian race of eastern Asia, and the North Pacific ocean, are far preferable to the Europeans and the Atlantic.

But enough of this. The country is vindicated: error is dispelled. Instead of worthlessness, the region of the Oregon is proved to have all the capabilities of an immense Power. Agricultural capabilities to sustain a great population, and to furnish the elements of commerce and manufactures—a vast and rich commerce and navigation at its hands—a peaceable sea to navigate—gentle and profitable people to trade with them—a climate of supreme and almost miraculous salubrity—a natural frontier of mountain ramparts—a triple barrier of mountains—to give her a military impregnability.

Having cleared away the errors which undervalued the country, and pointed out the advantages peculiar to it, I now come to another advantage, common to all North America, and long since the cherished vision of my young imagination. A Russian Empress said of the Crimea: Here lies the road to Byzantium. I say to my fellow-citizens: Through the valley of the Columbia, lies the North American road to India. . . .

God's Chosen People

The effect of the arrival of the Caucasian, or White race, on the western coast of America, opposite the eastern coast of Asia, remains to be mentioned among the benefits which the settlement of the Columbia will produce, and that a benefit, not local to us, but general and universal to the human race. Since the dispersion of man upon earth, I know of no human event, past or present, which promises a greater, and more beneficent change upon earth than the arrival of the van of the Caucasian race (the Celtic-

Anglo-Saxon division) upon the border of the sea which washes the shore of the eastern Asia. The Mongolian, or Yellow race, is there, four hundred millions in number, spreading almost to Europe; a race once the foremost of the human family in the arts of civilization, but torpid and stationary for thousands of years. It is a race far above the Ethiopian, or Black—above the Malay, or Brown, (if we must admit five races)—and above the American Indian, or Red: it is a race far above all these, but still, far below the White; and, like all the rest, must receive an impression from the superior race whenever they come in contact. It would seem that the White race alone received the divine command, to subdue and replenish the earth! for it is the only race that has obeyed it— the only one that hunts out new and distant lands, and even a New World, to subdue and replenish. Starting from western Asia, taking Europe for their field, and the Sun for their guide, and leaving the Mongolians behind, they arrived, after many ages, on the shores of the Atlantic, which they lit up with the lights of science and religion, and adorned with the useful and the elegant arts. Three and a half centuries ago, this race, in obedience to the great command, arrived in the New World, and found new lands to subdue and replenish. For a long time, it was confined to the border of the new field, (I now mean the Celtic-Anglo-Saxon division;) and even fourscore years ago the philosophic Burke was considered a rash man because he said the English colonists would top the Alleghanies, and descend into the valley of the Mississippi, and occupy without parchment if the Crown refused to make grants of land. What was considered a rash declaration eighty years ago, is old history, in our young country, at this day. Thirty years ago I said the same thing of the Rocky Mountains and the Columbia: it was ridiculed then: it is becoming history to-day. The venerable Mr. Macon has often told me that he remembered a line low down in North Carolina, fixed by a royal governor as a boundary between the whites and the Indians: where is that boundary now? The van of the Caucasian race now top the Rocky Mountains, and spread down to the shores of the Pacific. In a few years a great population will grow up there, luminous with the accumulated lights of European and American civilization. Their presence in such a position cannot be without its influence upon eastern Asia. The sun of civilization must shine across the sea: socially and commercially, the van of the Caucasians, and the rear of the Mongolians, must intermix. They must talk together, and trade together, and marry together. Commerce is a great civilizer—social intercourse as great—and marriage greater. The White and Yellow races can marry together, as well as eat and trade together. Moral and intellectual superiority will do the rest: the White race will take the ascendant, elevating what is susceptible of improvement—wearing out what is not. The Red race has disappeared from the Atlantic coast: the tribes that resisted civilization, met extinction. This is a cause of lamentation with many. For my part, I cannot murmur at what seems to be the effect of divine law. I cannot repine that this Capitol has replaced the wigwam—this Christian people, replaced the savages—white matrons, the red squaws—and that such men as Washington, Franklin, and Jefferson, have taken the place of Powhattan, Opechonecanough, and other red men, howsoever respectable they may have been as savages. Civilization, or extinction, has been the fate of all people who have found themselves in the track of the advancing Whites, and civilization, always the preference of the Whites, has been pressed as an object, while extinction has followed as a consequence of its resistance. The Black and the Red races have often felt their ameliorating influence. The Yellow race, next to themselves in the scale of mental and moral excellence, and in the beauty of form, once their superiors in the useful and elegant arts, and in learning, and still respectable though stationary; this race cannot fail to receive a new impulse from the approach of the Whites, improved so much since so many ages ago they left the western borders of Asia. The apparition of the van of the Caucasian race, rising upon them in the east after having left them on the west, and after having completed the circumnavigation of the globe, must wake up and reanimate the torpid body of old Asia. Our position and policy will commend us to their hospitable reception: political considerations will aid the action of social and commercial influences. Pressed upon by the great Powers of Europe—the same that press upon us—they must in our approach see the advent of friends, not of foes—of benefactors, not of invaders. The moral and intellectual superiority of the White race will do the rest: and thus, the youngest people, and the newest land, will become the reviver and the regenerator of the oldest.

It is in this point of view, and as acting upon the social, political, and religious condition of Asia, and giving a new point of departure to her ancient civilization, that I look upon the settlement of the Columbia river by the van of the Caucasian race as the most momentous human event in the history of man since his dispersion over the face of the earth. . . .

≠ *JOSIAH ROYCE*

Squatter's Rights
and Manifest Destiny

Josiah Royce (1855–1916), professor of philosophy at Harvard University for nearly thirty-five years, spent his boyhood in a mining camp in the Sierras, and his youth in San Francisco during frontier days. He became involved in an attempt to find a solution to the paradox of liberty and authority in American life. Information for his book *California from the Conquest in 1846 to the Second Vigilance Committee in San Francisco* (1886) was obtained from the personal collections of H. H. Bancroft, famous frontier historian; from conversations with General and Mrs. John C. Frèmont; and from the proof sheets of Charles Shinn's *Mining Camps*. The chapter from Royce's book which is reprinted here shows how the doctrine of Manifest Destiny was interpreted by land-hungry immigrants.

From *California from the Conquest in 1846 to the Second Vigilance Committee in San Francisco* (Boston: Houghton Mifflin Company, 1886), chap. 6, pp. 469–480. Author's footnotes omitted. Editor's title.

In the winter of 1849 and in the spring of 1850 our rapacity first became noticeable under the new conditions. As it happened, the city of Sacramento grew up on land near Sutter's Fort, and, of course, within the boundaries of Sutter's own grant of land, which he had received from Governor Alvarado in 1841. In the first months of the town's life, numerous lots of land were sold under this title, and those who acquired the new property profited, of course, very greatly by the rapid growth of the place. But by the winter of 1849 there were enough landless, idle, and disappointed wanderers present in Sacramento to make the existence of land ownership thereabouts appear to these persons as an intolerable burden, placed upon the necks of the poor by rapacious land-speculators. Such reflections are, of course, the well-known expressions of human avarice and disappointment everywhere in the world. Here they assumed, however, a new and dangerous form. One asked, "How comes it that there is any ownership of land in this golden country at all? Is this not a free land? Is it not our land? Is not the public domain free to all American citizens?" The very simple answer was, of course, that this land was not public domain, but Sutter's former land, sold by him, in the free exercise of his rights, to the founders of Sacramento. And this answer was, moreover, especially significant in this particular case. For Sutter's ownership of "New Helvetia" was, by this time, a matter, so to speak, of world-wide notoriety. The young Captain Frémont's "Report," which, in various shapes and editions, had years before become so popular a book, and which the gold-fever made more popular than ever, had distinctly described Sutter as the notorious and indisputable owner of this tract of land in 1844. If occupancy without any rival for a term of years could make the matter clear to a new-comer, Sutter's title to his "establishment" seemed beyond shadow. Moreover, the title-papers of the Alvarado grant were on record. Governor Alvarado's authority to grant eleven leagues to Sutter was indubitable, and none the less clear seemed the wording of the grant, when it gave certain outer boundaries within which the tract granted was to be sought, and then defined the grant so as to include the "establishment at New Helvetia." Surely, one would say, no new-comer could attack Sutter's right, save by means of some purely agrarian contention. A settler might demand that all unused land in California should be free to every settler, and that Mexican land-ownership should be once for all done away with. But unless a man did this, what could he say against Sutter's title to New Helvetia?

The complaining idlers in Sacramento were, however, quite equal to the task of overthrowing this argument. What, after all, was a Mexican title worth beside the rights of an American citizen? This grant of Sutter's might indeed be a test case, but then so much the more must the test determine the worthlessness of all Mexican pretensions. The big Mexican grant was to this new party of agitators, who already delighted to call themsleves "squatters," an obviously un-American institution, a creation of a benighted people. What was the good of the conquest, if it did not make our enlightened American ideas paramount in the country? Unless, then, Congress, by some freak, should restore to these rapacious speculators, the heirs of a justly conquered and dispossessed race, their old benighted legal *status*, they would have no land. Meanwhile, of course, the settlers were to be as well off as the others. So their thoughts ran.

Intelligent men could hold this view only in case they had already deliberately determined that the new-coming population, as such, ought to have the chief legal rights in the country. This view was, after all, a very obvious one. Providence, you see, and manifest destiny were understood in those days to be on our side, and absolutely opposed to the base Mexican. Providence, again, is known to be opposed to every form of oppression; and grabbing eleven leagues of land is a great oppression. And so the worthlessness of Mexican land-titles is evident.

Of course the squatters would have disclaimed very generally so naked a statement as this of their position. But when we read in one squatter's card that "surely Sutter's grant does not entitle to a monopoly of all the lands in California, which were purchased by the treasure of the whole nation, and by no small amount of the best blood that ever coursed or ran through American veins," the same writer's formal assurance that Sutter ought to have his eleven leagues whenever they can be found and duly surveyed cannot blind us to the true spirit of the argument. What has this "best blood" to do with the Sutter grant? The connection in the writer's mind is only too obvious. He means that the "best blood" won for us a right to harass great land-owners. In another of these expressions of squatter opinion I have found the assertion that the land speculators stand on a supposed old Mexican legal right of such as themselves to take up the whole territory of California, in sections of eleven leagues each, by some sort of Mexican preemption. If a squatter persists in understanding the land-owners' position in this way, his contempt for it is as natural as his willful determination to make game of all native Californian claims is obvious.

The squatter party, as it appeared in the winter of 1849 in Sacramento, was encouraged to develop its ideas by reason of the unsettled condition of the country. It was easy for men to feel that in this land, where no very definite government yet existed, where even the new state, before its admission, must seem of doubtfully legal character, every man might do what seemed right to himself and every new party might propose any view, however subversive of good government. A respect for the old California order of things was not yet developed; a new-comer was often hardly conscious that there ever had been an old order. And when one heard about it from the men of the interregnum, one also heard the cruelly false tale, begotten of the era of our conquest, about the injustice, the treachery, and the wickedness of the old government and people. One felt, therefore, well justified in wishing a new and American order of things to replace every relic of Mexican wretchedness. And, just because such conquest as this of California was a new experience in our short national history, one was often wholly unmindful of the simple and obvious principles according to which the conqueror of a country does not, by virtue of his conquest, either dispossess private land-owners, or deprive the inhabitants of any other of their private rights. One was, in fact, so accustomed to our atrocious fashion of conquering, dispossessing, and then exterminating Indian tribes, that one was too much disposed, *a priori*, to think of our conquest of California as exemplifying the same cruel process.

The first scenes of the land agitation at Sacramento in the winter of 1849–50 have been but imperfectly described for us. Bayard Taylor mentions them briefly, and so does a later correspondent of the "New York Tribune." A recent article of my own on the topic has, since its publication [*Overland Monthly*, September, 1885], called out some very interesting contemporary letters which a pioneer, now living in Oakland, Cal., has preserved, and which bring the scenes of the early agitation well before us. I make one extract from them here. They were published in a late number of the "San Francisco Bulletin":—

"I will endeavor," says the writer of the letter, himself a newcomer in Sacramento, who is addressing an Eastern friend, "to give you some idea of life in Sacramento, by relating some events that occurred this evening: It is rather a dark one, and walking along the levee requires some care to avoid falling over the numerous obstructions, but it was a political meeting that I stumbled into as I passed up R Street. That you may understand the state of things, I will explain a little; the question of land-titles and squatter's rights is just now greatly agitating the public mind. In several instances where men have squatted upon land without the precincts of the city, others have pretended to own it and ordered them off, and in one case the city authorities, on a man's refusal to vamose, sent a force and pulled down his shanty.

"Last Saturday evening a meeting of squatters was held outdoors. I was not present, but hear that much opposition was expressed to the measures adopted by the city officers, some of whom were present, and replied in no very courteous terms. The meeting this evening was intended as an opposition to the other, and styled 'Law and Order.' The speaker's stand was on some boxes piled up against the 'Gem,' a bowling, drinking, and gambling saloon. A board nailed against it, about even with the speakers' heads, supported a row of candles, which burned without a flicker, so still was the air. A large and democratic crowd were assembled. A committee was appointed to draw up resolutions, which were read. In the preamble the squatters were spoken of as having acted lawlessly and in contempt of the authorities. The substance of the resolutions was that the city council should be sustained at all events; that a committee should be appointed to proceed to Monterey and obtain a copy of J. A. Sutter's title to the land claimed by him, attested to by the governor of California.

"This land comprises most of the territory on which the city is built. They were read with much interruption, and on the question being put, indignantly rejected.

"At this juncture, another speaker arose, and commenced, but was interrupted with cries of 'Your name?' 'My name is Zabriskie,' he replied. In a respectful manner he avowed his determination to speak his sentiments, and beginning with the hand-bills which had been printed, calling a meeting to sustain 'law and order' in the community, he considered it an insult to the people to suppose that any were otherwise inclined. Then, in regard to the preamble, which spoke contemptuously of 'squatters,' in an eloquent speech he asked who carried the 'Stars and Stripes,' the institutions and laws of our land into the far West, and have now borne them even to the shores of the far-off Pacific? Then arose from the crowd the reply, '*Squatters.*'

"He then moved that this preamble be rejected, and the motion was carried without a dissenting voice. So he went on with each resolution, speechifying and moving that some be rejected, some adopted, and some amended, most of his motions being carried unanimously, making altogether a different set of resolutions than the projectors had calculated upon. He went strongly for sustaining the authorities in carrying out such just laws as they should enact. On the resolution which so read, he experienced much opposition, the sovereign people being extremely jealous that laws should be made, which, however just in the eyes of their makers, would be otherwise in *their* view. He contended that a man might squat where he pleased, and leave for nobody who could not show a better title than himself; that when a judiciary was appointed over the State was the time to decide the validity of titles, until which time, society would be benefited, the squatter would be benefited, the land, and consequently, the owner, whoever he was, would be benefited by its being brought under cultivation."

After the river flood of January, 1850, had passed over the town of Sacramento, the quarrel was temporarily suspended, especially by the prosperous opening of the spring of 1850, which sent many of the malcontents early to the mines. But persistent spring floods forced many of these to return afresh to the now once more prosperous. The discontent broke out again, and the title-papers of Sutter's grant, when once found and published, were soon made the subject of very bitter and unfair quibbles and quasi-legal objections. By the beginning of summer the squatter movement had become formidable in Sacramento and in the adjacent country. Its followers had organized an association, had begun a regular system of squatting on all vacant lots in and near the town, and were already planning every even remotely feasible sort of resistance to the real owners who held under the Sutter title. As Congress had still done nothing to settle titles in California, and as the State had not yet been admitted, the squatters had the effrontery to pretend in their public utterances that there was no legal support actually in existence for the California grants. They declared that even the legislature, which had already once met, had had no business to pass laws bearing on the subject of land. Still less, they said, had the so-called city of Sacramento, in its corporate capacity, any right to interfere with squatters. And as for the processes of state courts, if worst came to worst, these must be defied. Breathing out such threatenings, the squatters met frequently during the summer, in a more or less public fashion. They excited the attention of many in other parts of the State, and the alarm of all wiser men that appreciated their purposes. They were ably led. Among others, Dr. Charles Robinson, of Fitchburg, Massachusetts, later so prominent as governor of Kansas, was especially noteworthy as a squatter leader. His conscientious motives in supporting the squatter doctrine, his sagacity in conducting the movement, and his personal courage in forcing it to an issue, are all obvious. Obvious also is his wicked and dangerous use in this connection of the then current abstractions about the absolute rights of Man and the higher will of God, together with his diabolical activity in resisting the true will of God, which was of course at that time and place simply the good order of California. Every moral force, every force, namely, that worked for the real future prosperity of the new commonwealth, was *ipso facto* against these lawless squatters. The "land-speculators," whom they directly attacked, were indeed as greedy for gold as anybody in California, and were as such no more worthy of esteem than their even Christians. But these speculators chanced, in just that case, to represent both the old California order of things, which we were bound in sacred honor to respect, and the majesty of the new-born State as well, to which every citizen owed the most devout allegiance, so long as he should dwell within its borders. To these two great obligations the squatters were traitors, and their movement was unfortunately the father of much more treason, which showed the same turpitude, if not the same frankness.

But for the time, they were unable to do more than to bring about a riot, and a consequent reaction of popular feeling against themselves; a reaction which ended the possibility of any general predatory conspiracy throughout the State against the old land-titles, and which therefore introduced the squatter movement to the second stage of its sinful life, so that it became thenceforth no longer an open public enemy, but a treacherous corrupter of legislation, and a persistent pettifogger in the courts of justice.

⚓ WILLIAM GILPIN

The Pacific Railway

William Gilpin (1813–1894), first territorial Governor of Colorado, saw the West, as Stegner noted, "through a blaze of mystical fervor, as part of a grand geopolitical design, the overture of global harmony." In grandiose rhetoric, Gilpin interpreted America's mission as an obligation "to carry the career of mankind to its culminating point—to cause stagnant people to be reborn—to perfect science—to emblazon history with the conquest of peace—to shed a new and resplendent glory upon mankind." His book The Central Gold Region (1860) was retitled Mission of the North American People: Geographical, Social, and Political (1873) as more appropriate

From Mission of the North American People (Philadelphia: J. B. Lippincott and Company, 1873), chap. 2, pp. 135–164 passim.

in the light of the Manifest Destiny of the United States. In the following selection, Gilpin represents the pioneer agriculturists in their demand for a national railroad. For further information about the author see H. H. Bancroft, *History of the Life of William Gilpin: A Character Study* (San Francisco, 1889). Further information about the national railroad may be obtained from Samuel Bowles, *Across the Continent* (Springfield, Mass., 1868).

Progress, political liberty, equality. These, the most ancient and cardinal rights of human society, perplexed in the obscurity of military despotism, and almost lost for many centuries, are now struggling throughout the world to re-establish their pre-eminence. In America they occupy the vantage-ground; for sovereignty resides in the suffrage, and with us it is universal.

Progress, then, in America has the intensity of the whole people, showing itself in forms as infinite as the thoughts of the human mind. But it is to that department of progress which creates for us new States in the wilderness, and expands the area of our Republic, that I here restrict myself. Let us understand *this*; what it is at the present hour—what stimulates—what retards it.

Since 1608 we have grown from nothing to 22,000,000: from a garden-patch, to be thirty States and many Territories! This, with agriculture, manufactures, commerce, power, and happiness, is our progress so far.

The annual yield in money of this agriculture and manufactures is now $2,000,000,000. This commerce vexes all the waters and penetrates to all the nations of the earth. This power, tranquilly complete on our own continent, compels peaceful deference abroad. This happiness, so beneficently felt at home, recruits us with the oppressed of all nations.

But the life of a nation is long. Unlike human life, briefly extinguished in the grave, a nation breathes ever on with the vigor of generations of men daily arriving at maturity, and then departing. A nation has then a *normal* law of growth; and it is this law which every American citizen ought familiarly to understand, for obedience to it is the first duty of patriotism.

Up to the year 1840, the progress whereby twenty-six States and

four Territories had been established and peopled, had amounted
to a solid strip of twenty-five miles in depth, added annually, along
the western face of the Union from Canada to the Gulf.

This occupation of wild territory, accumulating outward like the
annual rings of our forest trees, proceeds with all the solemnity
of a Providential ordinance. It is at this moment sweeping onward
to the Pacific with accelerated activity and force, like a deluge of
men, rising unabatedly, and daily pushed onward by the hand of
God.

It is from the statistics accumulated in the bureau at Washington (the decennial census, sales of public lands, assessments of
State and national taxes) that we deduce with certainty the law
of this deluge of human beings, which nothing interrupts and no
power can stop.

Fronting the Union on every side is a vast army of pioneers. This
vast body, numbering 500,000 at least, has the movements and
obeys the discipline of a perfectly organized military force. It is
momentarily recruited by single individuals, families, and, in some
instances, communities, from every village, county, city, and State
in the Union, and by emigrants from other nations.

Each man in this moving throng is in force a platoon. He makes
a farm upon the outer edge of the settlements, which he occupies
for a year and then sells to the leading files of the mass pressing
up to him from behind.

He again advances twenty-five miles, renews his farm, is again
overtaken, and again sells. As individuals fall out from the front
rank, or fix themselves permanently, others rush from behind,
pass to the front, and assail the wilderness in their turn.

Previous to the late war with Mexico, this busy throng was
engaged at one point in occupying the peninsula of Florida and
lands vacated by emigrant Indian tribes—at another in reaching
the copper region of Lake Superior—in absorbing Iowa and
Wisconsin.

From this very spot had gone forth a forlorn hope to occupy
Oregon and California: Texas was thus annexed: the Indian country pressed upon its flanks; and spy companies reconnoitring New
and Old Mexico.

Even then, obeying that mysterious and uncontrollable impulse
which drives our nation to its goal, a body of the hardiest race that

ever faced varied and unnumbered privations and dangers embarked upon the trail to the Pacific coast, forced their way to the end, encountering and defying dangers and difficulties unparalleled, with a courage and success the like to which the world has not heretofore seen.

Thus, then, *overland* sweeps this tide-wave of population, absorbing in its thundering march the glebe, the savages, and the wild beasts of the wilderness, scaling the mountains and debouching down upon the seaboard.

Upon the high *Atlantic* sea-coast, the pioneer force has thrown itself into ships, and found in the ocean-fisheries food for its creative genius. The whaling fleet is the *marine* force of the pioneer army.

These two forces, by land and sea, have both worked steadily onward to the North Pacific. They now reunite in the harbors of Oregon and California, about to bring into existence upon the Pacific a commercial grandeur identical with that which has followed them upon the Atlantic. . . .

We find more than *three-fifths* of our continent to consist of a limitless plain, intersected by countless navigable streams, flowing everywhere *from* the circumference towards common centres: grouped in close proximity: and only divided by what connects them into one homogeneous plan.

To the American people, then, belongs this vast interior space, covered over its uniform surface of 2,300,000 square miles, with the richest *calcareous* soil: touching the snows towards the north, and the torrid heats toward the south: bound together by an infinite internal navigation: of a temperate climate: and constituting, in the whole, the most magnificent dwelling-place marked out by God for man's abode.

As the complete beneficence of the Almighty has thus given to us, the owners of the continent, the great natural outlets of the Mississippi to the Gulf, and the St. Lawrence to the North Atlantic, so is it left to a pious and grateful people, appreciating this goodness, to construct through the gorge of the Sierra Madre, a great artificial monument, an iron path, a NATIONAL Railway to the *Western* Sea. . . .

The *scientific men* of the nation oppose the National Railroad—so did those of Europe persecute Galileo and Columbus. Science, like the army and navy, is fed from the national revenues, which maritime policy distributes to all that serve its ends. Science is rare; the spurious quackery of science redundant. It is not the scientific doctors of the schools, the bureaus and military wings of government, that have hewed out this republican empire from the wilderness.

This has been reared by the genuine heroism and sublime instincts of the *pioneer army*, unpaid, unblessed, nay, scoffed and loaded with burdens by government and its swarm of dependents. To bridle PROGRESS has been the policy of thirty years. To keep the people out of the wilderness. To refuse Territorial governments, and prevent Territories from becoming States.

At this moment *scientific* men are especially busy distracting us with multitudinous routes and invented difficulties: devised to perplex and scatter the energies of the citizens: whose unanimous resolve it is to plow open a great central trail to the Pacific.

Science cannot unmake the eternal ordinances of nature, and reset the universe to suit local fancies and idle fashion. It is the humble duty of science to investigate nature *as she is*, and promulgate the truths discoverable for the guidance of governments and men.

The experience gained from the great works constructed by the last generation, in digging through the Alleghanies routes for commerce to the Atlantic, settles for us the rules that shall guide us across the Sierra Madre to the Pacific.

In 1818 the State of New York cut through the low and narrow ridge between Rome and Syracuse, the former on an affluent of the Hudson, the latter of Lake Ontario. Thus the *first* expenditures, perforating the dividing mountain, let through that infant commerce, which in thirty years has grown to such a grandeur of quantity and profit, that this great thoroughfare is itself quadrupled in capacity and lengthened out to Montreal, to Boston, to New York City, and into Pennsylvania, towards the east.

Westward, it reaches through Ohio and Indiana to the Ohio River: and by the Illinois and Wisconsin Rivers to the Missouri and Mississippi. . . .

It is, then, I repeat, through the heart of our Territories, our population, our States, our farms and habitations, that we need this broad current of commerce. Where passengers and cargo may, at any time or place, embark upon or leave the vehicles of transportation.

It is foul treason to banish it from the land: from among the people: to force it on to the barren ocean: outside of society: through foreign nations: into the torrid heats and along solitary circuitous routes, imprisoned for months in great ships.

This central railroad is an essential domestic institution: more powerful and permanent than law, or popular consent; to thoroughly complete the great systems of fluvial arteries which fraternize us into one people; to bind the two seaboards to this one nation, like ears to the human head: to radicate the foundations of the UNION so broad and deep, and render its structure so solid, that no possible force or stratagem can shake its permanence: and to secure such scope and space to progress, that prosperity and equality shall never be impaired or chafe for want of room. . . .

What means that expression in the Declaration of Independence, "life, liberty, and *the pursuit of happiness*"? What brought the Cavaliers to Virginia in 1608? It was "the pursuit of happiness." What animated the Pilgrims to endure the rigors of Plymouth Rock? Why, "the pursuit of happiness." What sought Boone and his companions plunging a thousand miles into the wilderness? This same "pursuit of happiness." What secret motive now brings foreigners to our shores, and impels our own citizens onward to the Pacific? Again, it is "the pursuit of happiness."

Progress, then, is one of the immortal RIGHTS sanctified in the Charter of human liberty. Why, then, is advent into the wilderness—the field for the discontented, the oppressed, the needy, the restless, the ambitious, and the virtuous, thus closed by a policy at once sinister, nefarious, and unconstitutional?

Unquiet for our sacred Union is this present time, when political power, about to cross the Alleghanies, see-saws on their crests, counting the days that precede her eternal transit over them!

It is by the rapid propagation of new States: the immediate occupation of the broad platform of the continent: the aggregation of the Pacific Ocean and Asiatic commerce: the inquietude will be swallowed up, and the murmurs of discontent lost in the onward sound of advancement. Discontent, distanced, will die out. . . .

Everybody is acquainted with the commercial intercourse between the continent which fringe the Atlantic. The life, the vivacity, the grand energies which resound upon its buoyant waves. All this is the result of the discovery of America and its population with European stock—hence all this has its growth!

Antiquity had for its field the Mediterranean, and galleys sufficed. This was commerce in its infancy, confined to the nursery and content with toys. Since Columbus, America has become greater than the Europe of Columbus—and as this period has expanded the field of human activity from the Mediterranean to the Atlantic and Mediterranean, from Western Europe to America and Europe, blending all this vast space under one international relationship.

So now we advance to consummate the blending of the Pacific with these other seas:—Asia with these other continents—and urge to its goal that expanding progression, which marches on to complete the zodiac of the globes, and blend into bonds of confraternity all the continents, all the seas, and all the nations!

⌐ *WALT WHITMAN*

Passage to India

Speaking of his poem "Passage to India," Walt Whitman (1819–1892) said, "There's more of me, the essential me, in that than in any of the other poems." Published first in pamphlet form and then as an important addition to the 1871 edition of *Leaves of Grass*, this poem relates three important engineering accomplishments to the idea of spiritual progress and the unity of mankind: completion of the trans-Atlantic cable (1866), of the transcontinental railroad from Omaha to San Francisco (1869),

From *Passage to India* (New York: Smith and McDougal, 1871).

and of the Suez Canal (1869). "I have reserv'd that
poem with its cluster," said Whitman, "to finish and
explain much that, without them, would not be explain'd, and to take leave, and escape for good, from
all that has preceded them."

1

Singing my days,
Singing the great achievements of the present,
Singing the strong light works of engineers,
Our modern wonders, (the antique ponderous Seven outvied,)
In the Old World the east the Suez canal,
The New by its mighty railroad spann'd,
The seas inlaid with eloquent gentle wires;
Yet first to sound, and ever sound, the cry with thee O soul,
The Past! the Past! the Past!

The Past—the dark unfathom'd retrospect!
The teeming gulf—the sleepers and the shadows!
The past—the infinite greatness of the past!
For what is the present after all but a growth out of the past?
(As a projectile form'd, impell'd, passing a certain line, still keeps
          on,
So the present, utterly form'd, impell'd by the past.)

2

Passage O soul to India!
Eclaircise the myths Asiatic, the primitive fables.

Not you alone proud truths of the world,
Nor you alone ye facts of modern science,
But myths and fables of eld, Asia's, Africa's fables,
The far-darting beams of the spirit, the unloos'd dreams,
The deep diving bibles and legends,
The daring plots of the poets, the elder religions;
O you temples fairer than lilies pour'd over by the rising sun!
O you fables spurning the known, eluding the hold of the known,
          mounting to heaven!

You lofty and dazzling towers, pinnacled, red as roses, burnish'd
   with gold!
Towers of fables immortal fashion'd from mortal dreams!
You too I welcome and fully the same as the rest!
You too with joy I sing.

Passage to India!
Lo, soul, seest thou not God's purpose from the first?
The earth to be spann'd, connected by network,
The races, neighbors, to marry and be given in marriage,
The oceans to be cross'd, the distant brought near,
The lands to be welded together.

A worship new I sing,
You captains, voyagers, explorers, yours,
You engineers, you architects, machinists, yours,
You, not for trade or transportation only,
But in God's name, and for thy sake O soul.

3

Passage to India!
Lo soul for thee of tableaus twain,
I see in one the Suez canal initiated, open'd,
I see the procession of steamships, the Empress Eugenie's leading
   the van,
I mark from on deck the strange landscape, the pure sky, the level
   sand in the distance,
I pass swiftly the picturesque groups, the workmen gather'd,
The gigantic dredging machines.

In one again, different, (yet thine, all thine, O soul, the same,)
I see over my own continent the Pacific railroad surmounting every
   barrier,
I see continual trains of cars winding along the Platte carrying
   freight and passengers,
I hear the locomotives rushing and roaring, and the shrill steam-
   whistle,

I hear the echoes reverberate through the grandest scenery in the
     world,
I cross the Laramie plains, I note the rocks in grotesque shapes,
     the buttes,
I see the plentiful larkspur and wild onions, the barren, colorless
     sagedeserts,
I see in glimpses afar or towering immediately above me the great
     mountains, I see the Wind river and the Wahsatch
     mountains,
I see the Monument mountain and the Eagle's Nest, I pass the
     Promontory, I ascend the Nevadas,
I scan the noble Elk mountain and wind around its base,
I see the Humboldt range, I thread the valley and cross the river,
I see the clear waters of lake Tahoe, I see forests of majestic pines,
Or crossing the great desert, the alkaline plains, I behold enchant-
     ing mirages of waters and meadows,
Marking through these and after all, in duplicate slender lines,
Bridging the three or four thousand miles of land travel,
Tying the Eastern to the Western sea,
The road between Europe and Asia.

(Ah Genoese thy dream! thy dream!
Centuries after thou art laid in thy grave,
The shore thou foundest verifies thy dream.)

4

Passage to India!
Struggles of many a captain, tales of many a sailor dead,
Over my mood stealing and spreading they come,
Like clouds and cloudlets in the unreach'd sky.

Along all history, down the slopes,
As a rivulet running, sinking now, and now again to the surface
     rising,
A ceaseless thought, a varied train—lo, soul, to thee, thy sight they
     rise,
The plans, the voyages again, the expeditions,
Again Vasco da Gama sails forth,

Again the knowledge gain'd, the mariner's compass,
Lands found and nations born, thou born America,
For purpose vast, man's long probation fill'd,
Thou rondure of the world at last accomplish'd.

5
O vast Rondure, swimming in space,
Cover'd all over with visible power and beauty,
Alternate light and day and the teeming spiritual darkness,
Unspeakable high processions of sun and moon and countless stars
        above,
Below, the manifold grass and waters, animals, mountains, trees,
With inscrutable purpose, some hidden prophetic intention,
Now first it seems my thought begins to span thee.

Down from the gardens of Asia descending radiating,
Adam and Eve appear, then their myriad progeny after them,
Wandering, yearning, curious, with restless explorations,
With questionings, baffled, formless, feverish, with never-happy
        hearts,
With that sad incessant refrain, *Wherefore unsatisfied soul?* and
        Whither O mocking life?

Ah who shall soothe these feverish children?
Who justify these restless explorations?
Who speak the secret of impassive earth?
Who bind it to us? what is this separate Nature so unnatural?
What is this earth to our affections? (unloving earth, without a
        throb to answer ours,
Cold earth, the place of graves.)

Yet soul be sure the first intent remains, and shall be carried out,
Perhaps even now the time has arrived.

After the seas are all cross'd, (as they seem already cross'd,)
After the great captains and engineers have accomplish'd their
        work,

After the noble inventors, after the scientists, the chemist, the
        geologist, ethnologist,
Finally shall come the poet worthy that name,
The true son of God shall come singing his songs.

Then not your deeds only O voyagers, O scientists and inventors,
        shall be justified,
All these hearts as of fretted children shall be sooth'd,
All affection shall be fully responded to, the secret shall be told,
All these separations and gaps shall be taken up and hook'd and
        link'd together,
The whole earth, this cold, impassive, voiceless earth, shall be com-
        pletely justified,
Trinitas divine shall be gloriously accomplish'd and compacted by
        the true son of God, the poet,
(He shall indeed pass the straits and conquer the mountains,
He shall double the cape of Good Hope to some purpose,)
Nature and Man shall be disjoin'd and diffused no more,
The true son of God shall absolutely fuse them.

6

Year at whose wide-flung door I sing!
Year of the purpose accomplish'd!
Year of the marriage of continents, climates and oceans!
(No mere doge of Venice now wedding the Adriatic,)
I see O year in you the vast terraqueous globe given and giving all,
Europe to Asia, Africa join'd, and they to the New World,
The lands, geographies, dancing before you, holding a festival gar-
        land,
As brides and bridegrooms hand in hand.

Passage to India!
Cooling airs from Caucasus far, soothing cradle of man,
The river Euphrates flowing, the past lit up again.

Lo soul, the retrospect brought forward,
The old, most populous, wealthiest of earth's lands,

The streams of the Indus and the Ganges and their many affluents,
(I my shores of America walking to-day behold, resuming all,)
The tale of Alexander on his warlike marches suddenly dying,
On one side China and on the other side Persia and Arabia,
To the south the great seas and the bay of Bengal,
The flowing literatures, tremendous epics, religions, castes,
Old occult Brahma interminably far back, the tender and junior
        Buddha,
Central and southern empires and all their belongings, possessors,
The wars of Tamerlane, the reign of Aurungzebe,
The traders, rulers, explorers, Moslems, Venetians, Byzantium, the
        Arabs, Portuguese,
The first travelers famous yet, Marco Polo, Batouta the Moor,
Doubts to be solv'd, the map incognita, blanks to be fill'd,
The foot of man unstay'd, the hands never at rest,
Thyself O soul that will not brook a challenge.

The mediæval navigators rise before me,
The world of 1492, with its awaken'd enterprise,
Something swelling in humanity now like the sap of the earth in
        spring,
The sunset splendor of chivalry declining.

And who art thou sad shade?
Gigantic, visionary, thyself a visionary,
With majestic limbs and pious beaming eyes,
Spreading around with every look of thine a golden world,
Enhuing it with gorgeous hues.

As the chief histrion,
Down to the footlights walks in some great scena,
Dominating the rest I see the Admiral himself,
(History's type of courage, action, faith,)
Behold him sail from Palos leading his little fleet,
His voyage behold, his return, his great fame,
His misfortunes, calumniators, behold him a prisoner, chain'd,
Behold his dejection, poverty, death.

(Curious in time I stand, noting the efforts of heroes,
Is the deferment long? bitter the slander, poverty, death?
Lies the seed unreck'd for centuries in the ground? lo, to God's due
        occasion,
Uprising in the night, it sprouts, blooms,
And fills the earth with use and beauty.)

7

Passage indeed O soul to primal thought,
Not lands and seas alone, thy own clear freshness,
The young maturity of brood and bloom,
To realms of budding bibles.

O soul, repressless, I with thee and thou with me,
Thy circumnavigation of the world begin,
Of man, the voyage of his mind's return,
To reason's early paradise,
Back, back to wisdom's birth, to innocent intuitions,
Again with fair creation.

8

O we can wait no longer,
We too take ship O soul,
Joyous we too launch out on trackless seas,
Fearless for unknown shores on waves of ecstasy to sail,
Amid the wafting winds, (thou pressing me to thee, I thee to me,
        O soul,)
Caroling free, singing our song of God.
Chanting our chant of pleasant exploration.

With laugh and many a kiss,
(Let others deprecate, let others weep for sin, remorse, humilia-
        tion,)
O soul thou pleasest me, I thee.

Ah more than any priest O soul we too believe in God,
But with the mystery of God we dare not dally.

O soul thou pleasest me, I thee,
Sailing these seas or on the hills, or waking in the night,
Thoughts, silent thoughts, of Time and Space and Death, like
            waters flowing,
Bear me indeed as through the regions infinite,
Whose air I breathe, whose ripples hear, lave me all over,
Bathe me O God in thee, mounting to thee,
I and my soul to range in range of thee.

O Thou transcendent,
Nameless, the fibre and the breath,
Light of the light, shedding forth universes, thou centre of them,
Thou mightier centre of the true, the good, the loving,
Thou moral, spiritual fountain—affection's source—thou reservoir,
(O pensive soul of me—O thirst unsatisfied—waitest not there?
Waitest not haply for us somewhere there the Comrade perfect?)
Thou pulse—thou motive of the stars, suns, systems,
That, circling, move in order, safe, harmonious,
Athwart the shapeless vastnesses of space,
How should I think, how breathe a single breath, how speak, if out
            of myself,
I could not launch, to those, superior universes?

Swiftly I shrivel at the thought of God,
At Nature and its wonders, Time and Space and Death,
But that I, turning, call to thee O soul, thou actual Me,
And lo, thou gently masterest the orbs,
Thou matest Time, smilest content at Death,
And fillest, swellest full the vastness of Space.

Greater than stars or suns,
Bounding O soul thou journeyest forth;
What love than thine and ours could wider amplify?
What aspirations, wishes, outvie thine and ours O soul?
What dreams of the ideal? what plans of purity, perfection,
            strength,
What cheerful willingness for others' sake to give up all?
For others' sake to suffer all?

Reckoning ahead O soul, when thou, the time achiev'd,
The seas all cross'd, weather'd the capes, the voyage done,
Surrounded, copest, frontest God, yieldest, the aim attain'd,
As filled with friendship, love complete, the Elder Brother found,
The Younger melts in fondness in his arms.

9

Passage to more than India!
Are thy wings plumed indeed for such far flights?
O soul, voyagest thou indeed on voyages like those?
Disportest thou on waters such as those?
Soundest below the Sanscrit and the Vedas?
Then have thy bent unleash'd.

Passage to you, your shores, ye aged fierce enigmas!
Passage to you, to mastership of you, ye strangling problems!
You, strew'd with the wrecks of skeletons, that living, never
          reach'd you.

Passage to more than India!
O secret of the earth and sky!
Of you O waters of the sea! O winding creeks and rivers!
Of you O woods and fields! of you strong mountains of my land!
Of you O praires! of you gray rocks!
O morning red! O clouds! O rains and snows!
O day and night, passage to you!

O sun and moon and all you stars! Sirius and Jupiter!
Passage to you!

Passage, immediate passage! the blood burns in my veins!
Away O soul! hoist instantly the anchor!
Cut the hawsers—haul out—shake out every sail!
Have we not stood here like trees in the ground long enough?
Have we not grovel'd here long enough, eating and drinking like
          mere brutes?
Have we not darken'd and dazed ourselves with books long
          enough?

Sail forth—steer for the deep waters only,
Reckless O soul, exploring, I with thee, and thou with me,
For we are bound where mariner has not yet dared to go,
And we will risk the ship, ourselves and all.

O my brave soul!
O farther farther sail!
O daring joy, but safe! are they not all the seas of God?
O farther, farther, farther sail!

part 7

LITERARY SKETCHES

↗ *MORGAN NEVILLE*

The Last of the Boatmen

Morgan Neville (1783–1840), a journalist and scholar who was a frequent contributor to the Western press, is remembered principally for his securing a place in American literature for the inimitable Mike Fink and for the extravagant exploits of this heroic riverboatman. The stories of "The Last of the Boatmen," "Chevalier Dubac," and others, said one of his contemporaries, "are sufficient to stamp Neville as a man of genius." "The Last of the Boatmen" first appeared in James Hall's *The Western Souvenir*, a pioneer Western annual for 1829. Other Mike Fink legends appeared in the Western almanacs and in William T. Porter's *Spirit of the Times*. Franklin J. Meine has more recently prepared a provisional bibliography of this material.

I embarked a few years since, at Pittsburg, for Cincinnati, on board of a steam boat—more with a view of realising the possibility of a speedy return against the current, than in obedience to the call of either business or pleasure. It was a voyage of speculation. I was born on the banks of the Ohio, and the only vessels associated with my early recollections were the canoes of the Indians, which brought to Fort Pitt their annual cargoes of skins and bear's oil. The Flat boat of Kentucky, destined only to float with the current, next appeared; and after many years of interval, the Keel boat of the Ohio, and the Barge of the Mississippi were introduced for the convenience of the infant commerce of the West.

From *The Western Souvenir* (Cincinnati, Ohio: N. & G. Guilford, 1829).

At the period, at which I have dated my trip to Cincinnati, the steam boat had made but few voyages back to Pittsburg. We were generally skeptics as to its practicability. The mind was not prepared for the change that was about to take place in the West. It is now consummated; and we yet look back with astonishment at the result.

The rudest inhabitant of our forests;—the man whose mind is least of all imbued with a relish for the picturesque—who would gaze with vacant stare at the finest painting—listen with apathy to the softest melody, and turn with indifference from a mere display of ingenious mechanism, is struck with the sublime power and self-moving majesty of a steam boat;—lingers on the shore where it passes—and follows its rapid, and almost magic course with silent admiration. The steam engine in five years has enabled us to anticipate a state of things, which, in the ordinary course of events, it would have required a century to have produced. The art of printing scarcely surpassed it in its beneficial consequences.

In the old world, the places of the greatest interest to the philosophic traveller are ruins, and monuments, that speak of faded splendour, and departed glory. The broken columns of Tadmor—the shapeless ruins of Babylon, are rich in matter for almost endless speculation. Far different is the case in the western regions of America. The stranger views here, with wonder, the rapidity with which cities spring up in forests; and with which barbarism retreats before the approach of art and civilization. The reflection possessing the most intense interest is—not what has been the character of the country, but what shall be her future destiny.

As we coasted along this cheerful scene, one reflection crossed my mind to diminish the pleasure it excited. This was caused by the sight of the ruins of the once splendid mansion of Blennerhasset. I had spent some happy hours here, when it was the favorite residence of taste and hospitality. I had seen it when a lovely and accomplished woman presided—shedding a charm around, which made it as inviting, though not so dangerous, as the island of Calypso;—when its liberal and polished owner made it the resort of every stranger, who had any pretensions to literature or science. —I had beheld it again under more inauspicious circumstances:— when its proprietor, in a moment of visionary speculation, had abandoned this earthly paradise to follow an adventurer—himself the dupe of others. A military banditti held possession, acting "by authority." The embellishments of art and taste disappeared beneath the touch of a band of Vandals: and the beautiful domain which presented the imposing appearance of a palace, and which had cost a fortune in the erection, was changed in one night, into a scene of devastation. The chimneys of the house remained for some years—the insulated monument of the folly of their owner, and pointed out to the stranger the place where once stood the temples of hospitality. Drift wood covered the pleasure grounds; and the massive, cut stone, that formed the columns of the gateway, were scattered more widely than the fragments of the Egyptian Memnon.

When we left Pittsburg, the season was not far advanced in vegetation. But as we proceeded the change was more rapid than the difference of latitude justified. I had frequently observed this in former voyages: but it never was so striking, as on the present occasion. The old mode of traveling, in the sluggish flat boat seemed to give time for the change of season; but now a few hours carried us into a different climate. We met spring with all her laughing train of flowers and verdure, rapidly advancing from the south. The buck-eye, cottonwood, and maple, had already assumed, in this region, the rich livery of summer. The thousand varieties of the floral kingdom spread a gay carpet over the luxuriant bottoms on each side of the river. The thick woods resounded with the notes of the feathered tribe—each striving to outdo his neighbor in noise, if not in melody. We had not yet reached the region of paroquets; but the clear toned whistle of the cardinal was heard in every bush; and the cat-bird was endeavouring, with its usual zeal, to rival the powers of the more gifted mockingbird.

A few hours brought us to one of those stopping points, known by the name of "wooding places." It was situated immediately above Letart's Falls. The boat, obedient to the wheel of the pilot, made a graceful sweep towards the island above the chute, and rounding to, approached the wood pile. As the boat drew near the shore, the escape steam reverberated through the forest and hills, like the chafed bellowing of the caged tiger. The root of a tree, concealed beneath the water, prevented the boat from getting sufficiently near the bank, and it became necessary to use the paddles to take a different position.

"Back out! Mannee! and try it again!" exclaimed a voice from the shore. "Throw your pole wide—and brace off!—or you'll run against a snag!"

This was a kind of language long familiar to us on the Ohio. It was a sample of the slang of the keel-boatmen.

The speaker was immediately cheered by a dozen of voices from the deck; and I recognized in him the person of an old acquaintance, familiarly known to me from my boyhood. He was leaning carelessly against a large beech; and, as his left arm negligently pressed a rifle to his side, presented a figure, that Salvator would have chosen from a million, as a model for his wild and gloomy pencil. His stature was upwards of six feet, his proportions perfectly symmetrical, and exhibiting the evidence of Herculean powers. To a stranger, he would have seemed a complete mulatto. Long exposure to the sun and weather on the lower Ohio and Mississippi had changed his skin; and, but for the fine European cast of his countenance, he might have passed for the principal warrior of some powerful tribe. Although at least fifty years of age, his hair was as black as the wing of the raven. Next to his skin he wore a red flannel shirt, covered by a blue capot, ornamented with white fringe. On his feet were moccasins, and a broad leathern belt, from which hung, suspended in a sheath, a large knife, encircled his waist.

As soon as the steam boat became stationary, the cabin passengers jumped on shore. On ascending the bank, the figure I have just described advanced to offer me his hand.

"How are you, Mike?" said I.

"How goes it?" replied the boatman—grasping my hand with a squeeze, that I can compare to nothing, but that of a blacksmith's vise.

"I am glad to see you, Mannee!"—continued he in his abrupt manner. "I am going to shoot at the tin cup for a quart—off hand —and you must be judge."

I understood Mike at once, and on any other occasion, should have remonstrated, and prevented the daring trial of skill. But I was accompanied by a couple of English tourists, who had scarcely

ever been beyond the sound of Bow Bells; and who were travelling
post over the United States to make up a book of observation, on
our manners and customs. There were, also, among the passengers,
a few bloods from Philadelphia and Baltimore, who could conceive
of nothing equal to Chestnut or Howard streets; and who expressed
great disappointment, at not being able to find terrapins and oysters
at every village—marvellously lauding the comforts of Rubicum's.
My tramontane pride was aroused; and I resolved to give them an
opportunity of seeing a Western Lion—for such Mike undoubtedly was—in all his glory. The philanthropist may start, and
accuse me of want of humanity. I deny the charge, and refer for
apology to one of the best understood principles of human nature.

Mike, followed by several of his crew, led the way to a beech
grove, some little distance from the landing. I invited my fellow
passengers to witness the scene.—On arriving at the spot, a stout,
bull-headed boatman, dressed in a hunting shirt—but bare-footed
—in whom I recognized a younger brother of Mike, drew a line
with his toe; and stepping off thirty yards—turned round fronting
his brother—took a tin cup, which hung from his belt, and placed
it on his head. Although I had seen this feat performed before, I
acknowledge, I felt uneasy, whilst this silent preparation was going
on. But I had not much time for reflection; for this second Albert
exclaimed—

"Blaze away, Mike! and let's have the quart."

My "compagnons de voyage," as soon as they recovered from the
first effect of their astonishment, exhibited a disposition to interfere. But Mike, throwing back his left leg, levelled his rifle at the
head of his brother. In this horizontal position the weapon remained for some seconds as immovable, as if the arm which held
it, was affected by no pulsation.

"Elevate your piece a little lower, Mike! or you will pay the
corn," cried the imperturbable brother.

I know not if the advice was obeyed or not; but the sharp crack
of the rifle immediately followed, and the cup flew off thirty or
forty yards—rendered unfit for future service. There was a cry of
admiration from the strangers, who pressed forward to see if the
foolhardy boatman was really safe. He remained as immoveable,
as if he had been a figure hewn out of stone. He had not even

winked, when the ball struck the cup within two inches of his skull.

"Mike has won!" I exclaimed; and my decision was the signal which, according to their rules, permitted him of the target to move from his position. No more sensation was exhibited among the boatmen, than if a common wager had been won. The bet being decided, they hurried back to their boat, giving me and my friends an invitation to partake of "the treat." We declined, and took leave of the thoughtless creatures. In a few minutes afterwards, we observed their "Keel" wheeling into the current,—the gigantic form of Mike, bestriding the large steering oar, and the others arranging themselves in their places in front of the cabin, that extended nearly the whole length of the boat, covering merchandize of immense value. As they left the shore, they gave the Indian yell; and broke out into a sort of unconnected chorus—commencing with—

> "Hard upon the beech oar!—
> She moves too slow!
> All the way to Shawneetown,
> Long while ago."

In a few minutes the boat "took the chute" of Letart's Falls, and disappeared behind the point, with the rapidity of an Arabian courser.

Our travellers returned to the boat, lost in speculation on the scene, and the beings they had just beheld; and, no doubt, the circumstance has been related a thousand times with all the necessary amplifications of finished tourists.

Mike Fink may be viewed, as the correct representative of a class of men now extinct; but who once possessed as marked a character, as that of the Gypsies of England, or the Lazaroni of Naples. The period of their existence was not more than a third of a century. The character was created by the introduction of trade on the Western waters; and ceased with the successful establishment of the steam boat.

There is something inexplicable in the fact, that there could be men found, for ordinary wages, who would abandon the systematic, but not laborious pursuits of agriculture, to follow a life, of all others, except that of the soldier, distinguished by the greatest exposure and privation. The occupation of a boatman was more calculated to destroy the constitution and to shorten life, than any other business. In ascending the river, it was a continued series of toil, rendered more irksome by the snail like rate, at which they moved. The boat was propelled by poles, against which the shoulder was placed; and the whole strength, and skill of the individual were applied in this manner. As the boatmen moved along the running board, with their heads nearly touching the plank on which they walked, the effect produced on the mind of an observer was similar to that on beholding the ox, rocking before an overloaded cart. Their bodies, naked to their waist for the purpose of moving with greater ease, and of enjoying the breeze of the river, were exposed to the burning suns of summer, and to the rains of autumn. After a hard day's push, they would take their "fillee," or ration of whiskey, and having swallowed a miserable supper of meat half burnt, and of bread half baked, stretch themselves without covering, on the deck, and slumber till the steersman's call invited them to the morning "fillee." Notwithstanding this, the boatman's life had charms as irresistible, as those presented by the splendid illusions of the stage. Sons abandoned the comfortable farms of their fathers, and apprentices fled from the service of their masters. There was a captivation in the idea of "going down the river"; and the youthful boatman who had "pushed a keel" from New Orleans, felt all the pride of a young merchant, after his first voyage to an English sea port. From an exclusive association together, they had formed a kind of slang peculiar to themselves; and from the constant exercise of wit, with "the squatters" on shore, and crews of other boats, they acquired a quickness, and smartness of vulgar retort, that was quite amusing. The frequent battles they were engaged in with the boatmen of different parts of the river, and with the less civilized inhabitants of the lower Ohio, and Mississippi, invested them with that ferocious reputation, which has made them spoken of throughout Europe.

On board of the boats thus navigated, our merchants entrusted valuable cargoes, without insurance, and with no other guarantee than the receipt of the steersman, who possessed no property but his boat; and the confidence so reposed was seldom abused.

Among these men, Mike Fink stood an acknowledged leader for many years. Endowed by nature with those qualities of intellect, that give the possessor influence, he would have been a conspicuous member of any society, in which his lot might have been cast. An acute observer of human nature has said—"Opportunity alone makes the hero. Change but their situations, and Caesar would have been but the best wrestler on the green." With a figure cast in a mould that added much of the symmetry of an Apollo to the limbs of a Hercules, he possessed gigantic strength; and accustomed from an early period of life to brave the dangers of a frontier life, his character was noted for the most daring intrepidity. At the court of Charlemagne, he might have been a Roland; with the Crusaders, he would have been the favourite of the Knight of the Lion-heart; and in our revolution, he would have ranked with the Morgans and Putnams of the day. He was the hero of a hundred fights, and the leader in a thousand daring adventures. From Pittsburg to St. Louis, and New Orleans, his fame was established. Every farmer on the shore kept on good terms with Mike—otherwise, there was no safety for his property. Wherever he was an enemy, like his great prototype, Rob Roy, he levied the contribution of Black Mail for the use of his boat. Often at night, when his tired companions slept, he would take an excursion of five or six miles, and return before morning, rich in spoil. On the Ohio, he was known among his companions by the appellation of the "Snapping Turtle"; and on the Mississippi, he was called "The Snag."

At the early age of seventeen, Mike's character was displayed, by enlisting himself in a corps of Scouts—a body of irregular rangers, which was employed on the North-western frontiers of Pennsylvania, to watch the Indians, and to give notice of any threatened inroad.

At that time, Pittsburg was on the extreme verge of white population, and the spies, who were constantly employed, generally extended their explorations forty or fifty miles to the west of this post. They went out, singly, lived as did the Indian, and in every respect, became perfectly assimilated in habits, taste, and feeling, with the red men of the desert. A kind of border warfare was kept up, and the scout thought it as praiseworthy to bring in the scalp of a Shawnee, as the skin of a panther. He would remain in the woods for weeks together, using parched corn for bread, and depending on his rifle for his meat—and slept at night in perfect comfort, rolled in his blanket.

In this corps, whilst yet a stripling, Mike acquired a reputation for boldness, and cunning, far beyond his companions. A thousand legends illustrate the fearlessness of his character. There was one, which he told himself, with much pride, and which made an indelible impression on my boyish memory. He had been out on the hills of Mahoning, when, to use his own words, "he saw signs of Indians being about."—He had discovered the recent print of the moccasin on the grass; and found drops of fresh blood of a deer on the green bush. He became cautious, skulked for some time in the deepest thickets of hazel and briar; and, for several days, did not discharge his rifle. He subsisted patiently on parched corn and jerk, which he had dried on his first coming into the woods. He gave no alarm to the settlements, because he discovered with perfect certainty, that the enemy consisted of a small hunting party, who were receding from the Alleghany.

As he was creeping along one morning, with the stealthy tread of a cat, his eye fell upon a beautiful buck, browsing on the edge of a barren spot, three hundred yards distant. The temptation was too strong for the woodsman, and he resolved to have a shot at every hazard. Re-priming his gun, and picking his flint, he made his approaches in the usual noiseless manner. At the moment he reached the spot, from which he meant to take his aim, he observed a large savage, intent upon the same object, advancing from a direction a little different from his own. Mike shrunk behind a tree, with a quickness of thought, and keeping his eye fixed on the hunter, waited the result with patience. In a few moments, the Indian halted within fifty paces, and levelled his piece at the deer. In the meanwhile, Mike presented his rifle at the body of the savage; and at the moment the smoke issued from the gun of the latter, the bullet of Fink passed through the red man's breast. He uttered a yell, and fell dead at the same instant with the deer. Mike re-loaded his rifle, and remained in his covert for some minutes, to ascertain whether there were more enemies at hand. He then stepped up to the prostrate savage, and having satisfied himself, that life was extinguished, turned his attention to the buck, and took from the carcass those pieces, suited to the process of jerking.

In the meantime, the country was filling up with a white population; and in a few years the red men, with the exception of a few fractions of tribes, gradually receded to the Lakes and beyond the Mississippi. The corps of Scouts was abolished, after having acquired habits, which unfitted them for the pursuits of civilized society. Some incorporated themselves with the Indians; and others, from a strong attachment to their erratic mode of life, joined the boatmen, then just becoming a distinct class. Among these was our hero, Mike Fink, whose talents were soon developed; and for many years, he was as celebrated on the rivers of the West, as he had been in the woods.

I gave to my fellow travellers the substance of the foregoing narrative, as we sat on deck by moonlight and cut swiftly through the magnificent sheet of water between Letart and the Great Kanhawa. It was one of those beautiful nights, which permitted every thing to be seen with sufficient distinctness to avoid danger; —yet created a certain degree of illusion, that gave reins to the imagination. The outline of the river hills lost all its harshness; and the occasional bark of the house dog from the shore, and the distant scream of the solitary loon, gave increased effect to the scene. It was altogether so delightful, that the hours till morning flew swiftly by, whilst our travellers dwelt with rapture on the surrounding scenery, which shifted every moment like the capricious changes of the kaleidoscope—and listening to the tales of border warfare, as they were brought to mind, by passing the places where they happened. The celebrated Hunter's Leap, and the bloody battle of Kanhawa, were not forgotten.

The afternoon of the next day brought us to the beautiful city of Cincinnati, which, in the course of thirty years, has risen from a village of soldiers' huts to a town,—giving promise of future splendour, equal to any on the sea-board.

Some years after the period, at which I have dated my visit to Cincinnati, business called me to New Orleans. On board of the steam boat, on which I had embarked, at Louisville, I recognised, in the person of the pilot, one of those men, who had formerly been a patroon, or keel captain. I entered into conversation with him on the subject of his former associates.

"They are scattered in all directions," said he. "A few, who had capacity, have become pilots of steam boats. Many have joined the trading parties that cross the Rocky mountains; and a few have settled down as farmers."

"What has become," I asked, "of my old acquaintance, Mike Fink?"

"Mike was killed in a skrimmage," replied the pilot. "He had refused several good offers on steam boats. He said he could not bear the hissing of steam, and he wanted room to throw his pole. He went to the Missouri, and about a year since was shooting the tin cup, when he had corned too heavy. He elevated too low, and shot his companion through the head. A friend of the deceased, who was present, suspecting foul play, shot Mike through the heart, before he had time to reload his rifle."

With Mike Fink expired the spirit of the Boatmen.

➤ *ANDY ADAMS*

A Moonlight Drive

Andy Adams (1859–1935), while still a youth, left the Indiana farm where he was born and took off for Texas, transported, as he said, by an "incurable wanderlust." For over ten years he rode the open range "on the hurricane deck of a Texas horse," and learned the true meaning of haphazard potluck in

From *The Log of a Cowboy* (Boston: Houghton Mifflin Company, 1903). chap. 17, pp. 258–277.

the cow country. Later, overcome by the "Cripple
Creek fever," Adams drifted to Colorado and became a miner and then, suddenly, a writer. *The Log
of a Cowboy* (1903), a synthesized record of numerous cattle drives between the Texas border and the
Powder River country, is probably the most authentic
account of range life ever put on paper. The selection
reprinted here demonstrates the cowpuncher's ingenuity in coping with a problem that threatened the
successful completion of the "long drive."

The two herds were held together a second night, but after
they had grazed a few hours the next morning, the cattle were
thrown together, and the work of cutting out ours commenced.
With a double outfit of men available, about twenty men were
turned into the herd to do the cutting, the remainder holding the
main herd and looking after the cut. The morning was cool,
every one worked with a vim, and in about two hours the herds
were again separated and ready for the final trimming. Campbell
did not expect to move out until he could communicate with the
head office of the company, and would go-up to Fort Laramie for
that purpose during the day, hoping to be able to get a message
over the military wire. When his outfit had finished retrimming
our herd, and we had looked over his cattle for the last time, the
two outfits bade each other farewell, and our herd started on its
journey.

The unfortunate accident at the ford had depressed our feelings
to such an extent that there was an entire absence of hilarity by
the way. This morning the farewell songs generally used in parting
with a river which had defied us were omitted. The herd trailed
out like an immense serpent, and was guided and controlled by
our men as if by mutes. Long before the noon hour, we passed out
of sight of Forty Islands, and in the next few days, with the change
of scene, the gloom gradually lifted. We were bearing almost due
north, and passing through a delightful country. To our left ran
a range of mountains, while on the other hand sloped off the
apparently limitless plain. The scarcity of water was beginning to
be felt, for the streams which had not a source in the mountains

on our left had dried up weeks before our arrival. There was a gradual change of air noticeable too, for we were rapidly gaining altitude, the heat of summer being now confined to a few hours at noonday, while the nights were almost too cool for our comfort.

When about three days out from the North Platte, the mountains disappeared on our left while on the other hand appeared a rugged-looking country, which we knew must be the approaches of the Black Hills. Another day's drive brought us into the main stage road connecting the railroad on the south with the mining camps which nestled somewhere in those rocky hills to our right. The stage road followed the trail some ten or fifteen miles before we parted company with it on a dry fork of the Big Cheyenne River. There was a road house and stage stand where these two thoroughfares separated, the one to the mining camp of Deadwood, while ours of the Montana cattle trail bore off for the Powder River to the northwest. At this stage stand we learned that some twenty herds had already passed by to the northern ranges, and that after passing the next fork of the Big Cheyenne we should find no water until we struck the Powder River—a stretch of eighty miles. The keeper of the road house, a genial host, informed us that this drouthy stretch in our front was something unusual, this being one of the dryest summers that he had experienced since the discovery of gold in the Black Hills.

Here was a new situation to be met, an eighty-mile dry drive; and with our experience of a few months before at Indian Lakes fresh in our memories, we set our house in order for the undertaking before us. It was yet fifteen miles to the next and last water from the stage stand. There were several dry forks of the Cheyenne beyond, but as they had their source in the tablelands of Wyoming, we could not hope for water in their dry bottoms. The situation was serious, with only this encouragement: other herds had crossed this arid belt since the streams had dried up, and our Circle Dots could walk with any herd that ever left Texas. The wisdom of mounting us well for just such an emergency reflected the good cow sense of our employer; and we felt easy in regard to our mounts, though there was not a horse or a man too many. In summing up the situation, Flood said, 'We've got this advantage over the Indian Lake drive: there is a good moon, and the days are cool. We'll make twenty-five miles a day covering this stretch, as this herd has never been put to a test yet to see how far they could walk in a day. They'll have to do their sleeping at noon; at least cut it into two shifts, and if we get any sleep we'll have to do the same. Let her come as she will; every day's drive is a day nearer the Blackfoot Agency.'

We made a dry camp that night on the divide between the road house and the last water, and the next forenoon reached the South Fork of the Big Cheyenne. The water was not even running in it, but there were several long pools, and we held the cattle around them for over an hour, until every hoof had been thoroughly watered. McCann had filled every keg and canteen in advance of the arrival of the herd, and Flood had exercised suffi-cient caution, in view of what lay before us, to buy an extra keg and a bull's-eye lantern at the road house. After watering, we trailed out some four or five miles and camped for noon, but the herd were allowed to graze forward until they lay down for their noonday rest. As the herd passed opposite the wagon, we cut a fat two-year-old stray heifer and killed her for beef, for the inner man must be fortified for the journey before us. After a two hours' siesta, we threw the herd on the trail and started on our way. The wagon and saddle horses were held in our immediate rear, for there was no telling when or where we would make our next halt of any consequence. We trailed and grazed the herd alternately until near evening, when the wagon was sent on ahead about three miles to get supper, while half the outfit went along to change mounts and catch up horses for those remaining behind with the herd. A half hour before the usual bedding time, the relieved men returned and took the grazing herd, and the others rode in to the wagon for supper and a change of mounts. While we shifted our saddles, we smelled the savory odor of fresh beef frying.

'Listen to that good old beef talking, will you?' said Joe Stallings, as he was bridling his horse. 'McCann, I'll take my carne fresco a trifle rare to-night, garnished with a sprig of parsley and a wee bit of lemon.'

Before we had finished supper, Honeyman had rehooked the mules to the wagon, while the *remuda* was at hand to follow. Before we left the wagon, a full moon was rising on the eastern horizon, and as we were starting out Flood gave us these general directions: 'I'm going to take the lead with the cook's lantern, and one of you rear men take the new bull's-eye. We'll throw the herd on the trail; and between the lead and rear light, you swing men want to ride well outside, and you point men want to hold the lead cattle so the rear will never be more than a half a mile behind. I'll admit that this is somewhat of an experiment with me, but I don't see any good reason why she won't work. After the moon gets another hour high we can see a quarter of a mile, and the cattle are so well trail broke they'll never try to scatter. If it works all right, we'll never bed them short of midnight, and that will put us ten miles farther. Let's ride, lads.'

By the time the herd was eased back on the trail, our evening camp-fire had been passed, while the cattle led out as if walking on a wager. After the first mile on the trail the men on the point were compelled to ride in the lead if we were to hold them within the desired half mile. The men on the other side, or the swing, were gradually widening, until the herd must have reached fully a mile in length; yet we swing riders were never out of sight of each other, and it would have been impossible for any cattle to leave the herd unnoticed. In that moonlight the trail was as plain as day, and after an hour, Flood turned his lantern over to one of the point men, and rode back around the herd to the rear. From my position that first night near the middle of the swing, the lanterns both rear and forward being always in sight, I was as much at sea as any one as to the length of the herd, knowing the deceitfulness of distance of camp-fires and other lights by night. The foreman appealed to me as he rode down the column, to know the length of the herd, but I could give him no more than a simple guess. I could assure him, however, that the cattle had made no effort to drop out and leave the trail. But a short time after he passed me I noticed a horseman galloping up the column on the opposite side of the herd, and knew it must be the foreman. Within a short time, some one in the lead wig-wagged his lantern;

it was answered by the light in the rear, and the next minute the old rear song,

> 'Ip-e-la-ago, go 'long little doggie,
> You'll make a beef-steer by-and-by,'

reached us riders in the swing, and we knew the rear guard of cattle was being pushed forward. The distance between the swing men gradually narrowed in our lead, from which we could tell the leaders were being held in, until several times cattle grazed out from the herd, due to the checking in front. At this juncture Flood galloped around the herd a second time, and as he passed us riding along our side, I appealed to him to let them go in front, as it now required constant riding to keep the cattle from leaving the trail to graze. When he passed up the opposite side, I could distinctly hear the men on that flank making a similar appeal, and shortly afterwards the herd loosened out and we struck our old gait for several hours.

Trailing by moonlight was a novelty to all of us, and in the stillness of those splendid July nights we could hear the point men chatting across the lead in front, while well in the rear, the rattling of our heavily loaded wagon and the whistling of the horse wrangler to his charges reached our ears. The swing men were scattered so far apart there was no chance for conversation amongst us, but every once in a while a song would be started, and as it surged up and down the line, every voice, good, bad, and indifferent, joined in. Singing is supposed to have a soothing effect on cattle, though I will vouch for the fact that none of our Circle Dots stopped that night to listen to our vocal efforts. The herd was traveling so nicely that our foreman hardly noticed the passing hours, but along about midnight the singing ceased, and we were nodding in our saddles and wondering if they in the lead were never going to throw off the trail, when a great wigwagging occurred in front, and presently we overtook The Rebel, holding the lantern and turning the herd out of the trail. It was then after midnight, and within another half hour we had the cattle bedded down within a few hundred yards of the trail. One-hour guards was the order of the night, and as soon as our wagon and saddle horses came up, we stretched ropes and caught out our night horses. These we either tied to the wagon wheels or picketed near at hand, and then we sought our blankets for a few hours' sleep. It was half past three in the morning when our guard was called, and before the hour passed, the first signs of day were visible in the east. But even before our watch had ended, Flood and the last guard came to our relief, and we pushed the sleeping cattle off the bed ground and started them grazing forward.

Cattle will not graze freely in a heavy dew or too early in the morning, and before the sun was high enough to dry the grass, we had put several miles behind us. When the sun was about an hour high, the remainder of the outfit overtook us, and shortly afterward the wagon and saddle horses passed on up the trail, from which it was evident that 'breakfast would be served in the dining car ahead,' as the traveled Priest aptly put it. After the sun was well up, the cattle grazed freely for several hours; but when we sighted the remuda and our commissary some two miles in our lead, Flood ordered the herd lined up for a count. The Rebel was always a reliable counter, and he and the foreman now rode forward and selected the crossing of a dry wash for the counting. On receiving their signal to come on, we allowed the herd to graze slowly forward, but gradually pointed them into an immense 'V,' and as the point of the herd crossed the dry arroyo, we compelled them to pass in a narrow file between the two counters, when they again spread out fan-like and continued their feeding.

The count confirmed the success of our driving by night, and on its completion all but two men rode to the wagon for breakfast. By the time the morning meal was disposed of, the herd had come up parallel with the wagon but a mile to the westward, and as fast as fresh mounts could be saddled, we rode away in small squads to relieve the herders and to turn the cattle into the trail. It was but a little after eight o'clock in the morning when the herd was again trailing out on the Powder River trail, and we had already put over thirty miles of the dry drive behind us, while so far neither horses nor cattle had been put to any extra exertion. The wagon followed as usual, and for over three hours we held the trail without a break, when sighting a divide in our front, the foreman went back and sent the wagon around the herd with instructions to make the noon camp well up on the divide. We threw the herd off the trail, within a mile of this stopping place, and allowed them to graze, while two thirds of the outfit galloped away to the wagon.

We allowed the cattle to lie down and rest to their complete satisfaction until the middle of the afternoon; meanwhile all hands, with the exception of two men on herd, also lay down and slept in the shade of the wagon. When the cattle had had several hours' sleep, the want of water made them restless, and they began to rise and graze away. Then all hands were aroused and we threw them upon the trail. The heat of the day was already over, and until the twilight of the evening, we trailed a three-mile clip, and again threw the herd off to graze. By our traveling and grazing gaits, we could form an approximate idea as to the distance we had covered, and the consensus of opinion of all was that we had already killed over half the distance. The herd was beginning to show the want of water by evening, but amongst our saddle horses the lack of water was more noticeable, as a horse subsisting on grass alone weakens easily; and riding them made them all the more gaunt. When we caught up our mounts that evening, we had used eight horses to the man since we had left the South Fork, and another one would be required at midnight, or whenever we halted.

We made our drive the second night with more confidence than the one before, but there were times when the train of cattle must have been nearly two miles in length, yet there was never a halt as long as the man with the lead light could see the one in the rear. We bedded the herd about midnight; and at the first break of day, the fourth guard with the foreman joined us on our watch and we started the cattle again. There was a light dew the second night, and the cattle, hungered by their night walk, went to grazing at once on the damp grass, which would allay their thirst slightly. We allowed them to scatter over several thousand acres, for we were anxious to graze them well before the sun absorbed the moisture, but at the same time every step they took was one less to the coveted Powder River.

When we had grazed the herd forward several miles, and the sun was nearly an hour high, the wagon failed to come up, which caused our foreman some slight uneasiness. Nearly another hour passed, and still the wagon did not come up nor did the outfit put

in an appearance. Soon afterwards, however, Moss Strayhorn overtook us, and reported that over forty of our saddle horses were
missing, while the work mules had been overtaken nearly five miles
back on the trail. On account of my ability as a trailer, Flood at
once dispatched me to assist Honeyman in recovering the missing
horses, instructing some one else to take the *remuda*, and the
wagon and horses to follow up the herd. By the time I arrived,
most of the boys at camp had secured a change of horses, and I
caught up my *grulla*, that I was saving for the last hard ride, for
the horse hunt which confronted us. McCann, having no fire built,
gave Honeyman and myself an impromptu breakfast and two can-
teens of water; but before we let the wagon get away, we rustled a
couple of cans of tomatoes and buried them in a cache near the
camp-ground, where we would have no trouble in finding them on
our return. As the wagon pulled out, we mounted our horses and
rode back down the trail.

Billy Honeyman understood horses, and at once volunteered the
belief that we would have a long ride overtaking the missing saddle stock. The absent horses, he said, were principally the ones
which had been under saddle the day before, and as we both knew,
a tired, thirsty horse will go miles for water. He recalled, also, that
while we were asleep at noon the day before, twenty miles back on
the trail, the horses had found quite a patch of wild sorrel plant,
and were foolish over leaving it. Both of us being satisfied that
this would hold them for several hours at least, we struck a free
gait for it. After we passed the point where the mules had been
overtaken, the trail of the horses was distinct enough for us to
follow in an easy canter. We saw frequent signs that they left the
trail, no doubt to graze, but only for short distances, when they
would enter it again, and keep it for miles. Shortly before noon, as
we gained the divide above our noon camp of the day before, there
about two miles distant we saw our missing horses, feeding over
an alkali flat on which grew wild sorrel and other species of sour
plants. We rounded them up, and finding none missing, we first
secured a change of mounts. The only two horses of my mount in
this portion of the *remuda* had both been under the saddle the
afternoon and night before, and were as gaunt as rails, and Honeyman had one unused horse of his mount in the band. So when,
taking down our ropes, we halted the horses and began riding

slowly around them, forcing them into a compact body, I had my eye on a brown horse of Flood's that had not had a saddle on in a week, and told Billy to fasten to him if he got a chance. This was in violation of all custom, but if the foreman kicked, I had a good excuse to offer.

Honeyman was left-handed and threw a rope splendidly; and as we circled around the horses on opposite sides, on a signal from him we whirled our lariats and made casts simultaneously. The wrangler fastened to the brown I wanted, and my loop settled around the neck of his unridden horse. As the band broke away from our swinging ropes, a number of them ran afoul of my rope; but I gave the rowel to my *grulla*, and we shook them off. When I returned to Honeyman, and we had exchanged horses and were shifting our saddles, I complimented him on the long throw he had made in catching the brown, and incidentally mentioned that I had read of vaqueros in California who used a sixty-five foot lariat. 'Thunder,' said Billy, in ridicule of the idea, 'there wasn't a man ever born who would throw a sixty-five foot rope its full length—without he threw it down a well.'

The sun was straight overhead when we started back to overtake the herd. We struck into a little better than a five-mile gait on the return trip, and about two o'clock sighted a band of saddle horses and a wagon camped perhaps a mile forward and to the side of the trail. On coming near enough, we saw at a glance it was a cow outfit, and after driving our loose horses a good push beyond their camp, turned and rode back to their wagon.

'We'll give them a chance to ask us to eat,' said Billy to me, 'and if they don't, why, they'll miss a good chance to entertain hungry men.'

But the foreman with the stranger wagon proved to be a Bee County Texan, and our doubts did him an injustice, for, although dinner was over, he invited us to dismount and ordered his cook to set out something to eat. They had met our wagon, and McCann had insisted on their taking a quarter of our beef, so we fared well. The outfit was from a ranch near Miles City, Montana, and were going down to receive a herd of cattle at Cheyenne, Wyoming. The cattle had been bought at Ogalalla for delivery at the former point, and this wagon was going down with their ranch outfit to take the herd on its arrival. They had brought along about seventy-five saddle horses from the ranch, though in buying the herd they had taken its remuda of over a hundred saddle horses. The foreman informed us that they had met our cattle about the middle of the forenoon, nearly twenty-five miles out from Powder River. After we had satisfied the inner man, we lost no time getting off, as we could see a long ride ahead of us; but we had occasion as we rode away to go through their remuda to cut out a few of our horses which had mixed, and I found I knew over a dozen of their horses by the ranch brands, while Honeyman also recognized quite a few. Though we felt a pride in our mounts, we had to admit that theirs were better; for the effect of climate had transformed horses that we had once ridden on ranches in southern Texas. It does seem incredible, but it is a fact nevertheless, that a horse, having reached the years of maturity in a southern climate, will grow half a hand taller and carry two hundred pounds more flesh, when he has undergone the rigors of several northern winters.

We halted at our night camp to change horses and to unearth our cached tomatoes, and again set out. By then it was so late in the day that the sun had lost its force, and on this last leg in overtaking the herd we increased our gait steadily until the sun was scarcely an hour high, and yet we never sighted a dust-cloud in our front. About sundown we called a few minutes' halt, and after eating our tomatoes and drinking the last of our water, again pushed on. Twilight had faded into dusk before we reached a divide which we had had in sight for several hours, and which we had hoped to gain in time to sight the timber on Powder River before dark. But as we put mile after mile behind us, that divide seemed to move away like a mirage, and the evening star had been shining for an hour before we finally reached it, and sighted, instead of Powder's timber, the campfire of our outfit about five miles ahead. We fired several shots on seeing the light, in the hope that they might hear us in camp and wait; otherwise we knew they would start the herd with the rising of the moon.

When we finally reached camp, about nine o'clock at night, everything was in readiness to start, the moon having risen sufficiently. Our shooting, however, had been heard, and horses for a change were tied to the wagon wheels, while the remainder of the remuda was under herd in charge of Rod Wheat. The runaways were thrown into the horse herd while we bolted our suppers.

Meantime McCann informed us that Flood had ridden that afternoon to the Powder River, in order to get the lay of the land. He
had found it to be ten or twelve miles distant from the present
camp, and the water in the river barely knee deep to a saddle
horse. Beyond it was a fine valley. Before we started, Flood rode in
from the herd, and said to Honeyman, 'I'm going to send the
horses and wagon ahead to-night, and you and McCann want to
camp on this side of the river, under the hill and just a few hundred yards below the ford. Throw your saddle horses across the
river, and build a fire before you go to sleep, so we will have a
beacon light to pilot us in, in case the cattle break into a run on
scenting the water. The herd will get in a little after midnight, and
after crossing, we'll turn her loose just for luck.'

It did me good to hear the foreman say the herd was to be
turned loose, for I had been in the saddle since three that morning, had ridden over eighty miles, and had now ten more in sight,
while Honeyman would complete the day with over a hundred to
his credit. We let the *remuda* take the lead in pulling out, so that
the wagon mules could be spurred to their utmost in keeping up
with the loose horses. Once they were clear of the herd, we let the
cattle into the trail. They had refused to bed down, for they were
uneasy with thirst, but the cool weather had saved them any
serious suffering. We all felt gala as the herd strung out on the
trail. Before we halted again there would be water for our dumb
brutes and rest for ourselves. There was lots of singing that night.
'There's One more River to cross,' and 'Roll, Powder, roll,' were
wafted out on the night air to the coyotes that howled on our
flanks, or to the prairie dogs as they peeped from their burrows at
this weird caravan of the night, and the lights which flickered in
our front and rear must have been real Jack-o'-lanterns or Will-o'-
the-wisps to these occupants of the plain. Before we had covered
half the distance, the herd was strung out over two miles, and as
Flood rode back to the rear every half hour or so, he showed no
inclination to check the lead and give the sore-footed rear guard
a chance to close up the column; but about an hour before midnight we saw a light low down in our front, which gradually increased until the treetops were distinctly visible, and we knew
that our wagon had reached the river. On sighting this beacon,
the long yell went up and down the column, and the herd walked

as only long-legged, thirsty Texas cattle can walk when they scent water. Flood called all the swing men to the rear, and we threw out a half-circle skirmish line covering a mile in width, so far back that only an occasional glimmer of the lead light could be seen. The trail struck the Powder on an angle, and when within a mile of the river, the swing cattle left the deep-trodden paths and started for the nearest water.

The left flank of our skirmish line encountered the cattle as they reached the river, and prevented them from drifting up the stream. The point men abandoned the leaders when within a few hundred yards of the river. Then the rear guard of cripples and sore-footed cattle came up, and the two flanks of horesmen pushed them all across the river until they met, when we turned and galloped into camp, making the night hideous with our yelling. The longest dry drive of the trip had been successfully made, and we all felt jubilant. We stripped bridles and saddles from our tired horses, and unrolling our beds, were soon lost in well-earned sleep.

The stars may have twinkled overhead, and sundry voices of the night may have whispered to us as we lay down to sleep, but we were too tired for poetry or sentiment that night.

↙ *MARK TWAIN*

The Californian's Tale

Mark Twain (1835–1910) in *The Californian's Story* (1893) has probed below the surface features of frontier life to some psychological realities related to loneliness. In 1865, the author wrote the following entry in his notebook: "Baden, crazy, asking after

his wife who had been dead thirteen years—first
knowledge of his being deranged." Twenty-eight
years later, Mark Twain published the story. In one
sense, the story is a companion piece to James Hall's
"The Indian Hater," but more than that, it is the
story of a hopelessness that drives men out of their
minds.

Thirty-five years ago I was out prospecting on the Stanis-
laus, tramping all day long with pick and pan and horn, and
washing a hatful of dirt here and there, always expecting to make
a rich strike, and never doing it. It was a lovely region, woodsy,
balmy, delicious, and had once been populous, long years before,
but now the people had vanished and the charming paradise was
a solitude. They went away when the surface diggings gave out.
In one place, where a busy little city with banks and newspapers
and fire companies and a mayor and aldermen had been, was
nothing but a wide expanse of emerald turf, with not even the
faintest sign that human life had ever been present there. This
was down toward Tuttletown. In the country neighborhood
thereabouts along the dusty roads, one found at intervals the
prettiest little cottage homes, snug and cozy, and so cobwebbed
with vines snowed thick with roses that the doors and windows
were wholly hidden from sight—sign that these were deserted
homes, forsaken years ago by defeated and disappointed families
who could neither sell them nor give them away. Now and then,
half an hour apart, one came across solitary log cabins of the
earliest mining days, built by the first gold-miners, the predeces-
sors of the cottage-builders. In some few cases these cabins were
still occupied; and when this was so, you could depend upon it
that the occupant was the very pioneer who had built the cabin;
and you could depend on another thing, too—that he was there
because he had once had his opportunity to go home to the States
rich, and had not done it; had rather lost his wealth, and had
then in his humiliation resolved to sever all communication with
his home relatives and friends, and be to them thenceforth as one
dead. Round about California in that day were scattered a host

of these living dead men—pride-smitten poor fellows, grizzled and old at forty, whose secret thoughts were made all of regrets and longings—regrets for their wasted lives, and longings to be out of the struggle and done with it all.

It was a lonesome land! Not a sound in all those peaceful expanses of grass and woods but the drowsy hum of insects; no glimpse of man or beast; nothing to keep up your spirits and make you glad to be alive. And so, at last, in the early part of the afternoon, when I caught sight of a human creature, I felt a most grateful uplift. This person was a man about forty-five years old, and he was standing at the gate of one of those cozy little rose-clad cottages of the sort already referred to. However, this one hadn't a deserted look; it had the look of being lived in and petted and cared for and looked after; and so had its front yard, which was a garden of flowers, abundant, gay, and flourishing. I was invited in, of course, and required to make myself at home—it was the custom of the country.

It was delightful to be in such a place, after long weeks of daily and nightly familiarity with miners' cabins—with all which this implies of dirt floor, never-made beds, tin plates and cups, bacon and beans and black coffee, and nothing of ornament but war pictures from the Eastern illustrated papers tacked to the log walls. That was all hard, cheerless, materialistic desolation, but here was a nest which had aspects to rest the tired eye and refresh that something in one's nature which, after long fasting, recognizes, when confronted by the belongings of art, howsoever cheap and modest they may be, that it has unconsciously been famishing and now has found nourishment. I could not have believed that a rag carpet could feast me so, and so content me; or that there could be such solace to the soul in wall-paper and framed lithographs, and bright-colored tidies and lamp-mats, and Windsor chairs, and varnished what-nots, with sea-shells and books and china vases on them, and the score of little unclassifiable tricks and touches that a woman's hand distributes about a home, which one sees without knowing he sees them, yet would miss in a moment if they were taken away. The delight that was in my heart showed in my face, and the man saw it and was pleased; saw it so plainly that he answered it as if it had been spoken.

"All her work," he said, caressingly; "she did it all herself—every bit," and he took the room in with a glance which was full of affectionate worship. One of those soft Japanese fabrics with which women drape with careful negligence the upper part of a picture-frame was out of adjustment. He noticed it, and re-arranged it with cautious pains, stepping back several times to gauge the effect before he got it to suit him. Then he gave it a light finishing pat or two with his hand, and said: "She always does that. You can't tell just what it lacks, but it does lack something until you've done that—you can see it yourself after it's done, but that is all you know; you can't find out the law of it. It's like the finishing pats a mother gives the child's hair after she's got it combed and brushed, I reckon. I've seen her fix all these things so much that I can do them all just her way, though I don't know the law of any of them. But she knows the law. She knows the why and the how both; but I don't know the why; I only know the how."

He took me into a bedroom so that I might wash my hands; such a bedroom as I had not seen for years: white counterpane, white pillows, carpeted floor, papered walls, pictures, dressing-table, with mirror and pin-cushion and dainty toilet things; and in the corner a wash-stand, with real china-ware bowl and pitcher, and with soap in a china dish, and on a rack more than a dozen towels—towels too clean and white for one out of practice to use without some vague sense of profanation. So my face spoke again, and he answered with gratified words:

"All her work; she did it all herself—every bit. Nothing here that hasn't felt the touch of her hand. Now you would think— But I mustn't talk so much."

By this time I was wiping my hands and glancing from detail to detail of the room's belongings, as one is apt to do when he is in a new place, where everything he sees is a comfort to his eye and his spirit; and I became conscious, in one of those un-accountable ways, you know, that there was something there somewhere that the man wanted me to discover for myself. I knew it perfectly, and I knew he was trying to help me by furtive indications with his eye, so I tried hard to get on the right track, being eager to gratify him. I failed several times, as I could see out of the corner of my eye without being told; but at last I knew I must be looking straight at the thing—knew it from the pleasure issuing in invisible waves from him. He broke into a happy laugh, and rubbed his hands together, and cried out:

"That's it! You've found it. I knew you would. It's her picture."

I went to the little black-walnut bracket on the farther wall, and did find there what I had not yet noticed—a daguerreotype-case. It contained the sweetest girlish face, and the most beautiful, as it seemed to me, that I had ever seen. The man drank the admiration from my face, and was fully satisfied.

"Nineteen her last birthday," he said, as he put the picture back; "and that was the day we were married. When you see her —ah, just wait till you see her!"

"Where is she? When will she be in?"

"Oh, she's away now. She's gone to see her people. They live forty or fifty miles from here. She's been gone two weeks to-day."

"When do you expect her back?"

"This is Wednesday. She'll be back Saturday, in the evening— about nine o'clock, likely."

I felt a sharp sense of disappointment.

"I'm sorry, because I'll be gone then," I said, regretfully.

"Gone No—why should you go? Don't go. She'll be so disappointed."

She would be disappointed—that beautiful creature! If she had said the words herself they could hardly have blessed me more. I was feeling a deep, strong longing to see her—a longing so supplicating, so insistent, that it made me afraid. I said to myself: "I will go straight away from this place, for my peace of mind's sake."

"You see, she likes to have people come and stop with us— people who know things, and can talk—people like you. She delights in it; for she knows—oh, she knows nearly everything herself, and can talk, oh, like a bird—and the books she reads, why, you would be astonished. Don't go; it's only a little while, you know, and she'll be so disappointed."

I heard the words, but hardly noticed them, I was so deep in my thinkings and strugglings. He left me, but I didn't know. Presently he was back, with the picture-case in his hand, and he held it open before me and said:

"There, now, tell her to her face you could have stayed to see her, and you wouldn't."

That second glimpse broke down my good resolution. I would stay and take the risk. That night we smoked the tranquil pipe, and talked till late about various things, but mainly about her; and certainly I had had no such pleasant and restful time for many a day. The Thursday followed and slipped comfortably away. Toward twilight a big miner from three miles away came— one of the grizzled, stranded pioneers—and gave us warm saluta-tion, clothed in grave and sober speech. Then he said:

"I only just dropped over to ask about the little madam, and when is she coming home. Any news from her?"

"Oh yes, a letter. Would you like to hear it, Tom?"

"Well, I should think I would, if you don't mind, Henry!"

Henry got the letter out of his wallet, and said he would skip some of the private phrases, if we were willing; then he went on and read the bulk of it—a loving, sedate, and altogether charming and gracious piece of handiwork, with a postscript full of affec-tionate regards and messages to Tom, and Joe, and Charley, and other close friends and neighbors.

As the reader finished, he glanced at Tom, and cried out:

"Oho, you're at it again! Take your hands away, and let me see your eyes. You always do that when I read a letter from her. I will write and tell her."

"Oh no, you mustn't, Henry. I'm getting old, you know, and any little disappointment makes me want to cry. I thought she'd be here herself, and now you've got only a letter."

"Well, now, what put that in your head? I thought everybody knew she wasn't coming till Saturday."

"Saturday! Why, come to think, I did know it. I wonder what's the matter with me lately? Certainly I knew it. Ain't we all get-ting ready for her? Well, I must be going now. But I'll be on hand when she comes, old man!"

Late Friday afternoon another gray veteran tramped over from his cabin a mile or so away, and said the boys wanted to have a little gaiety and a good time Saturday night, if Henry thought she wouldn't be too tired after her journey to be kept up.

"Tired? She tired! Oh, hear the man! Joe, you know she'd sit up six weeks to please any one of you!"

When Joe heard that there was a letter, he asked to have it read, and the loving messages in it for him broke the old fellow all up; but he said he was such an old wreck that that would happen to him if she only just mentioned his name. "Lord, we miss her so!" he said.

Saturday afternoon I found I was taking out my watch pretty often. Henry noticed it, and said, with a startled look:

"You don't think she ought to be here so soon, do you?"

I felt caught, and a little embarrassed; but I laughed, and said it was a habit of mine when I was in a state of expectancy. But he didn't seem quite satisfied; and from that time on he began to show uneasiness. Four times he walked me up the road to a point whence we could see a long distance; and there he would stand, shading his eyes with his hand, and looking. Several times he said:

"I'm getting worried, I'm getting right down worried. I know she's not due till about nine o'clock, and yet something seems to be trying to warn me that something's happened. You don't think anything has happened, do you?"

I began to get pretty thoroughly ashamed of him for his childishness; and at last, when he repeated that imploring question still another time, I lost my patience for the moment, and spoke pretty brutally to him. It seemed to shrivel him up and cow him; and he looked so wounded and so humble after that, that I detested myself for having done the cruel and unnecessary thing. And so I was glad when Charley, another veteran, arrived toward the edge of the evening, and nestled up to Henry to hear the letter read, and talked over the preparations for the welcome. Charley fetched out one hearty speech after another, and did his best to drive away his friend's bodings and apprehensions.

"Anything happened to her? Henry, that's pure nonsense. There isn't anything going to happen to her; just make your mind easy as to that. What did the letter say? Said she was well, didn't it? And said she'd be here by nine o'clock, didn't it? Did you ever know her to fail of her word? Why, you know you never did. Well, then, don't you fret; she'll be here, and that's absolutely certain, and as sure as you are born. Come, now, let's get to decorating—not much time left."

Pretty soon Tom and Joe arrived, and then all hands set about adorning the house with flowers. Toward nine the three miners said that as they had brought their instruments they might as well tune up, for the boys and girls would soon be arriving now, and hungry for a good, oldfashioned break-down. A fiddle, a banjo, and a clarinet—these were the instruments. The trio took their places side by side, and began to play some rattling dance-music, and beat time with their big boots.

It was getting very close to nine. Henry was standing in the door with his eyes directed up the road, his body swaying to the torture of his mental distress. He had been made to drink his wife's health and safety several times, and now Tom shouted:

"All hands stand by! One more drink, and she's here!"

Joe brought the glasses on a waiter, and served the party. I reached for one of the two remaining glasses, but Joe growled, under his breath:

"Drop that! Take the other."

Which I did. Henry was served last. He had hardly swallowed his drink when the clock began to strike. He listened till it finished, his face growing pale and paler; then he said:

"Boys, I'm sick with fear. Help me—I want to lie down!"

They helped him to the sofa. He began to nestle and drowse, but presently spoke like one talking in his sleep, and said: "Did I hear horses' feet? Have they come?"

One of the veterans answered, close to his ear: "It was Jimmy Parrish come to say the party got delayed, but they're right up the road a piece, and coming along. Her horse is lame, but she'll be here in half an hour."

"Oh, I'm so thankful nothing has happened!"

He was asleep almost before the words were out of his mouth. In a moment those handy men had his clothes off, and had tucked him into his bed in the chamber where I had washed my hands. They closed the door and came back. Then they seemed preparing to leave; but I said: "Please don't go, gentlemen. She won't know me; I am a stranger."

They glanced at each other. Then Joe said:

"She? Poor thing, she's been dead nineteen years!"

"Dead?"

"That or worse. She went to see her folks half a year after she was married, and on her way back, on a Saturday evening, the Indians captured her within five miles of this place, and she's never been heard of since."

"And he lost his mind in consequence?"

"Never has been sane an hour since. But he only gets bad when that time of the year comes round. Then we begin to drop in here, three days before she's due, to encourage him up, and ask if he's heard from her, and Saturday we all come and fix up the house with flowers, and get everything ready for a dance. We've done it every year for nineteen years. The first Saturday there was twenty-seven of us, without counting the girls; there's only three of us now, and the girls are all gone. We drug him to sleep, or he would go wild; then he's all right for another year—thinks she's with him till the last three or four days come round; then he begins to look for her, and gets out his poor old letter, and we come and ask him to read it to us. Lord, she was a darling!"

✍ RICHARD MALCOLM JOHNSTON

The Goosepond School

Richard Malcolm Johnston (1822–1898) testified that his tales were drawn partly from incidents in the life that he knew, but mostly from imagination. In

From *Dukesborough Tales* (New York: D. Appleton & Company, 1892), chaps. 4, 5, 6, pp. 15–33.

"Dukesborough" the author preserved his memoirs of Powelton, Georgia, a small village near where he was born. *Dukesborough Tales* (1871) consists of regional stories that were largely ignored when they were first published as *Georgia Sketches* during the Civil War. The new volume, with some additions, was much more successful, and the author became recognized as a local-colorist of enviable skill. The characters in Johnston's tales are so sharply drawn as to be convincingly real. The situations are humorous, but in not such a boisterous manner as is apparent in the writings of Baldwin, Hooper, Harris, or Mark Twain. Johnston published his autobiography in 1900.

It was the custom of the pupils in the Goosepond, as in most of the other country schools of those times, to study aloud. Whether the teachers thought that the mind could not act unless the tongue was going, or that the tongue going was the only evidence that the mind was acting, it never did appear. Such had been the custom, and Mr. Meadows did not aspire to be an innovator. It was his rule, however, that there should be perfect silence on his arrival, in order to give him an opportunity of saying or doing anything he might wish. This morning there did not seem to be anything heavy on his mind which required to be lifted off. He, however, looked at Brinkly Glisson with an expression of some disappointment. He had beaten him the morning before for not having gotten there in time, though the boy's excuse was that he had gone a mile out of his way on an errand for his mother. He looked at him as if he had expected to have had some business with him, which now unexpectedly had to be postponed. He then looked around over the school, and said:

"Go to studyin'."

He had been in the habit of speaking but to command, and of commanding but to be obeyed. Instantaneously was heard, then and there, that unintelligible tumult, the almost invariable incident of the country schools of that generation. There were spellers and readers, geographers and arithmeticians, all engaged in their several pursuits, in the most inexplicable confusion. Sometimes the spellers would have the heels of the others, and sometimes the readers. The geographers were always third, and the arithmeticians always behind. It was very plain to be seen that these last never would catch the others. The faster they added or subtracted, the oftener they had to rub out and commence anew. It was always but a short time before they found this to be the case, and so they generally concluded to adopt the maxim of the philosopher, of being slow in making haste. The geographers were a little faster and a little louder. But the spellers and readers had it, I tell you. Each speller and each reader went through the whole gamut of sounds, from low up to high, and from high down to low again; sometimes by regular ascension and descension, one note at a time, sounding what musicians call the diatonic intervals; at other times, going up and coming down upon the perfect fifths only. It was refreshing to see the passionate eagerness which these urchins manifested for the acquisition of knowledge! To have heard them for the first time, one might possibly have been reminded of the Apostles' preaching at Pentecost, when were spoken the languages of the Parthians and Medes, Elamites and the dwellers in Mesopotamia, and in Judea and Cappadocia; in Pontus and Asia, Phrygia and Pamphylia; in Egypt and in the parts of Syria about Cyrene; and strangers of Rome, Jews and Proselytes, Cretes and Arabians. Sometimes these jarring tongues subsided a little, when half a dozen or so would stop to blow; but in the next moment the chorus would swell again in a new and livelier *accrescendo*. When this process had gone on for half an hour, Mr. Meadows lifted up his voice and shouted, "SILENCE!" and all was still.

Now were to commence the recitations, during which stillness like that of death was required. For as great a help to study as this jargon was, Mr. Meadows found that it did not contribute any aid to the doing of *his* work.

He now performed an interesting feat. He put his hand behind the lapel of his coat-collar, and then, after withdrawing it, and holding it up, his thumb and forefinger joined together, he said:

"There is too much fuss here. I'm going to drop this pin, and I shall whip every single one of you little boys that don't hear it when it falls. Thar!"

"I heered it, Mr. Meadows! I heerd it, Mr. Meadows!" exclaimed, simultaneously, five or six little fellows.

"Come up here, you little rascals. You are a liar!" said he to each one. "I never drapped it; I never had nary one to drap. It just shows what liars you are. Set down and wait awhile, I'll show you how to tell me lies."

The little liars slunk to their seats, and the recitations commenced. Memory was the only faculty of mind that got development at this school. Whoever could say exactly what the book said was adjudged to know his lesson. About half of the pupils on this morning were successful. The other half were found to be delinquent. Among these was Asa Boatright. That calculating young gentleman knew his words and felt safe. The class had spelled around three or four times, when lo! the contingency which Allen Thigpen had suggested did come to pass. Betsy Wiggins missed her word; Heneritter Bangs (in the language of Allen) hern, and Mandy Grizzle hern; and thus responsibilities were suddenly cast upon Asa which he was wholly unprepared to meet, and which, from the look of mighty reproach that he gave each of these young ladies as she handed over her word, he evidently thought it the height of injustice that he should have been called upon to meet. Mr. Meadows, closing the book, tossed it to Asa, who, catching it as it was falling at his feet, turned, and his eyes swimming with tears, went back to his seat. As he passed Allen Thigpen, the latter whispered:

"What did I tell you? You heerd the pin drap too!"

Now, Allen was in no plight to have given this taunt to Asa. He had not given five minutes' study to his arithmetic during the whole morning. But Mr. Meadows made a rule (this one with himself, though all the pupils knew it better than any rule he had) never to allow Allen to miss a lesson; and as he had kindly taken this responsibility upon himself, Allen was wont to give himself no trouble about the matter.

Brinkly Glisson was the last to recite. Brinkly was no great hand at pronunciation. He had been reading but a short time when Mr. Meadows advanced him into geography, with the purpose, as Brinkly afterward came to believe, of getting the half-dollar extra tuition. This morning he thought he knew his lesson; and he did, as he understood it. When called to recite, he went up with a countenance expressive of mild happiness, handed the book to Mr. Meadows, and, putting his hands in his pockets, awaited the questions. And now it was an interesting sight to see Mr. Meadows smile as Brinkly talked of is-lands and promonitaries, thismuses and hemispheries. The lad misunderstood that smile, and his heart was glad for the unexpected reception of a little complacency from the master. But he was not long in error.

"Is-lands, eh? Thismuses, eh? Take this book and see if you can find any is-lands and promonitaries, and then bring them to me. I want to see them things, I do. Find 'em, if you please."

Brinkly took the book, and it would have melted the heart of any other man to see the deep despair of his heart as he looked on it and was spelling over to himself the words as he came to them.

"Mr. Meadows," he said, in pleading tones, "I thought it was is-land. Here it is, I-s-is-l-a-n-d-land: is-land;" and he looked into his face beseechingly.

"Is-land, eh? *Is-land!* Now, thismuses and promonitaries and hemispheries—"

"Mr. Meadows, I did not know how to pronounce them words. I asked you how to pronounce 'em, and you wouldn't tell me; and I asked Allen, and he told me the way I said them."

"I believe that to be a lie." Brinkly's face reddened, and his breathing was fast and hard. He looked at the master as but once or twice before during the term, but made no answer. At that moment Allen leaned carelessly on his desk, his elbows resting on it, and his chin on his hands, and said dryly:

"Yes, I did tell him so."

The man reddened a little. After a moment's pause, however, he said:

"How often have I got to tell you not to ask anybody but me how to pronounce words? That'll do, sir; set down, sir."

Brinkly went back to his seat, and, looking gloomily toward the door a minute or two, he opened his book, but studied it no more.

Mr. Meadows now set about what was the most agreeable portion of the duties of his new vocation, the punishment of offenders. The lawyers tell us that, of all the departments of the law, the vindicatory is the most important. This element of the Goosepond establishment had been cultivated so much that it had grown beyond all reasonable proportion to the others. As for the *declaratory* and the *directory*, they seemed to be considered, when clearly understood, as impediments to a fair showing and proper development of the vindicatory, insomuch that the last was often by their means disappointed of its victim. Sometimes, when his urchins would not "miss," or violate some of his numerous laws, Mr. Meadows used, in the plenitude of his power, to put the vindicatory first—punish an offender, *declare* what the latter had done to be an offense and then *direct* him that he had better not do so any more. Mr. Meadows, indeed, seemed to owe a grudge to society. Whether this was because society had not given him a father as it had done to almost everybody else, or because it had interfered in the peaceful occupation which had descended from his grandfather (as if to avenge itself on him for violating one of its express commands that such as he should inherit from nobody), did not appear. But he owed it, and he delighted in paying it off in his peculiar way; this was by beating the children of his school, every one of whom had a father. Eminently combative by nature, it was both safest and most satisfactory to wage his warfare on this general scale. So, on this fine morning, by way of taking up another instalment of this immense debt, which like most other debts seemed as if it never would get fully paid, he took down his bundle of rods from two pegs in one of the logs on which he had placed them, selected one fit for his purpose, and taking his position in the midle of the space between the fireplace and the rows of desks, he sat down in his chair. A moderate smile overspread his countenance as he said:

"Them spellin' classes and readin' classes, and them others that's got to be whipped, all but Sam Pate and Asa Boatright, come to the circus."

Five or six boys and as many girls, from eight to thirteen years old, came up, and, sitting down on the front bench which extended all along the length of the two rows of desks, pulled off their shoes and stockings. The boys then rolled up their pants, and the girls lifted the skirts of their frocks to their knees, and, having made a ring around the master as he sat in his chair, all began a brisk trot. They had described two or three revolutions, and he was straightening his switch, when Asa Boatright ran up, and, crying piteously, said:

"Please, sir, Mr. Meadows—oh pray do, sir, Mr. Meadows—let me go into the circus!"

Mr. Meadows rose and was about to strike; but another thought seemed to occur to him. He looked at him amusedly for a moment, and pointed to his seat. Asa took it. Mr. Meadows resumed his chair, and proceeded to tap the legs, both male and female, as they trotted around him. This was done at first very gently, and almost lovingly. But as the sport warmed in interest, the blows increased in rapidity and violence. The children began to cry out, and then he struck the harder; for it was a rule (oh! he was a mighty man for rules, this same Mr. Meadows) that whoever cried the loudest should be hit the hardest. He kept up this interesting exercise until he had given them about twenty-five lashes apiece. He then ceased. They stopped instantly, walked around him once, then, seating themselves upon the bench, they resumed their shoes and stockings, and went to their seats. One girl, thirteen years old, Henrietta Bangs, had begged him to let her keep on her stockings; but he was too firm a disciplinarian to allow it. When the circus was over she put on her shoes, and, taking up her stockings and putting them under her apron, she went to her seat and sobbed as if her heart were broken.

Allen Thigpen looked at her for a moment, and then he turned his eyes slowly around and looked at Brinkly Glisson. He sat with his hands in his pockets and his lips compressed. Allen knew what struggle was going on, but he could not tell how it would end. Mr. Meadows rested three minutes.

It has possibly occurred to those who may be reading this little history that it was a strange thing in Asa Boatright, who so well knew all the ways of Mr. Meadows, that he should have expressed so decisive a wish to take part in this last described exhibition—an exhibition which, however entertaining to Mr. Meadows as it doubtless was, and might be perchance to other persons placed in the attitude of spectators merely, could not be in the highest degree agreeable to one in the attitude which Master Asa must have foreseen that he would be made to assume had Mr. Meadows vouchsafed to yield to his request. But Asa Boatright was not a fool, nor was he a person who had no care for his physical well-being. In other words, Asa Boatright knew what he was about.

"Sam Pate and Asa Boatright!" exclaimed Mr. Meadows, after his rest. "Come out here and go to horsin'."

The two nags came out. Master Pate inclined himself forward, and Master Boatright leaped with some agility upon his back. The former, gathering the latter's legs under his arms, and drawing as tightly as possible his pants across his middle, began galloping gayly around the area before the fireplace. Mr. Meadows, after taking a fresh hickory, began to apply it with force and precision to that part of Master Boatright's little body which in his present attitude was most exposed. Every application of this kind caused that young gentleman to scream, and even to make spasmodic efforts to kick, which Master Pate, being for the occasion a horse, was to understand as an expression on the part of his rider that he should get on faster, and so Master Pate must frisk and prance and otherwise imitate a horse as well as possible in the circumstances. Now, the circumstances being that as soon as Master Boatright should have ridden long enough to become incapacitated from riding a real horse with comfort, they were to reverse positions, Master Boatright becoming horse and himself rider, they were hardly sufficient to make him entirely forget his identity in the personation of that quadruped. He did his best, though, in the circumstances, and not only frisked and pranced, but neighed several times. When Asa was placed in the condition hinted at above, he was allowed to dismount. Sam having mounted on his back, it was stirring to the feelings to see the latter kick and the former prance. This was always the best part of the show. A rule of this exercise was that, when the rider should dismount and become horse, he was to act well his part or be made to resume the part of rider—a prospect not at all agreeable, each one decidedly preferring to be horse. Sam was about three years older and fifteen pounds heavier than Asa. Now, while Asa had every motive which as sensible a horse as he was could have to do his best, yet he was so sore, and Sam, with the early prospect of butting his brains out, was so heavy, that he had great difficulties. He exhibited the most laudable desire and made the most faithful efforts to prance, but he could not keep his feet. Finding that he could do no great things at prancing, he endeavored to make up by neighing. When Sam would cry out and kick, Asa would neigh. He would occasionally run against the wall and neigh as if he were delighted. He would lift up one foot and neigh. He would put it down, lift up the other and neigh. Then when he attempted to lift up both feet at once, he would fall down and neigh. Again would he neigh even in the act of rising, apparently resolved to convince the world that, notwithstanding appearances to the contrary, he was as plucky a little horse as had ever trotted. Never before had Asa acted his part so well in the horsin' at the Goosepond. Never had horse, with such odds on his back, neighed so lustily. Sam screamed and kicked. Asa pranced and neighed, until at last, as he stumbled violently against the bench, Sam let go his hold upon his neck, in order to avoid breaking his own, and fell sprawling on his belly under a desk. This sudden removal of the burden from Asa's back made his efforts to recover from his false step successful beyond all calculation, and he fell backward, head-foremost, upon the floor. Mr. Meadows, contrary to his wont, roared with laughter. He dropped his switch, and ordered them to their seats. They obeyed, and sat down with that graduated declension of body in which experience had taught them to be prudent.

After the close of the last performance, Mr. Meadows seemed to need another resting spell. He always liked to be as fresh as possible for the next scene. The most interesting, the most exciting, and in some respects the most delightful exercise was yet to follow. This was the punishment of Brinkly Glisson.

Now, Brinkly was one of the best boys in the world. He was the only son of a poor widow, who, at much sacrifice, had sent him to school. He had pitched and tended the crop of a few acres around the house, and she had procured the promise of a neighbor to help her in gathering it when ripe. Brinkly was the apple of her eye, the idol of her heart. He was to her as we always think of him of whom it was said, "He was the only son of his mother, and she was a widow." And Brinkly had rewarded her love and care with all the feelings of his honest, affectionate heart. He was more anxious to learn for her sake than his own. He soon came to read tolerably well, and was advanced to geography. How proud was the widow when she bought the new geography and atlas with the proceeds of four pairs of socks which she had knit with her own hands. What a world of knowledge, she thought, there must be in a book with five times as many pages as a spelling-book, and in those great red, blue, and pink pictures, covering a whole page a foot square, and all this knowledge to become the property of Brinkly! But Brinkly soon found that geography was above his present capacity, and so told Mr. Meadows. That gentleman received the communication with displeasure; said that what was the matter with him was laziness, and that laziness, of all the qualities which a boy had, was the one which he knew best what to do with. He then took to beating him. Brinkly, after the first beating, which was a light one, went home and told his mother of it, and intimated his intention not to take another. The widow was sorely distressed, and knew not what to do. On the one hand was her grief to know her son was unjustly beaten, and his spirit cowed; for she knew that he studied all the time he had, and, though uneducated herself, she was not like many other parents of her day who thought that the best means to develop the mind was to beat the body. But on the other hand would be his failing to obtain an education if he should leave the school, there being then no other in the neighborhood. This, thought the poor woman, was the worst horn of the dilemma; and so she wept, and begged him, as he loved her, to submit. He should have the more time for study; she would chop the wood and feed the stock; he should have all the time at home to himself; he could get it, she knew he could; it would come to him after awhile.

Brinkly yielded; but how many a hard struggle he made to continue that submission no one knew but he. Mr. Meadows could see this struggle sometimes. He knew that the boy was not afraid of him. He saw it in his eye every time he beat him, and it was this which imparted such eagerness to continue. He wished to subdue him, and he had not succeeded. Brinkly would never beg nor weep. Mr. Meadows often thought he was on the point of resisting him; but he knew the reason why he did not, and, while he hated him for it, he trusted that it would last. Yet he often doubted whether it would or not; and thus the matter became so intensely exciting that he continually sought for opportunities of bringing it up. He loved to tempt him. He had no doubt but that he could easily manage him in an even combat; but he did not wish it to come to that. He only gloried in goading him almost to resistance, and then seeing him yield.

Have we not all seen how the showman adapts himself to the different animals of the menagerie? How quickly and sharply he speaks to the lesser animals, which jump over his wand and back, and over and back again, and then crouch in submission as he passes by! But when he goes to the lion, you can scarcely hear his low tones as he commands him to rise and perform his part, and is not certain whether the king of the beasts will do as he is bidden or not. Doubts like these were in the mind of Mr. Meadows whenever he was about to set upon Brinkly Glisson; but, the greater these doubts, the more he enjoyed the trial. After a short rest from the fatigues of the last exercise, during which he curiously and seriously eyed the lad, he rose from his seat, paced slowly across the room once or twice, and taking a hickory switch, the longest of all he had, he stopped in the middle of the floor, and in a low, quiet tone, said:

"Brinkly Glisson, come."

Allen had been eying Brinkly all the time since the close of the circus. He noted the conflict which was going on in his soul, and he thought he saw that the conflict was going to end.

Slowly and calmly Brinkly rose from his seat, and walked up and stood before Mr. Meadows.

"Why, hi!" thought Allen.

"Off with your coat, sir"—low and gentle, and with a countenance almost smiling. Brinkly stood motionless. But he had done so once or twice before, in similar circumstances, and at length had yielded. "Off with it, sir"—louder and not so gentle. No motion on Brinkly's part, not even in his eyes, which looked steadily into the master's, with a meaning which he nearly, but not quite, understood.

"Ain't you going to pull off that coat, sir?"

"What for?" asked Brinkly.

"What for, sir?"

"Yes, sir; what for?"

"Because I am going to give you this hickory, you impudent scoundrel; and if you don't pull it off this minute, I'll give you sich a beatin' as'll make you feel like you never was whipped before since you was born. Ain't you going to pull it off, sir?"

"Not now, sir?"

Allen wriggled on his seat, and his face shone as the full moon. Mr. Meadows retreated a step, and holding his switch two feet from the larger end, he raised that end to strike.

"Stop one minute, if you please."

Mr. Meadows lowered his arm, and his face smiled a triumph. This was the first time Brinkly had ever begged. He chuckled. Allen looked disappointed.

"Stop, eh? I yi! This end looks heavy, does it? Well, I wouldn't be surprised if it warn't sorter heavy. Will you pull off your coat now, sir?"

"Mr. Meadows, I asked you to stop because I wanted to say a few words to you. You have beat me and beat me, worse than you ought to beat a dog" (Allen's face getting right again); "and God in heaven knows that, in the time that I have come to school to you, I have tried as hard as a boy ever did to please you and get my lessons. I can't understand that jography, and I ain't been readin' long enough to understand it. I have asked you to let me quit. Mother has asked you. You wouldn't do it; but beat me, and beat me, and beat me" (there is no telling whether Allen wants to laugh or cry), "and now, the more I study it, the more I don't understand it. I would have quit school long ago, but mother was so anxious for me to learn, and made me come. And now I have took off my coat to you the last time." (Ah! now there is a great tear in Allen's eye.) "Listen to me" (as the teacher's hand makes a slight motion); "don't strike me. I know I'm not learnin' anything, and your beatin' ain't going to make me learn any faster. If you are determined to keep me in this jography, and to beat me, just say so, and I'll take my hat and books and go home. I'd like to not come today, but I thought I knew my lesson. Now, I say again, don't, for God's sake, don't strike me." And he raised up both his hands, pale and trembling.

It would be impossible to describe the surprise and rage expressed on the face of Mr. Meadows during the delivery and at the close of this little harangue. He looked at the boy a moment. Brinkly's countenance expressed the deepest sadness; but there was nothing in it like defiance or threatening. It was simply sad and beseeching. The master hesitated, and looked around upon his school. It would not do to retreat now, he thought. With an imprecation, he raised his switch and struck with all his might.

"My God!" cried the boy; but in an instant sadness and beseeching passed from his face. The long-pent-up resentment of his soul gushed forth, and the fury of a demon glared from his eyes. He was preparing to spring upon Mr. Meadows, when the latter, by a sudden rush, caught him and thrust him backward over the front bench. They both tumbled on the floor, between the rows of desks, Mr. Meadows uppermost.

"It's come," said Allen quietly, as he rose and looked down upon the combatants; "it's been a long time acomin', and by good rights ought to a come long ago; but it's come now."

Mr. Meadows attempted to disengage himself and rise; but Brinkly would rise with him. After several attempts at this, Brinkly managed to get upon one knee, and, by a violent jerk, to bring his assailant down upon the floor, where they were, in the phraseology of the wrestling-ring, cross and pile. Mr. Meadows shouted to two or three of the boys to hold Brinkly until he could rise. They rose to obey, but Allen, without saying a word, put out his hand before them, and, motioning them to their seats, they resumed them. And now the contest set in for good, Mr. Meadows struggling to recover his advantage, and Brinkly to improve what he had gained. The former's right arm was thrown across the latter's neck, his right hand wound in and pulling violently his hair, while his left hand pressed against his breast. Brinkly's left leg was across Mr. Meadow's middle, and with his right against a stationary desk, his right arm bent and lying under him like a lizard's, and his left in Mr. Meadows' shirt-collar, he struggled to get uppermost; but whenever he attempted to raise his head, that hand wound in his hair would instantly bring it back to the floor. When Mr. Meadows attempted to disengage himself from underneath Brinkly's leg, that member, assisted by its brother from the desk, against which it was pressed, held it like the boa holds the bullock. Oh, Mr. Meadows, Mr. Meadows! you don't know the boy that grapples with you. You have never known anything at all about him. You blow, Mr. Meadows! See! Brinkly blows not half so hard.

Remember, you walk a mile to and from the school, and Brinkly seven, often running the first half. Besides, there is something in Brinkly's soul which will not let him tire now. The remembrance of long-continued wrongs, that cannot longer be borne; the long-subdued but now inextinguishable desire of revenge; every hostile feeling except fear—all these are now dominant in that simple heart, and they have made of him a man, and if you hope to conquer you must fight as you never have fought before, and never may have to fight again.

Your right hand pulls less vigorously at the hair of Brinkly's ascending head. Look there Brinkly's leg has moved an inch further across you! Wring and twist, Mr. Meadows, for right under that leg, if anywhere for you, is now the post of honor. Can't you draw out your left leg and plant it against the desk behind you, as Brinkly does with his right? Alas! no. Brinkly has now made a hook of *his* left, and his heel is pressing close into the cavity behind your knee. Ah! that was an unlucky move for you then, when you let Brinkly's hair go, and thrust both of your hands at his eyes. You must have done that in a passion. But see there, now! he has released his grasp at your shirt-collar, and thrown his left arm over you. Good-morning to you now, Mr. Meadows!

In the instant that Mr. Meadows had released his hold upon his hair, Brinkly, though he was being gouged terribly, released his hold upon his collar, threw his arm over his neck, and pushing with all his might with his right leg against the desk, and making a corresponding pull with his left, he succeeded in getting fully upon him; then, springing up quick as lightning, as Mr. Meadows, panting, his eyes gleaming with the fury of an enraged tiger, was attempting to rise, he dealt him a blow in the face with his fist which sent him back bleeding like a butchered beast. Once more the master attempted to rise, and those who saw it will never forget that piteous spectacle of rage, and shame, and pain, and fear. Once more Brinkly struck him back. How that boy's face shone out with those *gaudia certaminis* which the brave always feel when in the midst of an inevitable and righteous combat! Springing upon his adversary again, and seizing his arms and pinioning them under his knees, he wound his hands in his shaggy hair, and raising his head, thrust it down several times with all his might against the floor.

"Spare me! for God's sake, spare me!" cried Mr. Meadows, in tones never before heard from him in that house.

Brinkly stopped. "Spare you!" he said, now panting himself. "Yes! you who never spared anything that you could hurt! Poor coward! You loved to beat other people, and gloried in seeing them suffering, and when they begged you to spare them, you laughed —you did. Oh, how I have heard you laugh, when they asked you to spare them! And now, beat yourself and whipped, you beg like a dog. Yes, and I will spare you," he continued, rising from him. "It would be a pity to beat any such a poor cowardly human any longer. Now go! and make them poor things there go to horsin' again, and cut 'em in two again! and then get in the circus ring, and make them others, girls and all—yes, girls and all—hold up their clothes and trot around you, and when they cry like you, and beg you to spare 'em, do you laugh again!"

He rose and turned away from him. Gathering up his books, he went to the peg whereon his hat was hanging, and was in the act of taking it down, when a sudden revulsion of feeling came over him, and he sat down and wept and wept.

The feelings in that poor boy's breast! The recollection of the wrongs he had suffered: of the motives, so full of pious duty, which had made him endure them; the thought of how mistaken had been the wish of his mother that he should endure them; and then of how terribly they had been avenged: these all meeting at once in his gentle, untaught spirit, overcame it, and broke it into weeping.

Meanwhile, other things were going on. Mr. Meadows, haggard, bruised, bleeding, covered with dirt, slunk off toward the fireplace, sat down in his chair, and buried his face in his hands. The pupils had been in the highest states of alternate alarm and astonishment. They were now all standing about their seats, looking alternately at Brinkly and Mr. Meadows, but at the latter mostly. Their countenances plainly indicated that this was a sight which, in their minds, had never before been vouchsafed to mortal vision. A schoolmaster whipped! beat! choked! his head bumped! and that by one of his pupils! And that schoolmaster Mr. Meadows!—Mr.

Meadows, who, ten minutes before, had been in the exercise of sovereign and despotic authority! And then to hear him beg! A schoolmaster!—Mr. Meadows!—to hear him actually beg Brinkly to spare him! They actually began to feel not only pity, but some resentment at what had been done. They were terrified, and to some extent miserable, at the sight of so much power, so much authority, so much royalty dishonored and laid low. Brinkly seemed to them to have been transformed. He was a murderer! a REGICIDE!! Talk of the divine right of kings! There was never more reverence felt for it than the children in country schools felt for the kingly dignity of the schoolmaster of sixty years agone.

⤖ WALLACE STEGNER

Not a Drop of Rain in a Thousand Miles

Wallace Stegner (1909–   ), Professor of English and Director of the Creative Writing Center at Stanford University, spent five years, 1914–1919, in what he called "a really rough and unregenerate frontier hamlet" in Saskatchewan. His father had the "pioneering itch" in his bones, and Stegner's childhood was spent in one of the last of American frontiers. A story writer and novelist of distinction, Stegner has exploited frontier materials for the purpose of fiction. In The Big Rock Candy Mountain (1938), he has revealed the "fool's gold" in the glittering myth of abundance.

The Big Rock Candy Mountain (part 4, chap. 4). Copyright 1938, 1940, 1942, 1943 by Wallace Stegner. Reprinted by permission of Brandt and Brandt.

There were days in July when they went out together along the wheat field, the long narrow strip stretching almost a mile from the pasture fence to the Montana line. They all carried pails of wheat wet and swollen and sweetsmelling from strychnine, and dropped a tablespoonful at every gopher hole they found. This was the crucial time, as far as the gophers were concerned. The wheat was a foot high, and the gophers liked it best at that stage, when they could break down the spears and get at the tender joints. Already, in spite of the boy's trapping and snaring and poisoning, there were patches as big as a table along the edges of the field where the wheat was broken and eaten down close to the ground.

"You ought to get out here with your traps more," Bo said. "You spend too much time in the pasture, where it doesn't matter."

"They come down for water, though," the boy said. "There's one hole by the dam where I've caught nineteen already."

"Well, you aren't catching them all," said his father. "If this poison doesn't thin them down you'll have to trap all up and down this field."

"I'll get 'em. I sort of hate to poison them because then I don't get the tails."

"Forget about the tails. You've got to keep this field from looking as if it had the mange."

They went clear to the line, to the heavy iron post that marked the international boundary, along the foot of the field, and back up the other side between the wheat and the flax. The father was sweating heavily under his wide straw hat. "I was a sucker to make that field so long and narrow," he said. "It'd be a lot handier if it was wider and not so long."

Elsa looked at him and smiled. "You wanted to plow a furrow a mile long and straight as a string," she said.

"Well, I plowed her. Maybe I'm no farmer, but I plowed her a mile long and six inches deep and straight as the team could walk."

"I know," she said, and lifted her straw hat from her red hair to let the wind cool her. "You've done fine with it."

Reaching down for a clod, he crumbled it between his fingers. "Dry pretty far down," he said. "We could stand a rain."

"It'll rain," she said. "It has to. Even so, I think the wheat looks awfully good." She wiped her forehead on her sleeve and smiled.

"It better," he said. He looked down the green shimmer of the field and set the edges of his teeth precisely together. "By God," he said, "if it doesn't make for us this year I'll . . ." He could think of nothing bad enough to do. "It sure better rain," he said. "With wheat two and a half a bushel it better rain."

"If we get a crop will you fix up the house a little?" she said.

"Fix it up how?"

"Paint it, maybe. And rig some kind of water system so I could plant flowers and things."

"Old Mama," he said. "Wants a cottage with roses round the door."

"Well, I do. It's so barren the way it is. It's like camping in the place. Ever since we went to the mountains I've had the itch to fix it up."

"I tell you one thing," he said, "if we don't make it this year we won't even be camping in it. We'll be going some place where we can make a living."

"We've made a living. Even with the drouth last year and the rust the year before we made a living."

He stooped to lay a spoonful of poison at a gopher hole. "When we came up here," he said, "we didn't come up just to make a living. We came up to make a pile."

They watched the sky those days, watched the southeast where the June rains had come from. Nothing but the fitful glare of heat lightning rewarded their watching, but even without rain the wheat grew strongly. From day to day the boy thought he could see the difference, for the days were warm and endless, and when he dug into the ground it was warm for five or six inches down.

The gophers were under control, though there were still hundreds of them. He had almost fifteen hundred tails in the cigar box, tied into bundles of a hundred so that he didn't have to spend all afternoon counting them. And he had taken to drowning out gophers along the coulee by the dam. There were always some there, now that the dry spell was on, and it was fun to sic Spot on the hole while he ran with buckets. Spot learned fast. He would stand quivering with excitement, with his nose down the hole, while the boy was gone, and when the water came he backed up one step and waited, whining and watching the hole. When the gopher popped out, wet and slick and dark with the water, Spot would snap once, and that was the end of Mister Gopher.

There were days, during that hot July, when they got into the Ford and went down to the little stream by Pete and Emil and had a swim in the lukewarm, barely-running water. Those were good days. But as July passed and the rain held off a tension came into the house. His father sang less at breakfast-making, and he was likely to stand in the door facing another cloudless morning and swear under his breath. His mother went around often with her lips pressed together and her eyes worried, and he saw how she avoided talk whenever she could.

When thunderheads did build up, the tension pulled harder, and there was a difference in the way they stood and watched. In June they had waited confidently, because if this one blew over the ground was still good and moist, and there would be another one soon anyway. But now there was a half expectation that the clouds would come to nothing, because there had been false alarms a half dozen times. Once or twice they watched storms get near enough to drop a few heavy pellets of rain in the baked dooryard, and whistle their winds through the screens of the porch so that they ran to roll down the canvas blinds. But by the time they got the porch snug the pelting would have stopped, and they would stand in the doorway again and see blue sky coming like a falsely-smiling enemy behind the hopeful dark of the cloud.

That tension invaded the private life of the boy, too. The farm was no longer a world invented simply for his exploration and delight. Seeing his father glum, his mother silent, he felt a compulsion to do something. The only thing he could do was to destroy gophers, and though they were not the real danger now, their decimation at least gave him the sense of helping. He was in the pasture and along the field three or four times a day, and from his lookout in the sleeping porch he kept the coulee bank always under his eye when he was in the house. The minute a gopher showed on the tawny slope he was out with a bucket as if he belonged to a volunteer fire company.

"By God," his father would say irritably, looking up at the brassy summer sky, "there isn't a drop of rain in a thousand miles."

The boy's mother told him privately that there wasn't enough for Pa to do. If he had had stock to care for, or odd jobs to do, or anything, he wouldn't be so nervous. On an ordinary farm, if one crop failed, others would come through all right, and you would have your hogs or your cattle or your cowpeas or whatever even if your big crop didn't make. But here it was just sit and watch, and it was pretty hard on Pa, and if the wheat didn't make there was nothing.

He took to going out into the field alone, and they would see him walking along the edge of the wheat, green-bronze now, stooping and straightening and taking little excursions into the grain that reached around his waist like green water. The first year they had come out, the mother said—1915, that was—the wheat had been higher than Pa's head. He had just walked into Gadke's field and disappeared. Ever since then Pa had a great respect for Gadke as a farmer. But he hadn't had much of a field in that year himself, just twenty acres, because he was building the house and getting the fence in and getting the sod broken and everything. Even so, they had made over a thousand bushel of wheat that year, more than they had made since with two or three times the acreage in.

The boy dreamed about the wheat at night now. Once he dreamed that he went out across the coulee and there was the grain grown enormously, a wilderness, a woods of wheat, taller than tall, with great fat heads nodding far above him, and he ran back to the house with his mouth shouting words, calling his father to come and see, but when they got back the wheat had shrivelled and blackened and died, and the field looked like a dark and smoky place that fire had passed over. His father flew into a rage and cuffed him for lying, and he awoke.

As August moved on day by cloudless day, they began to watch the southwest rather than the southeast. The days were hot, with light hot fingering winds that bent the wheat and died again, and in the evenings there was always a flicker of heat lightning. The southwest was dangerous in August. From that direction came the hot winds, blowing for two or three days at a time, that had withered and scorched the wheat last year. They were like Chinooks, his father said, except that in summer they were hot as hell. You couldn't predict them and you couldn't depend on their coming, but if they came you were sunk.

What a God damned country, his father said.

The boy heard them talking in bed at night, when they thought he was asleep, but even without that he couldn't have missed how his father grew darker and more sullen and silent. The good humor was less frequent and never lasted. Even when he proposed a swim down by Pete and Emil he did it as if it were a last resort to keep from flying all apart with worry and impotence. "Let's get out of here and do something," he would say. "Sit around here much longer and the roof'll fall in on us."

"It's just this not being able to do anything," the boy's mother said. "It's this sitting, without being able to do anything but sit. . . ."

That was why, the boy knew, she proposed the visit to the Garfields, who had come two years before to take up a homestead four miles east of them. "We ought to know our neighbors better," she said. "They've lived there two years and we've never even met them."

"I've met him," Bo said.

"Where?"

"Down at Cree. He's a prissy-faced long-nosed Englishman."

"Well, but he's our nearest neighbor. And she might be nice."

"Have they got any kids, Ma?" the boy asked.

"I don't think so. I wish they had." She looked at the father and wheedled him. "You'll drive us over on Sunday, won't you?" she said. "Just to be neighborly. It'll do you good."

He shrugged and picked up a magazine, four months old and dog-eared from long use.

The boy was excited by the visit to Garfields'. The hot afternoon was still and breathless, the air harder to breathe than usual. He knew there was a change in weather coming, because the gingersnaps in their tall cardboard box were soft and bendable when he snitched a couple to stick in his pocket. He could tell too by his father's grumpiness that something was coming. If it was rain everything would be dandy, there would be humming and singing again before breakfast. Maybe his father would let him ride the mare down to Cree for the mail. But if it was hail or hot wind they'd have to walk soft and speak softer, and the crop might be ruined, and that would be calamity.

He found more than he looked for at Garfields'. Mr. Garfield was tall and bald with a big nose, and talked very softly and politely. The boy's father was determined not to like him right from the start.

When Mr. Garfield said, "Dear, I think we might have a glass of lemonade, don't you?" the boy saw his parents look at each other, saw the beginning of a smile on his father's face, saw his mother purse her lips and shake her head ever so little. And when Mrs. Garfield, prim and spectacled, with a habit of tucking her head back and to one side while she listened to anyone talk, brought in the lemonade, the boy saw his father taste his and make a little face behind the glass. He hated any summer drink without ice in it, and kept his own beer at home deep in the cellar hole where it would keep cool.

But Mr. and Mrs. Garfield were nice people. They sat down in their new parlor and showed the boy's mother the rug and the gramophone. When the boy came up curiously to inspect the little box with a petunia-shaped horn with a picture of a terrier and "His Master's Voice" painted on it, and when the Garfields found that he had never seen or heard a gramophone, they put on a cylinder like a big spool of tightly-wrapped black thread, and pushed a lever and lowered a needle, and out came a man's voice singing in Scotch brogue, and his mother smiled and nodded and said, "My land, Harry Lauder! I heard him once a long time ago. Isn't it wonderful, sonny?"

It was wonderful all right. He inspected it, reached out his fingers to touch things, wiggled the big horn to see if it was loose or screwed in. His father warned him sharply to keep his hands off, but Mr. Garfield smiled and said, "Oh, he can't hurt it. Let's play something else," and found a record about the saucy little bird on Nellie's hat that had them all laughing. They let him wind the machine and play the record over again, all by himself, and he was very careful. It was a fine machine. He wished he had one.

About the time he had finished playing his sixth or seventh record, and George M. Cohan was singing, "She's a grand old rag, she's a high-flying flag, and forever in peace may she wave," he glanced at his father and saw that he was grouchy about something. He wasn't taking part in the conversation, but was sitting with his chin in his hand staring out the window. Mr. Garfield was looking at him a little helplessly. His eyes met the boy's and he motioned him over.

"What do you find to do all summer, young man? Only child, are you?"

"No sir. My brother's in Whitemud. He's twelve. He's got a job."

"So you came out on the farm to help," Mr. Garfield said. He had his hand on the boy's shoulder and his voice was so kind that the boy lost his shyness and felt no embarrassment at all in being out there in the middle of the parlor with all of them looking at him.

"I don't help much," he said. "I'm too little to do anything but drive the stoneboat, Pa says. When I'm twelve he's going to get me a gun and then I can go hunting."

"Hunting?" said Mr. Garfield. "What would you hunt?"

"Oh, gophers and weasels. I got a pet weasel now. His name's Lucifer."

"Well," Mr. Garfield said. "You seem a manly little chap. What do you feed your weasel?"

"Gophers." He thought it best not to say that the gophers were alive when he threw them in. He thought that probably Mr. Garfield would be a little shocked at that.

Mr. Garfield straightened up and looked around at the grown-ups. "Isn't it a shame," he said, "that there are so many predatory animals and pests in this country that we have to spend our time destroying them? I hate killing things."

"I hate weasels," the boy said. "I'm saving this one till he turns white and then I'm going to skin him. Once I speared a weasel with a pitchfork in the chicken house and he dropped right off the tine and ran up my leg and bit me after he was speared clean through."

He finished breathlessly, and his mother smiled at him, motion-him not to talk so much. But Mr. Garfield was still looking at him kindly. "So you want to make war on the cruel things, the weasels and hawks," he said.

"Yes sir." The boy looked at his mother and it was all right. He hadn't spoiled anything by talking about the weasels.

"Now that reminds me," Mr. Garfield said, rising. "Maybe I've got something you would find useful."

He went into another room and came back with a .22 in his hand. "Could you use this?"

"I . . . yes sir!" the boy said. He had almost, in his excitement, said, "I hope to whisk in your piskers," because that was what his father said when he meant anything real hard.

"If your parents will let you have it," Mr. Garfield said, and raised his eyebrows at the boy's mother. He didn't look at the father, but the boy did.

"Can I, Pa?"

"I guess so," his father said. "Sure."

"Thank Mr. Garfield nicely," his mother said.

"Gee," the boy said. "Thanks, Mr. Garfield, ever so much."

"There's a promise goes with it," Mr. Garfield said. "I'd like you to promise never to shoot anything with it but the bloodthirsty animals, the cruel ones like weasels and hawks. Never anything like birds or prairie dogs."

"How about butcher birds?"

"Butcher birds?"

"Shrikes," said the boy's mother. "We've got some over by our place. They kill all sorts of other things, snakes and gophers and other birds. They're worse than the hawks, because they kill just for the fun of it."

"By all means," said Mr. Garfield. "Shoot the shrikes. A thing that kills for the fun of it. . . ." He shook his head and his voice got solemn, like the voice of Mr. McGregor, the Sunday school superintendent in town, when he was asking the benediction. "There's something about the way the war drags on, or maybe it's just being in this new, clean country," Mr. Garfield said, "that makes me hate killing. I simply can't bear to shoot anything any more, even a weasel."

The boy's father turned cold eyes away from Mr. Garfield and looked out the window. One big brown hand, a little dirty from the wheel of the car, rubbed against the day-old bristles of his jaws. Then he stood up and stretched. "We got to be going," he said.

"Oh, stay a while," Mr. Garfield said. "You just came. I wanted to show you my trees."

The boy's mother stared. "Trees?"

He smiled. "Sounds a bit odd out here, doesn't it? But I think trees will grow. I've made some plantings down below."

"I'd love to see them," she said. "Sometimes I'd give almost anything to get into a deep shady woods. Just to smell it, and feel how cool . . ."

"There's a little story connected with these," Mr. Garfield said. He spoke warmly, to the mother alone. "When we first decided to come out here I said to Martha that if trees wouldn't grow we shouldn't stick it. That's just what I said, 'If trees won't grow there we shan't stick it.' Trees are like the breath of life to me."

The boy's father was shaken by a sudden spell of coughing, and his wife shot a look at him and then looked back at Mr. Garfield with a light flush on her cheekbones. "I'd love to see them," she said again. "I was raised in Minnesota, and I never get used to a place as barren as this."

"When I think of the beeches back home in England," Mr. Garfield said, and shook his head with a puckering smile around the eyes.

The father lifted himself heavily out of his chair and followed the rest of them out to the coulee edge. Below them willows grew in a thin belt along the almost-dry creek, and farther back from the water there were perhaps twenty cottonwoods a dozen feet high.

"I'm trying cottonwoods first because they can stand drouth," Mr. Garfield said.

The mother was looking down with all her longing plain and naked in her face. "It's wonderful," she said. "I'd give almost anything to have some on our place."

"I found the willows near here," Mr. Garfield said. "Just at the south end of the hills they call the Old-Man-on-His-Back, where a stream comes down."

"Stream?" the boy's father said. "You mean that spring-month trickle?"

"It's not much of a stream," Mr. Garfield said apologetically. "But. . . ."

"Are there any more there?" the mother said.

"Oh yes. You could get some. Cut them slanting and push them into any damp ground. They'll grow."

"They'll grow about six feet high," Bo Mason said.

"Yes," said Mr. Garfield. "They're not, properly speaking, trees. Still . . ."

Bo Mason looked at the southwest. "It's getting pretty smothery," he said, rather loudly. "We better be getting on."

This time Mr. Garfield didn't object, and they went back to the car with Mrs. Garfield and the boy's mother exchanging promises of visits. The father turned the crank and climbed into the Ford, where the boy was sighting along his gun. "Put that down!" his father said. "Don't you know any better than to point a gun around people?"

"It isn't loaded."

"They never are. Put it down now."

The Garfields were standing with their arms around each other's waists, waiting to wave goodbye. Mr. Garfield reached over and picked something from his wife's dress.

"What was it, Alfred?" she said, peering.

"Nothing. Only a bit of fluff."

The boy's father coughed violently and the car started with a jerk. With his head down almost on the wheel, still coughing, he waved, and the mother and the boy waved as they went down along the badly-set cedar posts of the pasture fence. They were almost a quarter of a mile away before the boy, with a last flourish of the gun, turned around to see that his father was not coughing, but laughing. He rocked the car with his joy, and when his wife said, "Oh, Bo, you big fool," he pointed helplessly to his shoulder. "Would you mind," he said. "Would you mind brushing that bit o' fluff off me showldah?" He rocked again, pounding the wheel. "I cawn't stick it," he said. "I bloody well cawn't stick it, you knaow."

"It isn't fair to laugh at him," she said. "He can't help being English."

"He can't help being a sanctimonious old mudhen, either," he said. "Braying about his luv-ly, luv-ly trees. They'll freeze out the first cold winter."

"How do you know? Maybe it's like he says—if they get a start they'll grow here as well as anywhere."

"Maybe there's a gold mine in our back yard, too, but I'm not going to dig to see. I couldn't stick it."

"You're just being stubborn," she said. "Just because you didn't like him. . . ."

He turned on her in heavy amazement. "Well my God, did you?"

"I thought he was very nice," she said, and sat straighter in the back seat, speaking loudly above the jolting of the springs and the cough of the motor. "They're trying to make a home, not just a wheat crop. I liked them."

"Uh huh." He was not laughing any more now. Sitting beside him, the boy could see that his face had hardened and that the cold look had come into his eyes again. "So I should start talking like I had a mouthful of bran, and planting trees around the house that'll look like clothesline poles in two months."

"I didn't say that."

"You thought it, though." He looked irritably at the sky, misted with the same delusive film of haze or cloud that had fooled him for three days. "You thought it all the time we were there. 'Why aren't you more like Mr. Garfield, he's such a nice man.' " With mincing savagery he swung around and mocked her. "Shall I make it a walnut grove? Or a sugar orchard? Or maybe you'd prefer orange trees."

The boy was squinting down his gun, trying not to hear them quarrel, but he knew what his mother's face would be like—hurt and a little flushed, and her chin trembling into stubbornness. "I don't suppose you could bear to have a rug on the floor, or a gramophone?" she said.

He smacked the wheel hard. "Of course I could bear it if we

could afford it. I'd love it. But I don't know what you think is going to give us the dough for things like that if a wind comes up out of that heat-hole over there. And I'd a damn sight rather do without than be like that old sandhill crane."

"I don't suppose you'd like to take me over to the Old-Man-on-His-Back some day to get some willow slips, either."

"What for?"

"To plant down in the coulee, by the dam."

"That dam dries up every August. Your willows wouldn't live till snow flies."

"Well, would it do any harm to try?"

"Oh, shut up!" he said. "Just thinking about that guy and his fluff and his trees gives me the pleefer."

The topless Ford lurched, one wheel at a time, through the deep burnout by their pasture corner, and the boy clambered out with his gun in his hand to slip the loop of the three-strand gate. It was then that he saw the snake, a striped limp ribbon, dangling on the fence, and a moment later the sparrow, neatly butchered and hung by the throat on a barb. He pointed the gun at them. "Lookit!" he said. "Lookit what the butcher bird's been doing."

His father's violent hand waved at him from the car. "Come on! Get the wire out of the way."

The boy dragged the gate through the dust, and the Ford went through and up behind the house framed by the fireguard overgrown with Russian thistle. Walking across that yard a few minutes later, the boy felt its hard heat through his sneakers. There was hardly a spear of grass within the fireguard. It was one of his father's prides that the dooryard should be like cement. "Pour your wash-water out long enough," he said, "and you'll have a surface so hard it won't even make mud." Religiously he threw his water out three times a day, carrying it sometimes a dozen steps to dump it on a dusty or grassy spot.

The mother had objected at first, asking why they had to live in the middle of an alkali flat, and why they couldn't let grass grow up to the door. But he snorted her down. Everything around the house ought to be bare as a bone. Get a good grass fire going and it would jump that guard like nothing, and if they had grass to the door where would they be? She said why not plow a wider guard then, one a fire couldn't jump, but he said he had other things to do than plowing fifty-foot fireguards.

They were arguing inside when the boy came up the step to sit down and aim his empty .22 at a fencepost. Apparently his mother had been persistent, and persistence when he was not in a mood for it angered the father worse than anything. Their talk came vaguely through the boy's concentration, but he shut his ears on sight, right on it, and pulled the trigger, that old coyote would jump about eighty feet in the air and come down dead as a mackerel, and he could tack his hide on the barn the way Mr. Larson had one, only the dogs had jumped and torn the tail and hind legs off Mr. Larson's, and he wouldn't get more than the three-dollar bounty for its ears. But Mr. Larson had shot his with a shotgun, anyway, and the hide wasn't worth much even before the dogs tore it.

"I can't for the life of me see why not," his mother said inside. "We could do it now. We're not doing anything else."

"I tell you they wouldn't grow!" his father said, with emphasis on every word. "Why should we run our tongues out doing everything that mealymouthed fool does?"

"I don't want anything but the willows. They're easy."

He made his special sound of contempt, half-snort and half-grunt. After a silence she tried again. "They might even have pussies on them in the spring. Mr. Garfield thinks they'd grow, and his wife told me he used to work in a greenhouse."

"This isn't a greenhouse, for Chrissake. Go outside and feel that breeze if you think so."

"Oh, let it go," she said. "I've stood it this long without any green things around. I guess I can stand it some more."

The boy, aiming now toward the gate where the butcher bird, coming back to his prey, would in just a second fly right into Deadeye's unerring bullet, heard his father stand up suddenly.

"Abused, aren't you?" he said.

The mother's voice rose. "No, I'm not abused! Only I don't see why it would be so awful to get some willows. Just because Mr. Garfield gave me the idea, and you don't like him. . . ."

"You're right I don't like him. He gives me a pain right under the crupper."

"Because," the mother's voice said bitterly, "he calls his wife 'dear' and puts his arm around her and likes trees. It wouldn't occur to you to put your arm around your wife, would it?"

The boy aimed and held his breath. His mother ought to keep still, because if she didn't she'd get him real mad and then they'd both have to tiptoe around the rest of the day. He heard his father's breath whistle through his teeth, and his mincing, nasty voice: "Would you like me to put my arm around you now, *dear?*"

"I wouldn't let you touch me with a ten-foot pole," his mother said. She sounded just as mad as he did, and it wasn't often she let herself get that way. The boy squirmed over when he heard the quick hard steps come up behind him and pause. Then his father's hand, brown and meaty and felted with fine black hair, reached down over his shoulder and took the .22.

"Let's see this cannon old Scissor-Bill gave you," he said.

It was a single-shot, bolt-action Savage, a little rusty on the barrel, the bolt sticky with hardened grease when the father removed it. Sighting up through the barrel, he grunted. "Takes care of a gun like he sets a fence. Probably used it to cultivate his luv-ly trees."

He went out into the porch, and after a minute came back with a rag and a can of machine oil. Hunching the boy over on the step, he sat down and began rubbing the bolt with the oil-soaked rag.

"I just cawn't bear to shoot anything any more," he said, and laughed suddenly. "I just cawn't stick it, little man." He leered at the boy, who grinned back uncertainly. Squinting through the barrel again, his father breathed through his nose and clamped his lips together, shaking his head.

The sun lay heavy on the baked yard. Out over the corner of the pasture a soaring hawk caught wind and sun at the same time, so that his light breast feathers flashed as he banked and rose. Just wait, the boy said. Wait till I get my gun working and I'll fix you, you hen-robber. He thought of the three chicks a hawk had struck earlier in the summer, the three balls of yellow with the barred mature plumage just showing through. Two of them dead before he got there and chased the hawk away, the other with its crop slashed open and wheat spilling from it to the ground. His mother had sewed up the crop and the chicken had lived, but it always looked droopy, like a plant in drouth time, and sometimes it stood working its bill as if choking.

By golly, he thought, I'll shoot every hawk and butcher bird in twenty miles. I'll. . . .

"Rustle around and find me a piece of baling wire," his father said. "This barrel looks like a henroost."

Behind the house he found a piece of rusty wire, brought it back and watched his father straighten it, wind a piece of rag around the end, ram it up and down through the barrel, and peer through again. "He's leaded her so you can hardly see the grooves," he said. "But maybe she'll shoot. We'll fill her with vinegar and cork her up tonight."

The mother was behind them, leaning against the jamb and watching. She reached down and rumpled the father's black hair. "The minute you get a gun in your hands you start feeling better," she said. "It's just a shame you weren't born a hundred years sooner."

"A gun's a good tool," he said. "It hadn't ought to be misused. Gun like this is enough to make a guy cry."

"Well, you've at least got to admit it was nice of him to give it to Bruce," she said. It was the wrong thing to say. The boy had a feeling that she knew it was the wrong thing to say, that she said it anyway just to have one tiny triumph over him. Even before he heard his father's answer he knew it would make Pa mad again.

"Oh sure," he said. "Mr. Garfield's a fine man. He can preach a better sermon than anybody in Saskatchewan. God Almighty, I get sick of hearing his praises sung. If you liked it so well why don't you move over there?"

"If you weren't so blind stubborn. . . ."

He rose with the .22 in his hand and brushed past her into the house. "I'm not so blind," he said heavily in passing. "You've been throwing that bastard up to me for two hours. It doesn't take very good eyes to see what that means. It means I'm no good, I can't do anything right."

The mother started to say, "All because I want a few little. . . ." but the boy cut in on her, anxious to help the situation somehow. "Will it shoot now?" he said.

His father said nothing. His mother looked down at him, sighed, shrugged, smiled bleakly with a tight mouth. She moved aside when the father came back with a box of cartridges in his hand. He ignored her, speaking to the boy alone in the particular half-jocular tone he always used with him or with the dog when he wasn't mad.

"Thought I had these around," he said. "Let's see what this smoke-pole will do."

He slipped in a cartridge and locked the bolt, looking around for something to shoot at. Behind him the mother's feet moved on the floor, and her voice came purposefully. "I can't see why you want to act this way," she said. "I'm going over and get some of those slips myself."

There was a long silence. The angled shade lay sharp as a knife across the baked front yard, and a breeze stirred in the Russian thistle of the fireguard. The father's cheek was pressed against the stock of the gun, his arms and hands as steady as stone.

"How'll you get there?" he said, whispering down the barrel.

"I'll walk."

"Five miles and back."

"Yes, or fifty miles and back. If there was any earthly reason why you should mind. . . ."

"I don't mind," he said, his voice soft as silk. "Go ahead."

Close to his mother's long skirts in the doorway, the boy felt her stiffen as if she had been slapped. He squirmed anxiously, but his desperation could find only the question he had asked before. His voice squeaked on it: "Will it shoot now?"

"See that sparrow out there?" his father said. "Right out by that cactus?"

"Bo!" the mother said. "If you shoot that harmless little bird!"

Fascinated, the boy watched his father's dark face against the rifle stock, the locked, immovable left arm, the thick finger crooked inside the triggerguard almost too small to hold it. He saw the sparrow, gray, white-breasted, hopping obliviously in search of bugs, fifty feet out on the gray earth.

"I just . . . cawn't . . . bear . . . to . . . shoot . . . anything," his father said, his face like dark stone, his lips hardly moving. "I just . . . cawn't . . . stick it!"

"Bo!" his wife screamed.

The boy's mouth opened, a dark wash of terror shadowed his vision of the bare yard and the sharp angle of shade. "Don't, Pa!"

The rocklike figure of his father never moved. The thick finger squeezed down slowly, there was a thin, sharp report, and the sparrow jerked and collapsed into a shapeless wad on the ground. In the instant of the shot all its clean outlines vanished. Head, feet, the white breast, the perceptible outlines of the folded wings, disappeared all at once, crumbled together and were lost, and the boy sat beside his father on the step with the echo of the shot thin in his ears.

He did not look at either of his parents. He looked only at the crumpled sparrow. Step by step, unable to keep away, he went to it, stooped, and picked it up. Blood stained his fingers, and he held the bird by the tail while he wiped the smeared hand on his overalls. He heard the click as the bolt was shot and the empty cartridge ejected, and he saw his mother come swiftly out of the house past his father, who sat still on the step. Her hands were clenched, and she walked with her head down.

"Ma!" the boy said dully. "Ma, what'll I do with it?"

She stopped and turned, and for a moment they faced each other. He saw the dead pallor of her face, the burning eyes, the not-quite-controlled quiver of her lips. But her words, when they came, were flat and level, almost casual.

"Leave it right there," she said. "After a while your father will want to hang it on the barbed wire."

The boy dropped it and went straight away, as if by inspiration, to run his trap line. He hated his father and he would not even stay in the same yard with him, and he hated him all up through the pasture and back along the north end of the wheat field where the grain drooped in the withering sun. The wind, by the time he got back to the house toward evening, was blowing quite strongly from the southwest.

part 8

RELIGION

Great Revival in the West

James Bradley Finley (1781–1856) traveled down
the Ohio River to Kentucky with his father in 1788.
For years afterward, he was district superintendent
of the Western Conference of the Methodist
Church, and was an eyewitness to the "jerking, leaping, rolling" enthusiasm brought about by the
"Great Awakening." The account of the massive
revivals, reprinted here, begins with the first camp
meeting, which was held at Gaspar River, Logan
County, Kentucky, in July 1800.

Finley's *Autobiography* (Cincinnati, 1853) is a
valuable source of information about frontier life in
Ohio. See also *The Backwoods Preacher: An Autobiography of Peter Cartwright* (London, 1858).

In the spring of 1800 one of the most astonishing and
powerful revivals occurred that has ever been known in the
western country. This was also the most extensive revival that
perhaps ever was witnessed in this country. It was marked by
some peculiarities which had not been known to characterize
any revival in former times. The nearest approximation to it, of
which I can form any conception, was the revival on the day
of pentecost, when thousands were awakened and converted to
God under the most exciting circumstances.

The commencement of the revival is traceable to the joint
labors of two brothers in Cumberland county, Kentucky, one of

From W. P. Strickland, ed., *The Autobiography of Rev. James B. Finley:
Or Pioneer Life in the West* (Cincinnati, Ohio: Methodist Book Concern,
1853), chap. 21, pp. 362–373. Editor's title.

317

whom was a Presbyterian and the other a Methodist preacher. They commenced laboring together every Sabbath preaching, exhorting, and praying alternately. This union was regarded as quite singular, and excited the curiosity of vast multitudes, who came to the places of meeting to hear two men preach who held views in theology supposed to be entirely antagonistic. Nothing was discoverable in their preaching of a doctrinal character, except the doctrine of man's total depravity and ruin by sin, and his recovery therefrom by faith in Christ. All were exhorted to flee the wrath to come, and be saved from their sins. The word which they preached was attended with the power of God to the hearts of listening thousands. The multitudes who flocked from all parts of the country to hear them, became so vast that no church would hold them, and they were obliged to resort to the fields and woods. Every vehicle was put in requisition; carriages, wagons, carts and sleds. Many came on horseback, and larger crowds still came on foot.

As the excitement increased, and the work of conviction and conversion continued, several brought tents, which they pitched on the ground, and remained day and night for many days. The reader will here find the origin of camp meetings.

In the spring of 1801 Bishop M'Kendree was appointed presiding elder of the Kentucky district; and being thus brought in contact with this wonderful work, he was prepared to form a correct judgment of its character. That there were extravagances that constituted no part of religion, he was prepared to admit, but that it was all a wild, fanatical delusion, he was very far from conceding. Nay, he believed that it was the work of God's Spirit on the hearts of the people, and that thousands were genuinely converted to God.

These meetings began to follow one another in quick succession, and the numbers which attended were almost incredible. While the meetings lasted, crowds were to be seen in all directions, passing and repassing the roads and paths, while the woods seemed to be alive with people. Whole settlements appeared to be vacated, and only here and there could be found a house having an inhabitant. All ages, sexes, and conditions pressed their way to the camp meeting. At these meetings the Presbyterians and Methodists united. They were held at different places. On the 22d of May, 1801, one was held at Cabin creek; the next was held at Concord, in one of my father's old congregations; the next was at Point Pleasant, and the succeeding one at Indian creek, in Harrison county. At these meetings thousands fell under the power of God, and cried for mercy. The scenes which successively occurred at these meetings were awfully sublime, and a general terror seemed to have pervaded the minds of all people within the reach of their influences.

The great general camp meeting was held at Cane Ridge meeting-house. This house was built for my father, and here was my old home. I have elsewhere described this meeting, or, rather, attempted to do so. Language is utterly impuissant to convey any thing like an adequate idea of the sublimity and grandeur of the scene. Twenty thousand persons tossed to and fro, like the tumultuous waves of the sea in a storm, or swept down like the trees of the forest under the blast of the wild tornado, was a sight which mine own eyes witnessed, but which neither my pen nor tongue can describe.

During the religious exercises within the encampment, all manner of wickedness was going on without. So deep and awful is man's depravity, that he will sport while the very fires of perdition are kindling around him. Men, furious with the effects of the maddening bowl, would outrage all decency by their conduct; and some, mounted on horses, would ride at full speed among the people. I saw one, who seemed to be a leader and champion of the party, on a large, white horse, ride furiously into the praying circle, uttering the most horrid imprecations. Suddenly, as if smitten by lightning, he fell from his horse. At this a shout went up from the religious multitude, as if Lucifer himself had fallen. I trembled, for I feared God had killed the bold and daring blasphemer. He exhibited no signs whatever of life; his limbs were rigid, his wrists pulseless, and his breath gone. Several of his comrades came to see him, but they did not gaze long till the power of God came upon them, and they fell like men slain in battle. I was much alarmed, but I had a great desire to see the issue. I watched him closely, while for thirty hours he lay, to all human appearance, dead. During this

time the people kept up singing and praying. At last he exhibited
signs of life, but they were fearful spasms, which seemed as if
he were in a convulsive fit, attended by frightful groans, as if he
were passing through the intensest agony. It was not long, however, till his convulsions ceased, and springing to his feet, his
groans were converted into loud and joyous shouts of praise. The
dark, fiend-like scowl which overspread his features, gave way to
a happy smile, which lighted up his countenance.

A certain Dr. P., accompanied by a lady from Lexington, was
induced, out of mere curiosity, to attend the meeting. As they
had heard much about the involuntary jerkings and falling which
attended the exercises, they entered into an agreement between
themselves that, should either of them be thus strangely attacked
or fall, the other was to stand by to the last. It was not long till
the lady was brought down in all her pride, a poor sinner in
the dust, before her God. The Doctor, agitated, came up and felt
for her pulse; but alas! her pulse was gone. At this he turned pale,
and, staggering a few paces, he fell beneath the power of the
same invisible hand. After remaining for some time in this state,
they both obtained pardon and peace and went rejoicing home.
They both lived and died happy Christians. Thousands were affected in the same way.

These camp meetings continued for some time, the Presbyterians and Methodists uniting together as one in the army of
the Lord. Some ministers had serious doubts concerning the
character of the work; but its genuineness was demonstrated by
the fruits. Men of the most depraved hearts and vicious habits
were made new creatures, and a whole life of virtue subsequently
confirmed the conversion. To all but Methodists the work was
entirely strange. Some of the peculiarities had been witnessed
before by the preachers, and they were enabled to carry it on.

These meeting exhibited nothing to the spectator unacquainted
with them but a scene of confusion, such as scarcely could be
put into human language. They were generally opened with a
sermon or exhortation, at the close of which there would be a
universal cry for mercy, some bursting forth in loud ejaculations
of prayer or thanksgiving for the truth; some breaking forth in
strong and powerful exhortations, others flying to their careless

friends with tears of compassion, entreating them to fly to Christ for mercy; some, struck with terror and conviction, hastening through the crowd to escape, or pulling away from their relations, others trembling, weeping, crying for mercy; some falling and swooning away, till every appearance of life was gone and the extremities of the body assumed the coldness of death. These were surrounded with a company of the pious, singing melodious songs adapted to the time, and praying for their conversion. But there were others collected in circles round this variegated scene, contending for and against the work.

Many circumstances transpired that are worthy of note in reference to this work. Children were often made the instruments through which the Lord wrought. At one of these powerful displays of Divine power, a boy about ten years old broke from the stand in time of preaching under very strong impressions, and having mounted a log at some distance, and raising his voice in a most affecting manner, cried out, "On the last day of the feast Jesus stood and cried, If any man thirst, let him come unto me and drink." He attracted the main body of the congregation, and, with streaming eyes, he warned the sinners of their danger, denouncing their doom, if they persevered in sin, and strongly expressed his love for the salvation of their souls, and the desire that they would turn to God and live. By this time the press was so great that he was taken up by two men and held above the crowd. He spoke for near an hour with that convincing eloquence that could be inspired only from heaven; and when exhausted, and language failed to describe the feelings of his soul, he raised his handkerchief, and dropping it, cried, "Thus, O sinner, will you drop into hell unless you forsake your sins and turn to God." At this moment the power of God fell upon the assembly, and sinners fell as men slain in mighty battle, and the cries for mercy seemed as though they would rend the heavens, and the work spread in a manner which human language can not describe.

We will now try to give something in reference to the manner and the exercise of mind of those who were the subjects of this work. Immediately before they became totally powerless, they were sometimes seized with a general tremor, and often uttered several piercing shrieks in the moment of falling. Men and

women never fell when under this jerking exercise till they became exhausted. Some were unable to stand, and yet had the
use of their hands and could converse with companions. Others
were unable to speak. The pulse became weak, and they drew
a difficult breath about once a minute. In many instances they
became cold. Breathing, pulsation, and all signs of life forsook
them for hours; yet I never heard of one who died in this condition, and I have conversed with persons who have laid in this
situation for many hours, and they have uniformly testified that
they had no bodily pain, and that they had the entire use of their
reason and powers of mind. From this it appears that their falling
was neither common fainting nor a nervous affection. Indeed,
this strange work appears to have taken every possible turn to
baffle the conjectures and philosophizing of those who were unwilling to acknowledge it was the work of God. Persons have
fallen on their way home from meeting, some after they had
arrived at home, others pursuing their common business on their
farms, and others when they were attending to family or secret
devotions. Numbers of thoughtless, careless sinners have fallen
as suddenly as if struck by lightning. Professed infidels, and other
vicious characters, have been arrested, and sometimes at the very
moment when they were uttering their blasphemies against God
and the work, and have, like Saul, declared that to be God's work
which they so vehemently persecuted. . . .

It is generally known that in the early settlement of Kentucky,
the regular Baptists were by far the most numerous body of
Christians. It is also known that they adhered most rigidly to
the doctrines of unconditional election and reprobation, together
with the final and unconditional perseverance of the saints. The
same may be said of the Presbyterians, who firmly maintained
and preached these doctrines till the commencement of this revival. Indeed, the doctrine of unconditional election and reprobation was so generally taught by these denominations, that
there was rarely found any one sufficiently fearless and independent to call them in question. They had taken deep root, and
it might be said the doctrines of Calvin had filled the whole country. During the prevalence of these doctrines, supported as they
were on all sides by polemical divines, whose religion seemed to

consist almost entirely of a most dogged and pertinacious adherence to the creeds and confessions of faith, which had been
handed down from orthodox Puritan fathers, it was not a matter
of surprise that professors of religion, losing sight of the weightier
matters of the Gospel, while they attended to its "anise, and
mint, and cummin," would fall insensibly into antinomianism.
The inconsistency of the doctrines of Calvin became the subject
of the sarcastic sneers of infidels, and the inability of these
Churches to reconcile their doctrines with the justice of God and
the present order of things, made fearful inroads on the cause of
Christianity, and strengthened the hands of the wicked. The
friends of the truth were few. They were without influence, and
much persecuted; but, notwithstanding, they lifted up their voice.

It was at this juncture, and under these circumstances, that it
pleased the Lord to look down upon the western country. Man's
extremity was God's opportunity, and the wonderful manifestation
of Divine power swept away antinomianism, and infidelity, and
every refuge of lies. There were some in the Presbyterian Church
who did not preach a partial Gospel, but who lifted up their voice
like a trumpet, and invited all to come to Jesus for salvation, assuring them that he died for all. Of this number was that man of God,
Carey Allen. As a missionary he was "a flame of fire," and thousands were awakened under his fervent, soul-stirring appeals.

Not long after the revival commenced, several of the Presbyterian ministers renounced Calvinism, and being persecuted by
their brethren, they left the Church, and organized a new Presbytery, which was called the Springfield Presbytery. As is often the
case with those who separate from the Church because they
judge it needs reformation in doctrine or discipline, so these
brethren, unfortunately, did not stop in media res, but rushed
to another extreme. They ran into gross errors and heresies, as
was seen in their apology for renouncing the jurisdiction of the
Synod, the tract on the atonement by Mr. Stone, in 1804, and
their sermons. Methodists and Presbyterians both saw that an
enemy had come in, and was sowing tares broadcast over the
field, and they retired to their own stands, and defended their
own doctrines.

The party which had separated were styled Newlights, but they have subsequently taken the name of *Christian*. In June, 1804, these preachers dissolved their Presbytery, and drew up a very curious paper, which they signed, entitled "The last Will and Testament of the Springfield Presbytery." Of the six ministers who signed this paper, two went back to the Presbyterian Church, three joined the Shakers, and one the Campbellites. They published to the world, in the paper above alluded to, their belief; or, in other words, their non-belief, for they renounced all creeds, confessions of faith, and standards of doctrine, and started out on a crusade against all the Churches. . . .

This heresy spread and prevailed. The early settlers of Kentucky were most skeptical on the subject of religion. The more influential classes of citizens were infidel in sentiment, and they labored to bring all to their views. To accomplish their wishes more fully, they employed an Englishman to take charge of their seminary of learning at Lexington. He had an extensive library, and, from his position, exerted a great influence in society. Subsequently, the principal of the seminary was elected Secretary of State. The Governor, Mr. Garrard, was a celebrated Baptist preacher, and a gentleman of much respectability and influence. It was not long till the Secretary succeeded in converting the Governor to his faith; and, having accomplished a result so desirable to the infidel party, the next thing was to get the Governor to publish a tract on the doctrine of the Trinity. This made considerable noise. In 1802 the Rev. Augustin Easton and Governor Garrard commenced a meeting on Cooper's run, in Bourbon county. Here they proclaimed publicly the Arian and Socinian doctrines. The wavering separatists were excited and encouraged wonderfully by this movement, as is evident from their own confession and subsequent course. These unfortunate people—Newlights—from the time they first began to preach their doctrines, were beset in their meetings with those wild exercises that have been alluded to (See Benedict's *History of Baptist Church*, vol. ii, p. 252.)

These strange exercises that have excited so much wonder in the western country came in toward the last of the revival, and were, in the estimation of some of the more pious, the chaff of the work. Now it was that the humilating and often disgusting exercises of dancing, laughing, jerking, barking like dogs, or howling like wolves, and rolling on the ground, manifested themselves. To add to their misfortune, being ripe for such a catastrophe, a company of Shakers from New York found their way among them, and proselyted their most talented and useful preacher and not a few of their members. These fanatics for a season went on with a tremendous influence, threatening to sweep all men before them. But they, like all other wild and visionary people, had their day. . . .

The wild vagaries adopted by the Newlight preachers of Kentucky prepared them to gulp down all the ridiculous tenets of Shakerism, and this produced a general skepticism in that state, that, I fear, will not be done away for generations. It may seem strange that all grades of Arians and Socinians have adopted immersion as the only mode of baptism, and regard it as constituting a title to heaven.

The new isms that followed this great revival were many, and it seemed as if Satan had taken advantage of the excitement to drive the bewildered into darkness and the sanguine into error and folly. The Shakers drew off hundreds with them. Elder Holmes rose up with his pilgrims, and started out in quest of the Holy Land. He had many followers, and, after wandering about for some time, died on an island in the Mississippi River, and his band dissolved. Elder Farnum, also another fanatic, pretended to have received the spirit of immediate inspiration, and raised a party called the "screaming children." After flourishing for a season, this association dwindled away. Next came A. Sargent and his twelve disciples—all women. It was spread over the country that he was inspired and conversed with angels daily, from whom he received revelations. Then Elias Hicks, the Quaker, espoused Arianism, and split the Quaker Church, spreading confusion and schism every-where among the Friends.

Last, but not least in the train of evils, came Kidwell with the last edition of Universalism. He taught that there was no hell, no devil, no future judgment; that it was impossible for any one to commit any crime in this life that would possibly shut him out of heaven; that all souls at death enter at once into the heavenly state, and are happy with God forever, no matter how they have lived in this world.

The Camp Meeting

Edward Eggleston (1837–1902), whose literary fame
rests on *The Hoosier Schoolmaster* (1871), presented his fictional characters as products of the
frontier culture with which he was familiar. His
The Circuit Rider (1874) is more truly historical
than literary and is a classic in the folklore of Ohio
pioneer settlements. Of the itinerant preacher
Eggleston said, "In no other class was the real heroic
element so finely displayed." But the author was
careful to present the rude as well as the heroic side
of early Methodism, and by writing about people
without prejudice, he was able to produce what he
called the "higher form of history." W. P. Randel
wrote a biography of Eggleston in 1946.

The incessant activity of a traveling preacher's life did not
allow Morton much opportunity for the society of the convalescent
Ann Eliza. Fortunately. For when he was with her out of meeting
he found her rather dull. To all expression of religious sentiment
and emotion she responded sincerely and with unction; to Morton's highest aspiration for a life of real, self-sacrifice she only
answered with a look of perplexity. She could not understand him.
He was "so queer," she said.

But people whose lives are joined ought to make the best of
each other. Ann Eliza loved Morton, and because she loved him
she could endure what seemed to her an unaccountable eccentricity. If Goodwin found himself tempted to think her lacking in
some of the highest qualities, he comforted himself with reflecting
that all women were probably deficient in these regards. For men
generalize about women, not from many but from one. And men,

From *The Circuit Rider* (New York: J. B. Ford, 1874), chap. 27, pp. 252–
266.

being egotists, suffer a woman's love for themselves to hide a multitude of sins. And then Morton took refuge in other people's opinions. Everybody thought that Sister Meacham was just the wife for him. It is pleasant to have the opinion of all the world on your side where your own heart is doubtful.

Sometimes, alas! the ghost of an old love flitted through the mind of Morton Goodwin and gave him a moment of fright. But Patty was one of the things of this world which he had solemnly given up. Of her conversion he had not heard. Mails were few and postage cost a silver quarter on every letter; with poor people, correspondence was an extravagance not to be thought of except on the occasion of a death or wedding. At farthest, one letter a year was all that might be afforded. As it was, Morton was neither very happy nor very miserable as he rode up to the New Canaan campground on a pleasant midsummer afternoon with Ann Eliza by his side.

Sister Meacham did not lack hospitable entertainment. So earnest and gifted a Christian as she was always welcome; and now that she held a mortgage on the popular preacher every tent on the ground would have been honored by her presence. Morton found a lodging in the preacher's tent, where one bed, larger, transversely, than that of the giant Og, was provided for the collective repose of the preachers, of whom there were half-a-dozen present. It was always a solemn mystery to me, by what ingenious over-lapping of sheets, blankets and blue-coverlets the sisters who made this bed gave a cross-wise continuity to the bedclothing.

This meeting was held just six weeks after the quarterly meeting spoken of in the last chapter. Goodwin's circuit lay on the west bank of the Big Wiaki River, and this camp-meeting was held on the east bank of that stream.

It was customary for all the neighboring preachers to leave their circuits and lend their help in a camp-meeting. All detached parties were drawn in to make ready for a pitched battle. Morton had, in his ringing voice, earnest delivery, unfaltering courage and quick wit, rare qualifications for the rude campaign, and, as the nearest preacher, he was, of course, expected to help.

The presiding elder's order to Kike to repair to Jonesville circuit had gone after the zealous itinerant like "an arrow after a wild goose," and he had only received it in season to close his affairs on Pottawottomie Creek circuit and reach this camp-meeting on his way to his new work. His emaciated face smote Morton's heart with terror. The old comrade thought that the death which Kike all but longed for could not be very far away. And even now the zealous and austere young man was so eager to reach his circuit of Peterborough that he would only consent to tarry long enough to preach on the first evening. His voice was weak, and his appeals were often drowned in the uproar of a mob that had come determined to make an end of the meeting.

So violent was the opposition of the rowdies from Jenkinsville and Salt Fork that the brethren were demoralized. After the close of the service they gathered in groups debating whether or not they should give up the meeting. But two invincible men stood in the pulpit looking out over the scene. Without a thought of surrendering, Magruder and Morton Goodwin were consulting in regard to police arrangements.

"Brother Goodwin," said Magruder, "we shall have the sheriff here in the morning. I am afraid he hasn't got back-bone enough to handle these fellows. Do you know him?"

"Burchard? Yes; I've known him two or three years."

Morton could not help liking the man who had so generously forgiven his gambling debt, but he had reason to believe that a sheriff who went to Brewer's Hole to get votes would find his hands tied by his political alliances.

"Goodwin," said Magruder, "I don't know how to spare you from preaching and exhorting, but you must take charge of the police and keep order."

"You had better not trust me," said Goodwin.

"Why?"

"If I am in command there'll be a fight. I don't believe in letting rowdies run over you. If you put me in authority, and give me the law to back me, somebody'll be hurt before morning. The rowdies hate me and I am not fond of them. I've wanted such a chance at these Jenkinsville and Salt Fork fellows ever since I've been on the circuit."

"I wish you *would* clean them out," said the sturdy old elder, the martial fire shining from under his shaggy brows.

Morton soon had the brethren organized into a police. Every man was to carry a heavy club; some were armed with pistols to be used in an emergency. Part of the force was mounted, part marched afoot. Goodwin said that his father had fought King George, and he would not be ruled by a mob. By such fannings of the embers of revolutionary patriotism he managed to infuse into them some of his own courage.

At midnight Morton Goodwin sat in the pulpit and sent out scouts. Platforms of poles, six feet high and covered with earth, stood on each side of the stand or pulpit. On these were bright fires which threw their light over the whole space within the circle of tents. Outside the circle were a multitude of wagons covered with cotton cloth, in which slept people from a distance who had no other shelter. In this outer darkness Morton, as military dictator, had ordered other platforms erected, and on these fires were now kindling.

The returning scouts reported at midnight that the ruffians, seeing the completeness of the preparations, had left the camp-ground. Goodwin was the only man who was indisposed to trust this treacherous truce. He immediately posted his mounted scouts farther away than before on every road leading to the ground, with instructions to let him know instantly, if any body of men should be seen approaching.

From Morton's previous knowledge of the people, he was convinced that in the mob were some men more than suspected of belonging to Micajah Harp's gang of thieves. Others were allies of the gang—of that class which hesitates between a lawless disposition and a wholesome fear of the law, but whose protection and assistance is the right foot upon which every form of brigandage stands. Besides these there were the reckless young men who persecuted a camp-meeting from a love of mischief for its own sake; men who were not yet thieves, but from whose ranks the bands of thieves were recruited. With these last Morton's history gave him a certain sympathy. As the classes represented by the mob held the balance of power in the politics of the county, Morton knew that he had not much to hope from a trimmer such as Burchard.

About four o'clock in the morning one of the mounted sentinels who had been posted far down the road came riding in at full speed, with intelligence that the rowdies were coming in force from the direction of Jenkinsville. Goodwin had anticipated this, and he immediately awakened his whole reserve, concentrating the scattered squads and setting them in ambush on either side of the wagon tracks that led to the camp-ground. With a dozen mounted men well armed with clubs, he took his own stand at a narrow place where the foliage on either side was thickest, prepared to dispute the passage to the camp. The men in ambush had orders to fall upon the enemy's flanks as soon as the fight should begin in front. It was a simple piece of strategy learned of the Indians.

The marauders rode on two by two until the leaders, coming round a curve, caught sight of Morton and his right hand man. Then there was a surprised reining up on the one hand, and a sudden dashing charge on the other. At the first blow Goodwin felled his man, and the riderless horse ran backward through the ranks. The mob was taken by surprise, and before the ruffians could rally Morton uttered a cry to his men in the bushes, which brought an attack upon both flanks. The rowdies fought hard, but from the beginning the victory of the guard was assured by the advantage of ambush and surprise. The only question to be settled was that of capture, for Morton had ordered the arrest of every man that the guard could bring in. But so sturdy was the fight that only three were taken. One of the guard received a bad flesh wound from a pistol shot. Goodwin did not give up pursuing the retreating enemy until he saw them dash into the river opposite Jenkinsville. He then rode back, and as it was getting light threw himself upon one side of the great bunk in the preachers' tent, and slept until he was awakened by the horn blown in the pulpit for the eight o'clock preaching.

When Sheriff Burchard arrived on the ground that day he was evidently frightened at the earnestness of Morton's defence. Burchard was one of those politicians who would have endeavored to patch up a compromise with a typhoon. He was in a strait between his fear of the animosity of the mob and his anxiety to please the Methodists. Goodwin, taking advantage of this latter feeling, got himself appointed a deputy-sheriff, and, going before a magistrate, he secured the issuing of writs for the arrest of those whom he knew to be leaders. Then he summoned his guard as a posse, and, having thus put law on his side, he announced that if the ruffians came again the guard must follow him until they were entirely subdued.

Burchard took him aside, and warned him solemnly that such extreme measures would cost his life. Some of these men belonged to Harp's band, and he would not be safe anywhere if he made enemies of the gang. "Don't throw away your life," entreated Burchard.

"That's what life is for," said Morton. "If a man's life is too good to throw away in fighting the devil, it isn't worth having." Goodwin said this in a way that made Burchard ashamed of his own cowardice. But Kike, who stood by ready to depart, could not help thinking that if Patty were in place of Ann Eliza, Morton might think life good for something else than to be thrown away in a fight with rowdies.

As there was every sign of an approaching riot during the evening service, and as no man could manage the tempest so well as Brother Goodwin, he was appointed to preach. A young theologian of the present day would have drifted helpless on the waves of such a mob. When one has a congregation that listens because it ought to listen, one can afford to be prosy; but an audience that will only listen when it is compelled to listen is the best discipline in the world for an orator. It will teach him methods of homiletic arrangement which learned writers on Sacred Rhetoric have never dreamed of.

The disorder had already begun when Morton Goodwin's tall figure appeared in the stand. Frontier-men are very susceptible to physical effects, and there was a clarion-like sound to Morton's voice well calculated to impress them. Goodwin enjoyed battle; every power of his mind and body was at its best in the presence of a storm. He knew better than to take a text. He must surprise the mob into curiosity.

"There is a man standing back in the crowd there," he began, pointing his finger in a certain direction where there was much disorder, and pausing until everybody was still, "who reminds me of a funny story I once heard." At this point the turbulent sons of

Belial, who loved nothing so much as a funny story, concluded to postpone their riot until they should have their laugh. Laugh they did, first at one funny story, and then at another—stories with no moral in particular, except the moral there is in a laugh. Brother Mellen, who sat behind Morton, and who had never more than half forgiven him for not coming to a bad end as the result of disturbing a meeting, was greatly shocked at Morton's levity in the pulpit, but Magruder, the presiding elder, was delighted. He laughed at each story, and laughed loud enough for Goodwin to hear and appreciate the senior's approval of his drollery. But somehow—the crowd did not know how,—at some time in his discourse—the Salt Fork rowdies did not observe when,—Morton managed to cease his drollery without detection, and to tell stories that brought tears instead of laughter. The mob was demoralized, and, by keeping their curiosity perpetually excited, Goodwin did not give them time to rally at all. Whenever an interruption was attempted, the preacher would turn the ridicule of the audience upon the interlocutor, and so gain the sympathy of the rough crowd who were habituated to laugh on the side of the winner in all rude tournaments of body or mind. Knowing perfectly well that he would have to fight before the night was over, Morton's mind was stimulated to its utmost. If only he could get the religious interest agoing he might save some of these men instead of punishing them. His soul yearned over the people. His oratory at last swept out triumphant over everything; there was weeping and sobbing; some fell in uttering cries of anguish; others ran away in terror. Even Burchard shivered with emotion when Morton described how, step by step, a young man was led from bad to worse, and then recited his own experience. At last there was the utmost excitement. As soon as this hurricane of feeling had reached the point of confusion, the rioters broke the spell of Morton's speech and began their disturbance. Goodwin immediately invited the penitents into the enclosed pen-like place called the altar, and the whole space was filled with kneeling mourners, whose cries and groans made the woods resound. But at the same moment the rioters increased their noisy demonstrations, and Morton, finding Burchard inefficient to quell them, descended from the pulpit and took command of his camp-meeting police.

Perhaps the mob would not have secured headway enough to have necessitated the severest measures if it had not been for Mr. Mellen. As soon as he detected the rising storm he felt impelled to try the effect of his stentorian voice in quelling it. He did not ask permission of the presiding elder, as he was in duty bound to do, but as soon as there was a pause in the singing he began to exhort. His style was violently aggressive, and only served to provoke the mob. He began with the true old Homeric epithets of early Methodism, exploding them like bomb-shells. "You are hair-hung and breeze-shaken over hell," he cried.

"You don't say!" responded one of the rioters, to the infinite amusement of the rest.

For five minutes Mellen proceeded to drop this kind of religious aqua fortis upon the turbulent crowd, which grew more and more turbulent under his inflammatory treatment. Finding himself likely to be defeated, he turned toward Goodwin and demanded that the camp-meeting police should enforce order. But Morton was contemplating a master-stroke that should annihilate the disorder in one battle, and he was not to be hurried into too precipitate an attack.

Brother Mellen resumed his exhortation, and, as small doses of nitric-acid had not allayed the irritation, he thought it necessary to administer stronger ones. "You'll go to hell," he cried, "and when you get there your ribs will be nothing but a gridiron to roast your souls in!"

"Hurrah for the gridiron!" cried the unappalled ruffians, and Brother Mellen gave up the fight, reproaching Morton hotly for not suppressing the mob. "I thought you was a man," he said.

"They'll get enough of it before daylight," said Goodwin, savagely. "Do you get a club and ride by my side to-night, Brother Mellen; I am sure you are a man."

Mellen went for his horse and club, grumbling all the while at Morton's tardiness.

"Where's Burchard?" cried Morton.

But Burchard could not be found, and Morton felt internal maledictions at Burchard's cowardice.

Goodwin had given orders that his scouts should report to him the first attempt at concentration on the part of the rowdies. He had not been deceived by their feints in different parts of the camp, but had drawn his men together. He knew that there was some directing head to the mob, and that the only effectual way to beat it was to beat it in solid form.

At last a young man came running to where Goodwin stood, saying: "They're tearing down a tent."

"The fight will be there," said Morton, mounting deliberately. "Catch all you can, boys. Don't shoot if you can help it. Keep close together. We have got to ride all night."

He had increased his guard by mustering in every able-bodied man, except such as were needed to conduct the meetings. Most of these men were Methodists, but they were all frontiermen who knew that peace and civilization have often to be won by breaking heads. By the time this guard started the camp was in extreme confusion; women were running in every direction, children were crying and men were stoutly denouncing Goodwin for his tardiness.

Dividing his mounted guard of thirty men into two parts, he sent one half round the outside of the camp-ground in one direction, while he rode with the other to attack the mob on the other side. The foot-police were sent through the circle to attack them in a third direction.

As Morton anticipated, his delay tended to throw the mob off their guard. They had demolished one tent and, in great exultation, had begun on another, when Morton's cavalry rode in upon them on two sides, dealing heavy and almost deadly blows with their ironwood and hickory clubs. Then the footmen charged them in front, and the mob were forced to scatter and mount their horses as best they could. As Morton had captured some of them, the rest rallied on horseback and attempted a rescue. For two or three minutes the fight was a severe one. The roughs made several rushes upon Morton, and nothing but the savage blows that Mellen laid about him saved the leader from falling into their hands. At last, however, after firing several shots, and wounding one of the guard, they retreated, Goodwin vigorously persuading his men to continue the charge. When the rowdies had been driven a short distance, Morton saw by the light of a platform torch, the same strangely dressed man who had taken the money from his hand that day near Brewer's Hole. This man, in his disguise of long beard and wolf-skin cap, was trying to get past Mellen and into the camp by creeping through the bushes.

"Knock him over," shouted Goodwin to Mellen. "I know him —he's a thief."

No sooner said than Mellen's club had felled him, and but for the intervening brush-wood, which broke the force of the blow, it might have killed him.

"Carry him back and lock him up," said Morton to his men; but the other side now made a strong rush and bore off the fallen highwayman.

Then they fled, and this time, letting the less guilty rowdies escape, Morton pursued the well-known thieves and their allies into and through Jenkinsville, and on through the country, until the hunted fellows abandoned their horses and fled to the woods on foot. For two days more Morton harried them, arresting one of them now and then until he had captured eight or ten. He chased one of these into Brewer's Hole itself. The shoes had been torn from his feet by briers in his rough flight, and he left tracks of blood upon the floor. The orderly citizens of the county were so much heartened by this boldness and severity on Morton's part that they combined against the roughs and took the work into their own hands, driving some of the thieves away and terrifying the rest into a sullen submission. The camp-meeting went on in great triumph.

Burchard had disappeared—how, nobody knew. Weeks afterward a stranger passing through Jenkinsville reported that he had seen such a man on a keelboat leaving Cincinnati for the lower Mississippi, and it soon came to be accepted that Burchard had found a home in New Orleans, that refuge of broken adventurers. Why he had fled no one could guess.

Mormons and Mormonism

The migration of the Mormons from Nauvoo, Illinois, to the Great Salt Lake (1847) and the transformation of a desert into a fertile garden under the direction of Brigham Young (1801–1877), is a story of one of the most successful attempts at colonization in the history of the West. Horace Greeley (1811–1872), founder of the New York *Tribune* (1841), visited Salt Lake City in 1859. The following account is based on his personal observations and interviews. Greeley, for thirty years the "greatest single journalistic influence in America," is especially remembered for his employment of the slogan "Go west, young man, and grow up with the country."

Since my interview with Brigham Young, I have enjoyed opportunities for studying the Mormons in their social or festive and in their devotional assemblies. Of private social intercourse—that is, intercourse between family and family—I judge that there is comparatively little here; between Mormons and Gentiles or strangers, of course still less. Their religious services (in the tabernacle) are much like those that may be shared or witnessed in the churches of most of our popular sects; the music rather better than you will hear in an average worshiping assemblage in the states; the prayers pertinent and full of unction; the sermons adapted to tastes or needs different from mine. They seemed to me rambling, dogmatic, and ill-digested; in fact, Elder Orson Pratt, who preached last Sunday morning, prefaced his harangue by a statement that he had been hard at work on his farm throughout the week, and labored under consequent physical exhaustion. Elder John Taylor

---

From *An Overland Journey from New York to San Francisco in the Summer of 1859* (New York: C. M. Saxton, Barker and Co., 1860), chap. 22, pp. 219–229.

(I believe he is one of the Twelve; at all events he is a high dignitary in the church, and a man of decided natural ability) spoke likewise in the afternoon with little or no premeditation. Now, I believe that every preacher should be also a worker; I like to see one mowing or pitching hay in his shirt-sleeves; and I hear with edification an unlettered but devout and earnest evangelist who, having worked a part of the week for the subsistence of his family, devotes the rest of it to preaching the gospel to small school-house or wayside gatherings of hearers, simply for the good of their souls. Let him only be sure to talk good sense, and I will excuse some bad grammar. But when a preacher is to address a congregation of one to three thousand persons, like that which assembles twice each sabbath in the Salt Lake City Tabernacle, I insist that due regard for the economy of time requires that he should prepare himself, by study and reflection, if not by writing, to speak directly to the point. This mortal life is too short and precious to be wasted in listening to rambling, loose-jointed harangues, or even to those which severally consume an hour in the utterance, when they might be boiled down and clarified until they were brought within the compass of half an hour each. A thousand half-hours, Reverend Sir! have you ever pondered their value? Suppose your time to be worth ten times that of an average hearer; still, to take an extra half-hour from a thousand hearers in order to save yourself ten or fifteen hours' labor in the due and careful preparation of a sermon, is a scandalous waste, which I see not how to justify. Be entreated to repent and amend!

The two discourses to which I listened were each intensely and exclusively Mormon. That is, they assumed that the Mormons were God's peculiar, chosen, beloved people, and that all the rest of mankind are out of the ark of safety and floundering in heathen darkness. I am not edified by this sort of preaching. It reminds me forcibly of the Pharisee's prayer: "Lord, I thank thee that I am not as other men are—unjust, extortioners," etc. I do not think good men delight in this assumption of an exclusive patent for the grace of God; and I am quite sure it is not well adapted to the transformation of bad men into good. It is too well calculated to puff up its disciples with self-conceit and spiritual pride. That

Jesus Christ is about to re-appear on the earth in all the pomp and splendor of a mighty conqueror—that he will then proceed to take vengeance on his enemies (mankind in general, whether heathen or nominally Christians) and to glorify his elect (the Latter-Day Saints or Mormons) were treated by the Tabernacle preachers as propositions too self-evident to need demonstration. Having thus chastised his enemies and "gathered his elect from the four winds of heaven," the Saviour is to reign over them here on earth for a thousand years; at the end of which period, they are together to be transferred to heaven. Of course, I had heard the like of this before; but it always seems to me a very gross and wooden perversion of the magnificent imagery whereby the Bible foreshadows a great spiritual transformation. The spirit of the Mormon religion appears to me Judaic rather than Christian; and I am well assured that Heber C. Kimball, one of the great lights of the church, once said in conversation with a Gentile—"I do pray for my enemies: I pray that they may all go to hell." Neither from the pulpit nor elsewhere have I heard from a Mormon one spontaneous, hearty recognition of the essential brotherhood of the human race—one generous prayer for the enlightenment and salvation of all mankind. On the other hand, I have been distinctly given to understand that my interlocutors expect to sit on thrones and to bear rule over multitudes in the approaching kingdom of God. In fact, one sincere, devout man has to-day assigned that to me as a reason for polygamy; he wants to qualify himself, by ruling a large and diversified family here, for bearing rule over his principality in the "new earth," that he knows to be at hand. I think he might far better devote a few years to pondering Christ's saying to this effect, "He who would be least in the kingdom of heaven, the same shall be greatest."

I was undeceived with regard to the Book of Mormon. I had understood that it is now virtually discarded, or at least neglected, by the church in its services and ministrations. But Elder Pratt gave us a synopsis of its contents, and treated it throughout as of equal authority and importance with the Old and New Testaments. He did not read from it, however, but from Malachi, and quoted text after text from the prophets, which he cited as predictions of the writing and discovery of this book.

The congregation consisted, at either service of some fifteen hundred to two thousand persons—more in the morning than the afternoon. A large majority of them (not including the elders and chief men, of whom a dozen or so were present) were evidently of European birth; I think a majority of the males were past the meridian of life. All gave earnest heed to the exercises throughout; in fact, I have seldom seen a more devout and intent assemblage. I had been told that the Mormons were remarkably ignorant, superstitious, and brutalized; but the aspect of these congregations did not sustain that assertion. Very few rural congregations would exhibit more heads evincing decided ability; and I doubt whether any assemblage, so largely European in its composition, would make a better appearance. Not that Europeans are less intellectual or comely than Americans; but our emigrants are mainly of the poorer classes; and poverty, privation, and rugged toil plow hard, forbidding lines in the human countenance elsewhere than in Utah. Brigham Young was not present at either service.

Do I regard the great body of these Mormons as knaves and hypocrites? Assuredly not. I do not believe there was ever a religion whereof the great mass of the adherents were not honest and sincere. Hypocrites and knaves there are in all sects; it is quite possible that some of the magnates of the Mormon Church regard this so-called religion (with all others) as a contrivance for the enslavement and fleecing of the many, and the aggrandizement of the few; but I cannot believe that a sect, so considerable and so vigorous as the Mormon, was ever founded in conscious imposture, or built up on any other basis than that of earnest conviction. If the projector, and two or three of his chief confederates are knaves, the great body of their followers were dupes.

Nor do I accept the current Gentile presumption, that the Mormons are an organized banditti—a horde of robbers and assassins. Thieves and murderers mainly haunt the purlieus of great cities, or hide in caverns and forests adjacent to the great routes of travel. But when the Mormon leaders decided to set up their Zion in these parched mountain vales and cañons, the said valleys were utterly secluded and remote from all Gentile approach

—way from any mail-route or channel of emigration. That the Mormons wished to escape Gentile control, scrutiny, jurisprudence is evident; that they meant to abuse their inaccessibility, to the detriment and plunder of wayfarers, is not credible.

Do I, then, discredit the tales of Mormon outrages and crime—of the murder of the Parrishes, the Mountain Meadow massacre,[1] etc. etc.—wherewith the general ear has recently been shocked? No, I do not. Some of these may have been fabricated by Gentile malice—others are doubtless exaggerated—but there is some basis of truth for the current Gentile conviction that the Mormons have robbed, maimed, and even killed persons in this territory, under circumstances which should subject the perpetrators to condign punishment, but that Mormon witnesses, grand jurors, petit jurors, and magistrates determinedly screen the guilty. I deeply regret the necessity of believing this; but the facts are incontestable. That a large party of emigrants—not less than eighty—from Arkansas to California, were foully massacred at Mountain Meadows in September, 1857, more immediately by Indians, but under the direct inspiration and direction of the Mormon settlers in that vicinity —to whom, and not to the savages, the emigrants had surrendered, after a siege, on the strength of assurance that their lives at least should be spared—is established by evidence that cannot (I think) be invalidated—the evidence of conscience-smitten partakers in the crime, both Indian and ex-Mormon, and of children of the slaughtered emigrants, who were spared as too young to be dangerous even as witnesses, and of whom the great majority have been sent down to the states as unable to give testimony; but two boys are retained here as witnesses, who distinctly remember that their parents surrendered to white men, and that these white men at best did not attempt to prevent their perfidious massacre. These children, moreover, were all found in the possession of Mormons —not one of them in the hands of Indians; and, though the Mormons say they ransomed them from the hands of Indians, the children deny it, saying that they never lived with, nor were in the

---

[1] A detailed account of this "massacre" appears in J. H. Beadle's *Western Wilds and the Men Who Redeem Them*, Cincinnati, 1877, pp. 301–316. [Ed. Note]

keeping of savages; and the Indians bear concurrent testimony. So in the Parrish case: the family had been Mormons, but had apostatized—and undertook to return to the states; they were warned that they would be killed if they persisted in that resolution; they did persist, and were killed. Of course, nobody will ever be convicted of their murder; but those who warned them of the fate on which they were rushing know why they were killed, and could discover, if they would, who killed them.

The vital fact in the case is just this: The great mass of these people, as a body, mean to be honest, just, and humane; but they are, before and above all things else, Latter-Day Saints, or Mormons. They devoutly believe that they are God's peculiar and especial people, doing His work, up-building His kingdom, and basking in the sunshine of His peculiar favor. Whoever obstructs or impedes them in this work, then, is God's enemy, who must be made to get out of the way of the establishment of Christ's kingdom on earth—made to do so by lawful and peaceful means if possible, but by any means that may ultimately be found necessary. The Parrishes were apostates; had they been allowed to pursue their journey to the states, they would have met many Saints coming up the road, whose minds they would have troubled if not poisoned; and they would have told stories after reaching their destination which would have deepened the general prejudice against the Saints; so the up-building and well-being of Christ's kingdom required that they should die. The Arkansas emigrants slaughtered at Mountain-Meadows, had in some way abused the Saints, or interposed obstacles to the progress of God's work, and they were consequently given over to destruction. Far be it from me to hint that one-fifth, one-tenth, one-twentieth, of the Mormons ever bore any part in these bloody deeds, or even know to this day that they were perpetrated. The great body of the Saints undoubtingly believe all the current imputations of Mormon homicide and outrage to be abominable calumnies. Many of the highest dignitaries of the church may be included in this number. But there are men in the church who know that they are not calumnies —who know that Gentiles and apostates have been killed for the church's and for Christ's sake, and who firmly believe that they ought to have been. I grieve to say it, but I hold these more consistent and logical Mormons than their innocent and unsuspicious brethren. For if I were a Latter-Day Saint, undoubtingly believing all opposers of the Mormon Church to be God's enemies, obnoxious to His wrath and curse, and powerfully obstructing the rescue of souls from eternal perdition and torture, I should be strongly impelled to help put those opposers of God's purposes out of the way of sending any more immortal souls to everlasting fire. I should feel it my duty so to act, as a lover of God and man. And I confidently predict that not one Mormon who has killed a Gentile or apostate under a like view of his duty will ever be fairly convicted in this territory. No jury can be drawn here, unless in flagrant defiance of territorial laws, which is not mainly composed of Mormons; and no such jury will convict a Mormon of crime for any act done in behalf of God's kingdom—that is, of the Mormon church.

⤝ EDGAR WATSON HOWE

The Hell Question, and the Rev. John Westlock

Edgar Watson Howe (1853–1937) at the age of three traveled in a covered wagon from Indiana to Fairview, Missouri. The little prairie town furnished Howe with materials for Story of a Country Town (1882), one of the first if not the best realistic novel of small-town America ever published. It anticipated Sherwood Anderson's Winesburg, Ohio and Sinclair

From Story of a Country Town (Boston: Houghton Mifflin Company, 1884), chap. 2.

Lewis's *Main Street* by nearly four decades. The author was not an educated man, having never seen the inside of a high school, but his literary activities, including the editorship of the Atchinson, Kansas, *Globe* (at one time the "best known small town paper in America") and of *Howe's Monthly*, earned him two honorary Lit.B. degrees. Howe's autobiography, *Plain People*, was published in 1929.

My father's religion would have been unsatisfactory without a hell.

It was a part of his hope of the future that worldly men who scoffed at his piety would be punished, and this was as much a part of his expectation as that those who were faithful to the end would be rewarded. Everybody saved, to my father's thinking, was as bad as nobody saved, and in his well-patronized Bible not a passage for pleasurable contemplation which intimated universal salvation was marked, if such exists.

The sacrifices he made for religion were tasks, and his reward was a conviction that those who refused to make them would be punished, for he regarded it as an injustice of which the Creator was incapable to do as well by His enemies as by His friends. I believe that he would rather have gone to heaven without the members of his family than with them, unless they had earned salvation as he had earned it, and traveled as steadily as himself the hard road marked on his map as leading heavenward.

One of the best evidences to his mind of a compassionate and loving Saviour was the belief that all thoughts of unfortunate friends in torment was blotted from the memory of the redeemed, and the lake of fire he thought of as a remedy for the great number of disagreeable people with whom he was compelled to come in contact below, and of whom he would be happily rid above. Religion was a misery to be endured on earth, that a reward might be enjoyed after death. A man must spend the ages of his future in a very pleasant place, with comfortable surroundings and pleasant associates, or in a very unpleasant place, with uncomfortable surroundings and all the mean people turned into devils and imps for companions. It was the inevitable law; every man of moderate sense should be able to appreciate the situation at a glance, and do that which would insure his personal safety. If there was a doubt—the thought was too absurd for his contemplation, but admitting a doubt—his future would be equal to that of the worldly man, for one cannot rot more easily than another, or be more comfortable as dust; but if there was no doubt—and all the authorities agree that there was none—then the difference would be in his favor.

It was the best thing offering under the circumstances, and should therefore be accepted without hesitation. If the conditions were hard, he could not help it; he might have suggested changes in the plan of salvation had his judgment been invited, but the plan had been formulated before his time, and there was nothing left for him but obedience. If he thought he deserved credit for all he possessed, the Bible said it came from God. That settled the matter finally and forever—he gave thanks (for a punishment was provided if he did not, and a reward if he did), and pretended to have had nothing to do with accumulating his property.

Religion was a matter of thrift and self-interest as much as laying away money in youth and strength for old age and helplessness, and he called upon sinners to flee the wrath to come because he had been commanded to go out and preach to all the world, for it mattered little to him whether the people were saved or not. They had eyes, therefore let them see; ears, therefore let them hear. The danger was so plain that they ought to save themselves without solicitation.

That which he most desired seldom came to pass; that which he dreaded, frequently, but no matter; he gave thanks to the Lord because it was best to do so, and asked no questions. There were jewels for those who earned them, and as a thrifty man he desired a greater number of these than any other citizen of Fairview. He was the principal man in his neighborhood below, and desired to be a shepherd rather than a sheep above; therefore he was foremost in the church, and allowed no one to be more zealous in doing the service of the hard master he had, after careful thought and study, set out to serve, believing the reward worth the service, and determined to serve well if he served at all, as was his custom in everything else.

If I do him an injustice I do not intend it, but I have thought all

my life that he regarded children as troublesome and expensive—
a practical sort of punishment for sin, sent from time to time as
the case seemed to require; and that he had been burdened with
but two was no doubt evidence to his mind that his life had been
generally blameless, if, indeed, this opinion was not confirmed by
the circumstance that one of them had been taken from him in
return for good service in the holy cause. Once they had arrived,
however, he accepted the trust to return them to their Maker as
nearly like they came as possible, for that was commanded of him.

Because he frequently referred to the road to heaven as narrow
and difficult, and the highway in the other direction as broad and
easy, I came to believe that but for his religion he would have been
a man much given to money getting, and ambitious for distinction,
but he put such thoughts aside, and toiled away at his work as
if to get out of temptation's way. When he talked of the broad
and easy road it was with a relish, as though he could enjoy the
pleasant places by the way-side if he dared; and in his preaching I
think he described the pleasures of the world so vividly that his
hearers were taken with a wish to enjoy them, though it is not
probable that he knew anything about them except from hearsay,
as he had always been out of temptation's way—in the backwoods
during his boyhood, and on the prairie during his maturer years.
But when he talked of the narrow and difficult path, his manner
changed at once; a frown came upon his face; he looked determined and unforgiving, and at every point he seemed to build
signposts marked "Duty!" It has occurred to me since that he
thought of his religion as a vigorous, healthy, successful man
thinks in his quiet moments of a wife sick since their marriage;
although he may deserve a different fate, and desire it, he dares not
complain, for the more wearisome the invalid, the louder the call
of duty.

I think he disliked the necessity of being religious, and only accepted and taught religion because he believed it to be the best
thing to do, for it did not afford him the peace he professed. To
all appearances he was a most miserable man, although he taught
that only the sinful are miserable, and the few acquaintances he
had who were not equally devout (strangers passing through, or
those he met at the country town, for all were pious in Fairview)

lived an easy and contented life which he seemed to covet, but nobody knew it, for he reproved them with all the more vigor because of his envy.

When not engaged in reading at night, as was his custom, he sat for hours looking steadily into the fire, and was impatient if disturbed. I never knew what occupied his thoughts at these times; it may have been his preaching, or his daily work, but more likely he was seeing glimpses of forbidden pictures; caravans of coveted things passing in procession, or of hopes and ambitions dwarfed by duty. Perhaps in fancy he was out in the world mingling with people of a class more to his taste than Fairview afforded. I believe that during these hours of silent thinking he was tempted and beckoned by the invisible and mysteriously potent forces he pretended to despise, and that he was convinced that, to push them off, his religion must be made more rigorous and pitiless.

That he coveted riches could be easily seen, and but for his fear of conscience he could have easily possessed himself of everything worth owning in Fairview, for with the exception of Theodore Meek, the next best man in the neighborhood, he was about the only one among the people who read books and subscribed for newspapers. None of them was his equal in intelligence or energy, and had he desired he could have traded them out of the little they possessed, and sold it back again at a profit. But, "do unto others as you would have others do unto you," was commanded of him by his inexorable master, and he was called upon to help the weak rather than rob them; therefore he often gave them assistance which he could but poorly afford. This limited him so much that he had no other hope of becoming well-to-do than that the lands which he was constantly buying would finally become valuable by reason of the development and settlement of the country. This he regarded as honorable and fair, and to this work he applied himself with great energy.

I heard little of his father, except that he was noted where he lived as a man of a large family, who provided them all with warm clothes in winter and plenty to eat all the year round. His early history was probably as unimportant and eventless as my own. He seldom mentioned his father to any one, except in connection with a story which he occasionally told, that once, when his house was on fire, he called so loud for help that he was heard a mile. Evidently the son succeeded to this extraordinary pair of lungs, for he sang the religious songs common in that day with such excellence that no man attempted to equal him. While his singing was strong and loud, it was melodious, and he had as great a reputation for that as for piety and thrift. His was a camp-meeting voice, though he occasionally sang songs of little children, as "Moses in the Bulrushes," of which there were thirty-eight verses, and the cradle song commencing, "Hush, my dear, lie still and slumber," written by a noted hymn-writer, otherwise my father would not have patronized him. Besides a thorough familiarity with all the common, long, short, and particular meters, he had a collection of religious songs preserved in a leather-bound book, the notes being written in buckwheat characters on blue paper fast turning yellow with age, and the words on the opposite page. Feeling the necessity of a knowledge of notes once, he had learned the art in a few weeks, in his usual vigorous way, and sang at sight; and after that he preserved his old songs, and all the new ones he fancied, in the book I have mentioned. The songs to which I refer I have never seen in print, and he sang them on special occasions, as at a camp-meeting when a tiresome preacher had allowed the interest to flag. "Behold Paul a Prisoner," a complete history of the Apostle requiring almost an afternoon in its performance, or "Christ in the Garden," nearly as long, never failed to start the interest anew in an emergency, and if the case were very desperate, he called the members of his family into the pulpit, and sang a quartet called "The Glorious Eighth of April," using for the words the first hymn in the book.

This was usually sufficient to start some one to shouting, and after a short prayer he preached as vigorously and loudly as he sang, and with an equally good effect.

Of his brothers and sisters, although he had a great number, he seldom talked, and I scarcely knew the names of the States in which they lived, as they were scattered in every direction. I had heard him mention a Samuel, a Joseph, a Jacob, an Elias, a Rebecca, a Sarah and a Rachel, from which I came to believe that my grandfather was a religious man (his own name was Amos), and I once heard that his children on Sundays carried their shoes to the brook near the meeting-house before putting them on, that they might last the longer, which confirmed the belief that there had been religion in his family as there was in ours.

Of his mother he said nothing at all, and if they had neighbors he never mentioned them. In short, he did not seem proud of his family, which caused us to wonder why he was so much like his father, which we had come to believe without exactly knowing why. We were certain he was like his father in religion; in the hard way in which he worked; in his capacity to mend his own ploughs and wagons; and in the easy manner in which he adapted himself to his surroundings, whatever they were, for in all these particulars he was unlike any other man we had ever known, and different from his neighbors, who spent half a day in asking advice in a matter which could be remedied in half an hour. The people came to our house from miles around to borrow, and to ask the best time to plant and to sow, but the Rev. John Westlock asked advice of no one, and never borrowed. If he needed an extra harrow, he made one of wood to answer until such a time as he could trade to advantage for a better one; if he broke a plough, he managed somehow to mend it until a rainy day came, when he made it as good as new. Even in cases of sickness he usually had a bottle hid away that contained relief, and in all other things was equally capable and thrifty.

If it be to the credit of a man to say that he was a slave to hard work, I cheerfully add this testimony to the greatness of my father, for he went to the field at daylight only to return with the darkness, winter and summer alike; and never in my life have I seen him idle—except on the day appointed for rest—and even then he devoured the Bible like a man reading at so much per page. He worked hard when he preached, talking rapidly that he might accomplish as much as possible before the people became impatient, and he no sooner finished one song of warning, than he began another.

My father being large and positive, it followed naturally that my mother was small and weak, and thoroughly under his control. He managed his own affairs so well that she was willing he should manage hers, as he had given her good reason to respect his judgment. She probably argued—if she argued the question at all—

that as his ideas were good in everything else, he would of course know how to manage a boy, so my bringing up was left entirely to him.

She never corrected me except to say that father would not like what I was doing, and she might find it necessary to call his attention to it, but in the goodness of her heart she forgot it, and never told him unless the offence was a very grave one. While she frequently pleaded with me to be good, and cried in vexation if I would not, she never gave commands which were enforced with punishment, as he did; therefore I am afraid that I did not appreciate her kindness and favor, but rather enjoyed my freedom when under her care as a respite from restraint at other times. She was as quiet and thoughtful as her husband, but seemed sad rather than angry and discontented, as was the case with him, and it will be easily imagined that as a family we were not much given to happiness. While I never heard my father speak harshly to her, he was often impatient, as though he regretted he had not married a wife as ambitious and capable as himself; but if he thought of it, he gave it no other attention than to become more gloomy, and pacified himself by reading far into the night without speaking to any one.

I could find no fault with him except that he never spoke kindly to me, and it annoyed him if I asked him questions concerning what I read in his books. When Jo and I worked with him in the field, which we both began to do very early he always did that which was hardest and most disagreeable, and was not a tyrant in anything save the ungrumbling obedience he exacted to whatever he thought about the matter in hand, without reference to what others thought on the same subject. We had to be at something steadily, because he believed idle boys grew up into idle men. Other boys in the neighborhood built the early fires, and did the early feeding, but he preferred to do these things himself— whether out of consideration for us, or because it was troublesome to drive us to it, I do not know. After starting the fire in the room in which he slept, he stepped to our door and told us to get up, to which command we mumblingly replied and slept on. After returning from the stables, he spoke to us again, but we still paid no attention. Ten minutes later he would start up the stairs with angry strides, but he never caught us, for we knew that was final and hurried on our clothes. Seeing that we were up and dressing when he reached the head of the stairs, he would say, "Well, you'd better," and go down again, where we speedily followed. This was his regular custom for years; we always expected it of him, and were never disappointed.

After the morning devotions, which consisted of reading a chapter from the Bible and a prayer always expressed in exactly the same words, he asked a blessing for the meal by this time ready (the blessing was as unvarying as the prayer), and we ate in silence. Then we were warmly clothed, if it were winter, and compelled to go out and work until we were hungry again. I suppose we helped him little enough, but his reasoning convinced him that, to work easily and naturally, work must become a habit, and should be taught from youth up, therefore we went out with him every day and came back only with the darkness.

I think he was kinder with us when at work than at any other time, and we admired him in spite of the hard and exacting tasks he gave us to do—he called them stints—for he was powerful and quick to aid us when we needed it, and tender as a child if we were sick. Sometimes on cold days we walked rather than rode to the timber, where my father went to chop wood while Jo and I corded it. On one of these occasions I became ill while returning home at night—a slight difficulty, it must have been, for I was always stout and robust—and he carried me all the way in his arms. Though I insisted I could walk, and was better, he said I was not heavy, and trudged along like a great giant, holding me so tenderly that I thought for the first time that perhaps he loved me. For weeks after that I tried as hard as I could to please him, and to induce him to commend my work; but he never did, for whether I was good or bad, he was just the same, silent and grave, so that if I became indifferent in my tasks, I fear he was the cause of it.

Other families had their holidays, and owned guns and dogs, which they used in hunting the wild game then abundant; but there was little of this at our house, and perhaps this was the reason why we prospered more than those around us. Usually Jo and I were given the Saturday afternoons to ourselves, when we roamed the country with some of the idle vagabonds who lived in rented houses, visiting turkey roosts a great distance in the woods, and only returning long after night-fall. I do not remember that we were ever idle in the middle of the week, unless we were sent on errands, as buying young stock at low prices of the less thrifty neighbors, or something else in which there was profit; so that we had little time to learn anything except hard work, and if we learned that well it was because we were excellently taught by a competent master. During those years work became such a habit with me that ever since it has clung to me, and perhaps, after all, it was an inheritance for which I have reason to be thankful. I remember my father's saying to me once, as if intimating that I ought to make up by unusual industry for the years of idleness, that I was a positive burden and expense to him until I was seven years old. So it will readily be imagined that I was put to work early, and kept steadily at it.

part 9

POLITICS AND
GOVERNMENT

✍ DAVID CROCKETT

How To Win an Election

David Crockett (1786–1836), a backwoods politician
who had never seen a public document, "nor knew
there was such things," began his public career as a
local magistrate in Tennessee and wound up by serv-
ing three terms in Congress. The secret of his unparalleled success at the polls lay in his superior
ability at telling racy stories and directing his thirsty
constituents to the cider barrel. At one time a staunch
supporter of Andrew Jackson, Crockett eventually
turned on "Old Hickory" because of his autocratic
removal of the Indians. "Cut to the hollow" by his
disappointment in the hope that he might run for
the Presidency and by his failure to be re-elected to
Congress, Crockett turned his back on politics and
went to Texas, where he became a hero in defense
of the Alamo.

For further information about the hilarious exploits of this "braggart bearhunter and petty politician," consult any of the following: *The Adventures
of Davy Crockett Told Mostly by Himself* (New
York, 1934); *The Autobiography of David Crockett,*
edited by Hamlin Garland (New York, 1923);
Constance Rourke, *Davy Crockett* (New York,
1934); and *Davy Crockett: American Comic Legend*
edited by Richard M. Dorson (New York, 1939).

I begin this book on the 8th day of July, 1835, at Home,
Weakly county, Tennessee. I have just returned from a two week's
electioneering canvass, and I have spoken every day to large con-

---

From *Col. Crockett's Exploits and Adventures in Texas* (Philadelphia: T. K.
and P. G. Collins, 1836), chap. 1, pp. 15–22. Editor's title.

courses of people with my competitor. I have him badly plagued, for he does not know as much about "the Government," the deposites, and the Little Flying Dutchman, whose life I wrote, as I can tell the people; and at times he is as much bothered as a fly in a tar pot to get out of the mess. A candidate is often stumped in making stump-speeches. His name is Adam Huntsman; he lost a leg in an Indian fight, they say, during the last war, and the Government run him on the score of his military services. I tell him in my speech that I have great hopes of writing one more book, and that shall be the second fall of Adam, for he is on the Eve of an almighty thrashing. He relishes the joke about as much as a doctor does his own physic. I handle the administration without gloves, and I do believe I will double my competitor, if I have a fair shake, and he does not work like a mole in the dark. Jacksonism is dying here faster than it ever sprung up, and I predict that "the Government" will be the most unpopular man, in one year more, that ever had any pretensions to the high place he now fills. Four weeks from tomorrow will end the dispute in our elections, and if old Adam is not beaten out of his hunting shirt my name isn't Crockett.

While on the subject of election matters, I will just relate a little anecdote about myself, which will show the people to the east, how we manage these things on the frontiers. It was when I first run for Congress; I was then in favour of the Hero [Andrew Jackson], for he had chalked out his course so sleek in his letter to the Tennessee legislature, that, like Sam Patch, says I, "there can be no mistake in him," and so I went ahead. No one dreamt about the monster and the deposits at that time, and so, as I afterward found, many like myself were taken in by these fair promises, which were worth about as much as a flash in the pan when you have a fair shot at a fat bear.

But I am losing sight of my story. Well, I started off to the Cross Roads, dressed in my hunting shirt, and my rifle on my shoulder. Many of our constituents had assembled there to get a taste of the quality of the candidates at orating. Job Snelling, a gander-shanked Yankee, who had been caught somewhere about Plymouth Bay, and had been shipped to the west with a cargo of cod fish and rum, erected a large shantee, and set up shop for the occasion. A large posse of the voters had assembled before I arrived, and my opponent had already made considerable headway with his speechifying and his treating, when they spied me about a rifle shot from the camp, sauntering along as if I was not a party in the business. "There comes Crockett," cried one. "Let us hear the colonel," cried another; and so I mounted the stump that had been cut down for the occasion, and began to bushwhack in the most approved style.

I had not been up long before there was such an uproar in the crowd that I could not hear my own voice, and some of my constituents let me know, that they could not listen to me on such a dry subject as the welfare of the nation, until they had something to drink, and that I must treat 'em. Accordingly I jumped down from the rostrum, and led the way to the shantee, followed by my constituents, shouting, "Huzza for Crockett," and "Crockett for ever!"

When we entered the shantee, Job was busy dealing out his rum in a style that showed he was making a good day's work of it, and I called for a quart of the best, but the crooked critur returned no other answer than by pointing at a board over the bar, on which he had chalked in large letters, "Pay to-day and trust to-morrow." Now that idea brought me all up standing; it was a sort of cornering in which there was no back out, for ready money in the west, in those times, was the shyest thing in all nature, and it was most particularly shy with me on that occasion.

The voters, seeing my predicament, fell off to the other side, and I was left deserted and alone, as the Government will be, when he no longer has any offices to bestow. I saw, plain as day, that the tide of popular opinion was against me, and that, unless I got some rum speedily, I should lose my election as sure as there are snakes in Virginny,—and it must be done soon, or even burnt brandy wouldn't save me. So I walked away from the shantee, but in another sort from the way I entered it, for on this occasion I had no train after me, and not a voice shouted "Huzza for Crockett." Popularity sometimes depends on a very small matter indeed; in this particular it was worth a quart of New England rum, and no more.

Well, knowing that a crisis was at hand, I struck into the woods with my rifle on my shoulder, my best friend in time of need, and as good fortune would have it, I had not been out more than a quarter of an hour before I treed a fat coon, and in the pulling of a trigger he lay dead at the root of the tree. I soon whipped his hairy jacket off his back, and again bent my way towards the shantee, and walked up to the bar, but not alone, for this time I had a dozen of my constituents at my heels. I threw down the coon skin upon the counter, and called for a quart, and Job, though busy in dealing out rum, forgot to point at his chalked rules and regulations, for he knew that a coon was as good a legal tender for a quart, in the west, as a New York shilling, any day in the year.

My constituents now flocked about me, and cried "Huzza for Crockett," "Crockett for ever," and finding that the tide had taken a turn, I told them several yarns, to get them in a good humour, and having soon dispatched the value of the coon, I went out and mounted the stump, without opposition, and a clear majority of the voters followed me to hear what I had to offer for the good of the nation. Before I was half through, one of my constituents moved that they would hear the balance of my speech, after they had washed down the first part with some more of Job Snelling's extract of cornstalk and molasses, and the question being put, it was carried unanimously. It wasn't considered necessary to call the yeas and nays, so we adjourned to the shantee, and on the way I began to reckon that the fate of the nation pretty much depended upon my shooting another coon.

While standing at the bar, feeling sort of bashful while Job's rules and regulations stared me in the face, I cast down my eyes, and discovered one end of the coon skin sticking between the logs that supported the bar. Job had slung it there in the hurry of business. I gave it a sort of quick jerk, and it followed my hand as natural as if I had been the rightful owner. I slapped it on the counter, and Job little dreaming that he was barking up the wrong tree, shoved along another bottle, which my constituents quickly disposed of with great good humour, for some of them saw the trick, and then we withdrew to the rostrum to discuss the affairs of the nation.

I don't know how it was, but the voters soon became dry again, and nothing would do, but we must adjourn to the shantee; and as luck would have it, the coon skin was still sticking between the logs, as if Job had flung it there on purpose to tempt me. I was not slow in raising it to the counter; the rum followed of course; and I wish I may be shot, if I didn't, before the day was over, get ten quarts for the same identical skin, and from a fellow too, who in those parts was considered as sharp as a steel trap, and as bright as a pewter button.

This joke secured me my election, for it soon circulated like smoke among my constituents, and they allowed, with one accord, that the man who could get the whip hand of Job Snelling in fair trade, could outwit Old Nick himself, and was the real grit for them in Congress. Job was by no means popular; he boasted of always being wide awake, and that any one who could take him in was free to do so, for he came from a stock that sleeping or waking had always one eye open, and the other not more than half closed. The whole family were geniuses. His father was the inventor of wooden nutmegs, by which Job said he might have made a fortune, if he had only taken out a patent and kept the business in his own hands; his mother Patience manufactured the first white oak pumpkin seeds of the mammoth kind, and turned a pretty penny the first season; and his aunt Prudence was the first to discover that corn husks, steeped in tobacco water, would make as handsome Spanish wrappers as ever came from Havanna, and that oak leaves would answer all the purposes of filling, for no one would discover the difference except the man who smoked them, and then it would be too late to make a stir about it. Job himself bragged of having made some useful discoveries; the most profitable of which was the art of converting mahogany sawdust into cayenne pepper, which he said was a profitable and safe business; for the people have been so long accustomed to having dust thrown in their eyes, that there wasn't much danger of being found out. . . .

After the election was over, I sent Snelling the price of the rum, but took good care to keep the fact from the knowledge of my constituents. Job refused the money, and sent me word, that it did him good to be taken in occasionally, as it served to brighten his ideas; but I afterwards learnt that when he found out the trick that had been played upon him, he put all the rum I had ordered in his bill against my opponent, who, being elated with the speeches he had made on the affairs of the nation, could not descend to examine into the particulars of the bill of a vender of rum in the small way.

↫ *JAMES FENIMORE COOPER*

Leatherstocking's Encounter
with Justice

James Fenimore Cooper (1789–1851), whose place in American letters is secured by his penetrating social criticism, deserves more than honorable mention for his epic treatment of frontier themes in the Leatherstocking series: The Deerslayer (1841), The Last of the Mohicans (1826), The Pathfinder (1840), The Pioneers (1823), and The Prairie (1827). Natty Bumppo, the heroic frontiersman of the stories, chooses to live in the wilderness as a primitive rather than to conform to social regulations in civilized society. In this selection from The Pioneers, the Leatherstocking is captured, tried, convicted, and punished for having refused to conform to society's demands.

It has been already said that the "court of common pleas and general sessions of the peace," or, as it is commonly called, the "county court," over which Judge Temple presided, held one

From *Pioneers* (New York: Hurd and Houghton, 1866), chaps. 30–33, pp. 432–495 *passim*. Editor's title.

of its stated sessions on the following morning. The attendants of Richard were officers who had come to the village as much to discharge their usual duties at this court, as to escort the prisoners; and the Sheriff knew their habits too well, not to feel confident he should find most, if not all of them in the public room of the jail, discussing the qualities of the keeper's liquors. Accordingly he held his way through the silent streets of the village, directly to the small and insecure building, that contained all the unfortunate debtors, and some of the criminals of the county, and where justice was administered to such unwary applicants as were so silly as to throw away two dollars, in order to obtain one from their neighbours. The arrival of four malefactors in the custody of a dozen officers, was an event, at that day, in Templeton; and when the Sheriff reached the jail, he found every indication that his subordinates intended to make a night of it.

The nod of the Sheriff brought two of his deputies to the door, who in their turn drew off six or seven of the constables. With this force Richard led the way through the village, towards the bank of the lake, undisturbed by any noise, except the barking of one or two curs, who were alarmed by the measured tread of the party, and by the low murmurs that ran through their own numbers, as a few cautious questions and answers were exchanged, relative to the object of their expedition. When they had crossed the little bridge of hewn logs that was thrown over the Susquehanna, they left the highway, and struck into that field which had been the scene of the victory over the pigeons. From this they followed their leader into the low bushes of pines and chestnuts which had sprung up along the shores of the lake, where the plough had not succeeded the fall of the trees, and soon entered the deep forest itself. Here Richard paused, and collected his troop around him.

"I have required your assistance, my friends," he said, in a low voice, "in order to arrest Nathaniel Bumppo, commonly called the Leatherstocking. He has assaulted a magistrate, and resisted the execution of a search-warrant, by threatening the life of a constable with his rifle. In short, my friends, he has set an example of rebellion to the laws, and has become a kind of out-law. He is suspected of other misdemeanors and offences against private rights; and I have this night taken on myself, by the virtue of my office of Sheriff, to arrest the said Bumppo, and bring him to the county jail, that he may be present and forth-coming to answer to these heavy charges before the court to morrow morning. In executing this duty, my friends and fellow-citizens, you are to use courage and discretion. Courage, that you may not be daunted by any lawless attempts that this man may make with his rifle and his dogs, to oppose you; and discretion, which here means caution and prudence, that he may not escape from this sudden attack—and, for other good reasons that I need not mention. You will form yourselves in a complete circle around his hut, and at the word 'advance,' called aloud by me, you will rush forward, and, without giving the criminal time for deliberation, enter his dwelling by force, and make him your prisoner. Spread yourselves for this purpose, while I shall descend to the shore with a deputy, to take charge of that point; and all communications must be made directly to me, under the bank in front of the hut, where I shall station myself, and remain in order to receive them."

This speech, which Richard had been studying during his walk, had the effect that all similar performances produce, of bringing the dangers of the expedition immediately before the eyes of his forces. The men divided, some plunging deeper into the forest, in order to gain their stations without giving an alarm, and others continuing to advance, at a gait that would allow the whole party to get in order; but all devising the best plans to repulse the attack of a dog, or escape a rifle-bullet. It was a moment of dread expectation and interest.

When the Sheriff thought time enough had elapsed for the different divisions of his force to arrive at their stations, he raised his voice in the silence of the forest, and shouted the watch-word. The sounds played among the arched branches of the trees in hollow cadences; but when the last sinking tone was lost on the ear, in place of the expected howls of the dogs, no other noises were returned but the crackling of torn branches and dried sticks, as they yielded before the advancing steps of the officers. Even this soon ceased, as if by a common consent, when the curiosity and impatience of the Sheriff getting the complete ascendency over his discretion, he rushed up the bank, and in a moment stood on the little piece of cleared ground in front of the spot where Natty had so long lived. To his utter amazement, in place of the hut, he saw only its smouldering ruins!

The party gradually drew together about the heap of ashes and ends of smoking logs, while a dim flame in the centre of the ruin, which still found fuel to feed its lingering life, threw its pale light, flickering with the passing currents of the air, around the circle, now showing a face with eyes fixed in astonishment, and then glancing to another countenance, leaving the former shaded in the obscurity of night. Not a voice was raised in inquiry, nor an exclamation made in astonishment. The transition from excitement to disappointment was too powerful in its effects for speech, and even Richard lost the use of an organ that was seldom known to fail him.

The whole group were yet in the fulness of their surprise, when a tall form stalked from the gloom into the circle, treading down the hot ashes and dying embers, with callous feet, and, standing over the light, lifted his cap, and exposed the bare head and weather-beaten features of the Leatherstocking. For a moment he gazed at the dusky figures who surrounded him, more in sorrow than in anger, before he spoke.

"What would ye have with an old and helpless man?" he said. "You've driven God's creaters from the wilderness, where his providence had put them for his own pleasure, and you've brought in the troubles and diviltries of the law, where no man was ever known to disturb another. You have driven me, that have lived forty long years of my appointed time in this very spot, from my home and the shelter of my head, lest you should put your wicked feet and wasty ways in my cabin. You've driven me to burn these logs, under which I've eaten and drunk, the first of Heaven's gifts, and the other of the pure springs, for the half of a hundred years, and to mourn the ashes under my feet, as a man would weep and mourn for the children of his body. You've rankled the heart of an old man, that has never harmed you or your'n, with bitter feelings towards his kind, at a time when his thoughts should be on a better world; and you've driven him to wish that the beasts of the forest, who never feast on the blood of their own families, was his kindred and race; and now, when he has come to see the last brand of his hut, before it is melted into ashes, you follow him up, at midnight, like hungry hounds on the track of a wornout and dying deer! What more would ye have? for I am here—one to many. I come to mourn, not to fight, and, if it is God's pleasure, work your will on me."

When the old man ended, he stood, with the light glimmering around his thinly-covered head, looking earnestly at the group, which receded from the pile, with an instinctive and involuntary movement, without the reach of the quivering rays, leaving a free passage for his retreat into the bushes, where pursuit, in the dark, would have been fruitless. Natty seemed not to regard this advantage, but stood facing each individual in the circle, in succession, as if to see who would be the first to arrest him. After a pause of a few moments, Richard began to rally his confused faculties, and advancing, apologized for his duty, and made him his prisoner. The party now collected, and, preceded by the Sheriff, with Natty in their centre, they took their way towards the village.

During the walk, divers questions were put to the prisoner concerning his reasons for burning the hut, and whither Mohegan had retreated, but to all of them he observed a profound silence, until, fatigued with their previous duties, and the lateness of the hour, the Sheriff and his followers reached the village, and dispersed to their several places of rest, after turning the key of a jail on the aged and apparently friendless Leather-stocking.

The long days and early sun of July allowed time for a gathering of the interested, before the little bell of the academy announced that the appointed hour had arrived for administering right to the wronged, and punishment to the guilty. . . .

At the first stroke of the bell, Richard issued from the front door of the "Bold Dragoon," flourishing in his hand a sheathed sword, that he was fond of saying his ancestors had carried in one of Cromwell's victories, and crying, in an authoritative tone, to "clear the way for the court." The order was obeyed promptly, though not servilely, the members of the crowd nodding familiarly to the members of the procession, as it passed. A party of constables with their staves followed the Sheriff, preceding Marmaduke, and four plain, grave-looking yeomen, who were his associates on the bench. . . .

When the judges were seated, the lawyers had taken possession of the table, and the noise of moving feet had ceased in the area, the proclamations were made in the usual form, the jurors were sworn, the charge was given, and the court proceeded to hear the business before them. . . .

Natty was dressed in his buck-skin garments, without his coat, in place of which he wore only a shirt of coarse linen-check, fastened at his throat by the sinew of a deer, leaving his red neck and weather-beaten face exposed and bare. It was the first time that he had ever crossed the threshold of a court of justice, and curiosity seemed to be strongly blended with his personal feelings. He raised his eyes to the bench, thence to the jury-boxes, the bar, and the crowd without, meeting everywhere looks that were fastened on himself. After surveying his own person, as if in search of the cause of this unusual attraction, he once more turned his face around the assemblage, and then opened his mouth in one of his silent and remarkable laughs.

"Prisoner, remove your cap," said Judge Temple.

The order was either unheard or unheeded.

"Nathaniel Bumppo, be uncovered," repeated the Judge.

Natty started at the sound of his name, and raising his face earnestly towards the bench, he said—

"Anan!"

Mr. Lippet arose from his seat at the table, and whispered in the ear of the prisoner, when Natty gave him a nod of assent, and took the deer-skin covering from his head.

"Mr. District Attorney," said the Judge, "the prisoner is ready; we wait for the indictment." . . .

When Mr. Van der School arose to address the jury, he commenced by saying—

"Gentlemen of the jury, I should have interrupted the leading questions put by the prisoner's counsel, (by leading questions I mean telling him what to say,) did I not feel confident that the law of the land was superior to any advantages (I mean legal advantages) which he might obtain by his art. The counsel for the prisoner, gentlemen, has endeavoured to persuade you, in opposition to your own good sense, to believe that pointing a rifle at a constable (elected or deputed) is a very innocent affair; and that society (I mean the commonwealth, gentlemen,) shall not be endangered thereby. But let me claim your attention, while we look over the particulars of this heinous offence." Here Mr. Van der School favoured the jury with an abridgment of the testimony, recounted in such a manner as utterly to confuse the faculties of his worthy listeners. After this exhibition he closed as follows:—"and now, gentlemen, having thus made plain to your senses the crime of which this unfortunate man has been guilty, (unfortunate both on account of his ignorance and his guilt,) I shall leave you to your own consciences; not in the least doubting, that you will see the importance (notwithstanding the prisoner's counsel) . . . of punishing the offender, and asserting the dignity of the laws."

It was now the duty of the Judge to deliver his charge. It consisted of a short, comprehensive summary of the testimony, laying bare the artifice of the prisoner's counsel, and placing the facts in so obvious a light, that they could not well be misunderstood. "Living as we do, gentlemen," he concluded, "on the skirts of society, it becomes doubly necessary to protect the ministers of the law. If you believe the witnesses, in their construction of the acts of the prisoner, it is your duty to convict him; but if you believe that the old man, who this day appears before you, meant not to harm the constable, but was acting more under the influence of habit than by the instigations of malice, it will be your duty to judge him, but to do it with lenity."

As before, the jury did not leave their box, but, after a consultation of some little time, their foreman arose, and pronounced the prisoner—

"Guilty."

There was but little surprise manifested in the court-room at this verdict, as the testimony, the greater part of which we have omitted, was too clear and direct to be passed over. The judges seemed to have anticipated this sentiment, for a consultation was passing among them also, during the deliberation of the jury, and the preparatory movements of the "bench" announced the coming sentence.

"Nathaniel Bumppo," commenced the Judge, making the customary pause.

The old hunter, who had been musing again, with his head on the bar, raised himself, and cried, with a prompt, military tone—

"Here."

The Judge waved his hand for silence, and proceeded—

"In forming their sentence the courts have been governed as much by the consideration of your ignorance of the laws, as by a strict sense of the importance of punishing such outrages as this of which you have been found guilty. They have, therefore, passed over the obvious punishment of whipping on the bare back, in mercy to your years but as the dignity of the law requires an open exhibition of the consequences of your crime, it is ordered, that you be conveyed from this room to the public stocks, where you are to be confined for one hour; that you pay a fine to the state of one hundred dollars; and that you be imprisoned in the jail of this county for one calendar month; and furthermore, that your imprisonment do not cease until the said fine shall be paid. I feel it my duty, Nathaniel Bumppo,"—

"And where would I get the money?" interrupted the Leatherstocking, eagerly; "where should I get the money? you'll take away the bounty on the painters, because I cut the throat of a deer; and how is an old man to find so much gold or silver in the woods? No, no, Judge; think better of it, and don't talk of shutting me up in a jail for the little time I have to stay."

"If you have any thing to urge against the passing of the sentence, the court will yet hear you," said the Judge, mildly.

"I have enough to say ag'in it," cried Natty, grasping the bar on which his fingers were working with convulsed motion. "Where am I to get the money? Let me out into the woods and hills, where I've been used to breathe the clear air, and though I'm threescore and ten, if you've left game enough in the country, I'll travel night and day but I'll make you up the sum afore the season is over. Yes, yes—you see the reason of the thing, and the wickedness of shutting up an old man, that has spent his days, as one may say, where he could always look into the window of heaven."

"I must be governed by the law"—

"Talk not to me of law, Marmaduke Temple," interrupted the hunter. "Did the beast of the forest mind your laws, when it was thirsty and hungering for the blood of your own child! She was kneeling to her God for a greater favour than I ask, and he heard her; and if you now say no to my prayers, do you think he will be deaf?"

"My private feelings must not enter into—"

"Hear me, Marmaduke Temple," interrupted the old man, with a melancholy tone of voice, "and hear reason. I've travelled these mountains when you was no judge, but an infant in your mother's arms; and I feel as if I had a right and a privilege to travel them ag'in afore I die. Have you forgot the time that you come on to the lakeshore, when there wasn't even a jail to lodge in; and didn't I give you my own bear-skin to sleep on, and the fat of a noble buck to satisfy the cravings of your hunger? Yes, yes—you thought it no sin then to kill a deer! And this I did, though I had no reason to love you, for you had never done any thing but harm to them that loved and sheltered me. And now, will you shut me up in your dungeons to pay me for my kindness? A hundred dollars! where should I get the money? No, no—there's them that says hard things of you, Marmaduke Temple, but you an't so bad as to wish to see an old man die in a prison, because he stood up for the right. Come, friend, let me pass; it's long sin' I've been used to such crowds, and I crave to be in the woods ag'in. Don't fear me, Judge—I bid you not to fear me; for if there's beaver enough left on the streams, or the buckskins will sell for a shilling a-piece, you shall have the last penny of the fine. Where are ye, pups! come away, dogs! come away! we have a grievous toil to do for our years, but it shall be done—yes, yes, I've promised it, and it shall be done!"

It is unnecessary to say, that the movement of the Leatherstocking was again intercepted by the constable; but before he had time to speak, a bustling in the crowd, and a loud hem, drew all eyes to another part of the room.

Benjamin had succeeded in edging his way through the people, and was now seen balancing his short body, with one foot in a window and the other on the railing of the jury-box. To the amazement of the whole court, the steward was evidently preparing to speak. After a good deal of difficulty, he succeeded in drawing from his pocket a small bag, and then found utterance.

"If-so-be," he said, "that your honour is agreeable to trust the poor fellow out on another cruise among the beasts, here's a small matter that will help to bring down the risk, seeing that there's just thirty-five of your Spaniards in it; and I wish, from the bottom of my heart, that they was raal British guineas, for the sake of the old boy. But 'tis as it is; and if Squire Dickens will just be so good as to overhaul this small bit of an account, and take enough from the bag to settle the same, he's welcome to hold on upon the rest, till such time as the Leatherstocking can grapple with them said beaver, or, for that matter, for ever, and no thanks asked."

As Benjamin concluded, he thrust out the wooden register of his arrears to the "Bold Dragoon" with one hand, while he offered his bag of dollars with the other. Astonishment at this singular interruption produced a profound stillness in the room, which was only interrupted by the Sheriff, who struck his sword on the table, and cried—

"Silence!"

"There must be an end to this," said the Judge, struggling to overcome his feelings. "Constable, lead the prisoner to the stocks. Mr. Clerk, what stands next on the calendar?"

Natty seemed to yield to his destiny, for he sunk his head on his chest, and followed the officer from the court-room in silence. The crowd moved back for the passage of the prisoner, and when his tall form was seen descending from the outer door, a rush of the people to the scene of his disgrace followed.

✔ CHARLES HOWARD SHINN

The Earliest Mining Courts
and Their Influence
on State Life

Charles Howard Shinn (1852–1924), born in Texas, reared in California, educated at Johns Hopkins, did research for his B.A. degree on the significance of the mining camp as a phase of the development of frontier government in America. From his college papers, he compiled a book, *Mining Camps: A Study in American Frontier Government*, which was published by Scribner's in 1885. The book has become a classic of mining history and frontier government, and has furnished a strong support for Turner's famous frontier hypothesis, by showing that the American character developed in the process of establishing law and order in undeveloped regions of the West. For a more detailed sketch of Shinn's life and literary activities see Joseph Henry Jackson's introduction to the 1948 edition of *Mining Camps*.

The general features of the organization of the "mining courts" that were in many cases found necessary towards the close of 1848 can easily be described. There were no permanent officers, except where the alcalde plan was adopted, as in instances hereafter described; neither were there any written laws, or any records of proceedings. Anyone who desired could call a meeting. A person who thought himself wronged would tell his friends, and they would tell others, till the miners of the region would assemble if they thought the cause sufficient; but if not, would ignore the

---

From *Mining Camps* (New York: Charles Scribner's Sons, 1885), chap. 10. Author's footnotes omitted.

call. Some important meetings grew out of informal discussions, among groups of miners, as to the best regulations for mutual benefit and protection. As soon as "mining districts," so called, began to be laid out, they assumed exceedingly definite boundaries as regarded the actual gold-bearing territory, but were very indefinite regarding size and shape. Each district included certain gulches, ran to the top of certain divides, took in certain flats and ridges, and would have presented a very irregular appearance on a map. The district might include several camps or but one, according to convenience. The term "camp" is properly used to express the nucleus of the district, the tent town to which the miners returned at night. The discovery of new mines might at any time create new camps, but not necessarily new districts, until its miners in camp assembled made new laws and separated themselves from the jurisdiction of their former laws.

At the first meeting called to organize a camp in a recently discovered mineral belt, the boundaries of a district were drawn so as to include not only the claims of all the miners present, but also all the unclaimed ground that seemed easy of access and likely to be valuable. If, however, the district proved too large for convenience as a political unit, the dissatisfied miners would post up notices in several places and call a meeting of those who wished for a division of territory and a new district. If a majority favored such action, the district was set apart and named. The old district was not consulted on the subject, but received a verbal notice of the new organization. Local conditions, making different regulations regarding claims desirable, were the chief causes of such separations. In most of these earlier cases, district and camp were one and the same: the camp was the unit. Disagreements between two camps, as camps, were never heard of. Cases of lesser camps uniting themselves for governing purposes with larger ones were of later occurrence.

There were no county lines to consider, for this was before the organization of the state. A number of districts were therefore laid out, through which county lines were discovered to pass when surveyed a few years later; but they retained their organization as separate political units. There are in northern California, at the

present time, several mining districts that include within their
boundaries territory under the jurisdiction of two counties. The
State of Nevada, in its laws of 1866, ordained that previously
created districts through which county lines passed should be
allowed to retain their autonomy and continue to enact local laws.
In facts like these we find evidence of the institutional nature of
the early camps, or districts, which thus created a local government
area long before counties were established, and were able, when
they chose, to maintain it intact. The decay of placer mining was
perhaps the only thing that prevented the later adoption of districts as universal divisions of the township, or rather as areas of
local authority that should disregard township and county lines
much as English parishes, union, school districts, and various local
government areas intersect and overlap at the present time.

The "mining court" of the camp, in its earliest form, was
simply the assembly of the freemen in open council. All who
swung a pick, all who held a claim, boys of sixteen and men of
sixty, took part in its deliberations. It was the folk-moot of our
Germanic ancestors. If the citizens had been summoned to try an
important case, they elected a presiding officer and a judge, im-
paneled a jury of six or twelve persons, summoned witnesses, and
proceeded to trial forthwith. Sometimes there was no jury; and
the case was submitted to the assemblage without argument, and
irrevocably decided *viva voce*. Had A trespassed on B's claim?
Was C's possessory right forfeited by absence, or neglect to work?
and could D assume it, or was D a "claim-jumper"? Such were the
questions usually brought before the "folk-moots" of the Sierra.
Changes and developments in this method of procedure occurred
a year or two later, but the earlier camps seized upon the "folk-
moot" plan with a true race-instinct.

Two things there were, that no camp assemblage ever attempted
to regulate: no mining court ever collected debts either for or
against any individual, nor did it ever take cognizance of minor
personal difficulties. As regards the first of these, the miners felt
and said that it was disgraceful to dun a man for money. They
held that honor between men, and the strength of social and
business relations, are a far better protection to the lender than
bond of Shylock and execution of sheriff. In one case, in one of

the camps of '48, a miner, dunned for a small debt at an unseasonable hour of the night, took a lantern, went to his claim, washed out more than sufficient, tied it up in a shot-bag, and, returning to the tent, flung it in his creditor's face with all the force of a sinewy arm. Men had to settle their financial affairs and their petty quarrels among themselves: that was mining-camp doctrine. Of course friends would interfere to separate drunken men, or to prevent a fight; but the camp as an organization set out to protect life and property, not to meddle with what seemed trivialities; so it winked at pugnacious tendencies, and possessed the most liberal definition of eccentricity conceivable. How else should it secure its Sunday-afternoon amusements, and maintain its clowns and oddities?

Crimes against society found swift enough punishment. The thief, for instance, was publicly flogged, and expelled from camp; forfeiting, of course, whatever mining ground he had occupied. But the thieves were usually the hangers-on of the camp, the idle Mexicans, or South Sea Islanders, not the men who owned and worked claims. Stealing, as we have previously stated, involved a greater degree of crime than it possibly could in a more highly organized commonwealth; because the social compact was simpler, and more clearly understood by all men.

Late in 1848 the foreign element began to find its way to the mines, and compelled better organization on the part of the Americans. When Mexicans settled the noted "Sonoranian Camp," now the town of Sonora, in Tuolumne County, nineteen white men—twelve of them Americans—followed, and, a little later, held a miners' meeting, elected R. S. Ham as alcalde, and agreed to support his authority. This district, Jamestown, was known as the "American Camp." The Mexicans and Chilians were greatly in the majority in the region, and their numbers increased during the next year. Many of them were men of the worst character, and only the closest organization prevented a reign of lawlessness. The real struggle for control of the southern mines was, however, at a later period than '48. "Sonoranian Camp" obeyed the mandates of Alcalde Ham with reasonable cheerfulness, and the few miners' meetings held were devoted to making laws regarding claims. There was no official communication between Alcalde Ham and

Colonel Mason, then acting governor of California: the camp was
left to govern itself.

In the camps of '48, Americans learned what strength there
was in organization; but systematic development of mining courts,
alcalde courts, and other forms of camp government can hardly
be said to have existed until the next year. The work of the better
class of miners during the winter of 1848-9 was closely connected
with the beginnings of that larger life—state organization. The
miners returning to their homes, forced by winter storms to desert
their camps in the mountain gulches, began to seek for a remedy
for certain no longer endurable evils that were afflicting the body
politic. American miners who had lived in peace and friendliness
all summer in their camps, had formed new bonds of fellowship,
had more closely cemented former bonds, and had proved their
ability to protect and govern themselves were now to take the
initiative in several remarkable organizing efforts.

A "memorial," at a later period presented to Congress, reviews
the political history of California. It says, in effect, that, "as early
as 1847," many Americans in California advocated the establishment of a civil territorial form of government; that in October of
that year the military-contribution tariff was established in Californian ports, and rigorously enforced, but never once resisted
though extremely onerous; that the overland immigration of 1847
strengthened the desire for a more American form of government;
that the military power continued taxation without representation,
and afforded inadequate protection to life and property; that the
gold-discovery occurred, and in April the towns were deserted, all
industrial pursuits were abandoned, and "a pall seemed to settle
upon the country"; that in August the news of the treaty with
Mexico was received, but the existing order of things was nevertheless continued. It describes an unsettled and unstable order of
things, and a dissatisfaction and even a profound discontent as
existing along the California coast in the summer and fall of
1848. It then proceeds to use the following remarkable language
regarding the influence of the miners:

"Upon the coming-on of winter, the great majority of the miners
returned to their homes in the towns. They came rich in gold-
dust; but a single glance at the desolate and unthrifty appearance

of the territory convinced them that other pursuits than that of gold-digging must receive a portion of their care and labor. . . . They felt, as all Americans feel, that the most important step they could take, and that most imperatively called for by the wants of the inhabitants, was the establishment of a stable system of government, which would command the respect and obedience of the people whose property it protected, and whose rights it preserved. Congress had adjourned without providing a Territorial government; and the public had settled into the firm conviction that the *de facto* government was radically defective, and incapable of answering the public wants."

This ample recognition of the important place in state organization taken by the returned miners appears to be fully borne out by the facts. A large public meeting was held at San José, December 11, 1848, at which the people of California were asked to organize in districts, and elect delegates to a convention for the purpose of forming a "provisional Territorial government," to go into immediate operation, and remain in full force until superseded by Congressional action. The plan was heartily welcomed and endorsed at massmeetings held in San Francisco, December 21 and 23; in Sacramento, January 6 and 8; in Monterey, January 31; and in Sonoma, February 5. Returned miners were prominent men in all these meetings. The very inclement weather and impassable condition of the roads had caused nearly two months to intervene between the San José meeting and the Sonoma meeting, and had prevented proposed meetings in other districts; but the five districts mentioned comprised more than three fifths of the whole population of California, and they elected delegates to a convention to be held early in March. Part also of this movement was the election, early in the year 1849, of "district legislative assemblies" for Sacramento and Sonoma. The legislature elected in San Francisco, for local reasons, was of a somewhat different type, and was chosen at a later date. The earlier assembly of Sacramento, which aimed to govern the entire surrounding region, was more directly the result of mining organizations than were the Sonoma and San Francisco assemblies. But all three of them disbanded peaceably in obedience to Governor Bennett Riley's orders. By the time the Territorial Convention assembled, the majority saw that California was too wealthy and populous for a territorial government; and they at once issued an address to the people, recommending a Constitutional Convention, which took place in September 1849, at the old pueblo of Monterey.

In all the important political events which began with the San José meeting of December 1848 and ended with the adoption of a state constitution, the men who had toiled, struggled, suffered, and "stood by each other" in the mining camps were leading spirits. Some of them returned to the mines; some engaged in other and more profitable occupations in the valleys and coast towns, for few of the pioneers of '48 had accumulated fortunes.

The preceding pages have in no wise exaggerated the intrinsic value of the work done by the "men of '48" in settling the foundations of society. Throughout our examination into the methods of later camps and the laws made by various districts we shall be constantly finding traces of earlier institutional organization. The debt of the Pacific coast to the few thousands of miners who first explored the Sacramento and El Dorado placers is greater than historians have heretofore acknowledged. They were the pioneers of the pioneers: without their brave and loyal work as American citizens, the greater and more dazzlingly successful work of that strange and complex era which followed could never have been accomplished.

part 10

LANGUAGE

⤅ THOMAS LOW NICHOLS

The Lingo of the West

Thomas Low Nichols (1815–1901), American liber-
tarian and social reformer, was no linguist in any
strict sense of the word, yet he had a sharp ear for
the nuances of folk idiom and of regional varieties
of American English. A chapter in his book, *Forty
Years of American Life* (1864), points out some of
the identifying characteristics of western speech. This
chapter, "Peculiarities and Eccentricities," is one of
the early discussions of language in the literature of
the West.

Englishmen know the Yankee chiefly as he appears in literature and on the stage. He is well drawn in the novels of John
Neal, Cooper, Paulding, and Mrs. Stowe, and in the writings of
the author of *Sam Slick* and James Russell Lowell. Hackett, Hill,
Jefferson, and other American actors and artists, have given us
pretty good Yankees on the stage. We imagine that literary and
dramatic portraitures are overdone. I do not think so. I have never
seen a stage Irishman, Cockney, Yankee, or negro that came fully
up to the genuine article. The trouble is not in overdoing, but in
doing falsely. Many English writers confuse the American idioms
and peculiarities of the East, West, and South. It is as if one
should mix up Scotchmen, Irishmen, and Cockneys.

It is possible to travel through America without meeting many
specimens of the thorough Yankee, the broad Western man, or
the distinctive Southerner of the strongest type; but they all exist

From *Forty Years of American Life* (Harrisburg, Pa.: The Stackpole Company, copyright 1937). Editor's title.

abundantly. There are districts in New England, in the rough mountain regions, where the Yankee flourishes as grotesque in the attire and speech as was ever described in story or seen upon the stage. Western and Southern peculiarities are still more common.

I know of no physiological reason why a Yankee should talk through his nose, unless he got the habit of shutting his mouth to keep out the cold fog and drizzling north-easters of Massachusetts Bay. It is certain that men open their mouths and broaden their speech as they go West, until on the Mississippi they tell you "thar are heaps of bar (bears) over thar, whar I was raised." Southern speech is clipped, softened, and broadened by the negro admixture. The child learns its language from its negro nurse, servants, and playmates, and this not unpleasant patois is never quite eradicated. Southerners drawl: the Northern people accent sharply and are very emphatic.

Besides peculiarities of articulation and enunciation, there are forms of expression peculiar to and characteristic of each section of the American States. An old fashioned Yankee is shy of swearing; he says, "I vum," "I swon," "I swow," "I vow," "darn it," "gaul darn your picter," "by golly," "golly crimus;" and uses other ingenious and cowardly substitutes for profanity. The Western man rips out remorseless oaths, swearing a blue streak with a remarkable breadth of expression. Whereas a Hoosier describes himself as "catawampously chawed up," the Yankee is merely a "gone sucker." Inquire about his health, and he tells you he is "so as to be crawlin'!" He talks of "spunkin' up to an all-fired, tarnation slick gall, clean grit, I tell yeou neow;" and, naturally, he has "a kinder sneakin notion arter her." If she were to tell him to "hold his yawp," he would admit that he felt "kinder streaked, by golly!" He describes a man as being "handsome as a picter, but so damnation ugly;" or as "a thunderin fool, but a clever critter as ever lived"—ugly being Yankee for wicked, and clever for good-natured. A plain girl is "as homely as a hedge-fence." A Yankee brags that he is "a hull team and a hoss to let." You can't "tucker him eout." It "beats all natur heow he can go it when he gets his dander up." He has "got his eyeteeth cut, true as preachin'." He gets "hoppin' mad," and "makes all gee agin." He is "dreadful glad to see you," and is "powerful sorry you enjoy such poor health;" but read Lowell's Zeke Bigelow or Mr. Stowe's Sam Lawson.

I am inclined to think the Western vocabulary more copious than that of the Yankee proper. The language, like the country, has a certain breadth and magnitude about it. A Western man "sleeps so sound, it would take an earthquake to wake him." He is in danger "pretty considerable much," because "somebody was down on him, like the whole Missouri on a sand-bar." He is a "gone 'coon." He is down on all "cussed varmints," gets into an "everlasting fix," and holds that "the longest pole knocks down the persimmons." A story "smells rather tall." "Stranger," he says, "in bar hunts I am numerous." He says a pathetic story sunk into his feelings "like a snagged boat into the Mississippi." He tells of a person "as cross as a bar with two cubs and a sore tail." He "laughs like a hyena over a dead nigger." He "walks through a fence like a falling tree through a cobweb." He "goes the whole hog." He raises "right smart of corn" and lives where there is "a smart chance of bars." "Bust me wide open," he says, "if I didn't bulge into the creek in the twinkling of a bedpost, I was so thunderin' savagerous."

In the south-west is found the combination of Western and Southern character and speech. The south-western man was "born in old Kaintuck, raised in Mississippi, is death on a bar, and smartly on a painter fight." He "walks the water, out hollers the thunder, drinks the Mississippi," "calculates" that he is "the genuwine article," and that those he don't like "ain't worth shucks." He tells of "a fellow so poor and thin he had to lean up agin a saplin' to cuss." He gets "as savage as a meat axe." He "splurges about," and "blows up like a steamboat."

The Southerner is "mighty glad to see you." He is apt to be "powerful lazy," and "powerful slow;" but if you visit him where he has located himself, he'll "go for you to the hilt agin creation." When people salute each other at meeting, he says they are "howdyin' and civilizin' each other." He has "powerful nice corn." The extreme of facility is not as easy as lying, but "as easy as shootin'." A man who has undressed has "shucked himself." To make a bet with a man is to "size his pile." Yankees guess everything, past, present and future; Southerners reckon and calculate.

All these peculiarities of speech would fill a small volume. Most of the Yankeeisms can be found in the districts of England from which the country was first settled. The colloquialisms of the South and West are more original. Miners, gamblers, and all sorts of adventurers attracted by gold to California and the Rocky Mountains, have invented new forms of expression which will be found in the poems and prose writings of Colonel Hay, Bret Harte, and others.

American humour consists largely of exaggeration, and of strange and quaint expressions. Much that seems droll to English readers is very seriously intended. The man who described himself as "squandering about permiscuous" had no idea that his expression was funny. When he boasted of his sister—"She slings the nastiest ankle in old Kentuck," he only intended to say that she was a good dancer. To escape rapidly, west of the Mississippi, might be "to vamose quicker'n greased lightnin' down a peeled hickory." "Vamose," and "vamose the ranch," were brought from Mexico by the Santa Fé traders. "Cut stick," and "absquatulate," are indigenous. A man cuts a stick when about to travel. Absquatulate comes from *a* or *ab* privative, and squat, western for settle. When a squatter removes, he absquatulates. As for the greased lightning and peeled hickory, Americans have a passion for making improvements on everything. The Mississippi boatmen improved the name of *Bois Brulé* into something they could understand, when they called it Bob Ruly's Woods. The story of land so rich that a squash vine, in its rapid growth, overtook and smothered a drove of pigs, was a western exaggeration. The evidence of a witness in a life insurance case, when the death was caused by the blowing-up of a steamboat on the Ohio, is droll, just because it is characteristic. The witness knew the missing man. He saw him on the deck of the steamboat just before the explosion. "When," asked the lawyer, "was the last time you saw him?" "The very last time I ever set eyes on him," said the careful witness, "was when the biler burst, and I was going up, *and I met him and the smoke pipe coming down!*"

I do not think that American peculiarities of language are so remarkable as those of character and manners—or, in other words, that Americanism is so much in speech as in thought, feeling, and action. Our language is English, modelled mainly upon English literature; but we are more independent in other matters.

Some one has said—"A Yankee stands up at prayers, takes his coat tail under his arms, turns his back on the minister, and winks at the gals in the singing seats." It is true that reverence is an uncultivated faculty in America, and finds little expression. I can remember when people stood up in prayer-time, at present they sit very quietly in their seats. This is true of the majority even in Episcopal Churches. In none do all, or even the larger number, kneel, except in the Roman Catholic or Ritualist Churches. Theodore Parker said in one of his sermons that New England was one of the few places in the civilized world where there were no Jews. The Yankees are too sharp for the children of Israel. Jews, however, flourish in New York, and still more in the South and West. The Irish do well in New England, because they are willing to do plenty of hard, rough work. When I first lived in New York the Irish kept all the corner groceries. Now nearly all such places are kept by Germans, who are more frugal than Yankees, and nearly as sharp. Irishmen, as a rule, are neither sharp nor frugal. Yankees are ingenious, enterprising, persevering, self-confident, and possess in an eminent degree that happy faculty which Sydney Smith attributed to Earl Russell, when he said his lordship would take command of the Channel fleet at an hour's notice. A genuine Yankee is always ready to go any possible where, or do any possible thing. Mr. Lincoln must have had Yankee blood in his veins, or he would never have taken the nomination for President. Mr. Seward was a Yankee New Yorker. General Banks and General Butler were Yankee civilians, a shoemaker and a lawyer, without the least military knowledge, but they were ready to command armies. Mr. Welles, the Secretary of the Navy during the late war, was a Yankee printer.

Barnum, who has been somewhat well known in England, is one sort of a model Yankee. He was born in Connecticut, kept store, edited a newspaper, preached the Gospel, became a showman, sold Bibles, invented the nurse of General Washington, exhibited the Fejee mermaid, organized and engineered the American tour of Jenny Lind, brought out General Tom Thumb, lectured on temperance, became a clock manufacturer, and made and lost several fortunes. One of his adventures on the Mississippi, not contained in his published autobiography, always seemed to me as Yankee as any of those he has related. He was on his way up the river from New Orleans, where he had been to spend the winter in some speculation. Some of the sporting gentlemen who make their home on the river engaged him in the favourite betting game of poker, a bluff or brag game, in which the skill consists in managing so as to have the best cards, or in boldly betting on the worst. It was hard, I think, to beat the great showman in either, but luck was against him, and he was dead broke. He landed at a small town in Mississippi, where he found the chances of winning money at play very small, in consequence of a revival of religion that was going forward. But "P.T." had more than one string to his bow. Not long before this time he had been a preacher —as it happened, a Universalist. He announced his profession, and obtained a place to preach, but found his creed anything but popular. The Southerners are orthodox in their religious notions, and like strong doctrine. The revival was attracting crowds to the Presbyterian Meeting-house. Something had to be done, and the exhibitor of dwarfs and prima donnas was equal to the occasion. He dismissed his small and indifferent congregation, walked over to the Presbyterian meeting, and announced to the astonished and delighted assembly that he had been converted from his errors. There was great rejoicing: he was invited to preach, was rewarded with a good collection, resumed his voyage, and had good luck at poker all the way to St. Louis.

This seems rather a tough story, and, as Barnum told it, it may not be true; but the man who could invite the Baptist ministers of Boston to administer the ordinance of the Lord's Supper to Joyce Heth, a poor drunken old negress, whom he palmed off upon the public by forged papers as the nurse of Washington; who got up a public wedding of two giants at the Broadway Tabernacle, to which the public was admitted at fifty cents a head, and who later managed the wedding of two dwarfs as a public spectacle in the most fashionable Episcopal Church in New York, may have really had the adventure on the Mississippi. It is certainly true that he was at one period selling Bibles in New York every day, and managing a saloon with negro dancing in the evening, with a genuine negro boy, blacked and wigged so as to pass for a make-believe one, because the New Yorkers, who applauded what they supposed a white boy in a blacked face and woolly wig, would have driven a real negro from the stage and mobbed his exhibitor.

≁ *M. SCHELE DE VERE*

A Rich Harvest
of New Words

Maximilian Schele De Vere (1820–1898), professor of modern languages at the University of Virginia for fifty-one years, was a native of Sweden, and was educated at the Universities of Berlin and Bonn. Coming to the United States in 1843, he studied Greek at Harvard before accepting the position in Virginia where he stayed until retirement. His keen interest in American folk speech made him one of the country's first linguists devoted to a study of indigenous speechways. De Vere published *Americanisms* in 1871, followed by *The English of the New World* in 1873. For further discussions of the language of America see, for example, Albert H. Marckwardt, *American English* (New York, 1958).

The language of Western men has been called high-flown, overwrought, grandiloquent—it may be so, but it is so only as a fair representation of the Western world, which God created on a

From *Americanisms: The English of the New World* (New York: Charles Scribner's Sons, 1871), chap. 3, pp. 161–181 *passim*. Editor's title.

large scale, and which in its turn grows faster, works harder, achieves more than any other land on earth has ever done. Nor must it be forgotten that the West has no severe critic to correct abuses, no court and no polite society to taboo equivocal words, no classic writers to impart good taste and train the ear to a love of gentle words and flowing verse. Speech, there, is free as the air of heaven, and moves with the impulsive energy of independent youth, conscious of matchless strength, and acknowledging no master in word or deed. It is an intensified, strangely impulsive language, just as the life's blood of the whole West throbs with faster pulse, and courses with fuller vigor through all its veins. There is no greater difference between the stately style of Milton and the dashing, reckless lines of Swinburne, than between the formal, almost pedantic echo of Johnsonian rhythm in Haw-thorne's work, and the free and easy verses of Bret Harte. Hence, New England has wit, and what can be more caustic than Lowell's deservedly famous political squibs? But the West has humor, golden humor, full of poetry, dramatizing dry facts into flesh and blood, but abounding in charity and good-will to all men.

So it is with their sounds, that come full and hearty from broad chests, breathing freely the pure air that sweeps down from Rocky Mountains unhampered, across broad prairies, over a whole con-tinent. Words are as abundant as food, and expressions grow in force and extent alike, till they sound extravagant to the more economical son of the East. Speech is bold, rejecting laws and rules, making one and the same word answer many purposes, and utterly scouting the euphemistic shifts of a sickly delicacy. If it becomes vulgar—and it will become so, as the sweetest milk turns sour when the thunder rolls on high—the vulgarism is still what J. R. Lowell so happily calls "poetry in the egg." Its slang, also, is as luxurious as the weeds among the rich grasses, but at least it is home-made, and smells of the breath of the prairie or the blood of the Indian, and is not imported from abroad or made in the bar-room and betting-ring.

Hence the student of English finds in the West a rich harvest of new words made to answer new purposes, often in the most sur-prising way, and of phrases full of poetical feeling, such as could only arise amid scenes of great beauty, matchless energy, and sublime danger.

There is a strange perfume about the very term *backwoods*, which brings up before our mind's eye at a glance the forest of primeval trees, those formidable giants which the *pioneer* has to encounter at once with his trusty weapon, the axe. For it used to mean—real *backwoods* no longer exist—the partially cleared woods on the Western frontiers of the union, which were considered the *back* of the new country, as the coast of the Atlantic constituted the *front*. The *East* having been first settled, and having furnished, to a large extent, the sinews and brains for the new States, was naturally looked upon as the representative of wealth, intelligence, and progress; and the *back country* became, from that time onward, synonymous not only with regions lying back, *i.e.*, to the West of the seaboard States, but also with a state of civilization somewhat behindhand. The nearest districts became early known—and are still very generally designated—as the *Up Country*, a term, when used as an adjective, peculiar to this continent. It is employed all along the seaboard from Maine to the Gulf of Mexico, with varying meaning, but always suggesting a certain inferiority to the seaboard population, because up the rivers, toward the headwaters, population becomes scarce, civilization imperfect, and schools few in number. Of this peculiar belt, J. R. Lowell says: "I imagined to myself such an *up country* man as I had often seen at anti-Slavery meetings, capable of district-school English, but always instinctively falling back into the national stronghold of his homely dialect, when heated to the point of self-forgetfulness" (*Preface to Biglow Papers*), and the result of this imagination was one of the most brilliant creations of American genius. In Southern States the inhabitant of the large seaboard city speaks with ineffable contempt of the *up country people*, and formerly used to rank them with Crackers and mean whites, till they made their political influence felt at elections.

The *back country* seems to have receded back from the Eastern States as civilization advanced westward, but it still retains the character of a region, where lands and living are cheap, and people simple and unsophisticated. An opulent family, reduced in circumstances, and compelled to remove to a place where social claims were unknown and wants few and easily supplied, is thus alluded to in the *Letters from the South*: "The family were in great distress, though we helped them on a little to get to the *back country*, where I hear they are doing pretty well again"; and even in more recent days a traveller in the West says: "The hotel was a roomy log-house, commanding a view of the *back country*, a prairie stretching off into the western horizon." (*Putnam's Magazine*, November, 1868.) . . .

When the immigrant looks around for the kind of land he would choose, he is generally guided by a preference for districts where neighbors of his own race or faith are found; but if he cannot indulge in this luxury and must go to what is called *New Lands*, he has to be careful in his selection. Fraudulent companies will sell him *water-lots*, tempting enough on the map, but found, upon reaching the place, to be swamp or morass, and half the year under water, while rascally *runners* will sell him tickets to the State of Virginia, which he may reach in twenty-four hours, instead of the town of Virginia, in Nevada, which he cannot reach under several days. He will, of course, prefer prairie-land, if it is to be had, and look out for an *island*, a grove in the midst of the prairie, or at least for a *bottom*, as the richest land is apt to be called. Their vicinity is generally marked by those high banks with precipitous fronts, which, from their resemblance to bold promontories jutting out into the sea, are in America called *Bluffs*. The term was already thus used by Lewis and Clark in their famous *Travels to the Pacific Ocean* (1804), and the bold, steep front is thus referred to by W. Irving: "The mountains were broken and precipitous, with huge *bluffs*, projecting from among the forests." (*Astoria*, II, p. 270) . . .

If the settler find no home on an *island* or in a *cove* of a prairie, he prefers, especially if he be a German, a *Knob*, as from its resemblance to a knob (Germ. Knopf), any rising is called in the West. Originally the term was limited to certain peculiar, round hills in Kentucky, the result of the material, soft sandstone and shale, having been worn by wind and rain into a rounded form. The word, however, soon extended over the whole West, and a hilly region is very apt to be called a *knobby* country in Western parlance. Should he build his cabin in a forest, he will soon find his neighborhood designated as a *neck of the woods*, that being the name applied to any settlement made in the well-wooded parts of the Southwest especially. Should he dread the *bush*, he may choose one of those beautiful forest glades called *oak openings* and found in the Northwest. They are undulating plains, covered with close, rich turf, and dotted all over with groups of fine, well-grown oaks, looking for all the world like a well-kept English park, though apparently endless. It is they which have given Mr. Cooper a title for one of his latest, though not most interesting novels. They are very differt from the *Barrens*, with which they are occasionally confounded. The latter are elevated plains of poor soil, either having no growth on them at all, or barely supporting stunted trees unfit for timber. Such waste lands abounded formerly in some of the Eastern and Central States even, but were soon brought under subjection to man by energy and ingenuity. Thus, when Ohio began to be settled, some seventy years ago, most of its territory outside of the rich valleys of the two Miamis, the Scioto and Maumee, was in *barrens*. No foliage could be discovered for hundreds of miles, save on the banks of a few streams; fires having consumed, year after year, the young trees which Nature had tried to bring forth there. Today, land in that State, everywhere, has advanced a hundred-fold, and yet one of the most profitable uses to which it has been put, and can now be put, is the growth of timber! It is from a vast stretch of such barren lands in the North-eastern corner of America, known as the *Barren Grounds*, that a variety of reindeer (Tarandus arcticus), derives its melancholy name of *Barren Ground Reindeer*, which it bears also if found in Greenland and other localities.

Where trees at all succeed in growing on such neglected lands, the latter are known as *Oak-barrens*, straggling forests of poor, stunted oak-trees, which show by their low growth and gnarled branches the poverty of the soil on which they have to subsist. The Southern States have, in like manner, *Pine Barrens*, which are still more desolate tracts, covered with light, loose sand, and bearing a wretched growth of pine-trees; the people who live here are called *sand-hillers*, and belong, generally, to the lowest class of whites. In the Southeastern States a similar kind of land, but of somewhat better quality, is known as the *Piny Woods*, the resort of poor people who cannot obtain lands elsewhere, while in the North and Northwest the superb tracts of noble woodland, which furnish the finest timber in the country, are called *Pineries.* Here loggers and lumberers in great numbers congregate during the season, and a recent traveller says admiringly: "No stimulants stronger than tobacco and tea are allowed in the *pineries;* the woods had not yet received enough of the influence of civilization to admit a bar within their hallowed shade." (*Minnesota Pineries.*) Thus hill and dale, valley and prairie, are open to the new-comer, and soon filled; the mountain alone seems to be shunned, as the rains wash all the rich soil from top and slope into the valley below, and thus it has come about that the words, *Over the Mountain,* are frequently used with a very sad meaning. . . . *Sloughs* also are dreaded, whether they are pronounced like "ploughs" or *slews,* since the sudden changes in the American climate, with alternate fierce droughts and terrific rains, make them dangerous neighbors to cultivated lands. California boasts of them in proportions which would elsewhere entitle them to a very different name, for we are told: "Passing from this summit, on a gently descending grade, we reached the *slough* which joins the upper lakes with Tulare. This *slough* is about forty miles long and two hundred feet wide. The stream has a sluggish current to the Northwest, and both of its banks, for nearly the whole distance, are covered with tules." (*Overland Monthly,* Aug. 1870, p. 155.) *Wild Lands* are by no means undesirable, as they are merely so called because not yet cultivated; they embrace all the land yet unappropriated, though generally meaning the forest by preference. It is different with the *Bad Lands,* which border the Missouri for about twenty miles, and were called, by the first French settlers, *Mauvaises Terres,* because, as a recent explorer, General Cuvier Grover, says, "they present a picture of Nature's wild deformities, a masterpiece in its way, characterized by a total absence of anything which could, by any possibility, give pleasure to the eye, or gratification to the mind, by any associations of utility. . . . Colonnades and detached pillars of partially cemented sand, capped by huge globes of light-brownish sandstone, tower up from the steep sides of the bluffs to the height of a hundred feet or more."

Even where the land looks fair and a stream promises comfort in times of drought, care has to be taken to ascertain if the latter is not, perhaps, in summer a *Dry Creek*. This apparent anomaly is very common in the Southern and Western parts of the Union, and rivers, which have no other name but that of *Dry Creek*, are found in nearly every State from Virginia to California. It is from these frequent periods of suffering that the two words *drought* and *dry* are so much used in the country. The former retains very frequently the sound, and quite as often the manner of writing, which were once considered orthodox in England; *drouth*, as even the verb to *dry*, reverts at times to its ancient form to *drow*. Sandys says: "As torrents in the drowth of summer fail," and Milton uses *drouth* as he writes *highth*. "The great but only drawback to these fertile regions (in Virginia) is the almost certainty of a *drouth* during the summer months." (Richmond *Enquirer*, August 7, 1866.) As the drying up of a river makes more or less efficiently an end to all agricultural operations, the verb *to dry up* has become synonymous with to make an end. "*Dry up!*" is a familiar slang term for the more considerate Hush! "*Dry up!*—no, I won't dry up. I'll have my rights, if I die for 'em, and I'll stand here until I get's 'em, too; so you had better *dry up* yourself." (*The Student's Speaker*, P. Reeves, p. 79.) . . .

↗ *DAVID CROCKETT*

One January Morning

Frontier language was often shockingly grotesque. David Crockett (1786–1836) has supplied American lexicographers with innumerable linguistic items

From an anonymous passage, quoted in Constance Rourke, *American Humor* (New York: Harcourt, Brace & Company, Inc., 1931), pp. 55–56. Editor's title.

that, except for the narratives and almanacs of the
frontier humorist, might never have been recorded.
The "blustiferous" nature of tall talk is most adequately represented in the following anonymous
passage, credited to Crockett. The text is quoted in
Constance Rourke, *American Humor* (New York,
1931), pages 55–56.

One January morning it was so all-screwen-up cold that the
forest trees war so stiff that they couldn't shake, and the very daybreak froze fast as it war tryin' to dawn. The tinder-box in my
cabin would no more ketch fire than a sunk raft at the bottom o'
the sea. Seein' that daylight war so far behind time, I thought
creation war in a fair way for freezin' fast.

"So," thinks I, "I must strike a leetle fire from my fingers, light
my pipe, travel out a few leagues, and see about it."

Then I brought my knuckles together like two thunder clouds,
but the sparks froze up afore I could begin to collect 'em—so out
I walked, and endeavored to keep myself unfriz by goin' at a hop,
step and jump gait, and whistlin' the tune of "fire in the mountains!" as I went along in three double quick time. Well, arter I
had walked about twenty-five miles up the peak o' Daybreak Hill,
I soon discovered what war the matter. The airth had actually friz
fast in her axis, and couldn't turn round; the sun had got jammed
between two cakes o' ice under the wheels, an' thar he had bin
shinin' and workin' to get loose, till he friz fast in his cold sweat.

"C-r-e-a-t-i-o-n!" thought I, "this are the toughest sort o' sus-
pension, and it mustn't be endured—somethin' must be done, or
human creation is done for."

It war then so antediluvian and premature cold that my upper
and lower teeth an' tongue war all collapsed together as tight as
a friz oyster. I took a fresh twenty pound bear off o' my back that
I'd picked up on the road, an' beat the animal agin the ice till the
hot ile began to walk out on him at all sides. I then took an' held
him over the airth's axes, an' squeezed him till I thaw'd 'em loose,
poured about a ton on it over the sun's face, give the airth's cog-
wheel one kick backward, till I got the sun loose—whistled "Push
along, keep movin'!" an' in about fifteen seconds the airth gin a

grunt, and begun movin'—the sun walked up beautiful, salutin'
me with sich a wind o' gratitude that it made me sneeze. I lit my
pipe by the blaze o' his top-knot, shouldered my bear, an' walked
home, introducin' the people to fresh daylight with a piece of
sunrise in my pocket, with which I cooked my bear steaks, an'
enjoyed one o' the best breakfasts I had tasted for some time. If I
didn't, jist wake some mornin' and go with me to the office o'
sunrise!

part 11

HUMOR

The Horse-swap

Augustus Baldwin Longstreet (1790–1870), Dean of American frontier humorists, was praised by Poe for his "penetrating understanding of character in general, and of Southern character in particular." Longstreet claimed that his *Georgia Scenes* (1835) "consist of nothing more than fanciful combinations of real incidents and characters." The book stands as an important landmark in the history of American realism. Longstreet was a judge, a politician, a minister of the gospel, four times a college president, a newspaper editor, and a businessman. For an analysis of his techniques of humor see Walter Blair, *Native American Humor* (New York, 1937).

During the session of the Supreme Court, in the village of —— about three weeks ago, when a number of people were collected in the principal street of the village, I observed a young man riding up and down the street, as I supposed, in a violent passion. He galloped this way, then that, and then the other; spurred his horse to one group of citizens, then to another; then dashed off at half speed, as if fleeing from danger; and, suddenly checking his horse, returned first in a pace, then in a trot, and then in a canter. While he was performing these various evolutions, he cursed, swore, whooped, screamed, and tossed himself in every attitude which man could assume on horseback. In short, he *cavorted* most magnanimously (a term which, in our tongue, expresses all that I have described, and a little more), and seemed to be setting all

From *Georgia Scenes*, 2d ed. (New York: Harper & Brothers, 1855), pp. 23–31.

creation at defiance. As I like to see all that is passing, I determined to take a position a little nearer to him, and to ascertain, if possible, what it was that affected him so sensibly. Accordingly, I approached a crowd before which he had stopped for a moment, and examined it with the strictest scrutiny. But I could see nothing in it that seemed to have anything to do with the cavorter. Every man appeared to be in good humour, and all minding their own business. Not one so much as noticed the principal figure. Still he went on. After a semicolon pause, which my appearance seemed to produce (for he eyed me closely as I approached), he fetched a whoop, and swore that "he could out-swap any live man, woman, or child that ever walked these hills, or that ever straddled horse-flesh since the days of old daddy Adam. Stranger," said he to me, "did you ever see the *Yellow Blossom* from Jasper?"

"No," said I, "but I have often heard of him."

"I'm the boy," continued he; "perhaps a *leetle*, jist a *leetle*, of the best man at a horse-swap that ever trod shoe-leather."

I began to feel my situation a little awkward, when I was relieved by a man somewhat advanced in years, who stepped up and began to survey the "*Yellow Blossom's*" horse with much apparent interest. This drew the rider's attention, and he turned the conversation from me to the stranger.

"Well, my old coon," said he, "do you want to swap *hosses?*"

"Why, I don't know," replied the stranger; "I believe I've got a beast I'd trade with you for that one, if you like him."

"Well, fetch up your nag, my old cock; you're jist the lark I wanted to get hold of. I am perhaps a *leetle*, just a *leetle*, of the best man at a horse-swap that ever stole *cracklins* out of his mammy's fat gourd. Where's your *hoss?*"

"I'll bring him presently; but I want to examine your horse a little."

"Oh! look at him," said the Blossom, alighting and hitting him a cut; "look at him. He's the best piece of *hoss*flesh in the thirteen united universal worlds. There's no sort o' mistake in little Bullet. He can pick up miles on his feet, and fling 'em behind him as fast as the next man's *hoss*, I don't care where he comes from. And he can keep at it as long as the sun can shine without resting."

During this harangue, little Bullet looked as if he understood it all, believed it, and was ready at any moment to verify it. He was a horse of goodly countenance, rather expressive of vigilance than fire; though an unnatural appearance of fierceness was thrown into it by the loss of his ears, which had been cropped pretty close to his head. Nature had done but little for Bullet's head and neck; but he managed, in a great measure, to hide their defects by bowing perpetually. He had obviously suffered severely for corn; but if his ribs and hip bones had not disclosed the fact, he never would have done it; for he was in all respects as cheerful and happy as if he commanded all the corn-crib and fodder-stacks in Georgia. His height was about twelve hands; but as his shape partook somewhat of that of the giraffe, his haunches stood much lower. They were short, strait, peaked, and concave. Bullet's tail, however, made amends for all his defects. All that the artist could do to beautify it had been done; and all that horse could do to compliment the artist, Bullet did. His tail was nicked in superior style, and exhibited the line of beauty in so many directions, that it could not fail to hit the most fastidious taste in some of them. From the root it dropped into a graceful festoon, then rose in a handsome curve; then resumed its first direction; and then mounted suddenly upward like a cypress knee to a perpendicular of about two and a half inches. The whole had a careless and bewitching inclination to the right. Bullet obviously knew where his beauty lay, and took all occasions to display it to the best advantage. If a stick cracked, or if any one moved suddenly about him, or coughed, or hawked, or spoke a little louder than common, up went Bullet's tail like lightning; and if the going up did not please, the coming down must of necessity, for it was as different from the other movement as was its direction. The first was a bold and rapid flight upward, usually to an angle of forty-five degrees. In this position he kept his interesting appendage until he satisfied himself that nothing in particular was to be done; when he commenced dropping it by half inches, in second beats, then in triple time, then faster and shorter, and faster and shorter still, until it finally died away imperceptibly into its natural position. If I might compare sights to sounds, I should say its *settling* was more like the note of a locust than anything else in nature.

Either from native sprightliness of disposition, from uncontrollable activity, or from an unconquerable habit of removing flies by the stamping of the feet, Bullet never stood still; but always kept up a gentle fly-scaring movement of his limbs, which was peculiarly interesting.

"I tell you, man," proceeded the Yellow Blossom, "he's the best live hoss that ever trod the grit of Georgia. Bob Smart knows the hoss. Come here, Bob, and mount this hoss, and show Bullet's motions." Here Bullet bristled up, and looked as if he had been hunting for Bob all day long, and had just found him. Bob sprang on his back. "Boo-oo-oo!" said Bob, with a fluttering noise of the lips; and away went Bullet, as if in a quarter race, with all his beauties spread in handsome style.

"Now fetch him back," said Blossom. Bullet turned and came in pretty much as he went out.

"Now trot him by." Bullet reduced his tail to "customary;" sidled to the right and left airily, and exhibited at least three varieties of trot in the short space of fifty yards.

"Make him pace!" Bob commenced twitching the bridle and kicking at the same time. These inconsistent movements obviously (and most naturally) disconcerted Bullet; for it was impossible for him to learn, from them, whether he was to proceed or stand still. He started to trot, and was told that wouldn't do. He attempted a canter, and was checked again. He stopped, and was urged to go on. Bullet now rushed into the wide field of experiment, and struck out a gait of his own, that completely turned the tables upon his rider, and certainly deserved a patent. It seemed to have derived its elements from the jig, the minuet, and the cotillion. If it was not a pace, it certainly had pace in it, and no man would venture to call it anything else; so it passed off to the satisfaction of the owner.

"Walk him!" Bullet was now at home again; and he walked as if money was staked on him.

The stranger, whose name, I afterward learned, was Peter Ketch, having examined Bullet to his heart's content, ordered his son Neddy to go and bring up Kit. Neddy soon appeared upon Kit; a well-formed sorrel of the middle size, and in good order. His *tout ensemble* threw Bullet entirely in the shade, though a glance was sufficient to satisfy any one that Bullet had the decided advantage of him in point of intellect.

"Why, man," said Blossom, "do you bring such a hoss as that to trade for Bullet Oh, I see you're no notion of trading."

"Ride him off, Neddy!" said Peter. Kit put off at a handsome lope.

"Trot him back!" Kit came in at a long, sweeping trot, and stopped suddenly at the crowd.

"Well," said Blossom, "let me look at him; maybe he'll do to plough."

"Examine him!" said Peter, taking hold of the bridle close to the mouth; "he's nothing but a tacky. He an't as *pretty* a horse as Bullet, I know; but he'll do. Start 'em together for a hundred and fifty *mile*; and if Kit an't twenty mile ahead of him at the coming out, any man may take Kit for nothing. But he's a monstrous mean horse, gentleman; any man may see that. He's the scariest horse, too, you ever saw. He won't do to hunt on, no how. Stranger, will you let Neddy have your rifle to shoot off him? Lay the rifle between his ears, Neddy, and shoot at the blaze in that stump. Tell me when his head is high enough."

Ned fired, and hit the blaze; and Kit did not move a hair's breadth.

"Neddy, take a couple of sticks, and beat on that hogshead at Kit's tail."

Ned made a tremendous rattling, at which Bullet took fright, broke his bridle, and dashed off in grand style; and would have stopped all farther negotiations by going home in disgust, had not a traveller arrested him and brought him back; but Kit did not move.

"I tell you, gentlemen," continued Peter, "he's the scariest horse you ever saw. He an't as gentle as Bullet, but he won't do any harm if you watch him. Shall I put him in a cart, gig, or wagon for you, stranger? He'll cut the same capers there he does here. He's a monstrous mean horse."

During all this time Blossom was examining him with the nicest scrutiny. Having examined his frame and limbs, he now looked at his eyes.

"He's got a curious look out of his eyes," said Blossom.

"Oh yes, sir," said Peter, "just as blind as a bat. Blind horses always have clear eyes. Make a motion at his eyes, if you please, sir."

Blossom did so, and Kit threw up his head rather as if something pricked him under the chin than as if fearing a blow. Blossom repeated the experiment, and Kit jerked back in considerable astonishment.

"Stone blind, you see, gentlemen," proceeded Peter; "but he's just as good to travel of a dark night as if he had eyes."

"Blame my buttons," said Blossom, "if I like them eyes."

"No," said Peter, "nor I neither. I'd rather have 'em made of diamonds; but they'll do, if they don't show as much white as Bullet's."

"Well," said Blossom, "make a pass at me."

"No," said Peter; "you made the banter, now make your pass."

"Well, I'm never afraid to price my hosses. You must give me twenty-five dollars boot."

"Oh, certainly; say fifty, and my saddle and bridle in. Here, Neddy, my son, take away daddy's horse."

"Well," said Blossom, "I've made my pass, now you make yours."

"I'm for short talk in a horse-swap, and therefore always tell a gentleman at once what I mean to do. You must give me ten dollars."

Blossom swore absolutely, roundly, and profanely, that he never would give boot.

"Well," said Peter, "I didn't care about trading; but you cut such high shines, that I thought I'd like to back you out, and I've done it. Gentlemen, you see I've brought him to a hack."

"Come, old man," said Blossom, "I've been joking with you. I begin to think you do want to trade; therefore, give me five dollars and take Bullet. I'd rather lose ten dollars any time than not make a trade, though I hate to fling away a good hoss."

"Well," said Peter, "I'll be as clever as you are. Just put the five dollars on Bullet's back, and hand him over; it's a trade."

Blossom swore again, as roundly as before, that he would not give boot; and, said he, "Bullet wouldn't hold five dollars on his back, no how. But, as I bantered you, if you say an even swap, here's at you."

"I told you," said Peter, "I'd be as clever as you; therefore, here goes two dollars more, just for trade sake. Give me three dollars, and it's a bargain."

Blossom repeated his former assertion; and here the parties stood for a long time, and the by-standers (for many were now collected) began to taunt both parties. After some time, however, it was pretty unanimously decided that the old man had backed Blossom out.

At length Blossom swore he "never would be backed out for three dollars after bantering a man;" and, accordingly, they closed the trade.

"Now," said Blossom, as he handed Peter the three dollars, "I'm a man that, when he makes a bad trade, makes the most of it until he can make a better. I'm for no rues and after-claps."

"That's just my way," said Peter; "I never goes to law to mend my bargains."

"Ah, you're the kind of boy I love to trade with. Here's your hoss, old man. Take the saddle and bridle off him, and I'll strip yours; but lift up the blanket easy from Bullet's back, for he's a mighty tender-backed hoss."

The old man removed the saddle, but the blanket stuck fast. He attempted to raise it, and Bullet bowed himself, switched his tail, danced a little, and gave signs of biting.

"Don't hurt him, old man," said Blossom, archly; "take it off easy. I am, perhaps, a leetle of the best man at a horse-swap that ever catched a coon."

Peter continued to pull at the blanket more and more roughly, and Bullet became more and more *cavortish:* insomuch that, when the blanket came off, he had reached the *kicking* point in good earnest.

The removal of the blanket disclosed a sore on Bullet's back-bone that seemed to have defied all medical skill. It measured six full inches in length and four in breadth, and had as many features as Bullet had motions. My heart sickened at the sight; and I felt that the brute who had been riding him in that situation deserved the halter.

The prevailing feeling, however, was that of mirth. The laugh became loud and general at the old man's expense, and rustic witticisms were liberally bestowed upon him and his late purchase. These Blossom continued to provoke by various remarks. He asked the old man "if he thought Bullet would let five dollars lie on his back." He declared most seriously that he had owned that horse three months, and had never discovered before that he had a sore back, "or he never should have thought of trading him," &c., &c.

The old man bore it all with the most philosophic composure. He evinced no astonishment at his late discovery, and made no replies. But his son Neddy had not disciplined his feelings quite so well. His eyes opened wider and wider from the first to the last pull of the blanket; and, when the whole sore burst upon his view, astonishment and fright seemed to contend for the mastery of his countenance. As the blanket disappeared, he stuck his hands in his breeches pockets, heaved a deep sigh, and lapsed into a profound revery, from which he was only roused by the cuts at his father. He bore them as long as he could; and, when he could contain himself no longer, he began, with a certain wildness of expression which gave a peculiar interest to what he uttered: "His back's mighty bad off: but dod drot my soul if he's put it to daddy as bad as he thinks he has, for old Kit's both blind and *deef*. I'll be dod drot if he *eint*."

"The devil he is," said Blossom.

"Yes dod drot my soul if he *eint*. You walk him, and see if he *eint*. His eyes don't look like it; but he'd *jist as leve go agin* the house with you, or in a ditch, as any how. Now you go try him." The laugh was now turned on Blossom; and many rushed to test the fidelity of the little boy's report. A few experiments established its truth beyond controversy.

"Neddy," said the old man, "you oughtn't to try and make people discontented with their things. Stranger, don't mind what the little boy says. If you can only get Kit rid of them little failings, you'll find him all sorts of a horse. You are a *leetle* the best man at a horse-swap that ever I got hold of; but don't fool away Kit. Come, Neddy, my son, let's be moving; the stranger seems to be getting snappish."

An Affair of Honor

Joseph Glover Baldwin (1815–1864) was one of the
fortune-seekers who stampeded into the new Gulf
states of Alabama and Mississippi during the period
of the cotton boom. The inflation of the times was
"fantastic," and speculation ran rampant. Baldwin's
accounts of his observations in this frontier territory,
published in *The Flush Times of Alabama and Mississippi* (1853), are set forth in the humorous style
of Crockett, Longstreet, Harris, and Hooper. Unlike
these writers, however, Baldwin makes little use of
direct discourse, being principally an essayist. "An
Affair of Honor" is no exception to the author's usual
manner of overgeneralization.

In the pleasant village of Patton's Hill, in the *Flush
Times*, there were several resorts for the refreshment of the weary
traveller, and for the allaying of the chronic thirst of more than
one of the inhabitants of the place and the country adjacent. They
are closed now, as the gaping portals of those who were wont in
the wild days to "indulge" in exciting beverages. A staid, quiet,
moral and intelligent community have supplied the place of many
of the early settlers "who left their country for their country's
good," and churches, schoolhouses and Lodges now are prominent where the "doggery" made wild work with "the peace and
dignity of the State," and the respectability and decency of particular individuals.

In the old times there came into the village of a Saturday
evening, a company more promiscuous than select, who gathered,
like bees at the mouth of a hive, around the doors of the grocery.
On one of these occasions a scene occurred, which I think worthy

From *The Flush Times of Alabama and Mississippi* (New York: D. Appleton & Co., 1853), pp. 192–196.

of commemoration; and it may be relied upon as authentic, in the main, as it came regularly before the Court as a part of the proceedings of a trial in a State case.

Jonas Sykes was a very valiant man when in liquor. But Jonas, like a good many other valiant men, was more valiant in peace than in war. He was a very Samson in fight—but, like Samson, he liked to do battle with that description of weapon which so scattered the Philistine hosts—*that* jaw-bone—one of which Nature had furnished Jonas with. Jonas was prodigal in the jaw-work and wind-work of a fight, and he could outswear "our army in Flanders." He had method in his madness, too, as he showed in selecting his enemies. He always knew, or thought he knew, how much a man would stand before he commenced "abusing" him, and his wrath grew the fiercer according as the patience of his enemy grew greater, and he was more fierce—like a bulldog chained—as he was the more held off.

Jonas had picked a quarrel with a quiet, demure fellow of the name of Samuel Mooney, and lavished upon that gentleman's liver, soul and eyes, many expressions much more fervid than polite or kind. Sam stood it for some time, but at length, like a terrapin with coals on his back, even his sluggish spirit could stand it no longer. He began to retort on Jonas some of the inverted compliments with which Jonas had besprinkled him. Whereupon Jonas felt his chivalry so moved thereat, that he challenged him to mortal combat.

Now, Jonas, as most bullies did at that time, went armed. Samuel had no *weepins*, as he called those dangerous implements, and gave that fact as an apology for not accepting Jonas's kind invitation. But Jonas would not "hear to" any such paltry excuse; he denounced Sam, for a white-livered poltroon, who would insult a gentleman (thereby meaning himself), and then refuse him satisfaction, and swore he would post him up all over town; regretting that he did not have the chance of blowing a hole through his carcass with his "Derringer" that "a bull-bat could fly through without tetching airy wing," and giving him his solemn word of honor that if he, (Sam), would only fight him, (Jonas), he, (Jonas), wouldn't hit him, (Sam) an inch above his hip-bone—which certainly was encouraging.

Sam still protested he was weaponless. "Well," said Jonas, "you shan't have that excuse any longer. I've got two as good pistols as ever was bought at *Orleens*, and you may have choice." And pulling one out of either side pocket, he produced two pistols very much alike, and, advancing to Sam, put his hands behind him and shuffled them from hand to hand a moment or two, and then held them forward—one rather in advance of the other—towards Sam, telling him to take which he chose. Sam took the one nearest to him, and Jonas called out to Bob Dobbs, who stood by, "to put them through in a fair duel," and called the crowd to witness "that he done it to the — rascal accordin to law." Bob willingly accepted the honorable position assigned him; commanded order; made the crowd stand back;—measured off the ground—ten paces—and stationed the combatants sidewise in dueling position. Bob then armed himself with a scythe blade, and flourishing it in the air, swore death and destruction to all who should interfere by word, look, or sign.

Bob took his position at a right angle between the two, and gave out in a loud and sonorous voice the programme of proceedings. "Gentlemen," said he, "the rules are as follows: the parties are to be asked—'Gentlemen are you ready'—answering 'Yes', I, as mutual second, will then pronounce the words slowly, 'Fire: one—two—three;' the parties to fire as they choose between the words *Fire* and *three*, and if either fires before or after the time, I shall proceed to put him to death without quarter, bail or main prize." Micajah F., a lawyer present, suggested, "or benefit of clergy." "Yes," said Bob, "or the benefit of a clergyman."

Bob then proceded to give the words out. At the word *two* Jonas's pistol snapped, but Sam's went off, the ball striking a button on Jonas's drawers and cutting off a little of the skin. Jonas fell—his legs flying up in the air, and shouting, "Murder! Murder! he's knocked off all the lower part of my abdomen. Send for a doctor! quick! quick! Oh! Lordy! oh! Lordy! I'm a dead man; the other fellow got the—wrong—pistol!" (And so he had; for on examining Jonas's pistol, it was found to have had no load in it. Jonas, by mistake in shuffling, having given the *loaded* one to Sam and kept the empty one himself.)

The testimony in the case was related with such comic humor by one of the witnesses, that the jury were thrown into convulsions of laughter; and the case being submitted without argument, the verdict was a fine of one cent only against the combatants.

Jonas immediately retired from the bullying business after that time, and as soon as he could get his affairs wound up, like "the star of Empire," "westward took his way."

✐ JOHNSON J. HOOPER

Simon Suggs Attends
a Camp-Meeting

Johnson J. Hooper (1815–1862), by creating the picaresque hero, Simon Suggs, made for himself a prominent place in the front row of American humorists. Suggs has been called "as clear-cut a figure as is to be found in the whole field of American humor." There is no question but that he furnished a model for Mark Twain's Huck Finn. Hooper's hero "lives as merrily and comfortably as possible at the expense of others." He has a way of cashing in on the inherent weaknesses of the human animal, which are the prime materials for effective satire. The Simon Suggs stories and sketches, appearing originally in William T. Porter's *Spirit of the Times* during the 1840s, were collected in *Some Adventures of Captain Simon Suggs, Late of the Tallapoosa Volunteers* (1845).

From *Adventures of Simon Suggs* (Philadelphia: Carey and Hart, 1846), pp. 118–133.

Captain Suggs found himself as poor at the conclusion of the Creek war, as he had been at its commencement. Although no "arbitrary," "despotic," "corrupt," and "unprincipled" judge had fined him a thousand dollars for his proclamation of martial law at Fort Suggs, or the enforcement of its rules in the case of Mrs. Haycock; yet somehow—the thing is alike inexplicable to him and to us—the money which he had contrived, by various shifts, to obtain, melted away and was gone forever. To a man like the Captain, of intense domestic affections, this state of destitution was most distressing. "He could stand it himself—didn't care a d——n for it, no way," he observed, "but the old woman and the children; *that* bothered him!"

As he sat one day, ruminating upon the unpleasant condition of his "financial concerns," Mrs. Suggs informed him that "the sugar and coffee was nigh about out," and that there were not "a dozen j'ints and middlins, *all put together*, in the smokehouse." Suggs bounced up on the instant, exclaiming, "D——n it! *somebody must suffer!*" But whether this remark was intended to convey the idea that he and his family were about to experience the want of the necessaries of life; or that some other, and as yet unknown, individual should "suffer" to prevent that prospective exigency, must be left to the commentators, if perchance any of that ingenious class of persons should hereafter see proper to write notes for this history. It is enough for us that we give all the facts in this connection, so that ignorance of the subsequent conduct of Captain Suggs may not lead to an erroneous judgment in respect to his words.

Having uttered the exclamation we have repeated—and perhaps, hurriedly, walked once or twice across the room—Captain Suggs drew on his famous old green-blanket overcoat, and ordered his horse, and within five minutes was on his way to a camp-meeting, then in full blast on Sandy Creek, twenty miles distant, where he hoped to find amusement, at least. When he arrived there, he found the hollow square of the encampment filled with people, listening to the mid-day sermon, and its dozen accompanying "exhortations." A half-dozen preachers were dispensing the word; the one in the pulpit, a meek-faced old man, of great simplicity and benevolence. His voice was weak and cracked, notwithstanding which, however, he contrived to make himself heard occasionally, above the din of the exhorting, the singing, and the shouting which were going on around him. The rest were walking to and fro (engaged in the other exercises we have indicated), among the "mourners"—a host of whom occupied the seat set apart for their especial use—or made personal appeals to the mere spectators. The excitement was intense. Men and women rolled about on the ground, or lay sobbing or shouting in promiscuous heaps. More than all, the negroes sang and screamed and prayed. Several, under the influence of what is technically called "the jerks," were plunging and pitching about with convulsive energy. The great object of all seemed to be, to see who could make the great noise—

> And each—for madness rules the hour–
> Would try his own expressive power.

"Bless my poor old soul!" screamed the preacher in the pulpit; "ef yonder aint a squad in that corner that we aint got one outen yet! It'll never do"—raising his voice—"you must come outen that! Brother Fant, fetch up that youngster in the blue coat! I see the Lord's a-workin upon him! Fetch him along—glory—yes! —hold to him!"

"Keep the thing warm!" roared a sensual seeming man, of stout mould and florid countenance, who was exhorting among a bevy of young women, upon whom he was lavishing caresses. "Keep the thing warm, breethring!—come to the Lord, honey!" he added, as he vigorously hugged one of the damsels he sought to save.

"Oh, I've got him!" said another in exulting tones, as he led up a gawky youth among the mourners—"I've got him—he tried to git off, but—ha! Lord!"—shaking his head as much as to say, it took a smart fellow to escape him—"ha! Lord!"—and he wiped the perspiration from his face with one hand, and with the other, patted his neophyte on the shoulder—"he couldn't do it! No! Then he tried to argy wi' me—but bless the Lord!—he couldn't do that nother! Ha! Lord! I tuk him, fust in the Old Testament— bless the Lord!—and I argyed him all thro' Kings—then I throwed him into Proverbs,—and from that, here we had it up and down, kleer down to the New Testament, and then I begun to see it work him!—then we got into Matthy, and from Matthy right straight along to Acts; and thar I throwed him! Y-e-s—L-o-r-d!"— assuming the nasal twang and high pitch which are, in some parts, considered the perfection of rhetorical art—"Y-e-s L-o-r-d! and h-e-r-e he is! Now g-i-t down thar," addressing the subject, "and s-e-e ef the L-o-r-d won't do somethin' f-o-r you!" Having thus deposited his charge among the mourners, he started out, summarily to convert another soul!

"Gl-o-ree!" yelled a huge, greasy negro woman, as in a fit of the jerks, she threw herself convulsively from her feet, and fell "like a thousand of brick," across a diminutive old man in a little round hat, who was speaking consolation to one of the mourners.

"Good Lord, have mercy!" ejaculated the little man earnestly and unaffectedly, as he strove to crawl from under the sable mass which was crushing him.

In another part of the square a dozen old women were singing. They were in a state of absolute ecstasy, as their shrill pipes gave forth:

> I rode on the sky,
> Quite ondestified I,
> And the moon it was under my feet!

Near these last, stood a delicate woman in that hysterical condition in which the nerves are incontrollable, and which is vulgarly—and almost blasphemously—termed the "holy laugh." A hideous grin distorted her mouth, and was accompanied with a maniac's chuckle; while every muscle and nerve of her face twitched and jerked in horrible spasms.

Amid all this confusion and excitement Suggs stood unmoved. He viewed the whole affair as a grand deception—a sort of "opposition line" running against his own, and looked on with a sort of professional jealousy. Sometimes he would mutter running comments upon what passed before him.

"Well now," said he, as he observed the full-faced brother who was "officiating" among the women, "that ere feller takes my eye! —thar he's been this half-hour, a-figurin amongst them galls, and's never said the fust word to nobody else. Wonder what's the reason

these here preachers never hugs up the old, ugly women? Never
seed one do it in my life—the sperrit never moves 'em that way!
It's nater tho'; and the women, they never flocks round one o' the
old dried-up breethring—bet two to one old splinter-legs thar,"—
nodding at one of the ministers—"won't git a chance to say turkey
to a good-lookin gall today! Well! Who blames 'em? Nater will
be nater, all the world over; and I judge ef I was a preacher, I
should save the purtiest souls fust, myself!"

While the Captain was in the middle of this conversation
with himself, he caught the attention of the preacher in the pulpit,
who inferring from an indescribable something about his appearance that he was a person of some consequence, immediately
determined to add him at once to the church if it could be done;
and to that end began a vigorous, direct personal attack.

"Breethring," he exclaimed, "I see yonder a man that's a sinner;
I know he's a sinner! Thar he stands," pointing at Simon, "a
missubble old crittur, with his head a-blossomin for the grave! A
few more short years, and d-o-w-n he'll go to perdition, lessen the
Lord have mercy on him! Come up here, you old hoary-headed
sinner, a-n-d git down upon your knees, a-n-d put up your cry for
the Lord to snatch you from the bottomless pit! You're ripe for
the devil—you're b-o-u-n-d for hell, and the Lord only knows
what'll become on you!"

"D——n it," thought Suggs, "ef I only had you down in the
krick swamp for a minit or so, I'd show you who's old! I'd alter
your tune mighty sudden, you sassy, 'saitful old rascal!" But he
judiciously held his tongue and gave no utterance to the thought.

The attention of many having been directed to the Captain by
the preacher's remarks, he was soon surrounded by numerous
well-meaning, and doubtless very pious persons, each one of whom
seemed bent on the application of his own particular recipe for
the salvation of souls. For a long time the Captain stood silent,
or answered the incessant stream of exhortations only with a
sneer; but at length, his countenance began to give token of inward
emotion. First his eye-lids twitched—then his upper lip quivered—
next a transparent drop formed on one of his eye-lashes, and a
similar one on the tip of his nose—and, at last, a sudden bursting
of air from nose and mouth, told that Captain Suggs was over-

powered by his emotions. At the moment of the explosion, he made a feint as if to rush from the crowd, but he was in experienced hands, who well knew that the battle was more than half won.

"Hold to him!" said one—"it's a-workin in him as strong as a Dick horse!"

"Pour it into him," said another, "it'll all come right directly!"

"That's the way I love to see 'em do," observed a third; "when you begin to draw the water from their eyes, taint gwine to be long afore you'll have 'em on their knees!"

And so they clung to the Captain manfully, and half dragged, half led him to the mourner's bench; by which he threw himself down, altogether unmanned, and bathed in tears. Great was the rejoicing of the brethren, as they sang, shouted, and prayed around him—for by this time it had come to be generally known that the "convicted" old man was Captain Suggs, the very "chief of sinners" in all that region.

The Captain remained grovelling in the dust during the usual time, and gave vent to even more than the requisite number of sobs, and groans, and heart-piercing cries. At length, when the proper time had arrived, he bounced up, and with a face radiant with joy, commenced a series of vaultings and tumblings, which "laid in the shade" all previous performances of the sort at that camp-meeting. The brethren were in ecstasies at this demonstrative evidence of completion of the work; and whenever Suggs shouted "Gloree!" at the top of his lungs, every one of them shouted it back, until the woods rang with echoes.

The effervescence having partially subsided, Suggs was put upon his pins to relate his experience, which he did somewhat in this style—first brushing the tear-drops from his eyes, and giving the end of his nose a preparatory wring with his fingers, to free it of the superabundant moisture:

"Friends," he said, "it don't take long to curry a short horse, accordin' to the old sayin', and I'll give you the perticklers of the way I was 'brought to a knowledge' "—here the Captain wiped his eyes, brushed the tip of his nose and snuffled a little—"in less'n no time."

"Praise the Lord!" ejaculated a bystander.

"You see I come here full o' romancin' and devilment, and jist to make game of all the purceedins. Well, sure enough, I done so for some time, and was a-thinkin how I should play some trick—"

"Dear soul alive! don't he talk sweet!" cried an old lady in black silk—"Whar's John Dobbs? You Sukey!" screaming at a negro woman on the other side of the square—"ef you don't hunt up your mass John in a minute, and have him here to listen to this 'sperience, I'll tuck you up when I git home and give you a hundred and fifty lashes, madam!—see ef I don't! Blessed Lord!"—referring again to the Captain's relation—"ain't it a *precious* 'scource!"

"I was jist a-thinkin' how I should play some trick to turn it all into redecule when they began to come round me and talk. Long at fust I didn't mind it, but arter a little that brother"—pointing to the reverend gentleman who had so successfully carried the unbeliever through the Old and New Testaments, and who Simon was convinced was the "big dog of the tanyard"—"that brother spoke a word that struck me kleen to the heart, and run all over me, like fire in dry grass—"

"I—I—I can bring 'em!" cried the preacher alluded to, in a tone of exultation—"Lord thou knows ef thy servant can't stir 'em up, nobody else needn't try—but the glory aint mine! I'm a poor worrum of the dust," he added, with ill-managed affectation.

"And so from that I felt somethin' a-pullin' me inside—"

"Grace! grace! nothin' but grace!" exclaimed one; meaning that "grace" had been operating in the Captain's gastric region.

"And then," continued Suggs, "I wanted to git off, but they hilt me, and bimeby I felt so missuble, I had to go yonder"—pointing to the mourner's seat—"and when I lay down thar it got wuss and wuss, and 'peared like somethin' was a-mashin' down on my back—"

"That was his load o' sin," said one of the brethren—"never mind, it'll tumble off presently, see ef it don't!" and he shook his head professionally and knowingly.

"And it kept a-gittin heavier and heavier, ontwell it looked like it might be a four year old steer, or a big pine log, or somethin' of that sort—"

"Glory to my soul," shouted Mrs. Dobbs, "it's the sweetest talk I ever hearn! You Sukey! aint you got John yit? never mind, my lady, I'll settle wi' you!" Sukey quailed before the finger which her mistress shook at her.

"And arter awhile," Suggs went on, " 'peared like I fell into a trace, like, and I seed—"

"Now we'll git the good on it!" cried one of the sanctified.

"And I seed the biggest, longest, rip-roarenest, blackest, scaliest —" Captain Suggs paused, wiped his brow, and ejaculated "Ah, L-o-r-d!" so as to give full time for curiosity to become impatience to know what he saw.

"*Sarpent!* warn't it?" asked one of the preachers.

"No, not a sarpent," replied Suggs, blowing his nose.

"Do tell us *what* it war, soul alive!—whar *is* John?" said Mrs. Dobbs.

"Allegator!" said the Captain.

"Alligator!" repeated every woman present, and screamed for very life.

Mrs. Dobbs' nerves were so shaken by the announcement, that after repeating the horrible word, she screamed to Sukey, "You Sukey, I say, you S-u-u-k-e-ey! ef you let John come a-nigh this way, whar the dreadful alliga—shaw! what am I thinkin' 'bout? 'Twarn't nothin' but a vishin'!"

"Well," said the Captain in continuation, "the allegator kept a-comin and a-comin' to'ards me, with his great long jaws a-gapin' open like a ten foot pair o' tailor's shears—"

"Oh! oh! oh! Lord! gracious above!" cried the women.

"Satan!" was the laconic ejaculation of the oldest preacher present, who thus informed the congregation that it was the devil which had attacked Suggs in the shape of an alligator.

"And then I concluded the jig was up, 'thout I could block his game some way; for I seed his idee was to snap off my head—"

The women screamed again.

"So I fixed myself jist like I was perfectly willin' for him to take my head, and rather he'd do it as not"—here the women shuddered perceptibly—"and so I hilt my head straight out"—the Captain illustrated by elongating his neck—"and when he come up and was a gwine to *shet* down on it, I just pitched in a big rock which choked him to death, and that minit I felt the weight slide off, and I had the best feelins—sorter like you'll have from good sperrits—any body ever had!"

"Didn't I *tell* you so? Didn't I *tell* you so?" asked the brother who had predicted the off-tumbling of the load of sin. "Ha, Lord! fool *who!* I've been *all* along thar!—yes, *all along thar!* and I know every inch of the way jist as good as I do the road home!" —and then he turned round and round, and looked at all, to receive a silent tribute to his superior penetration.

Captain Suggs was now the "lion of the day." Nobody could pray so well, or exhort so movingly, as "brother Suggs." Nor did his natural modesty prevent the proper performance of appropriate exercises. With the reverend Bela Bugg (him to whom, under providence, he ascribed his conversion) he was a most especial favorite. They walked, sang, and prayed together for hours.

"Come, come up; thar's room for all!" cried brother Bugg, in his evening exhortation. "Come to the 'seat,' and ef you won't pray yourselves, let *me* pray for you!"

"Yes!" said Simon, by way of assisting his friend; "it's a game that all can win at! Ante up!, boys—friends I mean—don't back out!"

"Thar aint a sinner here," said Bugg, "no matter ef his soul's black as a nigger, but what thar's room for him!"

"No matter what sort of a hand you've got," added Simon in the fullness of his benevolence; "take stock! Here am *I*, the wickedest and blindest of sinners—has spent my whole life in the sarvice of the devil—has now come in on *narry pair* and won a *pile!*" and the Captain's face beamed with holy pleasure.

"D-o-n-'t be afeard!" cried the preacher; "come along! the meanest won't be turned away! humble yourselves and come!"

"No!" said Simon, still indulging in his favourite style of metaphor; "the bluff game aint played here! No runnin' of a body off! Every body holds four aces, and when you bet, you win!"

And thus the Captain continued, until the services were concluded, to assist in adding to the number at the mourner's seat; and up to the hour of retiring, he exhibited such enthusiasm in the cause, that he was unanimously voted to be the most efficient addition the church had made during that meeting.

The next morning, when the preacher of the day first entered the pulpit, he announced that "brother Simon Suggs," mourning over his past iniquities, and desirous of going to work in the cause as speedily as possible, would take up a collection to found a church in his own neighbourhood, at which he hoped to make himself useful as soon as he could prepare himself for the ministry, which the preacher didn't doubt, would be in a very few weeks, as brother Suggs was "a man of mighty good *judgment*, and of a great discorse." The funds were to be collected by "brother Suggs," and held in trust by brother Bela Bugg, who was the financial officer of the circuit, until some arrangement could be made to build a suitable house.

"Yes, breethring," said the Captain, rising to his feet; "I want to start a little 'sociation close to me, and I want you all to help. I'm mighty poor myself, as poor as any of you—don't leave, breethring"—observing that several of the well-to-do were about to go off—"don't leave; ef you aint able to afford any thing, jist give us your blessin' and it'll be all the same!"

This insinuation did the business, and the sensitive individuals reseated themselves.

"It's mighty little of this world's goods I've got," resumed Suggs, pulling off his hat and holding it before him; "but I'll bury *that* in the cause any how," and he deposited his last five-dollar bill in the hat.

There was a murmur of approbation at the Captain's liberality throughout the assembly.

Suggs now commenced collecting, and very prudently attacked first the gentlemen who had shown a disposition to escape. These, to exculpate themselves from anything like poverty, contributed handsomely.

"Look here, breethring," said the Captain, displaying the bank-notes thus received, "brother Snooks has drapt a five wi' me, and brother Snodgrass a ten! In course, 'taint expected that you *that aint as well off as them*, will give *as much*; let every one give accordin' to ther means."

This was another chain-shot that raked as it went! "Who so low" as not to be able to contribute as much as Snooks and Snodgrass?

"Here's all the *small* money I've got about me," said a burly old fellow, ostentatiously handing to Suggs, over the heads of a half dozen, a ten dollar bill.

"That's what I call maganimus!" exclaimed the Captain; "that's the way every rich man ought to do!"

These examples were followed, more or less closely, by almost all present, for Simon had excited the pride of purse of the congregation, and a very handsome sum was collected in a very short time.

The reverend Mr. Bugg, as soon as he observed that our hero had obtained all that was to be had at that time, went to him and inquired what amount had been collected. The Captain replied that it was still uncounted, but that it couldn't be much under a hundred.

"Well, brother Suggs, you'd better count it and turn it over to me now. I'm goin' to leave presently."

"No!" said Suggs—"can't do it!"

"Why?—what's the matter?" inquired Bugg.

"It's got to be *prayed* over, fust!" said Simon, a heavenly smile illuminating his whole face.

"Well," replied Bugg, "less go one side and do it!"

"No!" said Simon, solemnly.

Mr. Bugg gave a look of inquiry.

"You see that krick swamp?" asked Suggs—"I'm gwine down in *thar*, and I'm gwine to lay this money down so"—showing how he would place it on the ground—"and I'm gwine to git on these here knees"—slapping the right one—"and I'm *n-e-v-e-r* gwine to quit the grit ontwell I feel it's got the blessin'! And nobody aint got to be thar but me!"

Mr. Bugg greatly admired the Captain's fervent piety, and bidding him God-speed, turned off.

Captain Suggs "struck for" the swamp sure enough, where his horse was already hitched. "Ef them fellers aint done to a cracklin," he muttered to himself as he mounted, "I'll never bet on two pair agin! They're peart at the snap game, theyselves; but they're badly lewed this hitch! Well! Live and let live is a good old motter, and it's my sentiments adzactly!" And giving the spur to his horse, off he cantered.

GEORGE W. HARRIS

Tripetown: Twenty Minutes
for Breakfast

George Washington Harris (1814–1869), author of
the hilarious *Sut Lovingood's Yarns* (1867), was
familiar with the raw facts of life on the frontier in
Tennessee. The rough mountaineers of the Great
Smoky Mountain region furnished material for many
of his stories, which are characterized by vivid
imagination, comic plot, satire, exaggeration, psychological action, artful artlessness, and sheer fun.
His work has been called the "nearest thing to the
undiluted oral humor of the Middle West that has
found its way into print."

For discussions of Harris's techniques, see Walter
Blair, *Native American Humor 1800–1900* (New
York, 1937); Franklin J. Meine, *Tall Tales of the
Southwest* (New York, 1930); Constance Rourke,
American Humor (New York, 1930); Bernard De
Voto, *Mark Twain's America* (Boston, 1932); and
Brom Weber's introduction to *Sut Lovingood* by
George Washington Harris (New York, 1954).

"I wer onst a-ridin ontu the ers ove a raleroad, an' hed
been livin on nuffin but sum bites ove whisky fur a hole day an'
nite, an' felt like a congrigashun ove rats wer a-bildin thar nestes
outen sifter wire in my stumick, an' a hive ove bees wer a-fixin tu
swarm in my head, when the conducter run his fore-aind intu the
door, up tu the butt ove his watch-chain, an' holler'd—

" 'Tripetown—twenty minutes fur breakfus'.'

" 'That's me,' I said, an' I went over. I jis' tell yu this case tu

From *Sut Lovingood's Yarns* (New York: Dick and Fitzgerald, 1867), pp.
193–197.

show yu that the sarmint I hev been preachin, wif Catfishe Tavrins
fur a tex, wer pervok'd outen me.

"I sot down, an' oh, lordy! sich a breakfus! My talk, bad es yu
sez hit wer, about the Catfishe peopil, don't begin tu du jestice
tu this mess ove truck. A hungry dorg wudn't hev smelt, nur a
sperienced buzzard even lit ontu hit, ef thar wer a ded hoss in
a hundred mile. I tried a bite, an' hit flew outen my mouf like
ther'd been a steel mattrass spring quiled in my froat; so ove
course I wer the fust wun outen thar. Thar he wer, the everlastin
'perpryiter,' a-standin in the door, wif his paw full ove notes,
a-lickin the ball ove his tuther thumb, like he wer hungry tu begin,
that bein the chief aind ove (the Catfishe) man.

" 'Two dullars an' a 'alf; yu mus' make the change,' sed he, all
in wun breff.

"I thor't I'd see ef *all* his feelins wer seared wif a red hot
iron, an' so I sed—lookin mity serus an' pius like, rite squar intu
the middil ove the glass ove his specks, what kivered a par ove
es mean an' muny-luvin eyes es ever star'd at the eagle ontu a
dime ontil that ar bird shot his'n up wif shame—

" 'Yu keep a all-fired good hous', Mister—good biskit, an' coffee
tu match; hit gins a man a appertite tu jis' look et yu; hit gins
him a appertite an' a stumick tu look et yur wife, an' hit sets
em bof a-rarin an' a-squealin tu smell yer tabil. This am a holesum
place. An' es I hes far'd so well, about yu, I wants tu tell yu a
valerabil secret; how tu make yer coffee, good es hit is, still better,
an' not cos' a cent more.'

" 'Much obleged, indeed,' sez he, an' lookin es sweet roun the
mouf es ef he'd been a-tastin good brandy an' white sugar, an'
wer wantin ove more.

"Now the travelers wer cumin out, ni ontu eighty ove em, an'
wantin me outen the way, so they cud pay fur what nastiness an'
pizen they'd swaller'd, an' git outen the smell ove hit es soon es
possibil. I jis' kep on talkin 'bout my 'provement ontu coffee till
I tho't mos' ove em wer in year shot, when I rais's my soun, an'
sed—

" 'Ef yu want tu make that good coffee ove yourn better, jis'
yu, instead ove makin hit all outen ole boot-laigs, put in about

half ove a ole wool hat, chopp'd fine, finer nur yu chops yer hash say, intu pieces a inch square; hit will help the taste pow'ful, an' not set the smell back a bit,' I flung down my munny an' put fur the train. I swar, es I went, I cud feel the fokis ove them specks a-burnin intu the back ove my head, an' I smelt my har swingin. I know'd that he wer tryin tu look thru me, an' the peopil, men an' wimmen, wer screamin a-larfin et sumthin. Tu help his mad to a head, wun feller hed sot down ontu the step, wif a segar clamp't atween his knees, a biskit intu each han, whetin away, tryin tu strike fire outen them ontu hit. Anuther hed fired wun ove the biggest an hardes' biskit at the smoke-hous', an' hit went thru the wether boardin like a grape shot. Anuther perlite, bowin, smilin feller cum out wif the drum-stick aind ove the hine laig ove a ole gander 'twixt his finger an' thumb, an' narrated hit that hit wer ole Powhattan's war club, an' he wer gwine tu start hissef a museum; while out in the yard, lay a long feller flat ontu his belly, wif his laigs wide apart, an' his paws locked roun a par-biled beef rib, an' he wer gnawin at tuther aind ove his fust in wun side ove his mouf, an' then tuther, growlin like a dorg, an' a-eyein sidewise the picter sot in the door-frame all the while. A long-necked passenger, top'd off wif a seal-skin cap, cum rushin out in a shanghi trot, wif a stripe ove tuff tripe es long es a sirsingle. He hed hit by the middil in his mouf, an' wer a-splashin an' a-slapin the aind agin everybody what he pass'd by, vigrusly shakin his head, jis' like a dorg dus when he's a-killin snakes, ur a sow playin wif rags afore a storm. All these shines didn't stop the larfin a bit, ef I noticed right.

"Well, when I'd got off about thuty yards, I venter'd tu look back. Thar he stood, the mos' orful picter ove onregenerated rath, mortal man ever seed. He looked like he'd weigh five hundred pounds; he wer swell'd all over, ni ontu bustin, an' the door wer chock full ove him, all in a strut. His arms stuck out like a settin hen's wings, his hat cocked before, his feet wide apart, an' he wer a-lookin at me sure enuf. Them specks blazin like two red lamps, his lips a-flutterin es he blow'd out the hot breff an' foam ove his onbearabil pent up rath, what my onekeled an' on-hearn ove imperdence tu *him, the perpryiter* hed sot a-bilin in his in'ards, ontil he wer ni ontu burnt out, thru tu the har, an' waiscoat. The smoke ove his torment wer-a-cumin out in whiffs frum his breeches pockets, an' button holes.

"My lookin back toch the trigger; an idear, an' speech now cum tu him fur the fust time, an' he exploded. He jis' bellered like a bull bawlin in a tunnel, a-flingin big splotches ove foam an' spittil way ofen the step et every word.

" 'Spose—yu—go—tu—h—ll—yu—dam—raskill.'

"He wer ontu his tip-toes when he sed this, an' as he ainded the word 'raskill,' he cum down ontu his heels, till he made the winders chatter, an' his big watch-seals dance agin.

"I jis' kep ontu the kers, an' didn't du what he tole me tu. Arter we'd run two miles, I looked back, an we wer so fur that the door looked like a black spot on the hous', an' I wish I may be tetotally durn'd, cordin tu law, ef I didn't still see them hot specks, rite in the middil ove hit, blazin away like two leetle red stars. Sum orful calamity tuck place at that rail road troff tu sumbody, afore he simmered down."

⇌ *ANONYMOUS*

A Dakota Winter

During frontier days, newspapers and magazines gave writers and scribblers an outlet for their creative impulses and emotional pressures. Much of Western humor appeared initially in one or more of the country's newspapers. Often the author of such pieces hid behind a pseudonym. The following anonymous selection first appeared in the Chicago *Ledger* under the name "Cowboy." The text as reprinted here is from *State Vidette* (Crete, Nebraska), November 5, 1885.

From *State Vidette* (Crete, Neb.), November 5, 1885. Editor's title.

A great many very intelligent people of the east never mention Dakota in winter time without feeling a cold wave blow through their minds at the same instant.

They have read reports from newspapers interested in steering the course of emigrants in other direction, that for nine months of the twelve Dakota is an iceberg; her lakes and rivers iced clear through, her soil congealed a half mile deep, and her inhabitants semi-frozen, living on the fat of the land—boiled blizzards, surrounded by mountains of drifted snow.

That this erroneous impression may be thawed out of their heads, we have concluded to let the subject of truth flash upon them from a red-hot pen. It is true that the mercury has a disposition to lie low a few weeks on both sides of the holidays, but the climate is so dry that a person can be very comfortable with the temperature diving down to 50 degrees below zero.

If a man is well dressed, he can stay out of doors and keep warm all day, although the heat is not oppressive, and there are very few sunstrokes after 35 below zero. After a cold spell, when it warms up to 25 below zero, it feels positively hot, and you intuitively begin thinking about mosquitos and garden sass. No one who has not actually tasted the joy of a Dakota winter can have the slightest idea how pleasant they are. No breathing of damp air, no chilly sensations racing up and down your spinal marrow, forming icicles of the blood in your veins. The air is fresh and pure, invigorating and dry, health-giving and bracing, an appetizer and a promoter of digestion. Mud is a stranger, and rain a foreign element, until the balmy month of April sets in. This is highly appreciated by one who has waded through the labyrinth of slush and mud in the south for four months of winter. The extra twists of freezing prepare the soil for producing 45 bushels of wheat to the acre, and other crops in proportion. This is a quick country, everything is on the jump. The people and all the animals move on a quick schedule, no loitering by the wayside. It is an even run between the frost and wild flowers which gets out of the ground first. Consumptives grow fat and dyspeptics good-natured here during the winter. We have no drownings from breaking through the ice, although it is quite thin—not more than thirty inches thick now. There is a big crop of ice-cream raised every winter. We were out during the last of January hunting for wild flowers; didn't find any though. Dakota winters are a luxury that ye easterners would delight to revel in, and southerners can never afford without they can borrow our ice machine. It is actually too warm on the 28th of January to wear a buffalo coat in the house.

—*Cowboy, in Chicago Ledger*

part 12

THE FRONTIER
IN RETROSPECT

Pioneers! O Pioneers!

Walt Whitman (1819–1892) considered *Drum-Taps* (1865) his best volume. Among other fine poems, it contained "Pioneers! O Pioneers!" which eulogizes the dauntless spirit and united effort of the pioneers in the conquest of the American continent, and predicts further accomplishments to follow in the wake of the westward movement.

Come my tan-faced children,
Follow well in order, get your weapons ready,
Have you your pistols? have you your sharp-edged axes?
    Pioneers! O pioneers!

For we cannot tarry here,
We must march my darlings, we must bear the brunt of danger,
We the youthful sinewy races, all the rest on us depend,
    Pioneers! O pioneers!

O you youths, Western youths,
So impatient, full of action, full of manly pride and friendship,
Plain I see you Western youths, see you tramping with the fore-
    most,
    Pioneers! O pioneers!

Have the elder races halted?
Do they droop and end their lesson, wearied over there beyond
    the seas?

From *Drum-Taps* (1865).

We take up the task eternal, and the burden and the lesson,
    Pioneers! O pioneers!

All the past we leave behind,
We debouch upon a newer mightier world, varied world,
Fresh and strong the world we seize, world of labor and the
    march,
    Pioneers! O pioneers!

We detachments steady throwing,
Down the edges, through the passes, up the mountains steep,
Conquering, holding, daring, venturing as we go the unknown
    ways,
    Pioneers! O pioneers!

We primeval forests felling,
We the rivers stemming, vexing we and piercing deep the mines
    within,
We the surface broad surveying, we the virgin soil upheaving,
    Pioneers! O pioneers!

Colorado men are we,
From the peaks gigantic, from the great sierras and the high
    plateaus,
From the mine and from the gully, from the hunting trail we
    come,
    Pioneers! O pioneers!

From Nebraska, from Arkansas,
Central inland race are we, from Missouri, with the continental
    blood intervein'd,
All the hands of comrades clasping, all the Southern, all the
    Northern,
    Pioneers! O pioneers!

O resistless restless race!
O beloved race in all! O my breast aches with tender love for all!
O I mourn and yet exult, I am rapt with love for all,
    Pioneers! O pioneers!

Raise the mighty mother mistress,
Waving high the delicate mistress, over all the starry mistress,
       (bend your heads all,)
Raise the fang'd and warlike mistress, stern, impassive, weapon'd
       mistress,
       Pioneers! O pioneers!

See my children, resolute children,
By those swarms upon our rear we must never yield or falter,
Ages back in ghostly millions frowning there behind us urging,
       Pioneers! O pioneers!

On and on the compact ranks,
With accessions ever waiting, with the places of the dead quickly
       fill'd,
Through the battle, through defeat, moving yet and never stop-
       ping,
       Pioneers! O pioneers!

O to die advancing on!
Are there some of us to droop and die? has the hour come?
Then upon the march we fittest die, soon and sure the gap is fill'd,
       Pioneers! O pioneers!

All the pulses of the world,
Falling in they beat for us, with the Western movement beat,
Holding single or together, steady moving to the front, all for us,
       Pioneers! O pioneers!

Life's involv'd and varied pageants,
All the forms and shows, all the workmen at their work,
All the seamen and the landsmen, all the masters with their slaves,
       Pioneers! O pioneers!

All the hapless silent lovers,
All the prisoners in the prisons, all the righteous and the wicked,
All the joyous, all the sorrowing, all the living, all the dying,
       Pioneers! O pioneers!

I too with my soul and body,
We, a curious trio, picking, wandering on our way,

Through these shores amid the shadows, with the apparitions press-
        ing,
        Pioneers! O pioneers!

        Lo, the darting bowling orb!
Lo, the brother orbs around, all the clustering suns and planets,
All the dazzling days, all the mystic nights with dreams,
        Pioneers! O pioneers!

        These are of us, they are with us,
All for primal needed work, while the followers there in embryo
        wait behind,
We to-day's procession heading, we the route for travel clearing,
        Pioneers! O pioneers!

        O you daughters of the West!
O you young and elder daughters! O you mothers and you wives!
Never must you be divided, in our ranks you move united,
        Pioneers! O pioneers!

        Minstrels latent on the prairies!
(Shrouded bards of other lands, you may rest, you have done your
        work),
Soon I hear you coming warbling, soon you rise and tramp amid us,
        Pioneers! O pioneers!

        Not for delectations sweet,
Not the cushion and the slipper, not the peaceful and the studious,
Not the riches safe and palling, not for us the tame enjoyment,
        Pioneers! O pioneers!

        Do the feasters gluttonous feast?
Do the corpulent sleepers sleep? Have they lock'd and bolted
        doors?
Still be ours the diet hard, and the blanket on the ground,
        Pioneers! O pioneers!

        Has the night descended?
Was the road of late so toilsome? did we stop discouraged nodding
        on our way?

Yet a passing hour I yield you in your tracks to pause oblivious,
  Pioneers! O pioneers!

    Till with sound of trumpet,
Far, far off the daybreak call—hark! how loud and clear I hear it
    wind,
Swift! to the head of the army!—swift! spring to your places,
  Pioneers! O pioneers!

↙ *FRANK NORRIS*

The Frontier Is Gone

Frank Norris (1870–1902), who is especially remembered for his naturalistic novels *McTeague*
(1899) and *The Octopus* (1901), was a strong advocate of the brotherhood of man. In this essay,
Norris shows how our race pushed the frontier westward around the world and how it now moves eastward again. This new direction suggests for the
author a new point of view and a broader patriotism:
a change from a national to an international orientation. Considered in the light of twentieth-century
developments, the author's astute remarks on the
brotherhood of man seem unbelievably prophetic.

Suddenly we have found that there is no longer any
Frontier. Until the day when the first United States marine landed
in China we had always imagined that out yonder somewhere in
the West was the border land where civilization disintegrated and
merged into the untamed. Our skirmish line was there, our posts

From *World's Work*, vol. 3 (February, 1902), 1728–1831.

that scouted and scrimmaged with the wilderness, a thousand miles in advance of the steady march of civilization.

And the Frontier has become so much an integral part of our conception of things that it will be long before we shall all understand that it is gone. We liked the Frontier; it was romance, the place of the poetry of the Great March, the firing line where there was action and fighting, and where men held each other's lives in the crook of the forefinger. Those who had gone out came back with tremendous tales, and those that stayed behind made up other and even more tremendous tales.

When we—we Anglo-Saxons—busked ourselves for the first stage of the march, we began from that little historic reach of ground in the midst of the Friesland swamps, and we set our faces Westward, feeling no doubt the push of the Slav behind us. Then the Frontier was Britain and the sober peacefulness of land where are the ordered, cultivated English farmyards of today was the Wild West for the Frisians of that century; and for the little children of the Frisian peat cottages, Hengist was the Apache Kid and Horsa Deadwood Dick—freebooters, law-defiers, slayers-o-men, epic heroes, blood brothers if you please to Boone and Bowie.

Then for centuries we halted and the van closed up with the firing line and we filled all England and all Europe with our clamor because for a while we seemed to have gone as far Westward as it was possible; and the checked energy of the race reacted upon itself, rebounded as it were, and back we went to the Eastward again— crusading, girding at the Mohammedan, conquering his cities, breaking into his fortresses with mangonel, siege engine and catapult—just as the boy shut indoors finds his scope circumscribed and fills the whole place with the racket of his activity.

But always, if you will recall it, we had a curious feeling that we had not reached the ultimate West even yet, that there was still a Frontier. Always that strange sixth sense turned our heads toward the sunset; and all through the Middle Ages we were peeking and prying at the Western horizon, trying to reach it, to run it down, and the queer tales about Vineland and that storm-driven Viking's ship would not down.

And then at last a naked savage on the shores of a little island in what is now our West Indies, looking Eastward one morning, saw the caravels, and on that day the Frontier was rediscovered, and promptly a hundred thousand of the most hardy rushed to the skirmish-line and went at the wilderness as only the Anglo-Saxon can.

And then the skirmish-line decided that it would declare itself independent of the main army behind and form an advance column of its own, a separate army corps, and no sooner was this done then again the scouts went forward, went Westward, pushing the Frontier ahead of them, scrimmaging with the wilderness, blazing the way. At last they forced the Frontier over the Sierra Nevada down to the edge of the Pacific. And here it would have been supposed that the Great March would have halted again as it did before the Atlantic, that here at last the Frontier ended.

But on the first of May, eighteen hundred and ninety-eight, a gun was fired in the Bay of Manila, still further Westward, and in response the skirmish-line crossed the Pacific, still pushing the Frontier before it. Then came a cry for help from Legation Street in Peking and as the first boat bearing its contingent of American marines took ground on the Asian shore, the Frontier—at last after so many centuries, after so many marches, after so much fighting, so much spilled blood, so much spent treasure, dwindled down and vanished; for the Anglo-Saxon in his course of empire had circled the globe and had brought the new civilization to the old civilization, had reached the starting point of history, the place from which the migrations began. So soon as the marines landed there was no longer any West, and the equation of the horizon, the problem of the centuries for the Anglo-Saxon was solved.

So, lament it though we may, the Frontier is gone, an idiosyncrasy that has been with us for thousands of years, the one peculiar picturesqueness of our life is no more. We may keep alive for many years yet the idea of a Wild West, but the hired cowboys and paid rough riders of Mr. William Cody are more like "the real thing" than can be found today in Arizona, New Mexico or Idaho. Only the imitation cowboys, the college-bred fellows who "go out on a ranch" carry the revolver or wear the concho. The Frontier has become conscious of itself, acts the part for the Eastern visitor; and this self-consciousness is a sign, surer than all others, of the decadence of a type, the passing of an epoch. The Apache Kid and

Deadwood Dick have gone to join Hengist and Horsa and the heroes of the Magnusson Saga.

But observe. What happened in the Middle Ages when for awhile we could find no Western Frontier? The race impulse was irresistible. March we must, conquer we must, and checked in the Westward course of empire we turned Eastward and expended the resistless energy that by blood was ours in conquering the Old World behind us.

Today we are the same race, with the same impulse, the same power and, because there is no longer a Frontier to absorb our overplus of energy, because there is no longer a wilderness to conquer and because we still must march, still must conquer, we remember the old days when our ancestors before us found the outlet for their activity checked and, rebounding, turned their faces Eastward, and went down to invade the Old World. So we. No sooner have we found that our path to the Westward has ended than, reacting Eastward, we are at the Old World again, marching against it, invading it, devoting our overplus of energy to its subjugation.

But though we are the same race, with the same impulses, the same blood-instincts as the old Frisian marsh people, we are now come into a changed time and the great word of our century is no longer War but Trade.

Or if you choose it is only a different word for the same race-characteristic. The desire for conquest—say what you will—was as big in the breast of the most fervid of the Crusaders as it is this very day in the most peacefully-disposed of American manufacturers. Had the Lion-Hearted Richard lived today he would have become a "leading representative of the Amalgamated Steel Companies" and doubt not for one moment that he would have underbid his Manchester rivals in the matter of bridge girders. Had Mr. Andrew Carnegie been alive at the time of the preachings of Peter the Hermit he would have raised a company of gens-d'armes sooner than all of his brothers-in-arms, would have equipped his men better and more effectively, would have been first on the ground before Jerusalem, would have built the most ingenious siege engine and have hurled the first cask of Greek-fire over the walls.

Competition and conquest are words easily interchangeable, and the whole spirit of our present commercial crusade to the Eastward betrays itself in the fact that we cannot speak of it but in terms borrowed from the glossary of the warrior. It is a commercial "invasion," a trade "war," a "threatened attack" on the part of America; business is "captured," opportunities are "seized," certain industries are "killed," certain former monopolies are "wrested away." Seven hundred years ago a certain Count Baldwin, a great leader in the attack of the Anglo-Saxon Crusaders upon the Old World, built himself a siege engine which would help him enter the beleaguered city of Jerusalem. Jerusalem is beleaguered again today, and the hosts of the Anglo-Saxon commercial crusaders are knocking at the gates. And now a company named for another Baldwin—and for all we know a descendant of the count—leaders of the invaders of the Old World, advance upon the city, and, to help in the assault, build an engine—only now the engine is no longer called a *mangonel*, but a locomotive.

The difference is hardly of kind and scarcely of degree. It is a mere matter of names, and the ghost of Saladin watching the present engagement might easily fancy the old days back again.

So perhaps we have not lost the Frontier after all. A new phrase, reversing that of Berkeley's, is appropriate to the effect that "Eastward the course of commerce takes its way," and we must look for the lost battle-line not toward the sunset, but toward the East. And so rapid has been the retrograde movement that we must go far to find it, that scattered firing-line, where the little skirmishes are heralding the approach of the Great March. We must already go further afield than England. The main body, even to the reserves, are intrenched there long since, and even continental Europe is to the rear of the skirmishers.

Along about Suez we begin to catch up with them where they are deepening the great canal, and we can assure ourselves that we are fairly abreast of the most distant line of scouts only when we come to Khiva, to Samarcand, to Bokhara and the Trans-Baikal country.

Just now one hears much of the "American commercial invasion of England." But adjust the field glasses and look beyond Britain and search for the blaze that the scouts have left on the telegraph poles and mile posts of Hungary, Turkey, Turkey in Asia, Persia, Beloochistan, India and Siam. You'll find the blaze distinct and the road, though rough hewn, is easy to follow. Prophecy and presumption be far from us, but it would be against all precedent that the Grand March should rest forever upon its arms and its laurels along the Thames, the Mersey and the Clyde, while its pioneers and Frontiersmen are making roads for it to the Eastward.

Is it too huge a conception, too inordinate an idea to say that the American conquest of England is but an incident of the Greater Invasion, an affair of outposts preparatory to the real manœuvre that shall embrace Europe, Asia, the whole of the Old World? Why not? And the blaze is ahead of us, and every now and then from far off there in the countries that are under the rising sun we catch the faint sounds of the skirmishing of our outposts. One of two things invariably happens under such circumstances as these: either the outposts fall back upon the main body or the main body moves up to the support of its outposts. One does not think that the outposts will fall back.

And so goes the great movement, Westward, then Eastward, forward and then back. The motion of the natural forces, the elemental energies, somehow appear to be thus alternative—action first, then reaction. The tides ebb and flow again, the seasons have their slow vibrations, touching extremes at periodic intervals. Not impossibly, in the larger view, is the analogy applicable to the movements of the races. First Westward with the great migrations, now Eastward with the course of commerce, moving in a colossal arc measured only by the hemispheres, as though upon the equator a giant dial hand oscillated, in gradual divisions through the centuries, now marking off the Westward progress, now traveling proportionately to the reaction toward the East.

Races must follow their destiny blindly, but is it not possible that we can find in this great destiny of ours something a little better than mere battle and conquest, something a little more generous than mere trading and underbidding? Inevitably with constant change of environment comes the larger view, the more tolerant spirit, and every race movement, from the first step beyond the Friesland swamp to the adjustment of the first American theodolite on the Himalayan watershed, is an unconscious lesson in patriotism. Just now we cannot get beyond the self-laudatory mood, but is it not possible to hope that, as the progress develops, a new patriotism, one that shall include all peoples, may prevail? The past would indicate that this is a goal toward which we trend.

In the end let us take the larger view, ignoring the Frieslanders, the Anglo-Saxons, the Americans. Let us look at the peoples as a people and observe how inevitably as they answer the great Westward impulse the true patriotism develops. If we can see that it is so with all of them we can assume that it must be so with us, and may know that mere victory in battle as we march Westward, or mere supremacy in trade as we react to the East is not after all the great achievement of the races but patriotism. Not our selfish present-day conception of the word, but a new patriotism, whose meaning is now the secret of the coming centuries.

Consider then the beginnings of patriotism. At the very first, the seed of the future nation was the regard of family; the ties of common birth held men together and the first feeling of patriotism was the love of family. But the family grows, develops by lateral branches, expands and becomes the clan. Patriotism is the devotion to the clan, and the clansmen will fight and die for its supremacy.

Then comes the time when the clans, tired of the roving life of herders, halt a moment and settle down in a chosen spot, the tent becoming permanent evolves the dwelling house, and the encampment of the clan becomes at last a city. Patriotism now is civic pride, the clan absorbed into a multitude of clans is forgotten; men speak of themselves as Athenians not as Greeks, as Romans not as Italians. It is the age of cities.

The city extends its adjoining grazing fields, they include outlying towns, other cities, and finally the State comes into being. Patriotism no longer confines itself to the walls of the city, but is enlarged to encompass the entire province. Men are Hanoverians or Wurtemburgers not Germans; Scots or Welsh not English; are even Carolinians or Alabamans rather than Americans.

But, the States are federated, pronounced boundaries fade, State makes common cause with State and at last the nation is born. Patriotism at once is a national affair, a far larger, broader, truer sentiment than that first huddling about the hearthstone of the family. The word "brother" may be applied to men unseen and unknown, and a countryman is one of many millions.

We have reached this stage at the present, but if all signs are true, if all precedent may be followed, if all augury may be relied on and the tree grow as we see the twig is bent, the progress will not stop here.

By war to the Westward the family fought its way upward to the dignity of the nation, by reaction Eastward the nation may in patriotic effect merge with other nations, and others and still others, peacefully, the bitterness of trade competition may be lost, the business of the nations seen as a friendly *quid pro quo*, give and take arrangement, guided by a generous reciprocity. Every century the boundaries are widening, patriotism widens with the expansion, and our countrymen are those of different race, even different nations.

Will it not go on, this epic of civilization, this destiny of the races, until at last and at the ultimate end of all, we who now arrogantly boast ourselves as Americans, supreme in conquest, whether of battle-ship or of bridge-building, may realize that the true patriotism is the brotherhood of man and know that the whole world is our nation and simple humanity our countrymen?

⌁ WAYNE KERNODLE

The Last of the Rugged Individualists

R. Wayne Kernodle (1919–   ), Chairman of Sociology and Anthropology at William and Mary College, has in this essay combined an exciting narrative of frontier life among Southern highlanders

From *Harper's Magazine*, January 1960. By permission of the author.

with critical comments on the cultural changes
brought about by the encroachment of civilization
in our own time. The last act of the drama of
frontier life among the hillbillies, as presented by
Kernodle, is a tragicomedy of losses and gains.

That fierce individualist, the Southern mountaineer, has
long been one of America's favorite characters. He has given us a
whole series of folk heroes, from Andrew Jackson and Davy
Crockett to Li'l Abner. His songs have become a national fad. He
has inspired a considerable literature, ranging from serious fiction
to the hillbilly cartoon.

And now he is about to vanish, without hope of rescue. Even if
there were any practical way to save him, he wouldn't stand for it.
In his aggressive—some say arrogant—tradition of independence,
he would rather go under than stand beholden to any rescuer. I
know, because some of the last of these rugged individualists are
my friends.

As the new highways push into dozens of once-hidden coves,
they are destroying that isolation which, over the course of the
generations, molded the character of the Southern highlander. It
is a character which the rest of the country comprehended only
dimly. He was ridiculed for his insularity, and capriciously celebrated for qualities which he probably never had and doesn't have
now. What he is really like is well exemplified, I think, by the
McCalls of Pin Hook Gap.

Perhaps it is best not to locate the place too precisely, because
there is more than one Pin Hook Gap and more McCalls than the
particular family I know. It is enough to say that it lies in the
westernmost end of North Carolina, close to the high, craggy spine
of the Appalachians that shuts the mountain country off from the
coastal East. The Plott Balsams are here and Pisgah National Forest and the Blue Ridge Mountains and the Blacks. The Cherokee
Indian reservation is not far to the west. The mountains are high
—the highest east of the Mississippi—but they are not peaks but
domes, "balds," flat at the top and bare, or wooded with a kind of
low, torn pine. Many have barely been explored, but they have
names: Yellow Face, Dirty Britches, Inkem-Binkem. If you walk

northwest of these ridges you come into a good thirty miles of nearly impassable balsam slicks and rhododendron thickets, briars, and dog hobble.

It is dense country. It is also beautiful country, with perhaps the most glorious displays of floral vegetation of any part of the United States—dogwood and azalea and laurel and rhododendron, and about them cool pine forest and a tumble of waterfalls. This is also the land of the black bear and of the deer which once provided a main source of food for the Cherokee nation. There are frequent reports of panthers and wildcats, though few of these are actually seen these days.

Pin Hook Gap is, roughly, in between the cities of Asheville, North Carolina, and Knoxville, Tennessee. The needs of the cities have brought roads to connect them, and Pin Hook Gap has felt the glory and the sorrow of being on the route of march. But the cities have not been corruptors directly or intentionally. The boondocks themselves have conceived their own transfiguration.

The total population of Pin Hook is five McCalls plus an assortment of bears, panthers, rattlesnakes, and wild pigs.

Young John McCall, who is seventy-three years old, and his brother Charlie, who is seventy, live in a tight little cabin nestled into a cove under Devil's Courthouse. One brother and his wife live about two hundred yards away, and another brother lives by himself in a shack about a half-mile back in the thicket. Neither Young John nor Charlie has married, and only two of the McCalls have ever been more than fifty miles from Pin Hook during their entire lives. That time was almost forty years ago, when Charlie went into the Army and stayed at training camp for about three weeks before coming back home for good.

A friend of mine, Al Moore, who lives parttime in Brevard, knew a cousin of the McCalls. Through him Al got directions to Pin Hook and the proper passwords that would get us in to John and Charlie's place. It took the two of us and Al's sister, Martha Kate, the better part of the morning, in a jeep, to make it to the top of Pin Hook Ridge. Then we started to drop off into the cove at a remarkably steep angle.

Here, following instructions, we started blowing the jeep horn every minute. When we finally came in sight of the cabin, we stopped and sat on the horn until a figure appeared on the porch. Then we just sat there. It must have been thirty minutes before anything happened. The man on the porch stood in the doorway, leaning on a rifle, and we sat there in the jeep—waiting.

Then I got the feeling that someone was close to the jeep and looked around. There stood Charlie McCall. He had made no sound coming and had given no indication that he was there. Al Moore—who has hiked almost every inch of the territory in this section from Rough Butt to Tennessee Bald and then some—introduced us. We nodded and followed Charlie up to the cabin. From the yard we howdy-ed Young John, but I haven't shaken hands with him to this day.

The beginning was mighty slow. Neither of the McCalls was inclined to start any conversation. They answered questions with the fewest words possible. At first some of the words were unintelligible to me, but Al and Martha Kate seemed to understand them well enough.

Everything about the place expressed the independent way of life. Their father had built the cabin when he first came to Pin Hook. The furniture was all fashioned by hand from cherry and walnut. It had the simple, true lines of great workmanship and was both comfortable and as sturdy as the rocks which surrounded the cove. All of their belongings had been made with tools they had hammered out themselves. The long rifle which stood across the entrance to the house had a barrel made by Charlie McCall.

Both men were tall—more than six feet—and thin, but they were not skinny. Their blue eyes were clear and sharp and their hearing was acute. They were confident men but not arrogant, cunning but not slick. They manifested a serenity unmatched by anything I have seen in the urban world. We talked about their life, which included some mining for precious stones, mica, and minerals.

With some prompting, Charlie told us about a long and ferocious struggle with a panther the winter before.

"This painter used that aire place up thar," he said, pointing out a promontory which jutted out from the balsam thickets about two thousand feet above the cabin. "He was driv by hungry and cold—hit ud been asnowin' fur a week a more. One night we heerd bangin' on the roof. We'suns tuk the rifles and got outside. He come aflyin' off the roof at us. We shot at him and he tuk off. But he come back later and was tearin' and clawin' at the windows and doors and all over the top of the house. Finally he tore a hole in the roof and come pilin' in. We fit him with arn bars and sticks and finally driv him outa the front door. John hit him in the hint leg and he'uns scremt and wailed like a dyin' hog. We haint seen him since. He had tore up the place baddest."

In the summer the McCalls raise a plot of corn and some other vegetables, and kill a hog or two. The hogs are put into a barrel of salt brine to keep from "spiling." In late August and early September, when the berries are plentiful, they pick for days at a time and can them for winter, using an old wood-burning stove and hand-fashioned pots for cooking. During the long winter months they work at their mining, at making the various articles necessary to keep life and limb together. What they do and how they do it is entirely up to them. They are independent, but will share a real offer of friendship. Their wishes are simple but include the great wish not to be "a-dickertated to"—by men or panthers.

When we arrived, the McCalls were just getting ready to go do some mining, and seemed itchy to get on with it. By this time it had started to rain a bit. We noticed that they were going bareheaded and with only rough denim jackets on their backs. Martha Kate ran back to the jeep and got a couple of plastic tablecloths and held them out to the McCalls. Then for a moment we were sorry, because we feared they were insulted. After a few moments John McCall took one of the tablecloths and put it over his shoulders. Charlie turned and went into the cabin. A few minutes later he returned, and into Martha Kate's hand he placed a beautiful clear ruby. She could not refuse this gesture and still maintain his friendship, so she merely let it lie in her open palm as Charlie pulled the old plastic cloth over his shoulders and he and John McCall walked off toward the hills beyond their rough-hewn homestead. Al, Martha Kate, and I went to the jeep and began our trip back to the way of life that might some day swallow up the McCalls and the painter—if he's still alive.

For "progress" is on its way to Pin Hook Gap. Thirty miles

away from the McCall cabin you come out onto a good dirt road and to a little community in the valley. The people at the country store were talking about the engineers who had been making surveys for paving the road and connecting it with the Blue Ridge Parkway at Wagon Road Gap and thence to Routes 19 and 23. This will connect with Highway 441, which is known as the "Over the Smokies Highway," the most scenic route between Brevard, Waynesville, Newfound Gap, Gatlinburg, and Knoxville.

They were excited about the future and the new life it meant for them. And if you know something about the stringencies of their life, you can't blame them for looking forward to more money and the chance to buy the city things that ease the hardships. I just hope the engineers leave enough balsam, "rhododaniel," white spruce, and briar thickets between the road and the McCalls to drown out the whir of those great instruments of change, the automobiles, as they wind around Pin Hook on their way to the scenic beauties which await them at the parking lots of Tennessee Bald.

It is evident that this way of life is already doomed. Twenty-one years ago, when I made my first intimate contact with the people of this region, the individualistic spirit was the first thing you noticed about the people you met. They were not special people like the McCalls that you had to go out of your way to find. They were most everybody who lived there and they simply did what was to them right and natural.

It was on my first visit in 1938 that I met Turkey Plott and Sary Ellison. I was not a complete stranger to the hill country, but my previous visits had been confined to the protected atmosphere of a church-sponsored summer assembly for young people. This time I was more on my own, and I looked forward to the exploration of the vast and exciting depths of the Great Smoky Mountains, the Balsams Range, and Pisgah National Forest. My plan was to make contact with a man named Otie Moorefield, who had been described to me as knowing more about the deep woods in this area than any man alive. From him I hoped to get instructions on trails to take—or with luck even get him to take a hiking trip with me.

My search for Moorefield led indirectly to several people who later became intimate friends. For an hour after arriving, a total stranger, in this small mountain community some forty miles from Asheville, I had sought my guide in vain. Two gaunt men had ignored my questions completely, and another had "never heerd of him." Finally I got a lead from a one-eyed, gimpy-legged fellow.

"I haint saw him all day," he said, "but he mought be at Turkey Plott's."

This turned out to be the hamlet's only café, across the street and down the block. Moorefield was not there, so I decided to eat something since I had had a long, cold trip from Asheville. Here in two surprising episodes, I discovered the individualism which then characterized this community—but does not now.

Sary Ellison, the daughter of Long Butt Ellison, worked as a waitress for Turkey Plott in a defiant and condescending fashion. The place was not awfully clean, and a fairly rough-looking crowd was in the place. When I ordered a hot roast-beef sandwich, milk, and coffee, Sary took the order and went about getting it together rather pokily. Turkey made some remark about "was she gonna take all day." Sary squared off and blared out in front of everybody present:

"Who do you think you air—Hilter or somebody?"

She then threw a dishrag in my plate of food, took off her apron, wrapped it around Turkey's neck, and said, "If'n you'uns want hit on the table so fast—git it thar yourself." And stalked out.

Everybody in the café but Turkey guffawed. Turkey brought me some more food. One of the men said to him:

"Ain't nobody gonna boss Sary around."

Turkey nodded. I gathered that everybody, including Turkey, knew that Sary would be back in a day or two, but that she wouldn't stay long if anybody started acting like "Hilter." Turkey didn't seem to be particularly mad at her, either. As a matter of fact, he said he "guessed he'd a done the same thing if he'd been her." And it wasn't five minutes before he demonstrated that he would.

The grease on my hot roast-beef sandwich was just starting to congeal when two unshaven giants lurched into the café and plopped down on the counter stools beside me. They smelled of tobacco juice and corn whiskey.

Both men were visibly mad and it wasn't just the whiskey, though this had reduced their caution somewhat. Frank Gash, the biggest one, pounded his meat-axe fist on the counter so hard my glass of milk jumped and skidded off onto the floor. For some crazy reason it didn't break, but landed right side up and sat there sloshing up and down. Gash bellowed, "Whar's Turkey Plott? I'm agonna kill 'im."

Turkey had gone back into the kitchen to get an order, but he heard Gash. He came charging out between the swinging doors that separated the two rooms so fast he nearly tore them off the hinges. Plott was probably the biggest and strongest man in western North Carolina at that time.

"Who's agonna kill Turkey?" he shouted.

Without waiting for an answer, he grabbed the two men by their coat collars and banged their heads together with such force you could hear the bones crack. Then he dragged them over the counter one at a time, lifting them above his head, and threw them through the front glass window.

When the glass stopped breaking, there ensued a most remarkable and wonderful quiet. Everybody went back to eating, and Turkey went back to the kitchen. Gash and his friend were picked up by the sheriff and put in jail. When they had recovered and been released, they stopped by to apologize to Turkey for the trouble they had caused. I never did find out what had set them off in the first place, because nobody ever talked about it after that.

This kind of immediate, vigorous expression was typical and is explained in part by the special cultural environment in which such people lived.

The western North Carolina folk like Turkey, Sary, Frank Gash, and their kind were largely of Anglo-Saxon descent. As pioneers, their ancestors had pushed into these wilderness areas, staked out their claims, and settled in for good. Until 1920, and almost until after World War II, the strain was only slightly adulterated by the various migrations. Protected in their isolation by the mountains and by their own reluctance to mingle with strangers, these mountaineers escaped much of the change which was occurring elsewhere. Because economic opportunities were not abundant, education and "refinement" were neglected.

The result was a strange mixture of the proud and the shy, the ignorant and the astute, the wise and the uneducated. In a real sense they lived apart from the main stream of American culture and thus developed ways of doing things that emphasized the importance of self-reliance and responsibility for one's own fate. This difference has been widely misunderstood, since the peculiar or sensational aspects of these people have been focused upon in such ways as to make them appear either stupid or comical, or both.

But many thoughtful people in this region, who have themselves shared this history, are watching the present changes with regret. The great levelers which have invaded their hinterland are radio, television, movies, industry, labor unions, paved roads, parkways, and tourists. What these things have done to Turkey Plott and Sary Ellison illustrates in miniature what is happening to the customs, attitudes, and ambitions of the whole region.

While Turkey, Sary, and the other inhabitants were going their usual way, the community was being surveyed by outsiders who wanted to locate a textile mill there. They needed a wide expanse of land, pure water, and a supply of moderately cheap labor. They found the land and water in abundance at the foot of the hill about three miles from town. The first investment to build the mill amounted to more than three million dollars; later this was doubled for additions. New roads were built, workmen were brought in from the outside, and all the skilled labor in the community was put on the job. Executives and their families moved in, together with a myriad of white-collar workers and personnel experts to train the mountaineers who wanted to work in the mill.

At first this increased Turkey's business, and he added some booths "for ladies and gentlemen." He also hired two new waitresses. But a new, modern restaurant opened up near him and attracted most of the new people who wanted hygiene, soft music, tablecloths, and more courteous service. Turkey finally gave up. He sold his café, lock, stock, and swinging doors, and went to work as a construction foreman at the mill.

Sary married a young insurance salesman who later became

president of the parent-teachers association and a charter member of the garden club. Her husband was voted "young man of the year" twice in a row and is now raising funds for a new community center, which is supposed to cut down on juvenile delinquency and rowdyism in town.

Turkey found it rough going for a while at the mill. He was a good foreman but was almost fired several times for being too demanding and for losing his temper. But he got hold of himself in time and calmed down to make a good, steady worker. For years he has been the chief of new construction and is known to be back of several plans to build better homes for the mill workers, athletic fields, and other recreational facilities. About the only time I see the fire in his eyes these days is when some diehard native or stranger makes a crack about how the mill has taken over and ruined the place. But he talks hard now instead of hitting hard.

In varying ways such urban influences have begun to standardize the life of all mountaineers. Working hours, types of work, wages, clothes, speech, and manners that once were highly individualized are—in some places gradually, in others suddenly—becoming formalized.

There was, for example, Warrior Hull. He was a strong-minded man and able to back up what he said. You didn't have to wait a week to get his opinion, either. Warrior lived by himself in a rough-hewn cabin just outside a small mountain community near Pisgah Forest. He was an artisan in the old sense, and by experience an expert machinist. He put these talents to work at a small tannery in town, where he developed the reputation of being able to fix anything.

In time the tannery was bought by outside interests in the East, and a representative of the company made a visit to survey the investment and make suggestions for improvement. At one point he came upon Warrior working on a piece of equipment. After a while he said, "Look here, you—you can work more efficiently if you'll get organized better." No comment from Hull. The boss shouted:

"You listen to me! I mean business—I want this done differently."

Hull turned slowly, picked up a monkey wrench, and said:

"You git your damn ass outa here and stop a-dickertatin' to me —I'll bust your head with this here monkey wranch."

The gentleman withdrew and Hull went back to work.

There are bigger plants in Hull's town now. The population has doubled, from 3,500 to 7,000 or more, and two big mills dominate the community. Warrior Hull's type does not work for either one of them, so far as I can tell. The current residents of the town are a different breed entirely. Thirty years ago there were many Warrior Hulls, and today there are none, except those who have escaped further into the hills.

Warrior Hull is dead now. The shack he lived in, where I spent many a cold winter night sleeping in front of his open fireplace, was knocked down by a bulldozer. Over the top of Hull's way of life runs a new superhighway.

At the same time that Warrior Hull was resisting change to the end, however, there were others in the region who welcomed "progress" and allied themselves with it. Though raised in the pioneering traditions, they joined hands with those who offered new opportunities. Some of them had gone into the Army during World War I and returned home with new notions about how to improve their own lot and that of their town.

Calvern Jones was one of the men who helped bring "progress." As a boy he was just as tow-headed, barefooted, and snaggle-toothed as any of the kids of his age. He hauled many a fruit-jar of moonshine whiskey from his father's cabin to the town residents in his home-fashioned, two-wheeled cart. His regular missions were widely known and folks would often taunt him as he pulled his cart along the back streets. "What you got there, Cal—some fancy groceries?" Cal would stiffen, ball up his fists, and yell: "None of your God damn business—you yeller self-made son of a bitch."

The first world war did a lot for Cal. It got him out of the bootleg business and into the grocery store. His experience in the Army—the new ideas he picked up and the extra schooling he took—provided him with a new weave in his personality. Mr. Calvern Jones opened up a nice grocery store all his own and began to spout salesmanship and progress, along with the doctors, the lawyers, and the newspapermen.

And they finally got progress in the shape of two big mills which now threaten to choke out Calvern Jones and pollute the clear waters of the rivers with their dyes. A recent editorial in the town's weekly newspaper commented on poor business conditions. At present there is only one grocery store in the main business section and that is an A & P supermarket. There was a Dixie store and, of course, Calvern Jones' store. The Dixie was bought out by the A & P, and Jones was forced out because his building was condemned. Several relatively new buildings are still unrented and most of the clothing stores have gone broke. Only the eating places and the filling stations prosper.

This has happened at a time when the people of the community have much more money than they ever had before. Jones blames the two mills which progress brought. Nearly everybody works for one of the mills and makes good money. But with the new wide superhighways to Asheville and Hendersonville, people flock to the city to spend their wages. So it's good-by Jones' store, farewell to rat cheese, the cracker box, fresh country butter, and a ten-cent poke of cressy salad.

This orientation toward the city and the urban way of life seems to have become the dominant urge of the present population. It extends into their social, economic, religious, and recreational activities, and into customs, mannerisms, speech, and styles of dress.

The informal way of life has given way to formal organization. The social and civic activities are carried on by Rotary, Kiwanis, and Lions clubs which promote civic improvement—such as bigger and better highways into the towns and larger attractions for tourists.

Recreational activities of the old type like berry picking, mountain fox hunting, and folk dancing have also been disappearing under the onslaught of spectator sports. High-school football games on lighted fields, "huddle queen" contests, and folk festivals with imported rock-and-roll guitar players have crowded out many of the old-time street dances, informal hoedowns, and singing conventions which once were the major recreational outlets. Now

kids sport Elvis Presley haircuts, talk bop slang, and dress "sharp."
Their mothers belong to women's clubs.

The physical face of the communities in this region is changing,
too. The kind of cabin Warrior Hull built has been replaced by
rows of little white houses from Asheville to Toxaway. There is
a developing sameness about everything, including the manicured
camping sites for tourists, with neat piles of wood cut to the
proper length for the outdoor grills. A few pure specimens like
the McCalls remain. In another generation their type will disappear forever. Such men already are strangers in their own land.

✦ THOMAS HORNSBY FERRIL

Something Starting Over

Thomas Hornsby Ferril (1896–   ), called Poet
Laureate of the Rocky Mountains, has captured the
mystique of frontier days by kicking about among
the relics of the Colorado ghost towns. In a thin
volume of poems, titled *Westering* (1934), he has
re-created America's frontier past in terms of its
dynamic present. In the poem reprinted here, Ferril
has given expression to a spiritual quality of the
"westering" impulse.

You don't see buffalo skulls very much any more
On the Chugwater buttes or down the Cheyenne plains,
And when you roll at twilight over a draw,
With ages in your heart and hills in your eyes,

From *Westering* (New Haven, Conn.: Yale University Press, copyright
1934).

You can get about as much from a Model-T,
Stripped and forgotten in a sage arroyo,
As you can from asking the blue peaks over and over:
    "Will something old come back again tonight?
    Send something back to tell me what I want."

    I do not know how long forever is,
But today is going to be long long ago,
There will be flint to find, and chariot wheels,
And silver saxophones the angels played,
So I ask myself if I can still remember
How a myth began this morning and how the people
Seemed hardly to know that something was starting over.

Oh, I get along all right with the old old times,
I've seen them sifting the ages in Nebraska
On Signal Butte at the head of Kiowa creek.
    (You can drink from the spring where old man Roubadeau
    Had his forge and anvil up in Cedar Valley,
    You can look back down the valley toward Scottsbluff
    And still see dust clouds on the Oregon trail.)
I entered the trench they cut through Signal Butte,
And I pulled a buffalo bone from the eight-foot layer,
And I watched the jasper shards and arrowheads
Bounce in the jigging screen through which fell dust
Of antelope and pieces of the world
Too small to have a meaning to the sifters.
One of them said, when I held the bone in my hand:
    "This may turn out to be the oldest bison
In North America," and I could have added:
    "How strange, for this is one of the youngest hands
That ever squeezed a rubber bulb to show
How helium particles shoot through water vapor."
And the dry wind out of Wyoming might have whispered:
    "Today is going to be long long ago."

I know how it smells and feels to sift the ages,
But something is starting over and I say

It's just as beautiful to see the yucca
And cactus blossoms rising out of a Ford
In a sage arroyo on the Chugwater flats,
And pretend you see the carbon dioxide slipping
Into the poverty weed, and pretend you see
The root hairs of the buffalo grass beginning
To suck the vanadium steel of an axle to pieces,
An axle that took somebody somewhere,
To moving picture theaters and banks,
Over the ranges, over the cattle-guards,
Took people to dance-halls and cemeteries—
I like to think of them that way together:
Dance-halls and cemeteries, bodies beginning
To come together in dance-halls where the people
Seem hardly to know that hymns are beginning too;
There's a hymn in the jerk of the sand-hill crawl of the dancers,
And all the gods are shining in their eyes;
Then bodies separating and going alone
Into the tilting uphill cemeteries,
Under the mesas, under the rimrock shadows.

I can look at an axle in a sage arroyo,
And hear them whispering, the back-seat lovers,
The old myth-makers, starting something over.

DATE DUE

DEC 10 '65			
NOV 4 '66			
APR 28 '67			
NOV 30 '67			
MAY 8 '68			
OCT 15 '68			
OCT 30 '68			
OCT 8 '69			
NOV 13 '72			
GAYLORD			PRINTED IN U.S.A.